Francis William Newman

Christianity in its Cradle

Francis William Newman

Christianity in its Cradle

ISBN/EAN: 9783743305632

Manufactured in Europe, USA, Canada, Australia, Japa

Cover: Foto ©Lupo / pixelio.de

Manufactured and distributed by brebook publishing software (www.brebook.com)

Francis William Newman

Christianity in its Cradle

CHRISTIANITY

IN ITS CRADLE.

BY

FRANCIS WILLIAM NEWMAN,

ONCE FELLOW OF BALLIOL COLLEGE, OXFORD;

NOW EMERITUS PROFESSOR OF UNIVERSITY COLLEGE, LONDON.

SECOND EDITION

LONDON:
TRÜBNER & CO., 57 & 59, LUDGATE HILL.
NOTTINGHAM: STEVENSON, BAILEY, AND SMITH, PRINTERS.
M.DCCC.LXXXVI.

PREFACE TO SECOND EDITION.

UNDER pressure of criticism I hav enlarged Chapter VIII., not without misgiving. I hav long thought that we must wait for another generation, before any complete review of the character and work of Jesus, who has left not a scrap from his own pen, can be successfully undertaken. Therefor I wished to narrate nothing but what the narrators say who ar received as sacred, and by no means all that they say. I hav confessed, and I again confess, on how slippery ground we hav to proceed.

In the problem of pp. 62—3 below, I hav overlooked one possibility; viz., that Jesus himself at some moments thought himself commissioned to overrule and discard the law of Moses, but was not permanently sure enough to avow this distinctly. Thus his parables of patching a threadbare garment with new cloth, and of pouring new wine into old skins, suggest that he then was imagining an overthrow of Mosaism; and equally when he said that no eating of food defiles a man. Nevertheless, he may hav been unable *at all times* to maintain so high a claim, or to declare to his disciples that God through his voice abolished the law of Moses. Without a positiv and distinct avowal from himself that this was his aim, it was impossible for them to admit the thought, while he lived to teach them.

CONTENTS.

CHAPTER	PAGE
I.—GENERAL VIEW OF JUDAISM	1
II.—JUDAISM RESTORED	4
III.—MESSIAH, THE DESIRE OF ALL NATIONS	14
IV.—ROMAN CONQUEST OF JUDÆA	24
V.—JEWISH SECTS AND JUDAS GAULANITIS	29
VI.—JOHN THE BAPTIST	37
VII.—SOURCES OF THE ACCOUNT OF JESUS	41
VIII.—JESUS OF NAZARETH. FIRST PART	50
,, ,, SECOND PART	74
,, ,, APPENDIX	93
IX.—FIRST STAGE OF THE CHRISTIAN CHURCH	95
X.—PAUL AND JAMES	110
XI.—CLOSE OF THE APOSTOLIC ERA	136
XII.—DESTRUCTION OF JERUSALEM AND ITS EFFECTS ON CHRISTIANITY	149
XIII.—OUR MODERN PROBLEM	158

NOTICE.

In my First Edition of this Book I was under the belief that Editors of newspapers were likely to welcome all omission of useless letters. But this is true only within very narrow limits. I now learn that *to drop final* e *where it is not only superfluous but also misleading*, probably is the utmost that they can advance ahead of the public. To this therefor I confine myself at present, not without hope of elsewhere further pressing for cautious reform of our worst and indefensible irregularities. To the total revolution contemplated by the Pitman-school, I am on principle irreconcilable.

CHRISTIANITY IN ITS CRADLE.

CHAPTER I.

GENERAL VIEW OF JUDAISM.

History is a vast topic, of which few of us can know much; yet to know a little correctly is valuable. An obvious parallel is Geography. We must be contented with great ignorance, yet an outline map is superfluous to no one. To study the birth of a Religion is eminently instructiv, yet generally is very difficult from the absence of written documents contemporaneous and trustworthy. So much the more do we need to learn the people and the circumstances under which it rose; which in the case of Christianity are no wise obscure.

These pages do not compete with complete Christian histories, nor attempt continuous narrativ, but only aim to summarize what will throw most light on the topic, and thereby aid to sound judgment.

The peculiarity of the Jewish people has turned on two pivots, *Monotheism* and *Ceremonialism;* and in the secondary stage, which alone here concerns us, each principle has derived its energy from a belief in Sacred Books. In the earlier period, before and during the Hebrew Monarchy, an activ warfare was carried on against Polytheism, to which a majority of the people, surrounded by Polytheistic and Idolatrous nations, was inclined: but the chief champions of the characteristic Hebrew faith were then, not established Priests, but Prophets rising untaught, or reared in voluntary seminaries; men who professed to utter the voice of God, not to expound any sacred book, or rest upon any sacred law. The name of Moses is hard to find in these prophets, nor do they argue for the doctrin of One God by quoting the Pentateuch or the Decalogue.

An eminent Christian divine of this century avowed that it was scarcely possible to worship a God who had neither place nor form nor geometrical size, so that an incarnate God is a necessary condescension to human infirmity. Nevertheless the Hebrews (indeed, it seems, the Persians before them) had quite dispensed with incarnation. It is hard to understand how any one can read the Hebrew psalms, and not see that an intense devotion of soul to an omnipresent God pervades them.* Even the Roman Tacitus, malignant as he is to the Jews and full of slander, yet seems in spite of himself to admire, when he approaches their absolute monotheism.

"The Jews (says he) apprehend a single Deity, and that "by the mind alone; accounting those profane who out of "decaying substances fashion images of gods into the like- "ness of men, while that which is Supreme and Eternal "can neither change nor perish." From our modern point of view, we must call the attachment of the Jews to the sole worship of Jehovah a *fanaticism*; because it enacted death by stoning for any one who enticed to the violation of this paramount doctrin. But in that day all nations which had an established creed accounted its deliberate violation a deadly guilt. The asperity of Persians against idolatry and the still greater severity of the Jews, denote, not that they were more cruel than Egyptians or Greeks, but that they were more definit and earnest in religious belief.

---

* Ponder well that magnificent outburst of devout piety: "Whom hav I in heaven but Thee? there is none upon earth that I desire in comparison with Thee. My flesh and my heart faileth; but God is the strength of my heart and my portion for ever." Possibly the explanation of "*for ever*" is found in another Psalm; "I will bless my God, *as long as I hav any being.*"

But the Ceremonialism of Israel grew up in the Priesthood, which (as apparently in Syria, Asia Minor and Greece) had its origin in unconnected sacred temples, each accumulating and digesting its own routine. When union came about, selection and codification were sure to follow and gain national assent. Jewish history frankly informs us of an era (nearly at the close of the monarchy, while the pious King Josiah was still young) which first established the Book of the Law in permanence.* In the received narrativ there is no indication that any copy of this book was in the hands of the public, or even of the most esteemed and venerated kings. Zeal for Ceremonialism is scarcely found in rulers until this later era. The Passover, and the Sabbatical year, hav no rigid and continuous observance before the captivity. Early kings ministered at the altar, in Jerusalem equally as in old Greece. Levites were confounded with other tribes, and had no actual possession of lands or tithes. Yet a frightful tale is told concerning the very earliest time, in illustration of a law delivered by Jehovah to Moses (Exodus xxxi. 15), "Whosoever doeth any work on the "sabbath day, he shall surely be put to death." Accordingly, for the crime of *gathering sticks in the wilderness* on the sabbath day (Numbers xv. 32—36) Moses himself is represented to hav caused a man to be stoned to death. We may disbelieve the fact and acquit Moses; but it is told in the sacred book: the belief of it by the later Jews cannot be doubted, nor the evil of its belief denied. All other ceremonial offences had a ceremonial expiation; but "sabbath-breaking" was imagined to be a breach

---

* An exhaustiv analysis of this transaction from the pen of the late Rev. John Robertson, of Coupar Angus, with the title, "The Finding of the Book," was published by the late Mr. Thomas Scott, in 1870. It may not be easy to get this now. In my own history of the Hebrew Monarchy, as early as 1847, I commented largely on the matter, and concluded that to alledge a discovery is to confess an invention.

of the tie which united the Most High to his peculiar people (Exodus xxxi. 16, 17), a breach *of the covenant;* therefore to be worse than most immoralities.

In Ceremonialism of course must be included the rite of Circumcision. But this was imposed in infancy once for all. To be uncircumcised, was in the national estimate a disgrace, as with the Egyptians (Joshua v. 9, Herod. ii. 36), also probably with a majority of the Syrians and Arabians. It scarcely ever could come into prominence. Foreigners had no right to resent it. There is an opinion that nations so diverse adopted this strange practice from a prevailing medical theory. It has no proper place in our history. The Greeks believed it to hav been learned from Egypt; the Hebrews supposed it to hav come down as a solemn covenant and command of God to Abraham. It was cardinal to Judaism, yet not so peculiar as the Sabbatical Law, which forbad labour on the seventh day. One thing ought to be known, on which modern Jews pointedly insist;—that there never was any prohibition of *innocent pleasure and merriment* on the sabbath, nor of *learning and teaching* any form of knowledge, provided only that no money be earned by the teacher. All that is forbidden (they assure us) is servile work and work for gain; but the cultivation of the intellect is highly approved.

CHAPTER II.

JUDAISM RESTORED.

In different national stages Israel had different teachers; first Prophets, next Psalmists (who were apparently a growth out of musicians and priests at the temple of Jerusalem); thirdly, Doctors of the Law, whom we call Rabbis. The earlier priesthood, when it rose above mere ceremony, was virtually a political element, struggling to enforce constitutional rule on the kings; but seldom on good terms with the prophets. When the monarchy vanished, the Priesthood came into power, and coalesced with the Rabbis, who did not write sacred books, but expounded the older scriptures.

The final conquest of Jerusalem by the Babylonian king Nebuchadnezzar (about 600 B.C.) terminated the Hebrew Monarchy. The policy of the conqueror was, to carry away the whole population and replace it by foreigners; this obviously aimed at destroying the national spirit which resists Imperialism. It gained partial or at least temporary success. It had indeed earlier been carried out against Israel, whether by a Syrian or an Assyrian King: and somewhat later the whole northern district of Palestine was swamped by new comers, various in origin and creed; indeed as early as the prophet Isaiah we ar surprized to read of *Gentile* Galilee. But Babylon, which had assisted the Median monarchy to overthrow that of Assyria, and had eagerly effaced the great city of Nineveh, fell in her turn by the power which she had helped to make supreme. Cyrus the Persian, supplanting the Medes and wielding all their resources, conquered and annexed Babylon; then, by reversing the Babylonian policy won the allegiance of all the Jews. Probably indeed Cyrus, whose creed was Monotheism, felt a true sympathy for monotheistic Israel. He warmly encouraged the return of the Jews to their own land; nay, according to the book of Ezra, he lavishly gave vessels of gold and silver to re-establish splendour in their Temple when rebuilt. So delightful a change of policy roused up a new and glorious prophet, whose book has unhappily been tacked on to the work of Isaiah, which ended with the 39th chapter. The new prophet begins with the joyful announcement: "Comfort ye my people, saith your God," and continues to the end in a like strain of triumph, though without any hint of life in an after-world for individual saints. This anonymous prophet has so long been quoted as Isaiah, that it is hard to find any better title for him than "the later Isaiah." In obedience to the friendly edict of Cyrus, the most zealous of the nation flocked back. The law of Moses assumed in the eyes of all Israel a dignity and sacredness never before realized. The Jews who were dispersed north-eastward or in Egypt, looked up to Jerusalem with pride and joy, as in the days of David and Solomon. The central figure in that city for three centuries and a half was no longer a military king, but a professed High Priest, guided by Doctors of the Law. The law was in some matters (as other antique law) too severe; but how much better than Greek, Roman, Persian, or Assyrian!

The effects of the DISPERSION were vast and permanent. It had begun in detail by a harassing slave trade, as far as we can judge. In antiquity, to no nation had other nations any human rights, unless guaranteed by treaty and oath. Each preyed upon others as on wild game, even without previous enmity. But the Imperialist King David, son of Jesse, had left rankling hatred in all the petty tribes around. Whenever the Jewish power was weak, marauders infested the land; Tyre and Sidon were activ slave-markets, and every merchant was a slave-dealer. Oh! what hav not been the miseries of mankind in the past! History is the little book of the Apocalypse, sweet in the mouth, but most bitter of digestion. Grievous as ar human sufferings now, they were formerly far wider and more constant, if not more terrible.

A large migration of Jews into Egypt had probably risen out of commerce. Isaiah (xix. 18) expects five cities in Egypt to speak the Hebrew tongue and propagate widely the worship of Jehovah. Some centuries later, when a Macedonian dynasty ruled in Egypt, the Jewish residents confronted Greek philosophy in Alexandria, then the most learned of all Greek cities. Something must hav been imbibed in Jerusalem from that attempt to combine Moses with Plato, which culminated in the theosophy of Philo the Jew. The *word* of the Lord, so often mentioned in Hebrew prophets and psalmists, was compared with the *logos** of Plato. A deliberate effort was made to interpret Hebrew notions into harmony with Greek philosophy; an effort in which ingenuity was sure to overpower good sense, and strained analogies to be mistaken for sober logic.

But the great mass of the dispersed Jews were carried to the north-east, to Nineveh or Babylon. These, whenever they submitted to a rural life, were probably lost among the Gentiles; but when, clinging to their religion and to one another, they abode in towns, their families as they multiplied could only liv by successiv migrations eastward or westward. For they necessarily betook themselves to such employments as still ar familiar with Jews, and indeed with the similarly dispersed Armenians. (It is an axiom in Western Asia that Jews and Armemenians cannot flourish in the same town.) From this cause it happened, that in the course of six centuries Jews of every tribe† were found, westward as far as

---

* *Logos* in Greek *may* be rendered Word, as in Mark ii. 2, " He preached the "*word* unto them;" but the pervading idea in Plato is, that *Mind* is the cause of whatever goes on "by plan," which plan he calls Logos. Timaeus in Plato (§ 10) teaches that the Universe is a living creature endowed with a soul,— that it is *a god begotten by God* (§ 12), *eternal, perfect, and only begotten* (μονογενής, unigenitus.) Philo somehow adapted these epithets to the *Word* of Hebrew poetry.—The divine *logos* in the noble ode of Cleanthes the Stoic means " well ordered plan."

† The modern Jews undoubtedly ar descendants of the *twelve* tribes, as the dispersed Jews are entitled in Acts xxvi. 7, James i. 1. That they ar the descendants of the *two* tribes, is a baseless fiction, with nothing to make it even plausible. The search after "the ten tribes" is an ignorance which has become fanatical.

Italy, eastward we know not how far. The new generations, born amid men who believed in inferior gods and demons, in magic and witchcraft, necromancy and astrology, Furies and Tartarus,—imbibed grave additions to the national creed, even when they steadily retained Jehovah as the sole object of worship. The doctrin of a Devil and fiery Hell, of a future Life and Judgment, of demoniacal possessions and religious exorcisms, did not come to the Jews by *divine teaching*, if thereby we mean Moses and the prophets; for neither in Moses nor in the prophets under the monarchy ar these beliefs found. They were imbibed by the Jewish race during its dispersion among nations, whose superstitions it had despised,—as we despise them. The pedigree of these tenets is open to us and undeniable. The "lying spirit" of Micaiah's vision (1 Kings xxii. 19) and even the Satan of the book of Job, ar (strange as is the notion) base ministers of Jehovah, and cannot be identified with the Christian Devil. In Zechariah iii. 1 and 2, a step forward may perhaps be claimed; but Zechariah wrote in the time of King Darius, four generations after the captivity.

It much excited the wrath of Tacitus, that Jews everywhere looked up to restored Jerusalem as a mother city, and often had great success in converting Gentiles to their higher spiritual faith. He tells it in these bitter and slanderous words: "These ceremonies [of sacrifice] "are defended by their antiquity: all their other insti-"tutions, ill-omened and foul, hav prevailed by their "perversity. For *whoever was worst* [in any nation], "discarding his country's religion, used to carry to Jeru-"salem tributes and petty moneys; whereby the resources "of the Jews were enlarged."

But the restored Jews had much to suffer, both from petty neighbours and from great monarchies. Judæa was a passage-land between Syria and Egypt, and when the kings of those regions (Macedonian dynasties) fell into conflict, this small territory was trampled down. At length under Antiochus, called Epiphanes, a dreadful persecution fell upon them. This monarch of Syria, Babylon and nearly all Asia Minor, was resolved to break down by violence all their religious scruples; but thereby raised up against himself the Asmonean family; heroes, called by us "Maccabees" (about 167 B.C.), who in the time of this king and his successor, after immense suffering, defeated trained armies vastly superior, and at length established the new Jerusalem in a strength and glory which seemed miraculous.

The gratitude of the Jewish nation foolishly recognized the Asmonean family (that of Judas Maccabeus) as hereditary holders of the priesthood; but the High Priest, being not only head of the Civil Government, but trustee for the public defence, soon became in spirit a military king. Not only were cities in Hollow Syria and Idumea coveted, besides Ammon, Moab, and Philistia, but municipal rights were grudged to Jewish towns. The nation desired peace, and government according to the law of Moses; and to a great extent attained the latter: but like more than one modern European nation, the peaceable desires of the people were sadly thwarted by the ambition of hereditary chiefs.

Tacitus (Hist. book v. ch. 8) thus sums up the account of these times: "Then the Jews placed kings over themselves, who, expelled by the fickleness of the populace, regained dominion by force of arms, and shrank not from exile of citizens, destruction of cities, slaughter of brothers, of wives, of parents, and other enormities usual with kings. These men fostered superstition, because it added the honour of priesthood as a support to their power." This writer loves to retail malevolent folly concerning Judaism; and his words ar far from depicting the whole case fairly: yet most certainly their priest-kings were the bane of Judaism. Children of a patriotic chief do not inherit patriotism by birth in the purple. It does not appear that they had any standing army except for the defence of the temple and certain fortresses; yet in Josephus's narrativ their facility of getting troops surprizes a reader. Still, this Judaism had another side, widely diverse, of which Tacitus knew nothing. The law of Moses was the national code, and never was so sacredly observed. Its law of land was antique and rational. The land belonged to Jehovah. Each generation possessed and cultivated it in turn, but no one owned it, no one could sell it; only its *use*, until the next Jubilee, could be sold. There was no military aristocracy, no caste of landlords to sponge the tillers of the soil, no pensioned idlers. The aristocracy consisted of the learned,—moralists trained in the sacred law, recruited from all ranks, and (as it is believed) all were taught some manual trade; certainly none of them were disgraced if he so earned his living. From these institutions sprang an energetic patriotic peasantry, brave and devoted; also a highly popular and large class of doctors of the law, chiefly of the sect called Pharisees, who laboured diligently to soften the rigour of antique law by tradition and subtle comment.

Only after the restoration from Babylon did the Jews nationally become devoted to the "Book of the Law" and hereby imbibe that intensity both of Monotheism and of Ceremonialism which sharply divided them from all their neighbours. Their aversion to foreign diet as unclean was a great social separation: their moral shrinking from idolatry was felt by idolators as an insult. A sense of religious superiority as inevitably pervaded Israel then, as it pervades Christendom now: nor is it wonderful, that to Polytheists who in Art excelled the Jews this people appeared conceited, narrow-minded and unamiable. So indeed did the ancient Christians appear to Romans and others. Polytheists in general could tolerate foreign religions, and fancy that each, rightly interpreted, was right on its own soil; nay, could without compunction allow resident aliens to erect sacred edifices for strange rites nativ to themselves, if morally innoxious. But Jews, while glad to raise temples to Jehovah abroad, could not, at least in those days, willingly endure foreign religion on Jewish soil: indeed their sacred laws forbad it. All this is so like to Christendom, that Christians can ill afford to brand the Jews of that day for too much pride in their nativ religion, too much zeal to propagate it, or too abject a submission to their sacred books. But Polytheists, as known to us by Greeks and Romans, had neither exclusiveness nor any depth in their religious notions. Athenian Comedy bitterly resented serious criticism of the traditional Pantheon, and recklessly slandered Athenian teachers who were thought to undermine it; yet without moral scruple itself made impure fun out of its own creed, nor did any poet shrink from using it as material for wild fancy, and moral aspersion on its gods and goddesses. Of course such Pagans disliked a strict and serious religion, sharply set, morally confident, and eager to proselyte. The same causes seem to make modern Agnostics bitter against Jews, and greedy believers of every aspersion broad-cast on the ancient Pharisee. No one would expect our Agnostics to praise the Hebrews for upholding against heathenism the doctrin that the Supreme Power is righteous and loves righteousness in man: yet some might hav expected far less animosity from Christians, and fairer judgment of those whose excellencies and peculiar points they hav so largely inherited.

In spite of royal pride and violence (for the high-priest at last assumed the title of King) Palestine under the Mosaic doctors flourished greatly, until Roman tyranny galled, tormented and drove to madness a high-spirited and free people.

Soon after the death of that cruel Antiochus the prophecy called Daniel's must hav been written. Criticism for which we hav no room, shows abundantly that the narrativ is opposed to history and truth. The wars of the kings of Syria and Egypt ar detailed accurately in chapter xi. but at the very next step the prophecy *is false:* for, Resurrection of the dead follows, in which Jewish saints rise to everlasting life and glory: all earthly affairs seem suddenly to close. Special remarks on this "prophecy" may here be in place.

This book has astonishing diversities from all the previous Judaic literature. In Ezekiel, in Jeremiah, in the later Isaiah and all the earlier prophets, there is no word to suggest resurrection from the dead or renewed life for individuals. Jeremiah's endless laments hav no assuagement from that topic, which was needed then, if ever, for his bleeding and crushed people. He, like the rest, sees in their sufferings nothing but *the anger of Jehovah*, and *proof of their guilt.* No such idea is found in this book called Daniel's. The saints whom he records by name hav miraculous triumphs over their imperial persecutors; king Nebuchadnezzar (ii. 46) falls on his face and worships Daniel!! Concerning the rest, the tone is jubilant, even in looking forward to a time of unprecedented suffering (xii. 2). "At that time," says the Angel to Daniel, "thy people shall be delivered, "*every one that shall be found written in the book.*" Here the Apocalyptic "Lamb's book of life" is anticipated. It proceeds: "Many who sleep in the dust of the earth "shall awake, some to everlasting life, some to shame "and everlasting contempt." This magnificent announcement was unknown to Isaiah and his patron king Hezekiah; nothing like it appears in Ezra or Nehemiah. Then as to his notions of the human world: he represents each kingdom to hav its guardian angel, who is called *its prince.* Michael is the great prince of Israel. Another tutelary angel was "withstood" for 21 days by the prince of the kingdom of Persia, until Michael came to aid him in the conflict (x. 13). "Afterwards," says he, "I must return to *fight* with the prince of Persia "(x. 20) and when I am gone forth, the prince of Graecia "will come." These notions certainly ar not Judaic; apparently they ar Persian. One step more, and the guardian *angels* of Gentile powers were degraded into *demons,* thus completing the Rabbinical idea of "prin-"cipalities aloft," subject to Satan, potentate of the air. Here a vast mass of Oriental mythology corrupted Hebrew simplicity.

In the book of Daniel we also find a Theatrical Tribunal held by the Supreme God. In the Psalms and Prophets hitherto, the throne of judgment was but a metaphor and poetical ornament. *The thrones* ar cast down (angelic or human), the Ancient of Days takes his seat; a fiery stream issues from him, millions (of angels) minister to him, myriads of myriads (of mankind?) stand before him, the judgment is set, and *the books* ar opened,—as in an Egyptian trial? Beyond this, a novel annunciation is made. One like unto *a son of man**
comes *with the clouds* of heaven, and receives over all peoples, nations and languages a dominion which shall never pass away. This appears to be the earliest state-

---

* By some fatuity our translators here write "one like unto *the* Son of Man;" and in iii. 25 give us "*the* Son of God," where the sense clearly needs and the original plainly says, *a* son of God. [Both now corrected in the Revised Version.]

ment, that some one *in human shape*, but *coming in the clouds of heaven*, is to rule permanently over this earth and its inhabitants.—But *was* it the earliest statement? We cannot be sure; for we do not know the date of the prophecy called the Book of Enoch. Concerning this, a few words may be appropriate.

To some of us the chief interest of the Book of Enoch turns on the fact, that in the Canonical Epistle of Jude it is quoted as the writing of Enoch *the seventh from Adam* (14) without any suspicion that it was a recent fraud. German critics, whose pride it is to disintegrate ancient books, think it has been interpolated by Christians. When discovered, early in this century, it was translated by our Archbishop Lawrence. Unless large parts of it ar generated by fraud upon fraud, it may have co-operated with the book of Daniel in preparing the Jewish mind for the idea of *a son of man* who should be *a son of God*, a Judge of the dead, and a universal Ruler over the living. But the idea of Messiah is so important, as to deserve a chapter for itself.

CHAPTER III.

MESSIAH, THE DESIRE OF ALL NATIONS.

Who can read the miserable tale of Western Asia with intelligence and without sympathy? After nations hav begun to be consolidated, cultivated and softened, they ar again torn in pieces by imperial encroachment. Industry is interrupted, families ar broken up, prosperity is wrecked, those tenderly reared ar carried into exile or actual slavery; national as well as personal love is trampled down and dishonoured merely for the aggrandizement of some foreigner. The Assyrian, after conquering widely both eastward and northward, wielded a vast population of mountaineers as his weapon for western conquest. But the Medes and Persians revolt, and a Median dynasty rears its head. Babylon joins the Medes, and at length lays Assyria prostrate. Babylon clutches Syria and Palestine; indeed invades Egypt, with no advantage to herself. Cyrus the Persian subdues first in a civil war the Medes, next Babylonia and Syria, finally all Asia Minor and its highly cultivated population of many races and languages. His son conquers Egypt: after his death usurpers arise in ten different centres whom Darius conquers, one by one, in complex war. Darius next crosses the Bosporus and conquers all Thrace (the modern Roumelia), Paeonia and Macedonia. Incensed by Athenian attack (for the Athenians had as yet no understanding of his vast resources) he and his son made war on Greece. The Greeks ar saved by their mountains and by the enemy's pride, and forthwith begin an endless harassing of his innocent and injured subjects. This culminates in the irruption of Alexander the Great into Asia, who perpetrates cruelties and horrors unmatched in the Persian invasion of Greece. On his death, his generals carry on civil war for twenty years, till they can agree on a fourfold division of his kingdom. Great standing armies hav become the organ of empire. Greece has now nominally conquered Asia; but this merely means, that her youth ar dragged from home or migrate to be tools of bloodshed, and her population rapidly wastes. Barbarians whose nerves and hearts ar hard may think perpetual warfare the natural state; but with industrious populations, trained to gentleness and proud of nationality, a series of successiv Empires involves intense suffering.

No wonder that lamentation, mourning and woe came forth from many nations, whatever their religion, with aspirations for *a Deliverer*. What may giv some idea of the suffering of a civil population from capture by even a *Greek* enemy, (and the Greeks were far from being cruel, in comparison with other nations), we hav definit narrativs concerning more than one town, that when it found longer resistance impossible,—then, rather than encounter the fate of being sold into slavery, they killed their wives and children, burned their precious goods, and leapt into the fire themselves, or died on the spears of the enemy. Historians who record such horrors, hav no better comment than to remark,—What madmen and fools they were! As a general fact, whatever the origin of a war, if (as ordinarily) greed of conquest alone impelled the aggressor, yet resistance to his arms was resented and punished as a crime. The nobler the national spirit, the greater the sacrifices it made in defence of its hereditary prince or its rightful independence, so much the fiercer and more unrelenting was its conqueror, both in revenge for his own losses and in the hope of deterring like bravery in others. Thus did ambition in the conqueror demoralize the conquered.

Each nation looked to its own God to support its rights. Each, when vanquished, supposed it had encountered the anger of its God. Not least was this the case with Israel, which never admitted the other alternativ, that its God had proved inferior to his adversary. No Jew could impute to Jehovah military weakness; but every Jew unawares imputed to him the moral weakness of fearing discredit with the heathen, if his chosen people be trampled down. It runs through the whole Hebrew literature, that however much that people may *deserve* chastisement and get it, yet at last, *for the glory of his own name*, Jehovah must exalt them over their enemy. Hence in national misfortunes, repentance for real or imagined sin blended with intense supplication that Jehovah would avenge *his own dishonor* and send a Deliverer. A like aspiration under other phrases rose in many cruelly oppressed peoples; so this champion, to be sent by God, became *the Desire of all Nations*.

We hav no chronology for the earliest Greek literature, nor trustworthy remains of any of the Sibyls. It here suffices to go back to Isaiah, who wrote when the Assyrian power in Nineveh had become the formidable enemy, both a little before and after the capture of Samaria and the deportation of the ten tribes. He at once anticipates for Jerusalem herself the direst calamities, that ar to sweep off nine-tenths of the people (vii. 11—13), yet believes that from her all nations shall learn religious wisdom. "Out of Zion shall go forth the law: Jehovah "shall become Judge among the peoples: nation shall "not lift up sword against nation, neither shall they learn war any more." Calamity had thus taught the elect of Israel a far higher wisdom than that of King David. Among the latest deeds of Samaria, its king confederated with the king of Syria against Ahaz king in Jerusalem. Isaiah tried to inspire Ahaz with his own belief, that these two enemies were not to be feared. In vain he urged that *in a very few years*,—before a certain child should have learned to talk (viii. 3)—the king of Assyria would destroy them both. Ahaz could not afford to wait those few years, but at once sent tribute to Nineveh, and bribed its king to a work which he cheerfully undertook and completed,—the conquest of Damascus. The prophet was fully aware that Samaria would be the next victim (ix. 8-21) and that the Assyrian would overflow into Judæa; but he believed that, before long, a prince of the house of David would overthrow him, and apparently declares that a child just born was

B

to be the great Deliverer and mighty Restorer. "Under "him a new Eden shall be established, with righteouness "and universal peace (ch. xi.) Ephraim shall be re-"conciled to Judah and all the dispersed of Israel shall "be brought back in triumph."—The last touches to this prophecy must hav been given (xi. 16) after the Samaritans had been carried to Assyria.

It is not imagined that anything here written could carry general conviction as to the real meaning of Isaiah's mysterious announcement (ix. 6), "Unto us a child *is* "*born*, unto us a son *is given*." So much we may say: there is nothing in the known chronology to forbid, and there is much to suggest, that Hezekiah, heir to the throne of Ahaz, was just then born. An inaccurate, perhaps rather a fraudulent, translation deceives most English readers. No attempt to improve it can here be made. It suffices to state, that with German scholars the rendering differs essentially from ours, and that the Jewish translation into Greek, called the *Septuagint*, instead of "his name shall be called Wonderful," &c., &c., has "his name is called, *Messenger of Great* "*Counsel* (or Council): for I will bring peace upon the "rulers and health to him. Great is his rule; and to "his peace no limit, on the throne of David," &c. Nothing on the surface forbids our supposing the prophet to hav expected the realization of his glorious vision by the future reign of infant Hezekiah. *Be that as it may*, we here notice two facts; *first*, that Isaiah predicted a mighty Deliverer and a blessed time of justice and peace; *secondly*, that Hezekiah, though a pious king, did *not* fulfil this hope. The Deliverer was to be a legitimate offspring of David, seated on David's throne; consequently to be an Anointed king. In Hebrew the word Messiah means *anointed:* therefore after the continuous royalty had vanished, the epithet Messiah became peculiar to the expected Deliverer. The Greeks translated it by *Christos*.

Contemporary with Isaiah, but perhaps younger, was the prophet Micah, who adopts as in choral chant, Isaiah's grand prediction that the Gentiles shall become religious pupils of the Jews (Micah iv. 2, 3) and proceeds to glorify Jerusalem (8) as the centre of coming dominion. Zion shall dash the nations in pieces with her iron horn and trample them down with her brazen hoof: their gain and substance shall be consecrated to Jehovah (13); and though the king of Samaria shall suffer outrage (ch. v. 1), yet *out of Bethlehem shall come the mighty Ruler* of Israel, whose grandeur the prophet further describes.— This is the celebrated text, which declares that Messiah shall come out of little Bethlehem: but (sadly to our confusion) it goes on to assign *as his great function*, the ravaging of Assyria with the sword and turning the now captiv Israelites into a lion among the flocks of sheep.— While Assyria was still a terrible foe, those who revered these great prophets found the interpretation of Messiah to be clear. He was to be Israel's victorious leader *against that foe*. But after the Assyrian power had vanished by Babylonian and Median arms, where and what was Messiah?

The Hebrew Psalms ar full of bitter cries against the men who lie in wait to shed blood. Wild banditti had the land at their mercy for many long years. Prayers against *enemies* painfully color many otherwise beautiful pieces: and a great day is often predicted when Jehovah will avenge his people and rule over the earth (or land?) himself; but it is hard to lay the finger on one which puts forward a military chieftain, like unto Micah's Messiah, as Jehovah's agent and sub-ruler. The seventy-second Psalm most nearly harmonizes with the picture of restored Eden in Isaiah, and ascribes the righteous rule to a Hebrew king. The last verse, which implies the Psalm to be David's, may be believed, or may be rejected as spurious. That is of secondary importance: the fact remains, that the Psalm does *not* define when we ar to expect this great king, nor how to recognize him *before* he achieves his mighty deeds. The same remark applies to the second Psalm, which in the last verse shows a false translation ("Kiss the Son,") made with a Christian purpose. The LXX. have Δράξασθε παιδείας, "*Lay hold of instruction*, lest the Lord be angry." The king who is here brought forward, the Psalmist magnificently represents to hav been constituted "a son of God," on that day. For this reason he is claimed as Messiah by the Christian writer to the Hebrews (Hebrews i. 6). But that writer also seizes for Messiah the words of the eighth Psalm, that God hath made *man* a little lower than the angels (ii. 6–9): and (what here chiefly concerns us) the Psalm givs us no instruction how to know Messiah when he comes.

The very same complaint may be repeated concerning all the other texts called Messianic. It was therefore natural, indeed inevitable, that the Jewish doctors should be uncertain, and greatly divided, when interrogated concerning Messiah. To reply from Isaiah or Micah was possible, if single verses were quoted, as they would be by the unlearned, who had no access to the entire prophecy; but wise and learned men knew that after the Assyrian power and all the petty tribes contemporary had disappeared, such a reply was folly or fraud.

One collateral prophecy by Malachi rested in the popular memory: "Behold, I will send you Elijah the "prophet before the great and dreadful day of the Lord." According to the narrativ which has been received among the Jews for two thousand years, Elijah did not *die* as other men, but (like Romulus?) was carried up to heaven in a whirlwind by a chariot and horses of fire (2 Kings ii. 11). Therefore he did not need to be raised from the dead; he had only to come back from heaven. Thus the popular idea accepted him as the *forerunner of Messiah*, since Messiah was to introduce the great and terrible day of God's vengeance.

Another topic must be added. The final prophecy of [the true] Isaiah, given in our books as chapters xxxiv., xxxv., is an intense invectiv against the land and people of Edom. David, if we believe the frightful story (1 Kings xi. 15, 16) had kept his chief captain Joab with all Israel (that is, with his whole military force) six months on Idumean soil, "until he had cut off every "male in Edom." Such murderous attempts never succeed entirely, but they always succeed in bequeathing untractable enmity of the weaker nation against the generally innocent posterity of the stronger. Israel long suffered miseries from Edomite retaliation, and bitterly cursed these enemies, while herself mourning by the waters of Babylon (Psalm cxxxvii. 7—9). It cannot surprize us to find Isaiah, a century earlier, vehement against Edom,—predicting her utter desolation, and the joy of her deserts that nothing but wild beasts and birds liv there (xxxv. 1). It *does* surprize to find this utterance suddenly turn into a quasi-Messianic description of the ensuing kingdom of God. Messiah indeed (*i.e.* God's chosen captain) is not named: but in his own high poetry the prophet declares, "*Then* the eyes of the blind shall "be opened and the ears of the deaf shall be unstopped: "*then* shall the lame man leap as a hart, and the tongue "of the dumb shall sing." From these words* the

---

* Chapter xlii. 7, of [the later] Isaiah speaks of opening blind eyes in very obvious metaphor. It was quite pardonable *there* to believe that *the servant of the Lord* meant an individual Messiah, if one had no means of studying the whole series of the prophecy, and comparing xlix. 3, and other passages.

vulgar managed to deduce that *when Messiah came, he would work miracles of healing.*—That no Gamaliel so reasoned, we may infer with some confidence from Gamaliel's great pupil, Paul of Tarsus; who seems quite unaware of any Messianic miracles.

To turn from Israel to other nations, it is interesting to read Virgil's Eclogue called Pollio, which opens by suggesting that he is reproducing a *Cumæan* song; that is, one concerning the blessed age predicted by the *Sibyl* of Cumae. In Virgil the scene of Paradise does for a moment recall Isaiah to us, as likewise his announcement of an auspicious birth impending. But Virgil's picture is blurred by his dream that history recurs in a circle. The Argonautic expedition is to be repeated, and a second Achilles is to fight at Troy! This sweet poet barely shows how widely spread was the idea that a great Deliverer was about to be born; who would rule over the world with Justice and Glory.

In the pages of Tacitus and Suetonius it is curious to find traces of a Gentile Messiah in the person of a Roman Emperor. The expectation had been widely diffused, that a great deliverer would come from the East. After the tumultuous alarms and suffering from the contests for Empire caused by the death of Nero, Vespasian coming from the Roman armies in Judæa was by many believed to be this mighty saviour. Omens and oracles confirmed the idea, and Vespasian to his great perplexity found himself expected to work miracles on the sick. The two historians are in substantial agreement. Tacitus details two of the cases somewhat more amply, and it may be of interest to my readers to have the whole passage set before them. It occurs in his Histories, book iv. chapter 81.

" In the course of those days, while Vespasian was " waiting at Alexandria for summer seas and safe voyage,

"many marvels occurred, to display the favor of Heaven
"towards him. A certain man of the Alexandrian
"populace, known to suffer from wasted eyeballs, clasped
"his knees and with a moan claimed of him a remedy
"for his blindness. The goddess Serapis, whom above
"all other deities this superstitious race honors, had
"urged him to this step,—and he kept imploring the
"prince, to deign to spatter saliva on his cheeks and
"eyeballs. Another, who was crippled in the hand,
"prompted by the same deity, begged that the foot and
"step of Cæsar might trample on his limb. Vespasian
"at first laughed at it, and refused; but when the
"patients persisted, he at one moment dreaded the dis-
"credit of silly assumption; at the next was moved into
"hope by their urgent entreaties and by the flattering
"cheers from others. Finally, he ordered the physicians
"to form a judgment, whether such blindness and such
"disablement were within human aid. The physicians
"discussed the case on several sides, saying: that in the
"blind eye force of sight was not extinct, but only
"impeded: that the crippled limb was dislocated, yet
"possibly force wisely applied might restore it; that
"perhaps the gods had such a result at heart, and a
"Prince had been chosen for a divine ministration. In
"fine, if the remedy succeeded, Cæsar would win the
"glory: if it failed, the poor wretches would hav to
"bear the ridicule. Thereupon Vespasian, thinking all
"things open to his fortune, and nothing any longer
"incredible, put on a joyful countenance, and while the
"crowd around gave earnest attention, performed the
"bidding [of the patients.] Instantly the hand became
"manageable, and light re-illumined the blind eye.
"Each fact is asserted by bystanders, up to the present
"day, when falsehood has nothing to gain."—So far
Tacitus. As he probably wrote full thirty years later, it

is open to conjecture that in place of "bystanders" he ought to hav written, "those who ar said to profess to "hav been present."

But it is a fair inference that a belief had gone widely abroad in Western Asia and Egypt, even reaching to the Greek and Italian Sibyls, that a great Deliverer was to come from the East; also, that when he came, he would work miracles of healing on various classes of disease. No other *note of Messiah* can be named as popular in Asia.

CHAPTER IV.

ROMAN CONQUEST OF JUDÆA.

THE Greek monarchy in Syria received its first shock from the Romans (B.C. 190) under the two Scipios, which established in Asia Roman power from the coast to Mount Taurus. After this their predominance was undisputed, until their own Italian and domestic conflicts emboldened the Greek cities to insurrection, aided by Mithridates, king of Pontus or Cappadocia. This war lingered on until in B.C. 66 Pompey the Great was sent to conduct it, then at the height of his celebrity for his wonderful rapidity of success against the ubiquitous pirates of the seas. He was eminently mild and humane; but, entrusted with a great army, he was quite aware that more would be expected of him in Rome than to put the last stroke to an old war. He had traversed Armenia and approached the Caspian Sea, but now resolved to march into Syria. He did so, and conquered it from north to south; deposed the XIth Antiochus, and made a present of Syria and Palestine to the Roman people.

The Romans had been glad to win the Jews as allies against kings of Syria, and ordinarily accounted allies as a second morsel to be devoured. But this time the forciner invited the Roman commander in. There were three parties in Jerusalem; a popular party which disliked royalty, and two brothers, Hyrcanus and Aristobulus, in civil war for the pontifical throne. Pompey listened to the pleas of all three, but deferred his verdict until he could hear what the Idumean chief Aretas, ally of the *elder* brother Hyrcanus, had to plead. Meanwhile Pompey commanded abstinence from warlike action. Aristobulus was too fierce, or dreaded to lose all by losing time. His disobedience and activity seem to hav thrown Pompey on to the side of Hyrcanus. Before long, the Romans found self-defence needful, and a stubborn conflict ensued. Though Hyrcanus largely controuled the rural populace, and had many partizans in Jerusalem itself, yet from no city in Syria did Pompey meet with resistance so formidable. These Jews were stricter in observance of the sabbath than those of Maccabean times. At the earlier era, when it was perceived that to allow the enemy's works to proceed without molestation during the sabbath, was to yield themselves to slaughter, they had worked against him in those sacred hours, though reluctantly. But Pompey, besides important aid from one faction, encountered men too scrupulous to work against him on the sabbath; who indeed calmly continued their incense, their sacrifices or expiation, while slaughtered by his missiles. Finally, only in the third month of his siege was he able to surmount the inner wall of the temple, though at the head of a veteran army. He marvelled at the scene, as we in reading of it. He is not likely to hav reflected, as we do, on the mischiefs of a sacred code, which none may criticize and improve.

Much as we must honor the self-devotion of those Jews, it is clear that Reverence paralyzed their intellect. Men's good sense will struggle upwards against a misplaced reverence. Sacredness of the letter therefore generates a perverse logic, just as in lawyers whose problem it is to reconcile a barbarous code with maturer judgments. Fanciful analogies, arbitrary presumptions, subtle distinctions ar invoked and approved, in aid of justice or mercy. In the Mosaic books religion, law, medicin, agriculture were interfused. Gentile beliefs were superadded: out of this mass the Rabbi had to hammer results that satisfy utility and wisdom; and every bigot had advantage over a larger-hearted expounder. From this system proceeded much heroism and fanatical energy, also much crooked subtlety of the moderate and comparativly wise.

Pompey from curiosity entered the Holy of Holies, but refused to plunder the gold of the temple, and restrained his soldiers from violence. From rudeness and insult to Jewish scruples, to restrain them was impossible. Moreover the eagles on his standard, being worshipped as idols, were a dire abomination. Their very entrance into the Holy City was an affliction to Jewish sentiment.

This new conquest by an idolatrous foe was a painful wound, after a century of belief that under Jehovah's protection Jehovah's people were safe. Severe doubts awoke as to the lawfulness of professing allegiance. The book of Deuteronomy seemed expressly to forbid; for (xvii. 11) in allowing them to choose a king it imposes two conditions, *first*, the king must be the man whom Jehovah shall choose—(therefore could not be an idolater);

next, he must be "one of thy brethren; but a stranger "thou mayest not set over thee, who is not thy brother." This prohibition was to many decisiv. Besides, a fine Psalm (cxxv.) givs a powerful moral reason. The sceptre of the wicked shall not rest on the lot of the righteous, *lest the righteous put forth his hand to injustice.* From every province the Roman rule tore away the young men to fight in aggressiv wars against distant peoples. Jehovah seemed to affirm that he rested "like "the mountains around his people," to shield them from this base subservience. Tender consciences were pierced by this liability. Brave and ardent souls must hav braced themselves, like our Quakers, to refuse it, and to deny the rightfulness of allegiance and loyalty. Not many of the wisest would see how to reconcile the command of the law with the dictates of prudence; nor how in sincerity to make professions which the conqueror would not interpret to mean, "We shall rebel as soon as we "dare,"—if nothing but inability to resist justified submission. That the religion was an intense explosiv, was soon manifest, and the Romans felt towards it, in vehement combination, Fear, Disgust and Hatred. How else feel Britons toward Islam in India?

After so difficult a conquest, no one will wonder that heavier tribute was laid on the Jews than on the Syrian towns. Romans indeed could justify this by a very peculiar reason. Because of suspension of culture in the sabbatical *year*, it was impossible to collect taxes. Therefore if in six years they collected seven years' revenu, they did nothing unfair to this eccentric people. At the same time it gave a new stone to fling at the Jews, as *lovers of idleness.*

Pompey, with his uniform humanity, tried to conciliate good will, and to arrange all things by healing measures. After his departure, first a son of Aristobulus, next the father himself, escaping from Roman captivity, renewed civil war, with nothing but distress to the Jews. Presently, the Roman consul Crassus plundered all the treasures which Pompey had spared, and perished with the chief part of his army in an expedition against the Parthians. Tranquillity was chiefly restored through the energy and sagacity of an Edomite prince, Antipater, son-in-law to a powerful Arabian chieftain. Apparently he belonged to the part of Idumea, which had accepted with circumcision the whole Mosaic ceremonial; so that he and his family passed as Jews. He had been a vehement and serviceable partizan of Hyrcanus and Pompey; but after civil war had divided the Romans and Pompey was murdered in Egypt, he quickly espoused the side of Cæsar, and rendered him signal service in a dangerous crisis. For this he was made prefect of Judæa, and conducted affairs cautiously through the terrible struggle which still convulsed the empire. His son is known to us as Herod the Great.

The ascent of Herod to power was singularly rapid. His father made him governor of Galilee when he was twenty-five years old. Sextus Cæsar, being temporarily in command, added to him the rule over Hollow Syria, B.C. 43. Driven out by the Parthians, who invaded Syria after their success against Crassus, he escaped to Rome. By large bribes he had previously won favor with Mark Antony, whose influence now gained for him the title, King of Judæa. But to turn the name into a fact, a new war was needed, and a new capture of unhappy Jerusalem. His actual reign is dated B.C. 37. Twenty years later he began to rebuild the temple magnificently. His reign was energetic but violent; to his wife and kinsfolk murderous. He rebuilt the town called the Tower of Straton and named the new city Cæsarea, in honor of Augustus Cæsar. It had a temple in Greek fashion; but in his later years he cast off all pretence of Judaism, and brought in Roman customs. His death is computed to hav fallen in March, B.C. 4. It will be observed that, according to historians, the current reckoning of the Christian era is wrong by three years.*

CHAPTER V.

JEWISH SECTS AND JUDAS GAULANITIS.

THE prophet Isaiah looked forward with joy to the time, when, under the righteous rule of a king from the root of Jesse, Ephraim would not envy Judah and Judah would not vex Ephraim. The head of Ephraim was Samaria, and the head of Judah was Jerusalem. But alas! in five hundred years the enmity of these rivals did not come to an end. After the captivity of the ten tribes, miscellaneous Eastern colonists were planted in all the towns of Samaria, who never wholly accepted the religious law of Jerusalem. They ar mentioned in a contemptuous tone (2 Kings xvii. 32—41) as "fearing "Jehovah and serving graven images *unto this day*,"— probably full as late as Ezra. Even now no Samaritan can obtain a Jewess as his wife! They hav the Pentateuch in a character older than the square Chaldee type, and, it is believed, they do not accept any other writing as sacred. Circumcision did not suffice to unite them cordially with Jerusalem. Which was earlier to blame,

---

* As we admit *no year of zero*, the common chronology supposes Jesus to hav been born in B.C. 1, and to hav been *one* year old in A.D. 1. From B.C. x to A.D. y is not $(x+y)$ years, but $(x+y-1)$.

is unknown; but Samaria ill-endured subjection to Maccabean rule: we may conjecture that sufficient local freedom was denied to her. This system of centralization made other towns disaffected. She is said to hav preferred a Syrian master. Josephus narrates that (perhaps about B.C. 120) while two brothers, the VIIIth and IXth called Antiochus, were in long contest for the throne of Syria, a Jewish High Priest called Hyrcanus took the opportunity of revenge against Samaria for being the ally of Syria against Jerusalem. After a year's siege he not only captured the city (Antiq. xiii. 10, 3), but by diverting mountain torrents against the walls swept away all appearance that it had been fortified. Hereby the Samaritans were made more and more hostile, though the weaker party. Their town being in the high road from Upper Galilee to Jerusalem, they had opportunity to insult, vex and sometimes to murder; a crime which was imputed. Later, on the sacred day of Jerusalem, when the Holy Place was accessible to the multitude, Samaritans tumultuously rushed in and defiled it by throwing in dead men's bones. For this offence all Samaritans were excluded from the temple, and the Jews sought to avoid all needless dealings with them. When, through insurgency against Rome, banditti abounded in the land whom it was hard to distinguish from patriots, new opportunities arose to Samaritans for outbursts of vengeance and spite. Thus against the Romans the real force of Pan-Judæa was never united.

Among the Jews at large three religious sects were at this time reckoned: Sadducees, Pharisees, and Essenes. The Sadducees adhered to the old law and refused to accept the imported doctrins of future life and retribution, heaven and hell, genii or demons enthroned in the air and reigning over special nations, angels personally united to individuals (the Roman or Etruscan idea of each man's special genius? Compare Matthew xviii. 10), demons possessing men's bodies, and other tenets which the Jews of that day had imbibed. Against the doctrin of life renewed to an individual after death they were able to argu, that it had been in very early days the established dogma in Egypt; that Moses, being well educated in Egyptian lore, cannot hav been unacquainted with it; therefore his total omission of it in the Law is a virtual protest against it as false. If he had believed it, such suppression would hav been guilt and cannot be imputed to him. They refused all attempts to soften the asperities of his law; hereby were accounted very severe as judges. Moreover, they ar spoken of as existing chiefly among the richer, perhaps the haughtier, part of the community,—a sacerdotal caste, virtually royalist.

The Pharisees were far more numerous and far more popular. To them, apparently, belonged the majority of the Doctors of the Law or Rabbis. To the multitude the Sadducees did not appear devout; but the Pharisees much more commanded their veneration. These diligently cultivated moral science (no doubt with frequent over-subtlety) — and honored the maxims of deceased worthies, under the name of tradition. They largely adopted and systematized forein religious notions. Partly by tradition and partly by ingenious reasoning, they labored to adapt all the laws of the Pentateuch to the needs of the modern nation, and to soften down some of its very harsh punishments. We may conjecture from the apocryphal story in John viii., that they judged the punishments commanded by the law against female unchastity to be extreme and barbarous. Of course they could not avow this,—perhaps not even to themselves. A crooked ingenuity was their only practical resource, and such lawyer-like habit must somewhat pervert the intellect. Nevertheless to this sect mainly were due such prosperity and goodness as prevailed in domestic life, and such just and mild administration as largely conduced to the public welfare.

The third sect, the Essenes, is far more peculiar. That any establishment of it existed at Jerusalem we ar not informed. There were many of them in Syria and in Egypt, as attested by Philo. Their number is estimated (in Judæa) at four hundred thousand. They were Jews, yet they had peculiarities as to ceremonial practices which forbad their admission to the altar in Jerusalem. They were like an Order in Christendom, with separate government and stringent laws; a Church within a Church. The basis of their Union was common property. For any one who wished to join them the first step was, to throw his private property into their general fund. From it each had his equal share of food and clothes, as brethren. There was no one centre for the Order, but special Establishments in many towns. Each member was at home in any of them, and partook of all things on a par with residents. Hence in travelling they needed no baggage, or wallet of provisions, no purse, no second coat, only *arms for defence against robbers*. Thus they were not absolute Quakers. Their costume was probably simple and uniform; it was of pure white like that of priests in Egypt, and many in Syria and Crete. Their food was equally simple. Virtue they placed in superiority to appetite and pleasure. On Marriage a majority of them looked down as a weakness; yet they zealously adopted the children of others. They eagerly studied ancient books concerning the Soul and the Body, Philosophy and Health. From Greek poets they imported a belief concerning the Isles of the Blessed, and other notions; from Plato or from the East, ideas concerning Spirit and Matter. Though scrupulously cleanly, they yet avoided to oil the skin,—a process like our use of soap,—whether regarding it as luxurious, or because the oils in the market prevalently came from Syria, and were manufactured by idolaters.

The managers of their common property were elected by general vote; and in each establishment a special caretaker for strange members was appointed. Clothes and shoes they wore without change, until useless by time and rents. Among themselves they neither bought nor sold, but freely received and freely gave.

The routine of their work and meals as described in Josephus reminds one of a well-ordered Catholic friarhood or a community of American Shakers. At the common table they hav two meals in a day. Religion is everywhere prominent, and noble moral precepts ar inculcated. Silence, gravity and respect for Elders ar always maintained. They go to various work, under the despotic rule of a director, and hav no free action, save to bring Aid and Mercy to those who ar in need. Before entering the dinner-hall they bathe in cold water and dress in linen coverings, which after dinner they put off as sacred. At the beginning and end of the meal a priest says grace, and the whole company pays honor to God as the provider of food. Neither cries nor tumult pollute the house, but they concede alternate gentle talk. Anger they deal out justly, passion they restrain, good faith they uphold, to make peace they ar activ. Oaths among themselves ar superfluous and forbidden, but from candidates for admission they exact frightful oaths, with a probation lasting for three years. Each candidate swears to keep nothing from the community, and to suffer death rather than reveal its secrets. But these secrets must hav been quite harmless in ordinary times; for Peace, Truth, and Justice were the paramount principles of the Order, and, as it were its normal mottoes.

c

Yet such a community would seem to any Roman officer detestable, the moment he learned that it had oaths of secrecy; and after the insurrection of Judas, called the Galilean, he would think his horror and his hatred to be fully justified. A few words ar needed concerning this Judas, and we take up the tale from the death of Herod the Great.

War, says the earliest of philosophic historians, is a severe schoolmaster. The sufferings of the Jewish people, the hopelessness of revolt, the vehemence of Herod hushed for awhile the outbreaks of religious zeal: but on Herod's death new tumults arose. The dissensions among his children probably awakened in the discontented a hope that a time of redress was come: but the complexity of affairs is far too great here to detail. Archelaus, son of Herod, made promises which were perhaps interpreted as a sign of weakness. Strange movements followed, which frightened the Roman officers in the province; and, to inspire terror, *one* officer, Sabinus, is stated by Josephus to hav crucified about *two thousand* Jews as insurgents. (Bell. Jud. ii. 5, 8.) Their action being necessarily that of *guerilla*, the Romans treated them all as robbers. Yet we may hope that popular report or Roman policy exaggerated the number.

Archelaus, by the decision of Augustus Cæsar, succeeded to about half of his father's kingdom, with the title *ethnarch* (nativ magistrate); but after ten years of very unpopular rule, he was deposed by Augustus, and the whole of his territory *was absorbed in the Roman province of Syria*. Thus Judæa, Samaria and Galilee were placed for the first time *under direct Roman rule*, about A.D. 6 or 7, and Quirinius (or in Greek Cyrenius), governor of Syria, became also chief governor of the western half of Palestine. Augustus ordered the usual

Roman registration of income to be made with a view to taxation. Herod or his son Archelaus may in their irregular way hav fleeced the Jews as much in the past, as was to be feared in the future; but these Idumeans passed as nativ princes, being circumcised. The fact that a forein idolater was registering every field and farm-house with a view to tax it, brought home to the Galileans the completeness of their slavery as never before. Judas, of the city of Gamala, beyond Jordan, in the district of Gaulana, first stirred the hill people to resistance, in company with Sadok, a Pharisee. This Judas was an Essene, a religious devotee; Josephus calls him a *sophist*, that is, a student of science or wisdom. He not only roused his own sect, but spread revolt through the most thickly peopled part of Palestine, refusing to listen to the prudential counsels of the high priest at Jerusalem. His doctrin was mainly religious. The Jews, having God for their king, were base in enduring mortal lords; but he made also the political addition, that to submit to be registered for forein taxation was a first step to utter slavery. With brave men who were *not* zealots in religion, he was able to use the very effectiv argument—It is better to die, fighting for nativ law and liberty, than to be forced into the ranks of Rome, and sent abroad to die in fighting against the liberty of other brave nations. In Galilee his revolt was apparently most formidable, therefor he was popularly called Judas *of Galilee*. Galilee is inferior in acreage to that ultra-Jordan district,—the old land of Bashan, Ammon, and Moab, then called the *Peræa*, and included in Palestine; but Josephus says, Galilee was more populous. The soil remained soft in the driest summer, being watered by mountain streams. For fruit and for every kind of crop it was excellently suited. Petty towns or large villages abounded, the smallest

having a population of 5,000. Such a nativ mass of brave agriculturists made a Roman general tremble, if he heard the whisper of religious fanaticism. Though Judas belonged to the very peaceful and righteous sect of Essenes, yet, once launched into insurgency, he could not afford to reject brave and earnest allies from any quarter. Guerilla subject to a local captain ar ill-distinguishable anywhere from banditti and robbers; and when their fanaticism rose to the point of treating Jews who would not join them as partizans of the enemy,[*] they virtually became robbers and assassins, as the Romans describe them. It was a frightful struggle, but Roman resources gave to Rome the victory. The cruelty of her revenge may measure her losses and her alarm. The Roman commander thought to cut away future insurrection by crushing out the religion of the Essenes; with this object he insisted on their *blaspheming Moses* and *eating food forbidden by their ceremonial law*. Josephus summarizes their treatment in a few dreadful lines. After stating their great longevity,—many of them living above a hundred years,—and their astonishing contempt of pain and death, he adds the following:—
"The Romans racked and twisted, burnt and broke them, "and passed them through all instruments of torture, to "force them to blaspheme Moses, or eat some forbidden "food. They not only refused; but disdaining to coax "their tormentors, addressed them with irony, and "yielded up their lives cheerfully, as about soon to "recover them."

Augustus Cæsar would not have formally sanctioned any such violences against a national religion; but his subordinates well knew that he never punished provincial

---

[*] In the Anglo-American war of independence, the insurgents treated the "Tories" as spies and friends of England. But Lord Cornwallis pressed them into English ranks, and in so far exhibited them as marks for attack.

authorities even for enriching themselves unjustly; and that too great zeal in the public service was never resented. In short, while military weakness was a bar to promotion, high-handed cruelties in or after insurrection would be accepted as marking an energetic officer. But on the Jewish nation what must hav been the moral result? Who can blame them, if they more and more abhorred subjection to Rome? No doubt, they did hate *Roman* rule, as we should; perhaps they hated the sight of a Roman. Thereupon, Roman historians call them *haters of all mankind*, and believe themselves impartial and philosophic.

CHAPTER VI.

JOHN THE BAPTIST.

CONCERNING John the Baptist we learn not only from the books of the Christian Canon: we hav corroboration from the historian Josephus (Antt. xvii. 5, 1—2). No one has seen reason to doubt the substantial accuracy of all that will be here adduced concerning the career of this singular man.

Some hav plausibly maintained that he must hav belonged to the Essene sect; but whether rightly or wrongly, is of no importance whatever. He did *not* adopt the Essene costume, nor subject himself in any way to the authorities of that sect. His very partial clothing reminds one of an Egyptian monk. He had a gown of camel's hair and a girdle of leather; very insufficient in a winter of frost and snow: but as the description places him by the side of the river Jordan, probably in the plain of Jericho celebrated in antiquity for its palm trees, at a depth of many hundred feet below the Mediterranean sea, raiment so scanty may well hav suited that climate. His food is stated to hav been locusts and wild honey. Locusts make their appearance only for a very short season, and in exceptional years: hence it has been plausibly suggested that the *fruit of the locust tree* has been confounded with the insects. If on such fruit and on wild honey he subsisted for some time, this may hav been set down as his sole and uniform food. The likeness of his exterior to that which was believed to hav been assumed by ancient Hebrew prophets, caused a great sensation even in Jerusalem itself; especially when the topic of his preaching became known, for his great announcement was, " *The* " *kingdom of God* (or of Heaven) *is at hand.*" Most acceptable was such a message to a people who for above eighty years had groaned under Roman despotism—a power which had inflicted countless miseries not only on insurgents, but also on the most peaceable and submissiv, in the unrelenting and cruel struggle of ambition. Moreover, if in very truth the kingdom of God were at hand, the prophet Malachi warned them that God would send to them Elijah the prophet before that great and terrible day. Would it not appear that this strange and mysterious John was (somehow) Elijah in disguise?

But that was not all. John was a fervent preacher of righteousness and a rebuker of sin, and taught that the great day of God would bring destruction not only on forein oppressors and idolaters, but also on all wicked members of the Jewish nation itself. Therefor he cried to all who were conscious of sin, " *Repent ye;* for the "kingdom of Heaven is at hand." In token of repentance he urged them to adopt a rite employed by the Pharisees and others in the admission of proselytes (that is, converts) to Jewish religion,—the rite of *baptism;* a

Greek word which means *plunging* (or being plunged) under water. In that latitude, especially in the climate of Jericho, a dip under water could seldom be very disagreeable, often the contrary. "To wash away filth "of the flesh," (as an Apostle entitles it,) betokened the renunciation of all that defiles the soul. Numbers of the Jews flocked to John, "and were baptized of him in "Jordan, confessing their sins."

The belief further went abroad, *perhaps* even in this early stage, that certain other words of high prophecy pointed at this John. He whom we call the later Isaiah, exhorting his countrymen to return to Jerusalem when permitted by Cyrus, imagins Jehovah himself journeying back to Jerusalem, and *a voice in the desert* commanding a royal high road to be constructed for his easy passage. The multitude who had no access to the entire roll of the prophet, and no ability to interpret poetical imagery, easily believed John to be meant by "the voice crying "in the wilderness," in preparation of the coming *kingdom of God*.

The three first books which we call gospels agree that a vast multitude from Jerusalem as well as from other parts flocked to John, to confess sin and to be baptized. All three represent him as uttering severe rebuke, and predicting that every tree which bore no good fruit would be cut down and cast into the fire. Luke represents him as entitling the mixed concourse "a brood of "adders." Matthew says, he uttered the phrase against certain Pharisees and Sadducees from Jerusalem, scornfully asking them, "Who hath warned you to flee from "the impending wrath (of God)?" On the whole, his preaching is broadly clear. A day of fiery wrath and judgment is close at hand. Repent ye, and your sins will be remitted: so alone can ye find admission into the coming kingdom of God.

John uttered no direct word, so far as we know, against Roman rule. He attacked the sins of his own people. Its priestly rulers had been stripped by the Romans of the royal name, of royal revenues, and all the highest initiativ, by putting over them on one side a Roman prefect, on another Idumean ethnarchs. They remembered painfully that the scandalous controversy between two Jewish princes had helped these foreiners into their galling supremacy. Undeniably the nation was suffering through the sin of its chiefs, their predecessors. They bowed the head, at least in secret, to John's sharp invectivs. Besides, as Roman taxation seized for itself all the main revenues, it is very probable that the High Priest and his Great Council were unable to maintain their own dignity without severe exaction from petty sources, called in contempt, *mint* and *cummin*; exaction which perhaps seemed mean to themselves, even while they knew not how to dispense with it. Their conscience was uneasy, and an idea pervaded even Jerusalem that John was a prophet sent by God to rebuke them.

Out of this arose a new question in many minds, and especially in those least able to study the prophets carefully and intelligently; namely, Is not Messiah to be manifested as the Divine agent of Vengeance in the approaching Great Day of wrath and restitution? Must not John be a forerunner of Messiah, if the kingdom of God is really nigh at hand?

In the belief of a somewhat later generation,—a belief which may hav been correct,—John himself distinctly replied to this question, by avowing: "After me cometh "one mightier than I, whose shoe-latchet I am not "worthy to unfasten. I indeed baptize you with water: "he shall baptize you with the Holy Spirit;" words possibly alluding to the prophecy of diffused personal inspiration in the promised sacred era. (Jeremiah xxxi. 33, 34.) The Herod of that generation was at first impressed with much reverence for John; but when Herod proceeded to dismiss his own wife, and seduce his brother's wife, John faithfully rebuked him. Herod in anger first imprisoned, and finally beheaded John. War against Herod followed from the father of the divorced wife. Herod was defeated; and Josephus tells us, that from the universal reverence felt for John, the defeat was ascribed to a judgment of God.

CHAPTER VII.

SOURCES OF THE ACCOUNT OF JESUS.

WHEN John the Baptist vanishes from the page of Josephus, we ar cast upon the books called Gospels for information concerning the earthly life of Jesus. Justin Martyr, who wrote in defence of Christianity about A.D. 150,—hardly earlier,—is supposed to quote often from our Gospels, but seldom in exact words as we hav them. He does not name them as separate books, but calls them Memorials of the Apostles. Enormous study has been spent on the four books by modern theologians; and according to the positiv decision of those ostensibly best able to judge, the three first were compiled with *at least one common document* before all three writers' eyes. Luke had some additional documents. None of them can hav written as eye-and-ear witnesses. Some of the materials which they trusted *may* hav been penned in the earliest time. They *may* also hav been notes taken by hearers of the men called Evangelists, who orally recited to the first Gentile Churches the tales current among Jewish Christians. In the opening of the third Gospel we ar informed that *many* had already undertaken the same task. Luke's four first verses ar in a widely different Greek style from all that follows, showing that the writer of the preface is compiling, not composing. Of course this is favorable to his honesty of purpose; as showing that, in transmitting the account, he does not needlessly change its forms of expression.

To accept marvellous tales on the word of writers who do not define their grounds of assurance, the date and names of their authorities, nor giv to their own contemporaries any means of examining, — belongs to inexperience. We see that no idea of the necessity of Criticism had presented itself to them. If we happened to know that their date was much earlier than that of Justin Martyr, it would not accredit their books; chiefly, because they evidently count upon extreme credulity in their readers and hereby display their own credulity. They expect us to receive religious miracles with immense results, if true,—and very pernicious, if untrue,—solely because an unknown writer tells us he has carefully compiled them; or even without his saying so much as that. They could not so write unless they were ignorant of the deceptivness of report and the mischiefs of credulity;—ignorant that all the baneful follies of false religion rise out of the too great readiness of mankind to believe in marvel. As to the current pretence that these writers ar divinely shielded from error, it is sufficient to reply that they themselves advance no such claim. It is made *for* them,—for the convenience of Christian assumption. Of course, if they made it, that would no more *in itself* prove anything, than if made by any of us moderns. It would need proof, if made; and would be liable to disproof. In fact the disproof is in the case before us easy and obvious. The pretence to divine exemption from error is refuted by single clear instances; for God cannot be the author of falsehood. The frequent error of these writers in interpreting ancient prophecy is palpable. That it is impossible to reconcile the four Gospels has been discovered with dismay by many pious Christians, when they tried to interweave the four into a continuous narrativ. The demonstration has been set forth many times over. Space cannot here be allowed for an argument hard to exhaust. A few words on the first Gospel may be premised with the remark, that no Unitarian can (with the late Dr. Lant Carpenter) gain credit for the rest of the book by cutting away the two first chapters as unworthy of belief. All comes out of the same mint.

Matthew opens by an error in his genealogy. He has confounded Ahaziah with his great grandson Uzziah in the name of Ozias, and has omitted thereby three generations, and he counts fourteen where there ar seventeen or eighteen. He also confounds Jehoiakim with his son Jehoiachin or Jeconiah. Such blunders ar not made by the Spirit of God. He proceeds to narrate the miraculous conception on the strength of *a dream* which Joseph *is said to hav had* many years back; a miracle unheard of by the local public during the life of Jesus. This writer rests an event, on which he supposes the salvation of the world to depend, on evidence which *nowhere* would suffice to establish the most ordinary fact. In corroboration he misinterprets Isaiah's words, "A "maiden shall conceive," Isaiah vii. 14. But the prophet spoke of that which was to happen *immediately*. Before the child should be able to talk, the king of Assyria was to plunder Damascus. He evidently contemplated an ordinary birth, which apparently was fulfilled in his own son, Isaiah viii. 3. So easily is a miracle accepted and supposed to be confirmed!

Next follows a miraculous travelling star which conducts Persian Magi to the birthplace of Jesus; a tale which to no astronomer is plausible. A horrible cruelty is ascribed to Herod the Great, a public deed that must hav been notorious, and must hav been recorded by Josephus in narrating his great crimes;—the massacring of all infants under the age of two years, in and round Bethlehem. Here again he perverts prophecy to establish his apocryphal fact. Further, a journey of Joseph into Egypt is fabricated out of a ludicrous blunder. The prophet Hosea, alluding *historically* to the residence of the Israelites in Egypt, represents Jehovah as saying: "When Israel was a child, I loved him; and called my "son out of Egypt." Matthew misquotes it as a *prophecy* concerning Jesus; and from it invents for him a residence in Egypt during his infancy. Can there be any literary weakness greater, than to accept this writer as divinely guided?

Presently he givs us a calm narrativ of Satan carrying away Jesus to a pinnacle of the Temple, and again to the top of a high mountain whence all the kingdoms of the world, and the glory of them, *could be seen;* an absurdity which confutes itself. Philosophical divines may interpret this as an "allegory;" but the writer accepted it and transmits it as fact. But again, he omits to tell us, whence came the knowledge of it; whether from Satan or from Jesus,—the only two who were cognizant of it.

A general remark must not be omitted concerning a superstition pervading the three first gospels, a superstition imported from heathenism surrounding them. Diseases well-known to us ar ascribed to indwelling demons. As if to prevent philosophic divines from explaining it away, the demons ar said to hav a preternatural acquaintance with Jesus as the Holy One of God.

In one signal case told by all three, a legion of such demons obtain leave from Jesus to enter the bodies of swine, when he expels them from the bodies of men. The exchange is effected. To argu against a story worthy only of the "Arabian Nights" is hardly worth while.

One who in the present light of geographical, physical and historical culture,—to say nothing of sound principles of literary interpretation,—can accept miracles in a past day on the mere word of *such* writers, otherwise unknown, may be pious and estimable, no doubt; but his judgment in the immediate question is not worth a rush. We need not go so far as the celebrated doctrin of David Hume, taken in its extremest form. It suffices to say that marvellous tales cannot be accredited by writers of whom we know nothing certain, except their credulity and their tendency to make history out of fancied prophecy.

There is no end of proof as to imaginary miracle. It is not amiss to speak of what oneself can testify. (1) When I returned from abroad in 1833, a lady eagerly inquired the details of my miraculous recovery from sickness. I did not understand her question. She explained: "I was told that in desperate fever you were "anointed with oil in the name of the Lord, and that "restored you to health." Most true (I replied) that I was thus anointed, but the fever got worse. After a sixth violent sweating it finally left me, unable to rise from the bed for a fortnight; and only after six months, by help of riding, I gradually regained my muscle. That there was any miracle, never occurred to me.—The lady was much disappointed. I believe she had trumpeted the cure.—(2) Another lady, a Mrs. Cummings, cousin to the late Lady Powerscourt, gave me the following account of herself. While Edward Irving, Hugh McNeil, and other religious persons well-known in 1830-33 were full of debates about the Second Advent of Jesus, Lady Powerscourt's house was made a place of conference. Many assembled there, when (as happened) Mrs. Cummings was laid up in (supposed) pulmonary consumption. Edward Irving heard of it, and sent a message up to the lady's chamber, that he should like to pray over her, and hoped the prayer of faith might restore her. She sent down a flat refusal, begging him not to invade her privacy. Instead of obeying, he suddenly marched into her chamber, and began to pray aloud. She hid herself under the clothes, but presently by a stolen glance saw that he held both hands up to heaven while vociferating. Much relieved she was, when he, as abruptly, vanished; for *she had no belief* in his prayers. Yet, continuing her tale, "certain it seemed to others that every day after "his prayer I got a little better, until I rose from my "bed and was accounted well. Mr. Irving used to "reproach me with unbelief, that I did not recognize my "recovery as miraculous. I *never* had belief in the "efficacy of his prayer; I still do not know whether it "aided my recovery."—(3) While I write, placards in the shop windows of this town (Weston-super-Mare) profess to attest miraculous cures wrought by mere faith. To deny its power in *some* maladies seems unavailing.

That the original of Matthew xxiv. was first imagined during the siege of Jerusalem by Titus, is almost certain. Christian interpreters hav commented triumphantly on the close agreement of the prophecy with known history in verses 15—28; yet in the next verse, 29, it becomes manifestly and hopelessly false. For it predicts a convulsion of sun, moon, and stars, and *the appearance of the sign of* THE SON OF MAN *in heaven*. One might explain away sun, moon, and stars as oriental extravagance; but the Son of Man coming in the clouds was a definit miracle long earnestly expected, and incapable of being misunderstood. The text asserts that this great event shall be seen *immediately* after the tribulation; and Jesus is made to add (v. 34), "This generation shall not pass, till all these things be fulfilled." A prophecy of which the close is false, cannot be divine. If the earlier part is too close to actual history to hav been foreseen by human faculties, the whole must hav been composed after those historical events. (A like case was noticed in Daniel xi., xii.) Evidently then, Jesus *never uttered this prophecy at all;* but it was imagined for him during the terrible excitement of the war with Titus. The fact givs us a very definit warning as to the quality of these writings.

A few historical errors ar notorious, which may here be briefly indicated. Luke gravely mistakes the Roman census enforced by Cyrenius (Quirinius), both as to substance and as to time. Augustus (says he) ordered a census over the whole *inhabited world*—(wonderful extravagance of language); really over Syria and that part of Palestine which had been under Archelaus. This was not while Herod the Great was still alive, as Luke asserts; but when his son Archelaus was deposed by Augustus,—full ten years after Herod's death.—The same writer, in Acts v. 36, makes Gamaliel speak of the tumult of Theudas as preceding the insurrection of Judas Galilaeus; but the affair of Theudas was while Cuspius Fadus was prefect, in the reign of Claudius Cæsar. Gamaliel is made to speak *historically* of an event *then in the future.* Evidently his speech is an after-fiction. Such is the writer on whose word we ar to accept miracles!

Also, Jesus is made to speak historically of Zacharias, son of Barachias, as last of the martyrs; while in the actual history he was martyred thirty-seven years later, during the siege of Jerusalem by Titus.

Out of such documents no man can construct a tale claiming to be certain history—ascertained fact. The utmost that can be fairly asked or wisely undertaken, is, an account *possible and not improbable.* The three first Gospels, though full of tales that cannot reasonably be accepted as fact, and of facts that may justly be suspected as falsely colored, yet contain much beside which was hard to invent, and much which the writers would never hav willingly penned, had not a strong current of tradition floated it down to them as true. Such ar various small details which *prima facie* ar derogatory to Jesus.

Theodore Parker put forth the epigram, that it would take a Jesus to invent a Jesus: an epigram which has a measure of truth, but far less than he supposed. Every artist knows, that the more peculiar ar any man's features, the easier it is to caricature them. So, the more original a man's discourses and the more eccentric his conduct, the easier it is to interlard fictitious additions that shall be plausible. Given a first sketch of Jesus, and it needs no high genius to amplify and paint it up. Given an eccentric Jesus, time and oral tradition suffice for the genesis of a caricature, venerable to some, damaging with others. If any one can purge these narrativs of their dross, by all means let him do it, and that quickly: but to acknowledge that they ar full of false representations, yet to read them as sacred books, is "a mockery, "a delusion, and a snare."

Another topic here presses on us. The greater the value of the discourses of Jesus and the wider the authority they were to exercise, so much the more urgent was the need of a well-authenticated primitiv version. Nothing of the sort has been bequeathed by him. He has left us to guess how the narrativs were framed, preserved, compiled. Can he possibly hav foreseen the prominence which they were about to receive, and the malignant consequences in the far future of leaving his doctrin as matter of controversy?

Concerning the fourth gospel we may briefly say: (1) that it starts by contradicting the other three on a cardinal point, in representing the Messiahship of Jesus as notorious to Andrew, brother of Simon, before they became disciples of Jesus; (2) that it replaces demoniac cures chiefly by two stupendous miracles performed in Jerusalem under the immediate cognizance of the rulers, who in vain strove to confute them. If the first three writers had ever heard of them, they *must* hav recorded them. If they never heard of them, the tales ar fraudulent inventions. (3) The Greek style of the fourth gospel credibly fixes it to be the work of John the Elder, from whom we hav three epistles. The doctrin in both is that of the second century, not of the first. (4) By substituting the magnificent address and prayer in John xiv.—xvii. for the agony in the garden, he betrays his object to be, *not* historical truth, but the glorification of Jesus. (5) The tale of Thomas, if true, could not hav been omitted by the others. This also must hav been a wilful conscious fiction.

A learned Unitarian* tells us that all difficulties of the fourth gospel "fall away at once, when we note that "this gospel is not and does not intend to be a source of "information concerning the historical Jesus, but is a "profession and testimony of faith put forward a century "after his death."—How easy to say, *does not intend to be!* Forsooth, the writer did not wish readers to believe what he writes solemnly and earnestly! It is only *a testimony of faith!* Is it then matter of indifference to faith, whether the things told ar true or false? I respect

---

* *Modern Review*, July, 1881, p. 849.

the three first writers. I believe that, according to their faculties and culture, they aimed to write and propagate truth. If the fourth is regardless of truth and knowingly propagates false facts, surely we ought to warn the simple that he is base and fraudulent, not use smooth phrases that make light of pernicious delusion.

CHAPTER VIII.

JESUS OF NAZARETH.

FIRST PART.

SCARCELY was John thrown into prison, when a successor appeared who adopted John's own proclamation: "Repent "ye: for the kingdom of heaven is at hand." The recital of this formula is entitled: "preaching the Gospel "(or good news) of the Kingdom," and still more concisely, "preaching the word" (τόν λόγον—Mark ii. 2.) The new preacher was a young man of Nazareth, by name *Joshua*, (in Greek *Jesus)* but he assumed as his mystic title, "The Son of Man." Ezekiel in vision believed himself addressed by the phrase, "Oh Son of "Man," equivalent to Son of Adam, or mortal man. The prophecy called Daniel's represents one "like to a "Son of Man" coming in the clouds of Heaven in God's great day to receive universal dominion. Based on this was another prophetical book, which pretended to be written by Enoch, the seventh from Adam, and was accepted so widely as to deceive Jude, author of a Canonical Epistle. In this book Messiah is called both Son of Man and Son of God. Thus the title of Son of

Man was advantageously ambiguous. It could not be attacked as an assumption: for it was ostensibly humble. But if any one interpreted it magnificently, Jesus (unless the narrators wonderfully belie him) had no objection at all to that.

The first matter here needing notice, is, the prevalent ascription to him of miraculous power in healing the sick, especially (according to the superstition of the age) in casting out demons. To disentangle truth out of a mass of untrustworthy legends is (as above remarked) a task, to which at best we can but approximate. The following attempt at an outline givs certainly a *possible* solution; many will say,--one that is quite *probable*.

Much excitement had gone abroad, especially in the rural districts, through the preaching of John, who not only announced the kingdom of God to be nigh at hand, but added that one greater than himself would follow. Who could that be but Messiah? When therefor Jesus came forth, uttering the same note of warning, but accompanied by tones of comfort to the captiv and the prisoner, to the poor and the oppressed, he was readily believed to be the greater prophet foretold by John, and at once drew to himself a wide and eager audience. Reasons hav been given for believing that beyond the limits of Judaism a great deliverer was expected, who would relieve men's bodily diseases. In Jewish dialect, Messiah was to destroy all the works of the Devil; and in Jewish belief, such diseases were eminently Satan's work. Jesus in consequence found himself expected to open blind eyes and restore crippled limbs. One and another, avowing *faith* in his ability, implored him to heal them. Parents or kinsfolk brought to him paralytic patients, or pressed him to come and chase away fevers or epilepsy, and other maladies ascribed to demons.

That Jesus on many occasions reluctantly undertook

to work cures, is attested distinctly by statements which must hav been transmitted to the writers as *fact;* for none who believed in his power would forge reluctance for him. Sometimes, after effecting a cure, he strictly forbad the patient to disclose it; an unintelligible and misanthropic charge, as commonly understood. It admits of one reasonable explanation. Though he had been successful in the particular case, he yet had no confidence in his ability to repeat the cure, if a new case were brought, apparently alike, yet perhaps less tractable. On several occasions he emphatically says: " *Thy faith* "hath saved thee," as if disowning power in himself. He shuns the crowd, who beseech him for miraculous cure. He is often represented as *marvelling* at their faith. He repelled a Syrophœnician woman rather harshly, until overpowered by her faith. Further, when pressed to show some *sign,* i.e., some *external* display of his credentials from heaven, he severely rebukes the request, calling those who made it "an evil and "adulterous generation." If his words ar correctly reported, they necessarily imply that he made no pretension to miracles.

These statements ar not compatible with the theory that Divine Pity and Sympathy dictated the miracles of healing. (Indeed it cannot reasonably be believed that the Most High who leaves mankind at large to struggle against diseases unaided, was led by *Pity* to giv miraculous cure to a definit number of Jews in that one age.) But their very opposition to the popular theory givs to the statements an augury of truth. Evasiv as they appear, no one believing his miraculous power would hav originated them. By a still more formal deputation somewhat later he was asked for his authority. That must hav meant his "authority to use the high and "imperious tone of a prophet." Now if he had worked notorious miracles, he must hav appealed to them as his reply. Instead of this, he asks in turn: "What authority had John the Baptist?" putting himself on a par, as regards authority, with one to whom no miracles were imputed.— Matt. xxi. 23.

In summary then, we may believe, that Jesus, when pressed by patients and their friends for miraculous cures, as was Vespasian some forty years later,* yielded to their pressure, very doubtfully and anxiously. After he had found that some were apparently benefited, he attributed the benefit to *their faith*, while he marvelled at it. He gradually became less able to resist similar entreaties, but still was diffident, and unless he found *faith* to pre-exist, made no attempt whatever at miraculous cure.—Matt. xiii. 58. Also, on some occasions, when he had seemed to be successful in private, he so well knew the uncertainties of such affairs, that he charged the patient not to reveal the cure. If such was the true outline of facts, we might confidently predict how the tale would be painted up. The accretion of vague reports would become ever greater with the lapse of time. Fifty years later, narrators were sure to exaggerate the number, the nature and the completeness of the cures. We may add, that with the more enlightened even of the Jews, the casting out of demons was regarded as medical, not miraculous, nor would the rumour of occasional success easily raise religious expectation in their minds.—So much may here suffice concerning Demoniacs and their cure.

The *order* of events is various in different Gospels, therefor seldom can be trusted. We cannot be sure when first Jesus surrounded himself with twelve permanent companions. It is agreed that he very early called two

---

* See page 22.

brothers, Andrew and Simon, sons of Jonah, also two other brothers, John and James, sons of Zebedee. All were fishermen on the lake of Galilee. His previous celebrity as a preacher is implied in the fact, that at his call they abandoned their trade, and the second pair their father. Jesus himself had been a carpenter in Nazareth, a town of Galilee. If he had, merely as an aid to travel, taken some comrade, this would move no comment; but when he proceeded to augment his train of followers to *twelve*, which was the mythological number of the tribes of Israel, the case is altered. Afterwards we learn that when they asked what reward they should hav for abandoning their all, he promised that they should sit on twelve thrones, and judge the twelve tribes of Israel. It cannot be doubted that the number *twelve* was carefully planned in this aspect. It was a claim of supremacy on his part, such as no earlier prophet had made. The learned Christian historian Mosheim confidently interprets it as a silent claim of dominion over all Israel. Like the title "Son of Man," the procedure was eminently cautious. The deed implied much, but asserted nothing: it was enigmatic. It called on the multitude to interpret it themselves: it did not commit Jesus to anything. The twelve at once became *religious mendicants,* living on the pious for the honor of the Master; and if we believe our narrators, he threatened perdition to those who failed to giv them free entertainment. Matt. x. 15. See also x. 40.

Luke further ascribes to him the organization of *seventy* other disciples. The thought might occur, that they were a virtual bodyguard, too powerful for the feeble police of the Sanhedrin; a guard of whom the rulers were afraid. Mosheim thinks their number alluded to that of this sacred Council, and that this second appointment was also typical of dominion over Israel. But it is equally possible, that the "seventy" ar a later fiction, which deceived Luke.

The twelve in Matthew and the seventy in Luke ar sent on a mission with orders moulded on Essene travel. "Provide neither gold, nor silver, nor copper, in your "purses, nor wallet for your journey, nor two coats nor "shoes." Moreover he is said to hav endowed them with power over demons. (How little he trusted *his own* power in the matter, has been noticed.) When they tried and failed, he is made to ascribe their failure to the fact that that *sort* of demon needed *prayer* and FASTING as well as more *faith !* Yet his charge to them and his gift of power is represented as unhesitating and ample: "Heal the sick, cleanse the lepers, *raise the dead*, "cast out demons: *freely ye hav received;* freely giv." He either did not foresee that their lack of faith, lack of fasting or lack of prayer, would make his "free gift" useless; or else he never attempted at all to confer on them this wonderful and various power. The latter is the more respectful, as well as the obvious alternativ. The whole idea is a later fiction. From the apostolic epistles no hint of such a thing can be gathered. Indeed when the apostles ar supposed to be fullest of spiritual power, not one of them claims to raise the dead. Is it credible that they possessed it during the era of their imagined stupidity?

We can scarcely speak of any other Deeds of Jesus; we proceed therefor to his Words and Doctrin. As already said, following up John the Baptist, he announces the imminence of the Day of Wrath and God's Kingdom; but in one or two Parables (that is Comparisons) by which he chiefly taught, he introduced a strange deviation, which annuls the imminence of the day of wrath. In the Parable of the Tares, the "kingdom of heaven" seems to differ little from the evil rule which preceded it. For the Supreme Master forbids his servants to root up plants sown by the enemy (Satan). A day *yet future* is to be waited for, when the tares will be burned. Similarly as to the bad fish mixed with the good. Thus the day of wrath, which with John was nigh at hand and gave power to the call, Repent ye! is suddenly deferred to an era indefinitly distant,—*if* the narrativ is correct. Nevertheless, again and again the coming of Judgment is called imminent. What moral wisdom or lesson not previously well known is conveyed in Matthew's parables, is far from clear.

It is not in the parables, pervaded as most of them ar by a belief in the impending overthrow of all human rule, that we find the most valued elements of the teaching ascribed to Jesus. From his preaching we may plausibly date the turn of the tide in the whole Western world against the sacrifice of beasts as a religious ordinance. To us moderns this element of ancient piety seems monstrous. Not only in Hebrew, Egyptian, Greek and Roman ceremonies does it abound, but also in all the notices brought before us of outlying barbarism, whether African, German, Scythian or Tartar. In several of the Hebrew prophets and psalmists this practice is treated scornfully. "Thinkest thou that I will eat the "flesh of bulls or drink the blood of goats?" is a question implying that the vulgar in Israel were not free from the Homeric idea that the savoury smell of burning flesh gave pleasure in heaven. [See too Gen. viii. 21, indeed Gen. iv. 4, 5.] Balaam, a Moabite prophet, in the lifetime of Moses, taught a new doctrin, as we learn from the Hebrew prophet Micah. If Micah vi. 5—8 is correct, Balaam earlier than any Hebrew taught the vanity of Pagan offerings, and that God requires of man only acts of Justice and Mercy, and a sentiment of Humility. In spite of Micah and Isaiah, ceremonialism grew more intense, by reason of increased sacerdotal power in Jerusalem. In the time of Jesus, all sacrifice having long been confined to the Holy City, the rite itself could only be seen by a journey thither, especially at one of the great feasts. So short were the distances, that poverty seldom could forbid such pilgrimage. Nevertheless, it is remarkable that in our three Gospels no visit of Jesus himself to Jerusalem is mentioned until the last, and then he is a stranger whom the rulers found it difficult to identify. With all the modern facilities for travel, no entire rustic population is familiar with its local capital. Perhaps the peasants of Galilee and those beyond Jordan, and even the Samaritans, passed many years without seeing the sacrifices at Jerusalem. All local sanctuaries having been zealously suppressed ever since Samaria sank under Assyrian attack, the rural Israelites must hav grown up less accustomed to the religious slaughter of animals than ordinary Greeks or other heathens. It is not wonderful that a religious teacher who undervalued this practice and all the sacerdotal ceremonies found large sympathy among multitudes of rustic Galileans.

When we attempt to define the doctrin taught by Jesus, our first impression may be that he was consciously denouncing the Mosaic law and its whole system of ceremonies. But from this opinion we are held back by the effect of his teaching on his immediate disciples. If we advance the hypothesis that Jesus assailed the law itself, we clash with the undenied and undeniable fact, that the earliest Christian Church believed all the Mosaic ceremonies to be permanently binding;—with the fact also that Paul of Tarsus, while superseding these ordinances, never dares to assert that such was the teaching of Jesus himself. Had this been notorious, Paul could not hav remained ignorant of it, and must hav eagerly availed himself of this corroboration. To say that Jesus could not speak as plainly as Paul, if he had wished to impress the same idea on his disciples, is simply ridiculous. No one as yet, of any school, has broached the theory that Jesus was guilty of conscious duplicity, and that he purposely undermined the system which was esteemed Mosaic, while pretending to revere and establish it. With our imperfect means of knowledge, a full certainty may be unattainable; but to the present writer the opinion most commends itself, that Jesus had *an instinct* of hatred to ceremonies *without being aware* that he was in collision with the sacred Mosaism. Believing that submission to the law was the duty of every good Jew, he inculcated absolute submission, and this, in entire good faith. We hav no reason to believe that he possessed any private manuscript of the law, or had any habit of studying it. In the synagogues the Sabbath readings were likely to be selected for general edification. The merciful and miraculous dealings of Jehovah with his chosen people and the general history would doubtless be prominent; so would moral instruction and devout utterances: but no motive prompted obtrusion of mere ceremonialism or dry legalities. In every synagogue, we may presume, a complete copy of our "Old Testament" was found; but it is highly improbable that such a roll was habitually and intimately studied by any but professed Doctors of the Law. How few Englishmen, in this day of cheap Bibles, hav an accurate knowledge of any part of the books esteemed sacred! In that comparativly illiterate age, when with cumbrous parchment and elaborate copying the price of a complete roll was necessarily high, no one can reasonably assume that a young Galilean carpenter had either the means or the disposition to study the actual law. It is therefor not possible only, but probable, that Jesus in clashing rudely with the national teachers may not hav been aware that his assault was virtually against the law itself;—against "Moses," to use the current phrase. This theory will perhaps reconcile statements at first sight incongruous.

The direct, vehement, unmistakeable attack of Jesus on the legal sacrifices was not made until just the close of his career; but from the first the absence of everything *national to the Jews* is felt in his teaching. No allusion is made to the covenant of God with Abraham as of any present importance, nor of his covenant that a king from the line of David should rule over Israel, nor to the past history of the nation, nor to the promise of political supremacy over the heathen,—topics which abound in the Hebrew Psalms and in the later Isaiah. Nay, nor does he press the keeping of the Sabbath as the seal of the covenant between God and his chosen people, nor in any way regard religion as *a national affair*, as though the Church (or Sacerdotal System) were a Mediatrix through which the individual soul enters into relation with the Most High. Religion with him is *personal* and secret, not *corporate* and national. This is his greatest contrast to the prophets who went before him, and equally his greatest contrast to what is called the Catholic Christian Church.

The audience which Jesus systematically chose consisted of the less instructed and more rustic part of the community. He is stated to hav defined it as, "to the "*poor* the Gospel is preached." He does not care to teach any but those who will, like simple "children," look up to him. "Publicans and Sinners" ar imputed as his habitual audience. *Publicans* (Taxgatherers) denotes those who, by collecting taxes for the usurping power of Rome, violate the obvious prohibition of the law, and ar apt to drop all special care for Mosaism.

Sinners ar any who in general neglect Jewish scruples, *whether ceremonially or morally.* (There is absolutely no reason for supposing the word Sinners to mean females.) Both Publicans and Sinners were likely to be gratified by every attack made on the ceremonialism of Scribes and Pharisees by one who taught morals dogmatically and forcibly.

The first mention of a deputation from Jerusalem to the Galilean prophet is in Matthew xv. They enquire: "Why do thy disciples transgress the tradition of the "elders? for they wash not their hands *when they eat* "*bread.*" These words do not bring to an English ear the sense intended; which undoubtedly was: "They "wash not their hands *before joining in a meal*," which might involve dipping of fingers into a common dish. [See Matt. xxvi. 23, John xiii. 26.] Anyone who has seen an Arab company eating rice pilau, is aware how essential ar clean finger-tips for that very simple meal. A sacred law cannot go into all precepts of daily cleanliness, but wise teachers supply them. Elders among the Jews carefully inculcated *good manners* (as do Turkish teachers now) and *Tradition* gave weight to their precepts. They taught the grave *indecency* of putting unwashed fingers into a dish, whether of cooked grain or other food, on the common table. Knives or forks were not thought of, nor apparently even spoons: pieces of bread scooped up or sopped up even gravy. Fingers might really be already clean, but respect to the other guests required the visible act of washing; and then probably, as now, a jug of water was handed round with a basin for the purpose. This "tradition of the elders" did not counteract the law of God, nor did it tend to make social civility a substitute for obedience to that law. The precept was wise and blameless,—not at all superfluous; neglect of it seemed to imply coarse and unamiable rusticity. The question, "Why was this precept of "good manners neglected?" was (to say the least) natural. Ar we then really to believe what Matthew tells us? According to him, Jesus does not deny, explain, confess, or apologize, nor yet does he justify his disciples; but as if gravely offended and irritated that anyone should step in between him and them, he makes no answer to the question, but merely *recriminates* in words which Christians forbid me to call rude and fierce. "Why do *ye also* transgress the commandment "of God by your tradition? *Ye hypocrites*," &c.

Was this the reply of one "apt to teach, meek, patient" according to Paul's ideal? Did it tend to show to those whom he thus assailed his moral superiority? How strangely he wastes an opportunity of instructing his questioners, if they in any way misjudged the conduct of his disciples! How gratuitously he raises a barrier against their reception of the superior knowledge which he claims! Nay, and is not sweetness of temper and gentle kindliness far better than mere knowledge?—But this is not all. Jesus flings at his questioners the charge of Hypocrisy, based on an argument which severely wounds himself, unless the Evangelists slander him. For the sin which he imputes is that of violating the fifth commandment, in that the Elders had defined certain ecclesiastical purposes for which money might be given by a son, even when *prima facie* a parent might seem to hav a better claim to it. We hav not before us the Pharisaic doctrin, therefor cannot defend it: possibly if we knew the details, we might condemn it. But this would neither justify dirty fingers dipped into a common dish, nor shelter Jesus from his own imputation of "making void the commandment of God," by neglecting filial duty to parents. When two sons were aiding their father in his work of fishing, they abandoned him at the call of Jesus, and ar praised by him for obedience. Matthew and Luke say, he forbade a disciple to follow his father to the grave, and added the heartless precept, "Let the dead bury their dead." All is summed up in his extravagant avowal, "Unless a man hate his father, "he cannot be my disciple." However much we pare this down by urging "Oriental hyperbole," it cannot mean *less*, than that service to a parent must always yield to the personal claims of Jesus. Therefor if Matthew in ch. xv. correctly narrates his bitter recrimination, it virtually asserts: "For *my* service it is quite right to "neglect a parent,—even permanently to abandon him; "but if for the service of *God*, as taught in Mosaism, even "some partial diminution be made of support which a "parent may claim, the deed is unlawful and wicked: "nay, those who justify it ar HYPOCRITES precondemned "by the prophet Isaiah." Ar we really to accept such doctrin?

Matthew further tells us, that on this occasion Jesus uttered his aphorism, "Nothing that goeth into the "mouth defileth a man,"—a doctrin which utterly overthrows the Mosaic distinction of clean and unclean meats. His disciples told him that the Pharisees were offended at this revolutionary utterance. Well they might be: for it laid the axe to the root of the ceremonial law. They had a right to ask: "Does this teacher seriously "bid us to renounce our national lawgiver? If so, let "him state plainly that he is a prophet higher than "Moses, and is sent from God with loftier credentials. "Let him deal openly with us and expound his mission "and his grounds for claiming authority so high." But according to Matthew, Jesus does not frankly state his own claims, nor say a word to relieve the natural and reasonable offence of the Pharisees, nor did he effectivly instruct his disciples that the ceremonies ar of no religious value. All Jews, in every part of Palestine, nay, whithersoever carried in the Dispersion, distinguished clean and unclean meats. Jesus, if he spoke as here represented, not only opposed his entire nation, but must hav known that he was flatly condemning THE LAW; and the disciples must hav discerned it. Either our Gospels here exaggerate his actual words, or he *privately* retracted and softened them. He *may* hav meant only that men ar *worse* defiled by what comes out of the mouth than by forbidden food;—very unwise as it is to join a dogmatic tone to forms of speech which mislead the simple: but such interpretation of his words is mere guesswork. And side by side with utterances that seem to contradict the sacred law, he is represented as venting vague, uninstructive, arrogant scorn of the national teachers, saying: "Let them alone; they ar blind leaders of the blind, and "both will fall together into the ditch." And what led him on to this scornful attack? According to Matthew, a simple inquiry why his disciples dipt into a common dish with fingers possibly dirty.

Certain modern Christians, anxious to exhibit Jesus as a type of immaculate morals, accuse these Gospels of virtually slandering him. Much reason, no doubt, there is for distrust of them. They uniformly daub the Pharisees with cruel imputations; but if we drop the coloring and examin the facts as detailed, the worst they hav to tell us, is, that the Pharisees, *like modern Christians*, believed the Mosaic system to hav divine sanction. If Messiah came, these Jews did not deny that he might be greater than Moses: but whoever claimed to be this higher prophet, must giv them some intelligible *proof* of his right to overrule their sacred law. What less could any man of good sense demand? The actual conduct ascribed to the Pharisees and Chief Priests by these bitter assailants is respectful, prudent, moderate, forbearing under great provocation; while that which they ascribe to Jesus calls for widely different epithets. How much to disbelieve of the narrativ is a very uncertain problem; but any *general* distrust throws mist over the moral character of the events, and justifies the Mussulman contempt of the Christian books as corrupt. Moreover, in that case, what is it but actual guilt to read them solemnly in public worship as books especially sacred?

It was above remarked, that in the phrase *Sinners*, (joined to Publicans) the common idea that Sinners meant *females* is groundless. With regard to a certain woman of ill repute in one Simon's house,[*] it may be worth while to note that Luke's account is apparently a garbled remaking of Matthew and Mark's tale of what happened before the last supper: *that* was in the house of Simon the leper. The anonymous woman of the two first Evangelists has no aspersion cast on her. Luke tries to outdo the other tale by making the woman a notorious sinner, whose sin is forgiven *because* she has a personal love for Jesus; who is made to assert this in the least edifying style, at the same time reproaching his host Simon for not *kissing him*, and so on. Luke has tried to improve the story and has spoiled it. John has identified the woman told of in Matthew with Mary of *Bethany*. So careless ar Christian readers, that they infer *Luke's* woman to be Mary of *Magdala*, thereby blasting the good *Magdalen's* reputation down to this day. Putting aside this untrustworthy tale, there is absolutely no ground for supposing that Jesus ever had among his attached hearers so much as one woman of ill-repute.—There is another apocryphal tale in John viii. where Jesus *evades* the duty of a prophet higher than Moses,—that is, the duty

---

[*] Luke vii. 37, 38.

to confirm Moses, if Moses was right, or to correct Moses, if Moses was too severe; but this in no respect puts him into the relation of teacher to the guilty woman.

It would be quite superfluous here to make the patronizing remark that in the discourses attributed to Jesus "a great deal is good." Thoughtful and very able men who professed no allegiance to him, hav spoken their mind. Ram Mohun Roy translated "the Precepts "of Jesus" for his countrymen. John Stuart Mill in his latest writings caused surprize by his panegyric. If honor were claimed for Jesus as for Socrates, for Seneca, for Hillel, for Epictetus, we might apologize for his weak points as incident either to his era and country or to human nature itself; weakness to be forgiven and forgotten. But the unremitting assumption of superhuman wisdom, not only made for him by the moderns, but breathing through every utterance attributed to him, changes the whole scene, and ought to change our treatment of it. Unless his prodigious claim of Divine Superiority is made good in fact, it betrays an arrogance difficult to excuse, eminently mischievous and eminently ignominious.

It is hard to point to anything in the teaching of Jesus, at once *new* to Hebrew and Greek sages, and likewise in general estimate *true*. Forgivness of injuries, kindness to enemies, life after death, future retribution, had all been taught in Greece or in Egypt long ago. The pure attributes of God, his oversight of human conduct, his forgivness of penitent sinners, his love of righteousness, his judgments on the obstinately wicked, had been amply enforced by Hebrew prophets and psalmists. Voluntary poverty, equality of all disciples, had been vigorously exemplified among the Essenes; nay, perhaps long before in Pythagorean and Indian schools. One may search in vain through the Gospels for a precept or sentiment so novel and valuable, as to justify the grandiloquent boast: "*Blessed ar ye* who "hear now from me things which many prophets and "kings *hav in vain longed to hear.*"

It is asserted by some, that Jesus was *first* to teach a universal religion, which made no distinction of nation from nation, but embraced all as equals and brethren in the sight of God, with no local or ceremonial rite to divide them. Undoubtedly, as above observed, he had an instinct of hatred to ceremonialism, and at least once leans towards Universalism in slashing at the national teachers. When a Roman centurion (Matt. viii. 5—12) avows belief in his healing powers, he marvels at the man's faith, and takes opportunity to declare that many a Gentile shall *sit down* in the [banquet? or throne?] of the kingdom of heaven, when Jews ar shut out. But no general statement of Gentile equality is recorded of him. His address to the Canaanite (or Syrophœnician) woman leans to the other side; and it is certain that his own disciples never understood him to account Gentile and Jew equals in the "kingdom of heaven." To say that he was the *first* to teach a religion in which moral sentiment is paramount over ceremonies, is very unjust to his predecessors,—to Jewish proselyters contemporary with him; to many a Hebrew psalm, and utterances of Hebrew prophets: nay, we may ask, How much of ceremonialism is taught in the "Ode to Jupiter," of Cleanthes the Stoic? No speech of Jesus recorded for us approaches the sublime largeness of the true Isaiah in his prophecy concerning Egypt the idolatrous and Assyria the dangerous and bitter foe of Israel, "In that day "shall Israel be a third with Egypt and with Assyria; "of whom the Lord of Hosts shall say, Blessed be Egypt "my people and Assyria the work of my hands, and "Israel mine inheritance."

One piece of originality,—and that, highly important,—may indeed be claimed as a logical deduction from the tone and attitude of Jesus, or from the implied assumption in his teaching. Whether he himself intended and discerned it, is not clear.

All ancient nations, Gentile or Hebrew, accounted it a rightful function of the civil power to dictate religion to the community. The deep-thinking Aristotle agreed herein with received Mosaic doctrin. Among barbarians religious ideas ar only skin-deep. If their Chief adopts a new religion, the whole tribe easily follow him : but when time has consolidated institutions, the public religion, with all its barbarian error, is, as it were, burnt in and consecrated. Then the head of the State runs risk of deposition, if he be bold to innovate. If a citizen dare to decline a ceremony commanded by the nativ law, it is a high offence against the State. When indeed an Imperial power claims of the conquered a renunciation of their *hereditary* religion, this was in most cases judged to be tyranny, and has been resisted to death by Indian martyrs, as well as by Jews. But Antiquity certainly had not learned, that private men had any *right to a conscience* of their own in religion. The main reason was this : Religion in their idea was essentially external and corporate, not individual, personal, internal, as Jesus in every utterance assumes it to be. He never dilates on the covenant of Jehovah with *collectiv Israel*, but dwells on the relation of each separate worshipper to a Father in Heaven as a private affair. This was the fruitful germ, this was the "seed of mustard" by which he virtually called his countrymen to Free Thinking concerning their national institutions.

His preaching was dictatorial, but his example eminently encouraged Private Judgment. He did not parade his opposition to "Moses," and if we could trust

Matthew, he declared that every jot and tittle of the law is sacred. But in that same sermon "On the Mount," "Moses" himself is attacked, Matt. v. 38. "Ye hav "heard that it hath been said, An eye for an eye, and a "tooth for a tooth, but *I* say unto you," &c.—Now to whom does he here refer? Knowingly or unknowingly, to Deut. xix. 21. "Thine eye shall not pity, but life "shall go for life, eye for eye, tooth for tooth," &c. With the early prophets he agrees in not being dependent on Mosaism; but he differs from them herein: They conceal their own dogmatism by the formula, "Thus saith Jehovah," he reveals his dogmatism by "*I* say "unto you"—the Ego being paramount, and sometimes prefaced by *Surely, surely*, Ἀμὴν, Ἀμὴν. Few will doubt Matthew's word, that in Jesus this vehemence of self-assertion most struck the multitude, in contrast to the reverential modesty of their usual teachers. He persistently disparages and keenly assails the religious authorities of his own nation. He shows lofty contempt of the ancients in vague terms which do not exclude Moses; which certainly invite all to criticize ancient doctrin. He never appeals to the learned and cultivated intellect, but to the poor, as though "babes and sucklings" were the best judges. When in one matter Moses is quoted, he calmly sets aside that paramount authority, by the assertion that *this was an imperfect law, given to the people for the hardness of their hearts*. If that were true in one case, it might be true in twenty more: then what becomes of Mosaic authority? Scruples about the Sabbath,—that touchstone of a faithful Jew—he several times treats from a point of lofty independence. Once, if we can believe Mark (ii. 28) he claims as "Son of man" to be Lord of the Sabbath, *because* the Sabbath was made for man! Luke (vi. 5) omits this clause; and perhaps thought the logical conclusion required was: "Therefor

"*Man* is Lord of the Sabbath." Either utterance must to reverent and anxious doctors hav seemed profane in the extreme, who might comment as follows. "When "Moses commanded a man to be stoned to death for "picking sticks in the wilderness, did *he* look on the "sacredness of the sabbath with the same eyes as does "this Jesus? We *know* that God spake by Moses: but "as for this man, we cannot learn what is his authority "so to dogmatize."—Whenever the law is quoted, the virtual treatment of it by Jesus is suggested by the words, "Wherefor judge ye not of yourselves what is "right?" If in one breath (as in Matt. xxiii. 3) he bid to obey the religious teachers, in the next he teaches by his invectiv to despise them.

Such daring defiance of superior authority was in Jesus spontaneous and self-initiated. On the part of his disciples resistance shortly became inevitable, and, as time went on, was normal to the whole Church. Thus grew up the greatest moral novelty universal to Christendom,—separation of the two ideas, Church and State. Hence also the axiom cardinal to Protestantism: *Religion is not corporate, but is an inward allegiance of the individual to the Supreme Power of the Universe.*

Moreover, by emphatically declaring that of his disciples no one shall hav authority over another, nor be called Father or Rabbi, Jesus cast scorn on all Sacerdotalism. In no point has his teaching been more grossly reversed by historical Christianity. Even Toleration for those who ar satisfied to remain *outside* of the Church had to be fought out by weapons of war against Popes, Bishops, Presbyters and Cæsars, though it cannot be reasonably denied that in calling heathens to cast off the religion of their birth, Christian apostles did but imitate their Lord in judging the conscience and religious heart to belong to God, not to Cæsar. Undoubtedly Imperialists hav everywhere felt, that in men devoted to the precepts ascribed to Jesus they hav but a lame and partial allegiance. "Dissidents" ar the foul fly that corrupts the sacred ointment of royalty.

Into politics Jesus appears seldom to venture. The virtue cardinal to his moral system, the virtue without which no disciple can be *perfect*, is that fundamental one of the Essenes, the renunciation of private property. This pervades his discourses from end to end. Not many Christians in any age hav obeyed him, and the prevalent excuse is, that he intended this precept for *the twelve apostles only*. But the Sermon on the Mount cannot be reasonably so confined, and therein he enjoins: "Giv to him that asketh of thee, and from him who "would borrow of thee, turn not away." The precept has no limitation. He who *asks* may be idle, may be a worthless beggar or a drinker; no special case is suggested as ground for just refusal. That industry is a human duty, cannot be gathered from his doctrin: how could it, when he kept twelve religious mendicants around him? No one who obeys him will long be able to keep property. Indeed in Luke the passage parallel to one given by Matthew as on the Mount, is: "*Sell that ye* "*hav, and give alms:* provide yourselves bags that wax "not old, a treasure in the heavens that fadeth not;" &c. Almsgiving is prominent with him, as a sort of sanctification.

Many precepts of the law had a sanitary purpose, and the Pharisees, like Egyptian priests, were studious of cleanliness. Jesus, deriding them for it, says (Luke xi.31) "Giv alms of your substance, and all things ar clean "unto you." It is not mere compassion for the destitute that is enforced; much rather is wealth treated as unsaintly,—an unrighteous thing, that will lessen our COMPENSATION in heaven. This is forcibly brought out in the Parable of Dives and Lazarus; but without pressing that parable into the argument, we find in Luke that Jesus says: "Woe unto you that ar rich, for *ye hav "received your consolation*." Nay, he brands wealth with the title, "the mammon of unrighteousness." In a Parable which is the despair of those who teach simple folk, he insists, that, as by a clever *wrong* a certain steward won friends, so each rich man by a clever use of *wrongful* possessions ought to buy friends who will receive him into everlasting habitations. Good news for medieval barons, enriched by rapine ! By shovelling away wealth, they may buy treasures in heaven. Unless our narrators belie him, Jesus never warns hearers that to giv without a heart of charity does *not* prepare a soul for heaven nor "earn salvation ;" and that selfish pre-speculation turns virtue into despicable marketing. To forgiv that we may be forgiven, to avoid judging lest we be judged, to do good that we may buy extrinsic reward, to affect humility that we may be promoted, to lose life that we may gain it with advantage, ar precepts not needing a lofty prophet. But to return to the topic of wealth, the remarkable tale of a rich young man, narrated with close agreement in three Gospels, is quite decisiv. He asks: " What shall I do (besides keeping the command-"ments of the second table) that I may inherit eternal "life?" Jesus replies: "Thou lackest one thing. If "thou wilt be *perfect*, sell all that thou hast and dis-"tribute to the poor, and thou shalt hav treasure in "heaven." This corroborates his aphorism, that no one can be his disciple, who does not forsake all that he hath. Thus it is *not* on the twelve apostles *only* that he lays this charge, but upon all who will buy *the Pearl of Great Price*, all who desire to win heaven as the paramount object, whatever the sacrifice. He does not say, "*Rather* "lose all your possessions *than* be false to your religious "convictions," but "fling away your wealth, in order to "earn heavenly remuneration for your sacrifice:" a very different doctrin indeed.

Some other tenets deserve notice. The doctrin of Life after Death is often named as eminently due to his teaching. In the theory of Paul (2 Tim. i. 10)—who had no historical knowledge of Jesus,—"Christ abolished "Death and brought Life and Immortality to light." Yet Paul must hav known that human immortality was a doctrin of the Pharisees, imported from abroad before Jesus was born. At most he could but *establish* it. But how? The Sadducees (we ar told) plied him with an objection: thereupon he not only swept it away, but elicited immortality out of Jehovah's words to Moses, "I am the God of Abraham, &c. *God is not the God of* "*the dead, but of the living.*" With good reason the multitude "were *astonished* at his doctrin." Hitherto, the words had been interpreted: "I am *he*, who, when "Abraham was alive, *was* God to Abraham." They must hav been thus accepted by Isaiah and Jeremiah, who understood Hebrew well. If the Supreme Ruler condescended to speak in the Hebrew language to Moses, he was sure to speak intelligibly to all the great spiritual minds of the Hebrew nation. Sadducees were not likely to be convinced by the new interpretation. Even Luke found something deficient; for, to complete the argument, he makes Jesus add: "for all (*or*, for they all) liv (or ar "alive) unto him." Unfortunately this *reason* assumes the very thing to be proved. Besides, the argument avails only to those who believe that Moses duly reported the very words of Jehovah. Moses, who did not knowingly teach immortality, is made the Mediator through whom immortality is to be learned! Undoubtedly Jesus, like the Pharisees and Essenes, always *presumes* an after-life for man. This is all that can justly be said.

A Hebrew doctrin, false and mischievous, dominated in early days, ascribing to the anger of God against *sin* calamity of whatever kind, whether defeat in war, failure of crops, or bodily disease:—a folly which mars many of the Hebrew psalms. As to some on whom the tower of Siloam fell, Jesus (in Luke) opposed this error; but he startles one by entirely adopting it, when he identifies the two phrases, *Thy sins be forgiven thee*, and *Be thou healed of thy malady.*—But perhaps these words ar foolishly imputed, in the wish to glorify him. Nevertheless, if we accept the narrativs as *substantially* correct concerning his *doctrin*, there is much indeed to regret, much reason to wonder that thoughtful persons can approve. His vehement and frequent threat of a hell with unquenchable flames and undying worm, has above all things given vitality to this noxious doctrin, which darkens the character of God and hardens the hearts of men. From none of the other Christian writings could the dreadful idea of Eternal Sin, Eternal Despair and Eternal Agony be established. Therefor we must believe that it was a dominating idea characteristic of *him*,—as indeed, after him, of Mohammed. He threatens this doom to the simple townsfolk to whose conscience his message of "The Kingdom" did not commend itself:—a worse doom at the day of judgment than that of Sodom and Gomorrha. A preacher so dogmatic and so full of threat ought above all to be cautious in expression. With his enigmatic and hyperbolical style and precepts paradoxically framed, (such as, "Hate your father and mother for "my sake,") he must hav puzzled and *revolted* many hearers. A teacher with ordinary wisdom who expected docility and submission from simple folk, would know how dangerous ar hyperbolical and vague precepts. The writer whom we call Matthew gravely assures us that Jesus *purposely* made his teaching obscure, in order to fulfil prophecy; *lest* the people be converted and he should heal them ! ! (Matt. xiii. 11—17.) How grave the danger of ambiguous precept, is disagreeably shown in his panegyric on those who hav made themselves eunuchs for the kingdom of heaven's sake. To this day it is debated whether he spoke figurativly or literally. For the latter an Origen could plead that the zeal which adopts the cruel letter may carry the gospel into Eastern harems from which a mere celibate Paul is excluded. Whether here also the fault is thrown on the stupidity of reporters, I wait to learn.

In his teaching is a still more fundamental unsoundness. He repels by rudeness or evasion the more educated inquirers who may approach him; and then solemnly thanks God that "HE had hidden *these things*" (*i.e.* the divine mission of Jesus? or his divine wisdom?) "from the wise and prudent, and revealed them unto "babes. *Even so,* Father! *for so it seemed good in thy "sight."* Was he unaware that *Reasons* ar necessary to convince *the wise and prudent?* He demanded that his hearers should become babes, thus *identifying Credulity with Faith.* This rottenness at the core has been fatal to Christianity. Truth, even if nobly established at first, cannot maintain itself, if Credulity is consecrated as a virtue; but Fantasy overcrusts and smothers it, because Criticism is frowned down.

SECOND PART.

A TIME arrived, which, according to our three narrators, was critical to Jesus. Rumours favorable to him had thickened among the populace. He inquired of his apostles, what was the prevalent opinion. They replied: "Some think thee to be John the Baptist, others one of "the old prophets, or Elijah" (brought back from heaven). "But whom think *ye* that I am?" is his further question: to which Simon replied, "The Messiah of God." According to Matthew, Jesus hereon burst into the joyful utterance: "Blessed art thou, Simon son of "Jonah! for *flesh and blood hath not revealed it to thee,* "*but my Father which is in heaven.*" He proceeds to bestow on him the title Kefa (ROCK)—which we render by Peter or Cephas—and adds: "On this Rock will I "build my Church"—whether on Simon or Simon's confession is hotly debated:—"and the gates of *Hades* "shall not prevail against it." Mark and Luke ar here more concise: but all three agree that after accepting Simon's avowal, Jesus strictly charged them to tell no man of it. Only one reasonable explanation here offers itself; for such a dialogue will not be ascribed to wanton fancy. Jesus, while despising the doctors and daring to denounce them, had (like them) great difficulty in defining how Messiah was to be discerned. Though inwardly believing himself to be the pre-destined One, he had never dared to utter the claim. If he even had a complete copy of the old prophets, to reconcile them was so hard, that doubt was perhaps inevitable. Naturally he wished *others* to enunciate his Messiahship; hence his eager delight and exultation when Simon made the bold avowal. Nevertheless, after a short interval, old doubts recurred, with painful misgivings. He was frightened at his own elation; therefor he forbad them to tell any one.

But the word, as an arrow, stuck deep in his side. From this era he began to ponder on an ambitious career, which must lead either to glorious triumph or to violent and ignominious death. He is consistently said to hav tried *from this moment* to prepare his disciples for the worst, often warning them of the fate in store for him.

Here an interesting question arises, Hav we any clue that may suggest what was *his own* conception of the task and function of Messiah? If we may assume, that he discarded the idea of a warlike Messiah such as the prophet Micah suggested,—such a deliverer to Israel as Judas Maccabæus had been,—did he imagine Messiah to be prefigured by the "servant of God" in the later Isaiah, from which alone the idea of Messiah suffering death for his people could be gathered? In answer, a remark must be premised. It is not credible that Jesus should not hav discerned what were the expectations of his disciples, and should not hav corrected them, if he judged them to be wrong. Therefor, whatever error on this topic they all held down to his death, must hav been his error also. Several passages giv us information. In Luke xxii. 29, we read: "I appoint unto you a *kingdom;* as my Father "hath appointed unto me, that ye may *eat and drink* at "my table in my kingdom, and sit on thrones, judging "the twelve tribes of Israel." We should call a teacher mad, who used such words to simple men, and did not expect them to understand him literally. The royal table, and the chief ministers eating and drinking at it; the judicial thrones, and the same favored ministers dealing out awards to the inferior multitude,—precisely hit off the idea cardinal in those days to a heavenly monarchy planted on earth. As, in a Greek republic, to be dieted in the City Hall at public expense was the highest honor, so in a royalty to liv at the king's table. The *eating and drinking* distinctly marks that continued *life in the flesh* was intended. Bread and Wine were the normal food, as with king Melchisedek; and so a little above, Luke xxii. 18, Jesus says: "I will drink no "more of the fruit of the vine until the kingdom of God "is come." Moreover Acts i. 6 converges to the same result. The disciples there ask Jesus: "Lord! wilt "thou at this time *restore the kingdom to Israel?*" words on which it is useless to foist any spiritual sense. He does not reprove them for the belief, that the kingdom (now held by Rome) is to be restored to Israel, nor does he deny that he is himself God's champion to restore it; but simply avows that the *time* of the event is a secret with God, thus virtually asserting that earthly dominion is to be restored to Israel:—as indeed every Jew who accepted Isaiah was bound to believe. Of course it may be objected that this discourse was fictitious, being held after the death of Jesus; but it does not the less attest the sharply defined persistent tradition that *at that era* the disciples continued to believe such to be Messiah's function, though Messiah had first to suffer.

An indirect confirmation meets us in Zachariah's hymn, Luke i. 68. We cannot know when first it was penned; but Luke's authority (some earlier Christian) received it as *an inspired prophecy.* "Zachariah was filled with the "Holy Ghost and prophesied." We must infer that Zachariah uttered what the early Christian Church accepted as sound doctrin. Twice he distinctly intimates the great function of Messiah to be, deliverance of Israel from a heathen yoke; "that we should be saved from "our enemies and from the hand of all that hate us"— v. 71; again, v. 74, "that we, being delivered out of "the hand of our enemies might serve him without "fear," &c. Deliverance from the power of the heathen was *the first condition requisit* for the pure and permanent service of God; *therefor* is here put forward as the main result to be achieved by the new-born Messiah. It is called Redemption.— Such being the Christian belief when this hymn was first incorporated with Christian sacred writings, the belief must hav subsisted all along, first among those devout Jews who were precursors of Christianity; next, in the first Christian Church. It cannot hav been a secret to Jesus, neither can it hav been reproved by him. At the same time it is every way probable that on so obscure a matter as the career of Messiah the mind of Jesus varied from day to day. The fifty-third chapter of Isaiah may well hav weighed on him and given him the augury that Messiah would suffer death for his nation (as indeed may happen in war to a victorious general); hence his dark forebodings which astonished his disciples, and made them incredulous. Their very incredulity implies that he said absolutely nothing to unteach the universal belief that the great function of Messiah was to raise Israel to be the head of the Heathen, as abundantly attested concerning "God's "servant" in the later Isaiah.

One more broad historical fact ought to be considered in this connexion, *viz.*, that in the final war of the Jews under Hadrian, their leader Bar Coceb was accepted as Messiah; so persistent was the national belief that to deliver Israel from the oppressiv foreigner was Messiah's task. That it was the prevalent conviction in the time of Jesus is thus doubly confirmed; and of this he cannot hav been ignorant. Not to oppose it, was to acquiesce in it. If he had opposed it, such opposition *must* in some way hav been transmitted to us in his teaching.

The strong probability therefor is this. Jesus himself not merely knew that his nation in general and his disciples in particular expected Messiah to break the yoke of Rome and establish Israel in supremacy, but by his *occasional* distinct utterances he encouraged them in it; though at other moments when his fears prevailed over his hopes, he foreboded violent treatment, perhaps death, for himself. The stupidity imputed to them would be a natural result of his vacillation. While he lived, they could not believe that Messiah, instead of saving Israel from the proud and violent heathen, would himself be slain. But after his death, they wondered that they had not accepted his own plain words, which more than once had warned them that he was rushing voluntarily on destruction.

To that issue at length he hastened. He accepted a triumphal entrance into Jerusalem previously planned by himself according to the three first narrators. For he sent forward to provide a suitable ass, that he might fulfil the prophecy of Zechariah (ix. 9) and *represent himself as King of Jerusalem*. The words ar: "Behold, "thy king cometh to thee riding on an ass, and on a "colt* the foal of an ass." A crowd escorted him, a very great multitude, and spread their garments on the road before him, in acknowledgment of royalty. Others cut branches from the trees to hold as triumphant laurels amid shouts to him as Son of David. Knowingly or unknowingly, he hereby put himself into the power of those whom he regarded as his bitter enemies. They had now only to whisper to the Roman Prefect (Pontius Pilatus) "Do you intend to let this man pass himself off "to the multitude as King and Son of David? *Judas of* "*Galilee never went so far in daring.*"

Jesus had come up to Jerusalem by a very circuitous route, passing through Jericho.† If it be true that a very great multitude escorted him triumphantly into the Holy City, his escort may hav consisted largely of men from along the Jordan, baptized by John and ready to accept Jesus as Messiah. Since in the three gospels it is definitly stated that he of himself planned the triumphal

---

* Matthew is here supremely ridiculous. Misled by Hebrew parallelism, he thinks *two* animals ar intended; makes the disciples bring *two*, put their garments on *them* and seat Jesus upon *them*. Our translators, new and old, to disguise the absurdity, adopt the word *thereon* which hides the plural number of the Greek.

† Compare Matthew xix. 1, xx. 29, with Luke xviii. 35, xix. 1.

entry, it is not rash to infer that he had taken previous measures for its success by announcing his pretensions as he passed. For in Jerusalem itself, where his personality was scarcely known, he could not expect enthusiastic reception.

But after this royal parade, according to our three narrators, he forthwith displayed to the Holy City the presence of its paramount lord by an astonishing demonstration *against the Mosaic Law*. He proceeded to the courts of the temple, armed with a lash; drove out the money-changers, overturned their counters and the seats of those who sold doves; alledging that they made *his* Father's House a den of thieves. The traders seem to hav made no resistance, whether smitten by the report that the prophet of Nazareth was the anointed Son of David, or panic-struck by violence so unexpected. Mark adds, that he would not suffer any man to carry any vessel [or basket?] through the temple, that is, through the courts. To understand this proceeding, we ought to know accurately what routine of sacrifice then went on. If we judged by the Pentateuch and the books of Kings and Chronicles, he found in the temple-courts altars and huge fires, dishes and blood pans, sacrificial knives, bellowing and shrieks, with all the filth of butchery, odour of blood and of roast flesh, and banqueting of guests, while new victims were slaughtered; all gravely incongruous (as we judge) to cleanliness, decorum and sacred devotion. But none of these greater nuisances ar mentioned. Clearly he assumed authority (possibly unawares) to override the law, softened and improved into comparativ decency as it may hav been by the diligence of the prudent Pharisaic interpreters. Cattle-merchants, money-changers and dove-sellers were necessary for obedience to the law (Deut. xiv.) which, in order to centralize sacerdotalism and gather the tithe of all clean beasts and birds, as well as of crops, prescribed that the offerer and his household should partake of these firstlings in the sacred precinct. Moreover, anticipating the difficulty of driving cattle from a distance, the law itself suggested the carrying of money to buy oxen and sheep at the temple, and eating them "before the Lord." Hitherto the Sanhedrin had believed this routine to be required by the service of God. Did Jesus now intend to denounce the law of Moses? Did he claim, as Messiah, to overrule and supersede it, or what did his strange conduct mean? Unless he really were the long expected and much desired deliverer of Israel, he must be a very audacious and dangerous man.

Nevertheless they persevered in the quiet and dignified behaviour always previously ascribed to them. Children in the temple-courts, delighted with the novel turmoil, raised afresh the shout: "Hosannah to the Son of David," a dangerous war-cry to every Roman ear. The chief priests took the opportunity of mildly asking Jesus, "whether he heard" what the children were crying out. Promptly, and as it may seem, joyfully, he replied that he did hear and warmly approved; thereby attesting to them his personal complicity in the royal Messianic acclaim. Hereupon they withdrew for further consultation, and he went out to Bethany.

Next day, on his return to the city, the chief priests and elders put to him the formal question, "By what "authority had he been acting?" words which might refer solely to his violent dealing in the temple-courts, or also to his acceptance of the royal entry. This time he was not so frank, but evasively asked in turn, "What authority had John the Baptist?" On their confessing ignorance, he haughtily replied: "Then "neither do I tell you *my* authority." Not content with this scornful refusal to justify or explain conduct *utterly unlike that of John the Baptist*, he went on (if we may trust the narrativ) into new and gratuitous insult: saying to the chief priests and elders: "The tax-gatherers and "harlots go into the kingdom of God before you." Next; in his favorit way he told them a parable, by which he suggested much, and committed himself to nothing. Matthew tells us that they understood him well. "There were certain wicked husbandmen" (said he) " who, when the landlord's bailiffs came to receive "his rent, beat one, stoned or killed another, and finally "planned to kill the lord's own son." By the son of (Israel's) lord he meant himself. Thus, while evading responsibility for so grave a charge, he is made to impute to the chief priests a plot to murder him. Nevertheless, they ar said still to hav repressed natural indignation at his conduct.

Unless Matthew's narrativ is violently and disgracefully incorrect, we cannot be far wrong in imagining the secret conference which followed. No certainty is here pretended as to the belief then held by Caiaphas and Gamaliel concerning miraculous aid to be expected by God's chosen people; but our modern experience makes it highly probable, that they, like to ourselves, combined a firm belief that God had worked miracles for them in the past, with scarcely the faintest hope of miraculous aid in the present. The High Priests must hav known that the victories of Judas Maccabæus had no element of miracle. Every High Priest compared the resources of Rome and those of little Judæa in the prudential spirit of a statesman. He might not despair that the advent of Messiah might bring back miraculous agency; yet, after the bitter experience of the power and cruelty of Romans, caution and extreme timidity were prevalent in the policy of the Sanhedrin. With this assumption, we may imagin their conference as follows. The aged

Annas may hav opened by the ominous words: "If this "man persist in his claim to be the Anointed One, Son "of David and King of Israel, he will bring on us a "new Roman war, to which we ar quite unequal." Such foreboding may hav called out an opposit sentiment from some more hopeful elder, some Joseph of Arimathea: "True! most true! yet surely our wise elder must re- "member, that if we ar *ever* to be delivered, as our "prophets assure us, from the crushing yoke of our "enemies, it will be as when Judas Maccabæus was sent "from God. We shall hav war against foes far superior "to us: yet these Gentiles will learn that the Lord of "Hosts fights for Israel. Is it certain that this Jesus, "unwarlike hitherto, may not after all be the Messiah "who will breathe preternatural force into our people?" "Nay!" might the High Priest Caiaphas answer: "see "how he shuffled when we asked for his authority. He "overrules the law of Moses, yet does not plainly avow "himself greater than Moses; nor did he dare to repeat "that the babes and sucklings were right in hailing him "as the predestined Son of David. One who is to rouse "the armies of the Lord into enthusiasm must proclaim "himself God's elect and anointed; not skulk behind "parables and evasions." To such remark the wise Gamaliel was likely to assent, and to add: "We must "further put him to proof, and try of what metal he is "made. Let us ask whether he holds the doctrin of "our gallant, but alas! unsuccessful champion, Judas "Galilæus, concerning tribute and allegiance to a foreign "idolater. The reply is sure to give us insight into his "Messianic tone." This proposal was approved, as we know from our Gospels.

Of all difficulties pressing on a scrupulous Jew, most painful was the conviction that divine books forbad his recognition of an idolatrous and foreign prince. The words of the law (Deut. xvii. 11) were too distinct to explain away. These had in recent memory kindled a direful war, entraining Roman cruelties most horrible. The embers were still hot, and ready to flame anew. The popular sentiment against taxgatherers testifies that the Jewish conscience held their trade to be illegal. Of this grave difficulty some solution might be hoped, from one who presented himself as a heaven-sent, pre-eminent teacher, greater indeed than Moses, and now as the Royal successor of David. But when the question was propounded to Jesus very respectfully in the name of the chief religious authorities,—(if we ar to believe Matthew)—he replied in his own chosen dialect: "Ye "Hypocrites! why put ye me to the proof?". As if it were not their obvious duty to put him to proof, and a thing to be rejoiced in by a prophet equal to the occasion. How were they to obey his precept, "Beware of false "prophets!" if they did *not* put to proof the wisdom of one who claimed to be a prophet? *If we believe the tale*, Jesus proceeded to pronounce, that a coin is Cæsar's property, and must be handed to Cæsar as tribute, when demanded, if it bear Cæsar's image! Whether the new school of Christian advocates here condemn Matthew's narrativ as foolish, false and damaging, it will be interesting to learn. Meanwhile, it is reasonable to ponder, how, if Matthew be substantially correct, the chief priests must hav been affected by the reply of Jesus.

When a Frenchman, by giving an equivalent, has possessed himslf of an English sovereign, does he account the coin to be Queen Victoria's property, or admit that he is justly tributary to her? When the Queen or her ministers parted with the coin, they did not lend it, but sold it. The same was true of every coin stamped with Cæsar's head. Under the Roman republic every sound foreign coin was freely accepted as tribute. If it can be shown that Augustus or Tiberius Cæsar were more exacting, and refused all money unless it bore their stamp, it could not prove their right, but only their overwhelming power. The production of what is here called "the Tribute Money" was wholly *irrelevant* to the moral and religious question asked; and to call for a specimen of the coin, was merely a theatrical effort to throw dust into the eyes. No solution is thus to be had of the question proposed. If Jesus really thus replied, we may be confident of the effect produced on the chief priests. They would say among themselves: "This man "is an impostor, as well as impudent, slanderous and "reckless of the law of Moses. *He takes no notice at all* "*of the law*. He has no tenderness for our pious brethren, "who ar in agony from our perplexing subjection. He "assumes arrogant tones of superior wisdom; yet, when "interrogated on a pressing difficulty, he displays puerile "*un*wisdom: and because we (as is our duty) test him "by a very respectful and reasonable question, he insults "us as *hypocrites*. Truly we ar wrong in being respect- "ful to so ill-bred a churl. What further proof need we, "that such a man, pretending to be a divine messenger, "is really an impostor, or half mad? Into what mis- "chiefs may he not plunge us with Rome!" Will it be said, that Jesus did not foresee such a result of his reply? or that, foreseeing the result, he deliberately intended it?

The rulers, having thus felt their ground, saw distinctly at what they must aim,—*to exculpate themselves from any complicity* with Jesus in his claim to be the predestined Son of David and antagonist of Roman power. They believed that his Messianic pretensions could only involve the nation in defeat and misery. So galling was the Roman incubus, that a calamitous explosion might follow from the mere words of a weak pretender. Attack with a whip, as on the money-changers, while he claimed to be Messiah, might precipitate insurrection as fatally as a spear. Therefor their great anxiety was, to convince the Roman prefect and Cæsar himself, that they vehemently disapproved the claim of Jesus, and desired the stoppage of his carcer.*

After this, we cannot doubt that they attended carefully to his movements and his public speeches; and *if it be true* (as Matthew and Mark tell) that at this very crisis he uttered the speech given us in Matt. xxiii., the whole Sanhedrin must hav been immediately informed of it. An American lawyer has entitled this speech the most virulent invectiv known to us in history. We cannot imagin it to hav been taken down by a shorthand writer, and it may hav received exaggerating touches; but unless it had been very bitter, very fierce, no admiring disciple could hav produced such a memento of it. As we now read it, its sole purpose was, its sole result can hav been, to exasperate the rulers into the conviction that he was an implacable, untractable fanatic, whose carcer it was absolutely necessary to arrest. In its close the speaker seems aware that he has failed of keeping his hearers in sympathy with him. The students of sacred law whom he assailed so contemptuously were held in high esteem by the multitude in Jerusalem, in whom most probably his invectiv did but move indignation. He must hav felt that his words fell flat and dead upon them, when he closed with the dark threat, that *they should see him no more* until they were eager to receive him as blessed and coming in the name of the Lord.

Pious Christians hav accepted the defamatory epithets,

---

* Mr. Charles Hennell is the earliest English writer known to me who insisted that *political fears* were the main influence in the death of Jesus.

Hypocrites, Blind, Fools, Avaricious, Tyrannical, Children of Hell, as calm truth, stigmatizing pre-eminent wickedness of those Mosaic rulers: yet some of his utterances seem (if correctly reported to us) to convict themselves of bitter slander: they outdo Tacitus and Suetonius in malignity. The Hebrew doctrin of religion *may* in the origin hav been not much better than that of Greece or Rome; but certain it is, that with intellectual growth those Gentiles evolved by their most esteemed sages only a God who with high mind and power had no moral sympathy with man, and gave no aid to human virtue; while the Hebrew teachers, one and all, rose into the belief of a God "righteous and loving righteous-"ness," "holy and claiming holiness" from man. When Tacitus raves against Gentiles converted to Judaism, we disregard his words as folly. In special cases converts ar not morally improved by their change; but to a vast majority the effort of private judgment in religion and the sacrifices made for conscience' sake entrain a visible improvement: much more when made out of a Paganism full of impure and silly fables into the Hebraism of that day. Yet Jesus is made to denounce Woe! on the Pharisees for their zeal in proselyting, and to declare, "Ye make your proselytes two-fold more the CHILDREN "OF HELL than yourselves." Tacitus had no vocabulary spiteful enough for this. Again: (if we accept the narrativ) Jesus rudely insults them, calling them Hypocrites, for building tombs of deceased prophets and deploring the outrages of their ancestors against them. Yet what better could they do, than grieve for the past and honour their martyrs? and what indication of HYPOCRISY did it giv? what proof had he to alledge of so gross an imputation?

Two or three days passed, during which Jesus clung to the precincts of Jerusalem. From Matthew we learn that it was resolved now to bring him before Pilate the Roman prefect. He finally ate the Paschal Supper with his disciples in a secret upper room, yet migrated from it to the Mount of Olives and thence to a certain oliveyard (Geth Semane) when night came on. A strange scene is then revealed, which none of the narrators was likely to invent. From agitation of mind Jesus could not sleep, but woke his companions and chided them for not staying awake with him. He prayed earnestly against having to drink a certain cup;—no doubt he meant, Roman punishment for his Royal entry. When some proposed to defend him with the sword, he replied (according to Matthew) that by praying to his Father he could obtain twelve legions of angels. Such hope then had buoyed him up; and though his agitation showed that his confidence in miraculous aid was shaken, he still clung to the fond idea. If in his agony his sweat was like great drops of blood, (as Luke says), it denoted a terrible fall from high hope; but an immovable calm,—or shall we say? the apathy of exhaustion,—succeeded.

Though Jesus had been seen in Jerusalem many times in the few last days, the priests did not know his sleeping place, nor trust the power of constables to identify him in the night: and they had chosen night for his arrest. They therefor paid money to Judas Iscariot, one of his disciples, who conducted the constables to Geth Semane and indicated him by a kiss of honor. No angel guard defended him. The apostles found no mark of Messianic power and divine aid. Their faith naturally broke down, and they took to flight. He was led before the High Priest, who asked whether he had professed to be able to destroy the temple and rebuild it in three days: but Jesus refused to answer. Next, when asked whether he claimed to be Messiah and Son of God, he assented vehemently, in a tone triumphant, perhaps threatening. This the High Priest is said to hav called *blasphemy*: whether he did, or did not, is historically unimportant; for there was no legal issue. The further proceeding against Jesus turned *solely* on his assumption of an *earthly* royalty, which might draw after it a war with Rome.

Next morning, when Pilate took his seat in the judgment hall, complaint was made against Jesus of insurrectionary entry and royal pretensions. To all military tumult Pilate was bound to giv attention: to neglect the present accusation was impossible. Yet inasmuch as no armed force had been embattled by Jesus, Pilate could not believe that any serious insurrection was planned. He probably regarded the outcry about a son of David and king of Jerusalem as child's play and Jewish nonsense, so long as neither sword nor spear was forthcoming. On the other hand there was something formidable in the temperament of this eccentric people. Even in Jerusalem a strange prophet no sooner rides on a white ass, with a procession to call out Hosannah! (the war-cry, it is said, of a former insurrection) than a great multitude is ready to acknowledge him as king. If such a thing be possible by the side of the High Priest and Great Council, what may not happen if this man return to the warlike and more excitable population of Galilee, with the name of king, and with the report that he has been received as king in Jerusalem? One with whom in Jerusalem this was mere vanity, may be carried even against his intention into real insurrection, when urged on and elated by thousands of brave fanatics, who bitterly remember Roman cruelties.

Pilate condemned Jesus against his own convictions, through fear of being thought at Rome feeble against insurrection. That the offence for which Jesus was crucified (as were many hundreds of Jewish insurgents) was purely political, is proved by Pilate's inscription over him (Matt. xxvii. 37) "Jesus, king of the Jews." It is also notable that Pilate crucified *two robbers* with him. This can hardly hav been a gratuitous insult, while Pilate had no hostile animus against him. All insurgents were called "robbers" by the Romans: hence the obvious presumption is, that Pilate was making a demonstration to Cæsar of his zeal and activity in suppressing insurrection. This idea is corroborated by the conduct ascribed to the robbers. They said to Jesus, "If "thou be the Messiah, save thyself *and us*." This would be quite natural, if from patriotism they had taken up arms in the belief of his royal pretensions; and equally natural then was it for Pilate to punish them side by side with the king in whose name they had risen against Cæsar. Provisionally therefor this interpretation of the robbers' position is reasonable. Pilate would hav saved Jesus, if he could hav extorted any distinct renunciation of *earthly* royalty. Tiberius Cæsar would no more hav been troubled by any claim of *heavenly* grandeur, than by a Stoic's boast that he was a king, and the mass of mankind slaves. But Jesus, *after professing to be a king*, refused further utterance, and remained (as a Roman officer would call it) contumaciously silent; thus depriving Pilate of all excuse available at Rome, where the memory of Judas Galilæus might be his ruin. Nevertheless, even at the last, it seems, he tried to save the life of Jesus; for he took him from the cross prematurely and delivered him to his friends.

The two first Gospels ascribe to Jesus while on the cross the shriek of despair: "My God! why hast thou "forsaken me?" No one would invent this cry to glorify him; therefor it looks like truth. It implies that he had, up to the last, clung to the belief that legions of angels would carry him victoriously through the career into which he had plunged, and that, when struck down from lofty imaginations, a total collapse of mind ensued. The third and fourth narrators suppress his cry of despair, apparently as unworthy of him. Luke ascribes to him a nobler utterance: "Father! for-"giv them; for they know not what they do." But Luke is here quite untrustworthy: for he represents one of the "robbers" who was crucified with him as reproving the other, and making actual *prayer* to Jesus as Lord of Paradise, which is magnificently accepted. So marked a contrast of the two robbers could not hav been unknown to Matthew and Mark, who distinctly declare that both of them insulted him. The fourth narrator makes him die with the grand utterance: "It is finished;" certainly a great improvement. But how much is here historically true, will be judged differently by different minds.

That the priests could not easily identify Jesus denotes that he was very new in Jerusalem. Archbishop Whately (late of Dublin) teaches, that Judas expected his Lord to summon angels to his rescue, as soon as an arrest was attempted; and hanged himself in despair, when no such event followed. But how much to believe concerning Judas[*] is a hard problem, when we discern that our narrators hav made history out of misunderstood prophecy. Their "potter's field" is a blunder. The true sense of the Hebrew is probably given by the LXX., as the *foundry* or *mint;* and no sound exposition can connect the prophecy with the proceeding of Judas.

The inquiry may justly be made, whether Jesus, after accepting and applauding Simon's avowal that he was the Messiah, at all changed his ideas concerning the coming Kingdom of Heaven. That he ever for a moment

---

[*] Paul in 1 Corinth. xv., says that Jesus after his resurrection "was seen "by the *twelve*."

internally aspired to be a new Judas Maccabæus, no one is likely to assert. Perhaps an obscure utterance attributed to him bears on this question. I submit my interpretation with diffidence; for I hav to assume that the Greek given us in Matt. xi. 12 does not *to the letter* express his exact argument. I suppose him to hav meant to say: "There ar persons who wrongfully expect "the kingdom of heaven to be established by weapons of "war. Such men as was Judas of Gaulana *use violence*, "and think *to seize it by force:* and *even* after the "preaching of John the Baptist, who declared that it "must come *through national repentance of sin*, the error "continues to this day." That from the very beginning of his career Jesus believed himself higher than any preceding prophet and about to announce higher wisdom than any taught in the Mosaic law, cannot be doubted without a total rejection of our Gospels; but it may be asked, did his idea of the "kingdom of heaven" at all change, after he braced his courage to claim and act the part of Messiah? Apparently there *was* a change. The order of events in Luke is so untrustworthy, that we cannot press as belonging to the second stage his phrase *(found in Luke only*, xvii. 21), "the kingdom of heaven "*is within you.*" But in his many comparisons of this kingdom, which seem to belong to his earlier stage, its predicted triumphs ar by moral and spiritual growth. The comparison of its process to that of leaven, and to the growth of mustard, also the parable of the sower, ar in this respect very notable. "The Son of Man" in Matt. xiii. 41 may be adduced on the other side; yet in what appears to be his earlier teaching, there is nothing flatly political like the twelve thrones of Matt. xix. 28, set up over the twelve tribes for compensation of the twelve disciples. Indeed when the mother of John and James (in Matt. xxii. 20—24) comes to entreat ascendancy in his royalty for her two sons and hereby excites jealousy in the ten, Jesus warns them that these high posts must be earned by suffering and by service; yet drops no rebuke on this political ambition as a fundamental mistake. In his triumphal entry he assumes to be King of Israel, and again before Pilate avows himself to be a king, and allows Pilate to interpret the word as every Roman was sure to understand it. These ar indications that with the growth of his own ambition, his idea of "the kingdom" became more that of human royalty,—divinely established, no longer demoniacally. Indeed immediately after avowing himself to be Messiah, he claims (Matt. xvi. 27) to be the Heavenly Son of Man predicted in Dan. vii. 13. If that be rejected as spurious because the phrase "take up *his cross*" is anachronistic, yet no just suspicion rests on Matt. xxv. 31—46,—a discourse very characteristic of him, nor on his declaration (xxvi. 64) in reply to the solemn demand of the High Priest. Had he not explicitly claimed to be prefigured in Daniel's vision, it is unintelligible that this should immediately on his death become the cardinal doctrin on which thenceforth his Church was to rest. The duty of *watching* for the coming of the Son of Man in the clouds of heaven does not appear in his earlier stage, and *possibly* is spurious in the later stage,—an afterthought.

APPENDIX TO CHAPTER VIII.

It will not be overlooked that in many texts Jesus is represented as avowing that the Pentateuch has Moses for its author, and rests on divine authority. Christians hav in general accepted this as decisiv and final.

Nevertheless modern skill in literature has pursued

its diligent course. The life-labors of many scholars, eminently of Germans, hav established that the Pentateuch is the work of *at least* three different writers, who wrote at different times,—the last as late as King Josiah. English clergymen, no doubt, struggle to deny this. The learned Professor, Rev. George Rawlinson of Oxford, is a very uncompromising opponent of Bishop Colenso, who has set forth his own argument elaborately on the German lines; and Mr. Rawlinson in answering him *(Aids to Faith*, p. 251) distinctly admits (1) that Moses made up the book of Genesis from a number of records of more or less antiquity; (2) that the Pentateuch underwent authoritativ revision [a thousand years after Moses] by Ezra, who modernized it and introduced many parenthetic comments; (3) that the last chapter of Deuteronomy is not from Moses.—Ezra's dealing is merely conjectural, his authority so to deal is a fiction: but the admissions here made confess that the book is COMPOSIT and was worked up at a very late age; while no particle of historical evidence is produced in proof that Moses wrote *one line* in it.

The able German Professor Hupfeldt, commenting on the Sources of Genesis, avows that the discovery of the composit origin of the Pentateuch is as certain as it is important; that no retrograding of opinion is possible, as long as criticism exists; that we now start on this basis as already proved: proof is no longer needed, but at most, improvement in detail. Colenso equally, with unanswerable force, contrasting the versions of the Fourth Commandment in Exodus and in Deuteronomy, infers that the later writer knowingly alters the earlier, and supposed himself at liberty to do so, *i. e.*, regarded the composition not divine, but human. The pretence that the law was *recovered* under Josiah, was adverted to above, p. 3.

Unless we reject the testimony of these Gospels concerning the utterances of Jesus, we hav to believe *either* that he was misinformed on this literary question and was wrongfully dogmatic; *else*, that he knew the truth and concealed it. The latter is a most improbable imputation. To ascribe to him the knowledge which for us has been worked out by the co-operation of hundreds of students aided by libraries, is as unreasonable as to ascribe to him a knowledge of physical astronomy. On those who accept the Gospels as true, the conclusion presses that Jesus thought himself eminently wise in matters on which he had everything to learn. Therefor, when he assumed to be the Hebrew Messiah, there is no cause to wonder that he deceived himself and fell very deeply.

CHAPTER IX.

FIRST STAGE OF THE CHRISTIAN CHURCH.

DISMAY and Despair ar described as the first emotions in the disciples deprived of their Master; which were gradually dissipated, when the opinion gained currency, that the *soul* of Jesus, on leaving the body, had ascended to heaven, and *was there glorified*. That this was the original meaning of the doctrin, that "God raised him "from the dead" is attested by Peter's first Epistle, which says: "Christ was put to death in *flesh*, but was "made alive in *spirit*;" words that show the writer to hav no belief that the flesh of Jesus was called back into life. Indeed in Charles Knight's Cyclopædia the doctrin of Resurrection held by the *Pharisees* is described as consisting *not* in the re-animation of the *body*, but in the passage of the *soul* into some other body. We might therefor make sure that this was the current doctrin with those Jews. The same result may be confidently inferred concerning the belief of Paul (1 Cor. xv. 38, 44), who soon became the great apostle of the Gentiles. On so fundamental a topic neither apostle could differ from the collectiv church. No tale concerning the *flesh* of Jesus being made alive after death is found in any book which can be proved to hav existed in the life-time of those apostles. We know that the disciples accepted doctrin from what were called *visions;* which, being either simply dreams, or results of *abnormal* sleep, can bring no evidence as to exterior truth, certainly no proof of fact. The Church settled down into a belief that the *spirit* of Jesus had appeared to many, but (according to one tale in Luke) so *transformed* that he was not recognized by the outward likeness. When we further consider what is assumed by his ascending into heaven *in their sight*, with flesh and bones (as an Anglican article expresses it), *viz.*, that in the plumb-line vertical to the *Mount of Olives*, there is *a local heaven aloft*, into which his body soared, we ar warned as to the credulity of that age; yet, as in the "assumption" of Elijah and Romulus, we hav no reason to believe the tale to hav been current among actual contemporaries. "Pardon is given to "ANTIQUITY," says the historian Livy, " to mingle things "divine with human, and thus make the origin of cities" [or of religions?] "more august."

With what ease absurd stories were circulated concerning events of an earlier generation is instructivly shown in Matt. xxvii. 50—53. No sooner has Jesus uttered his despairing cry, than (we ar told) the earth quakes, rocks ar rent, the graves open; " and many *bodies* of the saints "which slept arose, and *came out of the graves* after his "resurrection, and went into the holy city and appeared "unto many." So vague and impossible a statement passed as fact fifty or seventy years later. Bodies coming out of the graves! By whom could they be recognized? [But only after his resurrection! We need not comment on this, though the words ar in the Sinaitic version; but they ar absent in some other, according to Titschendorf's note.] Criticism is superfluous.

Comparing our Gospels, we can see indications how stories *hav grown in telling*. Matthew, after saying that the disciples met Jesus on a mountain of Galilee after his death on the cross, honestly adds, that *some doubted*. He says nothing about the body of Jesus passing through closed doors. But in the twelve apocryphal verses added to Mark it is stated that Jesus appeared to the eleven as they sat at meat. Luke adds, they supposed it was a spirit, but Jesus showed them his hands and his feet, and said, "Handle me: a spirit hath not flesh and "bones, as ye see me hav." Thus the writer, unlike Peter and Paul, supposed Jesus to hav his old body; so notably had the story grown in two generations. But "John" goes far beyond. Out of "*some doubted*," he boldly manufactures the romance of Thomas. He invents a spear-wound in Jesus's side large enough to receive Thomas's hand, and makes Thomas exclaim, "My Lord and *my God*." The moderns, assuming that these Gospels were written in the very first age, ar naturally confounded, and see no reasonable intermediate hypothesis.

In this second stage it was necessary to modify and refashion the idea of Messiah. "He was to *suffer* "before entering into his glory." A truly new doctrin, quite irreconcilable with Isaiah ix. and xi., and with Micah v. 2—8, the very sources of Messianic expectation. Messiah was still to be personal Ruler on Earth, still to sit with his faithful saints on a royal throne; but he had now *to come back* from heaven and so assume his dominion.

Daniel's prophecy was made the basis. "One like a "Son of Man," (that is, he who had called himself *the* Son of Man) would come in the "clouds of heaven." This mythological picture was made cardinal, with the addition of " God's trumpet," of which the sound would wake the dead out of their graves.—(1 Thess. iv. 16.) Still the original cry was uttered, "The kingdom of God " is *at hand;* " which continued to be the touchstone of faith for more than fifty years. This earnest expectation and looking for "the Lord from heaven" was made *the primitiv Gospel* of the Church.

The doctrin of a suffering Messiah could only be maintained by arbitrary and uncritical interpretation of the old prophets. But one school of Rabbis was very fanciful. Their methods were available for obtruding the new tenet. By isolating the fifty-third chapter of Isaiah from the chain of prophecy in which it is one link, a specious beginning was made, and various Psalms of moaning and complaint were presently assumed to be "Messianic." The cry of despair which was imputed to the dying Jesus is a quotation from the first verse of Psalm xxii.; which was sufficient to suggest that the Psalm prefigured Messiah's bitter complaints. After this, ver. 18 of this Psalm was likely to be borrowed and *transmuted into history* as we see in so many other cases.—In modern England Daniel ix. 26 is thought to assert that Messiah shall be slain; but in the Greek version it is the Anoint*ing* (not the Anoint*ed*) that shall come to an end. Such also is the rendering by erudite German scholars. No school of Jews in high repute for learning has ever admitted that their prophets taught a suffering Messiah. Evidently Christians betook themselves to the idea, in order to find comfort in their blank disappointment.

But on the day of Pentecost which followed the death

of Jesus, *i.e.*, about seven weeks later, a new event suddenly broke out, of which a *garbled* account is given in the book of Acts. *Garbled* we may boldly pronounce it; for the learned Evangelical Professor Augustus Neander in his History abandons it as indefensible. After long strained religious emotion, many of those present babbled in unintelligible sounds, which were supposed to denote a *Divine Inspiration*. Paul (in 1 Cor.) givs a lucid account of what he personally knew : he makes plain that the strange sounds were not foreign languages, as the writer in the "Acts" pretends; but were explicable only by a new miracle, *i.e.*, by some one gifted divinely with a power of interpretation. All was closely similar to the phenomena displayed in Edward Irving's London Church from 1830 for several years. In modern England the delusion could not long abide unexposed, but it permanently deceived the early Christians. The idea that such carnal and morbid excitement was a special mark of the Divine presence and approval, and was "a gift of the Holy Spirit"— pervades the whole book of Acts. So little discrimination of healthy from morbid emotion do we find in those primitiv Christians, whose warmth of devotion and self-abandonment is often transcendent. We may honor their self-sacrifice and their many virtues, while deploring their weakness of understanding.

This outburst on the day of Pentecost gave a mighty impetus to new enthusiasm. It roused all the disciples into the belief that God was on their side. The Church was, as it were, set on flame. Among the apostles, Peter and John seemed suddenly to enter upon new life. Many new converts were made, and "were *baptized* in "the name of Jesus the Messiah for the remission of sins." These words call for remark. In the three first Gospels no one but John the Baptist baptizes. We ar not positivly informed that the Apostles and other disciples of Jesus had been baptized by John. It is probable that they were, if it be true that Jesus personally submitted to it and recommended it. We afterwards find in the Acts that baptized disciples of *John* pass as Christians. Jesus is twice made to prefigure his own coming sufferings as a new "Baptism" or Immersion: but in the three Gospels neither does he baptize nor the disciples for him. Only in the fourth Gospel (John iii. 22, and iv. 2) is this asserted. But after this Pentecostal excitement Baptism *in the name of Jesus* becomes the rite for admission to the new church; and the idea naturally went abroad that Jesus himself had instituted it for all future disciples.

The new zeal and enthusiasm kindled earnest remembrance of the preachings of Jesus against the retention of Wealth. Some of the richer men among them, seeking for *perfection* along the lines laid down by Jesus, sold their possessions and brought the proceeds to the apostles. Open tables were spread, at which all the converts, new and old, fed without charge, as in an Essene Establishment. But after a little while, the apostles felt the administration of such funds to be an invidious and unsuitable task, and begged the assembly to elect seven *deacons* (*i.e.*, ministers) for its due discharge. Seven were elected, of whom one was called Stephen. But Stephen presently showed himself far too high for this duty. He forthwith flamed out as a new apostle. His short career is of great importance, and deserves far more attention and closer detail than has been given to it. According to the narrator, "Being full of *faith* and *power*, he did great "*wonders* and *miracles* among the people." No details ar given of these miracles, nor even a hint of their nature; nor how his "*faith*" was displayed: but we learn that he stirred deep resentment in the Jewish rulers by the doctrin which he preached; resentment wholly new. This makes it important to examin the narrativ closely.

His offence (we ar told) was an avowal that Jesus would destroy the holy place and change the Mosaic law. Change of the law does seem to be implied in the coming kingdom of Messiah; yet no hostile emotion had been awakened when Peter announced this event as impending. Stephen is conjectured to hav added, that in Messiah's kingdom Jews would hav no advantage over Gentiles: but at this era Gentiles were not even admissible into the Church,—a fact which does not commend the conjecture as probable. What is more, the penalty of stoning is not commanded by the law against religious error except when anyone is guilty of introducing some new god; and it is manifest that on this occasion the tribunal was strictly judicial, with priests of high rank presiding. Thus a high probability arises, that the *introduction of the worship of Jesus* was the main guilt imputed. The writer of the "Acts" professes to giv us in great detail Stephen's actual speech of defence. Unless Stephen is maligned by the narrator, he must hav tried the patience of his judges sorely. It is impossible to find out from his speech that any offence was imputed to him. He denies nothing, he defends nothing, he explains nothing. He enters upon a tedious and very superfluous recital of events from Abraham in Mesopotamia downwards,—matters notorious to every boyish Jew; digresses to quote prophecy against the idolatrous; then goes back to Solomon and his temple. At last he bursts out into fierce attack on his judges, as resisting the Holy Spirit, now equally as of old, and entitles them "betrayers and "murderers of The Just One," and "transgressors of the "Law."—Up to this point the tribunal had controlled itself; but (we must infer) it now concluded that he had no defence to offer; that he knew himself guilty of the crime imputed, and, like a dashing captain of war, thought his best defence lay in counter-attack. Abundant time had been granted. He had used freedom of speech only to abuse it. Conviction of his guilt was now universal. The law of Moses (as alone known to them) strictly forbad mercy, and prescribed the dreadful form of punishment—namely in Deuter. xiii.; for by this chapter they evidently were guided. He discerned anger rising in the countenance of his judges, and aggravated it by declaring that he "saw the heavens opened, "and *the Son of man* standing at the right hand of God." They can hardly hav been ignorant that by *the Son of man* he meant that Jesus of whom he called them betrayers and murderers. A terrible scene followed,— the popular stoning to death, which the law strictly commanded against anyone who might try to bring-in the worship of a new god. It is not credible that the Christian account defines correctly the crime alledged against him. The last words ascribed to Stephen ar an invocation of the dead Jesus as a god: "Lord Jesus! "receive my spirit." We cannot suppose that Stephen now invoked Jesus for the first time. It must hav been his habit, and it can hardly hav been secret. The evident probability is, that *Invocation of Jesus* was the *main offence* imputed; but after such invocation had become universal in the Gentile Church and the Jewish Church was nowhere, the writer of the "Acts" was unwilling to record that the Jews had resented such invocation as *idolatrous*. Of course no Jew could see any difference between the Greek invocation of a dead hero, and the Christian invocation of a dead man, however saintly. If they had been physically unable (as they *may* hav been) to keep Greek hero-worship out of Cæsarea, this was no reason for conniving at the like in Jerusalem itself. Subtle devices which explain away the charge of idolatry, and evade the Jewish law of Monotheism, *had not yet been concocted* by Christians, nor in any case could hav weight with Jews. The plea that "Jesus is God," if it had been made, could only be understood as setting up two Gods. Hebrew doctors knew well, how idolatry crept in among the heathen by reverence to deceased parents, ancestors, heroes and kings, and that the fatal beginning was through Invocation of the Dead. No plausible fantasies can set aside the fact, that men who implore aid from an unseen spirit, treat that spirit as omnipresent on this globe and indefinit in power. Thus they virtually raise it into a second god, who in their hearts dethrones the One Supreme. Hence the unrelenting attack on Stephen. The words of the law rang in their ears, "Thine eye shall not pity him, "neither shalt thou spare, were it thy brother, the son "of thy mother." Let Christians attack the law: one might praise them for that. But when they call the law divine, and bitterly censure the Jews for obeying it, how can one then praise them?

This tragedy was the beginning of a wider persecution. No doubt, all Christians were suspected of complicity in Stephen's guilt. Saul, a disciple of Gamaliel, (Saul, better known to us as Paul) was eager in enmity, and went to distant cities as inquisitor of like criminality. No similar outbreak is recorded until about A.D. 63, which will be noticed below. Why Herod Agrippa put to death James the son of Zebedee (Acts xii. 2) no hint is given: only it is said, that by it Herod "pleased the "Jews." For no religious offence short of imputed idolatry, would the Jews approve. They *may* hav been glad that Herod relieved them from the odious necessity of another popular movement of violence; but this is only one possibility. We must be contented with ignorance why this James was slain. With this exception, the Christians of Jerusalem seem to hav long lived in peace with the priestly rulers. We must infer that none of them avowed themselves followers of Stephen's doctrin; which by reasonable interpretation seems to mean, that the Church in Jerusalem did not teach nor practise Invocation of Jesus. In the extant epistle of James, long President of that Church, no hint can be found to justify the practice; no allusion to it; not even such a formula as "The *favor* [grace] of our Lord Jesus "be with you," nor any word which could offend a Jew however bigoted. In "the Lord's Prayer" Jesus did not teach the disciples to introduce his name into their worship. Perhaps Stephen originated the practice.—This subject is brought up again in the doctrin of Paul's gospel.

Another remarkable event, cardinal to the history, soon followed,—namely, the admission of Gentile converts to the Church. The chief man was a Roman centurion (or petty captain) of the Italian band at Cæsarea, by name Cornelius, previously known by Jews to be devout. As the tale is given us in the "Acts," a discourse of the apostle Peter so moved the Italian audience, that the Holy Spirit fell upon them: whereupon "*they spake with tongues* and glorified God." Peter accepted the omen (as Greeks might phrase it), saw in it a manifestation of the divine will, proposed baptism and baptized them forthwith.

On his return to Jerusalem murmur arose against him. He had gone in to men uncircumcised and *had eaten with them*. The complaint implied that he had eaten some forbidden food. He justified himself (it is said) first, by a dream or vision which bade him kill and eat; a voice saying, "what God hath cleansed call not thou "unclean:" secondly, by narrating how the Holy Spirit had fallen upon his audience, just as on themselves at the first Pentecost. Those who had been thus baptized by the Holy Spirit (Peter argued) might surely be baptized with water. His arguments were convincing, and drew from his hearers the glad words: "Then hath "God granted to the Gentiles also repentance unto life."

Who of us can rightly call these early Christians of Jerusalem narrow-hearted and bigoted? Many such unjust epithets ar poured out against them. These ar they who ar branded by the epithet Judaizers, because they continued to believe their Sacred Scripture, which had taught that all descendants of Abraham must be circumcised, and that Circumcision had a religious value. Rather might one here deride them for the ease with which they resigned their old prejudices. Evidently they were glad to hav their hearts and minds enlarged: what more could we expect? Born and bred in that atmosphere, they inherited its errors with its wisdom. They could not be wide in knowledge, nor sage in caution, as ar we, eighteen centuries later. Their belief in the Holy Tongues, we must pity. Peter's vision they seem to hav interpreted metaphorically, not as abolishing ceremonial restrictions on food, but as establishing that comradeship with converted Gentiles was not a defilement. But it is possible that Peter himself was led by it to hold the prohibitions on food with a looser hand.

We here attain a critical fact defining a new error in the four Gospels. We now see that the disciples had never learned from Jesus, that Gentiles were to be admitted into his Church. Hitherto they had supposed that it was to consist of "a select remnant" of Jews only. A supernatural revelation (for so Peter's dream or vision was esteemed) had been necessary to teach them the opposit: to teach them indeed that the "Good "News" was to be preached to all nations, and that Gentiles were admissible to baptism. We infer that all passages in the Gospels which represent Jesus as contemplating a world-wide church ar later fictions; and in particular the close of Matthew's Gospel is anachronistic and untrue. Jesus cannot hav told them to go into all nations and baptize them in the name of the Holy Trinity. Had he done so, then neither Peter's dream nor the Holy Tongues would hav been needed. Peter, when arraigned for baptizing converted Gentiles, would simply hav pleaded the solemn last commands of Jesus as his sufficient justification. Since he makes absolutely no allusion hereto, the fact (as told in the "Acts") proves that Peter had never received such commands. We also now understand somewhat better why Jesus did not take precautions that his sacred words should be accurately conveyed to the many distant nations who were to be converted. Though Matthew makes him giv definit charge to teach his discourses to foreigners, yet in fact he had neither design nor foresight that his "Gospel" would be preached to foreigners; much less that his discourses would be preserved, transmitted and translated.

The argument by which modern Christians try to evade these inferences is truly astonishing. They say, that before the Holy Spirit in tongues of fire sat upon the disciples, the apostles were so carnal and dull of mind that they could not understand the words of Jesus, even when he spoke plainly. If our books ar at all credible, his speech was notoriously often far from plain; Matthew says, was purposely obscure. Grant that this rose out of the depth of spiritual mysteries in which he dealt: yet when he spoke of matters external, which a wholly unspiritual man or a child could understand, then it becomes ludicrous to impute the apostolic ignorance to dulness of mind. When Paul declared that Gentiles might enter the church without circumcision, every Jew, however carnal, understood him: yet *we ar expected to believe*, that when Jesus commanded his apostles to preach to the Gentiles and baptize them, these apostles, being very carnal and dull, could not understand him; —nay, not even after they had been illuminated by the Holy Spirit did they remember his commands.—But this is to expect stupidity in us.

After the principle had been established that the uncircumcised were admissible to the Christian church, a hope arose that, from among heathen proselytes to Judaism converts might be made to Christianity. Few of these received circumcision: but they had shown independence of mind in throwing off their hereditary mythology: they were presumably devout persons, and not likely to resist innovation in religion so stiffly as born Jews. In fact the first convert, Cornelius, seems to hav been previously "a proselyte of the gate." But of necessity every Christian Jew who believed in the only natural sense of the Hebrew prophets, and had not learned the art of blurring the contrast of Jew and Gentile therein established as sharply as possible, was led even by kindness and sympathy to wish that every converted Gentile should be incorporated into the Hebrew body; so that, instead of being one of the faithful Gentile vassals and servants, bringing tribute and performing menial offices for the Holy People under Messiah's reign, he should himself become one of the sacred ruling caste. One short passage from the later Isaiah is a clue to all beside: lxi. 5, 6,—"Strangers "shall stand and feed your flocks, and the sons of the "alien shall be your plowmen and your vinedressers: "but ye shall be named the Priests of the Lord; men "shall call you the Ministers of our God. Ye shall eat "the riches of the Gentiles, and in their glory shall ye "boast yourselves." Such was the exalted rank into which Jesus, descending from heaven with a shout, with the voice of the archangel and the trump of God, would establish his faithful Jewish disciples. While they believed this, love to Gentile converts made them long to embrace them as fully graduated Jews: and how *could* any of them throw off belief in that glorious later Isaiah? Nay, were they not now basing their belief in a Messiah *who had to suffer* before ruling in glorified Zion, mainly on the words of this very prophet?—We cannot therefor wonder,—we must almost take for granted—that a strong and powerful movement came forth from Jerusalem, *urging* in much love and seeking to *persuade* Gentile converts to adopt circumcision, the sabbath and all the peculiarities of Mosaism.

In fact, this was no question internal to Christianity. In the historian Josephus (Antiq. xx. 2 § 3—5) we hav a very interesting account concerning Izates, the young prince of Adiabênė and his mother Queen Helena. The prince, while residing abroad, was converted to Judaism by a Hebrew merchant called Ananias. At the same time his mother remaining at home was converted by *another* Jew. When, by the death of the king of Adiabênė, Izates was called home to take his father's place, mother and son were alike delighted to find their mutual zeal for the pure monotheistic faith. The young man was eager to become a complete Jew by circumcision. The mother dissuaded, and appeal was made to Ananias. He also dissuaded, saying that without circumcision Izates could do what was vastly better,—*revere God;* and with the mother he thought it unwise to stir up violent feeling in the nation by submitting to a *foreign* ceremony. But after this, came a third Jew, Eleazar from Galilee, whom the historian calls most exact as to Jewish customs. This man finding the young king to be reading the books of Moses, vehemently censured him, as "learning and not obeying." Izates was ambitious of perfection, accepted circumcision and thereby encountered much calamity, temporarily losing his throne and strangely regaining it. These events were under the empire of Claudius Cæsar. The sons and brothers of Izates were brought before Titus Cæsar after Jerusalem was captured. Thus the chronology is fixed. The three Jewish proselyters gained access to royal persons contemporaneously with the career of Paul of Tarsus. Queen Helena went on pilgrimage to the temple of Jerusalem. She arrived in the midst of a great famine, bringing with her much treasure. She at once sent to Alexandria for wheat and to Cyprus for dry figs. Her son, on hearing the news, sent large funds to the leading men in Jerusalem for public relief, and later they continued their liberalities.—Since all this was *after* the death of Jesus, we ar *not* forced to say, that these three Jewish devotees and their royal proselytes were accounted by him to be "children of hell."

Not a word has come down to us that can justly imply any sacerdotal terrors to hav been wielded by those who ar contemptuously called Judaizers: they had no power but kind argumentativ suasion. To us, of course, the suasion is empty of force. We do not believe in any secular domination promised to the Jewish race, or to others who hav accepted the Jewish ceremonial. But it is on the one hand unjust to call these Christians narrow and bigoted for desiring to hav the Gentile converts as *equals* and *partners;* on the other hand it is futile to censure them for believing the evident and plain sense of their great and magnificent prophet. This controversy concerning the value of the Jewish law, and the *advantage* of the Jew over the Gentile was presently to be quickened by the energies and enthusiasm of one man into a furious and deplorable heat. Here it may be added that in the book of Acts (xv.) a solitary occasion is reported, on which certain Christians from Jerusalem taught the Gentiles, that without circumcision "*they could not be saved.*" But the immediate result of this was (if we accept that narrativ) that the Church in Jerusalem collectivly reproved such teaching. If by "salvation" *acceptance with God* was meant, the doctrin was narrower than that of the Pharisees, who admitted proselytes of the gate. When the mother church so promptly disowned it, we may infer, even from the book of Acts itself, that the error was an exceptional indiscretion, and cannot hav had any deep roots or permanent strength. Yet another possibility must not be forgotten. If the Judaizers *only* taught that without circumcision converts could not take *equal rank with Jews* in Messiah's kingdom, this might be unfairly represented in *the oral tradition* of the Church fifty years later,—after Jerusalem had perished,—as teaching that without circumcision *they could not be saved.*

CHAPTER X.

PAUL AND JAMES.

The introduction of Gentiles into the Christian faith before long broke the Church in twain: but the actual process was not one of natural development. It could not hav been pre-imagined, and it needs special and detailed narrativ. Happily we ar here landed on solid historical ground. We hold Paul's own letters, the letters of that pupil of Gamaliel who played a leading part in the first persecution of Christians. We may rest on them with the same confidence as on those of our own contemporaries. But he writes as an eager controversialist against Christians of the earliest school. We hav not their statements. To accept his bitter accusations of them as a complete and final account, is not the way to truth or justice. With such light as we hav, we must do our best to *imagin* their side of the case.

This is not easy. For from childhood we hav been trained into contempt and aversion for the "Judaizers," that is, for the primitiv Christians of Jerusalem. Paul, we ar told, was "an apostle;" *therefor* all that he wrote must be true. But Paul sharply opposed Peter. Peter was made an apostle by Jesus; Paul had no credentials but his own. His apostleship rests on his *own assertion* that he was "called to be an apostle" (by a private vision?) after the death of Jesus. In a difference between two apostles, apostolic infallibility cannot be ascribed to either.

Paul was at first called Saul in the book of Acts; no reason is assigned for his change of name. But since he was by birth a Roman citizen, and Paullus is a well-known family name at Rome, we may conjecture that Saul was his personal Hebrew name and Paullus the name which as a Roman, he used and preferred.—In this second stage of Christianity, two names, *Paul* and *James*, represent the two contending schools. The collision between these two was not confined to the question of Justification as understood by Luther. It took a much wider sweep; namely, Did Christianity overthrow and annihilate the Mosaic law? James replied: "Certainly not; not one jot or tittle: we Jews ar bound "to the law, as well as to circumcision and the sabbath; "*only* Gentile Christians ar free." Paul replied: "Nay, "but all the ceremonies ar mere types and *shadows:* the "*substance* is in Christ; (Coloss. ii. 17) Jews ar free, "equally as Gentiles: Christ has made *me* free, *though*

"*I am a Jew.*"—It is natural, almost necessary, for us moderns to admire the breadth of Paul's view, just as we admire Pythagoras in Astronomy. But in the actual controversy we hav to consider by what arguments Paul vindicated his position, and what personal authority he assumed in pronouncing that he had a right to dictate. That the living Jesus never taught the doctrin of Paul, is so obvious that no words ar here needed. Paul professed to hav learnt it by a special revelation to himself: James continued reverently to obey his Master and Lord.

James son of Alphæus, (strangely entitled James *the less)* is supposed to hav been *first cousin* of Jesus, because both by Paul and by the historian Josephus he is called *brother* of Jesus. It is agreed that at least after the death of James son of Zebedee (of whom nothing is reported but that he was put to death by Herod Agrippa the first) this other James became *President*, or first Bishop, of the Church in Jerusalem. Paul was a far greater man than James, if greatness be measured by the magnitude and permanence of his doings; but if we ought to esteem men chiefly for modesty, for fairness and sobriety of mind, in these qualities James was apparently superior. We know Paul better by his numerous letters. This *controversy* is opened most sharply by himself in his Epistle to the Galatians, which splendidly reveals the man. Perhaps Martin Luther, who commented upon it at enormous length, judged it to be the most valuable of his epistles. To us it is certainly valuable as signally displaying all Paul's weakest points.

If he prided himself on anything, it was on his skill and sagacity in interpreting the Hebrew scriptures. It is worth while to examin his use of them in this epistle. (1) "Unto Abraham and his seed" (argues he, iii. 16) "were the promises made, He saith not *unto seeds*, as of "many, but as of one, and *to thy seed*, which is Christ." At first this strikes one with amazement. The writer seems not to know that a noun in the singular number may denote a collection of individuals. But on considering that Paul himself (Rom. ix. 7) calls the Jews *the seed* of Abraham, and does not say *seeds*, it appears that we ought not to impute this enormous and ridiculous blunder to real ignorance and stupidity, but only to haste. He fancies he sees an argument for his purpose, and he *jumps at it* without allowing himself time to think.—And ar we really to accept so hot-headed a writer as guided by a secret divine power too high for our criticism? This attempt at reasoning is so ludicrous, as to forbid deference to his judgment, however great our admiration of other qualities in him.

(2) He proceeds to build upon this by argument, with which few moderns would hav patience. It suffices to remark, that he closes with the wild words,—"The law "(of Moses) was ordained by angels in the hand of a "mediator. Now a mediator is not a mediator of one, "but God is one."—Was he going to sleep as he wrote? or will anyone maintain that words ar lost from the text?

(3) He undertakes to prove that the death of Christ has annihilated all the ceremonial of Moses, or as elsewhere he puts it, has nailed the ordinances to his cross. His proof is as follows. "*It is written*, Cursed is every "one that continueth not in all things that ar written in "the book of the law, to do them. Christ hath redeemed "us from the curse of the law, being made a curse for "us: *for it is written*, Cursed is every one that hangeth "on a tree." At first sight this argument is quite enigmatic. Most unwillingly we ar forced to see that he means, "So impotent was the law really to curse "Christ, that by cursing him, it has made its curse vain: "it has lost cursing power; it is like a bee which has

H

"tried to sting a buffalo, and has stung out its vitals:
"the law has thus lost all power of *prohibiting*, and may
"safely and rightly be disobeyed."

But if the curse fell *justly* on Messiah, how can this make the curse void? and if *unjustly*, then how is the law "holy, just and good"? Did Paul know what he was writing? Hardly. The law which he quotes (Deut. xxi. 23) on sanitary grounds commanded the early burial of a corpse. If a criminal was hanged, he must be buried before night. His body had become an accursed thing,—that is, a pollution,—'εναγὲs as a Greek would say. Snatching at the word *Curse*, Paul confounds physical pollution incident to the corpse of a saint with the moral offence of disobeying a sacred law: strange want of moral sensitivness! He argues: "The body "of Messiah (having been hanged) is pronounced by the "law to be an accursed thing: hereby the law has "manifestly *so put itself in the wrong*, that henceforth no "one need care what it curses or what it commands; all "its ordinances ar made null and void, as if nailed to "the cross." Among these ordinances he makes circumcision prominent, all through this epistle, and indeed everywhere; and forgets that circumcision is older than Moses! Forgets? but if in haste he forgot, he cannot hav been permanently ignorant. *In his belief* the Most High prescribed to the Hebrew nation by Abraham (Gen. xvii. 7—10), as AN EVERLASTING COVENANT, the duty of circumcision. That now goes for nothing with Paul, because Moses enacted a sanitary precaution on a wholly different matter! Those may justify Paul, who care not a straw what Jehovah is said to hav said to Abraham, nor what promises of high rank and grandeur the prophets made to Israel. The command of Jehovah to Abraham is so clear and positiv, that the attempt to argue it down might in those days seem a reckless profanity. We do not need high imagination to understand how outrageous such argument must hav seemed to Jews, devout or patriotic, whether Christian or not. It goes far beyond exempting Gentiles from the Mosaic ceremonies: it exempts Jews as completely as Gentiles, justifying the accusation in Acts xxi. 21; for Paul's *argument* goes as far, if his *intention* was otherwise.

Orthodox Christians surely ought to see that his argument is utterly delusiv. His boast that his doctrin on this subject was given him by divine revelation (Eph. iii. 3) must be accounted a folly, unless the Pentateuch is fundamentally renounced. Nay, Paul shows, that in calling the law "holy, just and good," his sentiment was transient and unsubstantial. In real fact he professes to look down upon it as childish lore, which he has outgrown—Gal. iv. 1—7. He had no more reverence for it than had any Greek philosopher. He tried to argue it down, not by philosophy, but *as a Rabbi*, by quoting its own texts against it: hence his manifest failure.

(4) His allegories ar equally wild. He complacently undertakes to *teach the law* to those Galatian converts who ar disposed to embrace it; and assures them that Abraham's two wives ar an allegory,—Hagar, the slave-concubine, typifies mount Sinai, who is in bondage with her children (thus *assuming* that all who observe the law ar *in bondage !)* — and that Sarah typifies Heavenly Jerusalem.—Anything can thus be proved.—In the same spirit he teaches in the first Epistle to Corinthians that the Israelites in the wilderness were baptized unto Moses *in the cloud and in the sea*, and drank of that spiritual *rock which followed them* — (a rock followed them ! ! a fancy of his own, it seems) and that rock was Christ.— Such argument can conjure up any amount of arbitrary mythology. It is the lowest type of Rabbinism.

Paul's notion of the law as "added because of trans-"gression," and as the centre of "sin, bondage and curse," is in wonderful contrast to the joyful delight in it expressed in the 19th, the 119th, and many other Psalms. It may be said, "Those Psalms were perhaps written "earlier than Josiah's reign. *The law of Moses was not* "*yet known.* The Psalmist by 'the law' meant the "general Hebrew precepts, known to them partly from "the prophets, partly by the traditions of daily life." Be it so: but how speaks James? Did *he* regard the law as a bondage, or a source of curses? Nay, remarkably enough, he entitles it "the law of *liberty.*"—But pass we now to the substance of the Epistle to the Galatians, and its occasion.

Paul had converted these Galatians to his own Gospel. He is careful to style it his own. Aware that it gravely differed from that which might be taught them from another quarter, he took the precaution of charging them *to account any man accursed* who should teach them any other Gospel than that which he had delivered to them. The report comes to him, *not* that they hav in heart thrown aside his Gospel, *but* that they hav adopted the law of Moses *concurrently with it.* They might naturally think it impossible for any Christian to hold Mosaism and Christianism incompatible. How could the union offend their first teacher, — himself of the tribe of Benjamin, and often acting as a law-abiding Hebrew, when he wished to ingratiate himself with strict Jews? —But Paul resented it gravely. Having learned Christ from him, their minds became his property. They were not free to learn anything from anyone else. He reminds them of the solemn *curse* which he had pronounced upon all who taught any other Gospel than that which he had taught: and that there may be no mistake, he defines this as applying to certain FALSE BRETHREN "who came "from James" and "trouble them," and of these he says (v. 12) "I wish that *they were even cut off.*" He elsewhere complains of persecution incited by the Jews: but it would appear from these words that Paul would hav been, not sorry, but even glad, if some Herod or Nero had put to death these troublesome advocates of the law of Moses.

James beautifully answers Paul's monstrous curse of brother Christians. While defining True Religion as depending on Deed, that is, on Kindness and Purity, not on notions or knowledge [called or miscalled Faith], he presses the danger of rash words, saying that a man's religion is vain, who bridles not his tongue; that the tongue is a fire, a world of iniquity, an unruly evil, full of deadly poison; wherewith at one moment we bless God, in the next *we curse man!* My brethren, these things ought not to be. Who is a wise man? Let him show out of good conduct his works *with meekness of wisdom.* But if ye hav bitter envying and strife in your hearts, THIS wisdom cometh not down from above, but is earthly, from the carnal intellect, such as even a devil may hav.

Paul richly earned these censures. As here he calls the brethren who came from James "false brethren "privily brought in" and curses them; so in 2nd Corinthians he styles the same class "false apostles, deceitful "workers, transforming themselves into the apostles of "Christ; and no marvel: for Satan himself also is trans-"formed into an angel of light." Moreover to the Galatians he sneers at "James, Peter and John, who "*seemed to be somewhat; but whatever they were, it maketh* "*no matter to me.*" Evidently he knew that on one or other important matter he had the weight of the apostles at Jerusalem against him; and he glories in the public rebuke which he gave to Peter at Antioch.—We hav not Peter's account of the affair.

When Paul was so vehement, so self-confident, so insulting, it must not be assumed that the opposit party was always meek. In the outset they were wrong, according to Acts xv. 1. Rather must we expect that some of them sharply retaliated, and that the bitterness and strife which James deprecated was shown on both sides. But the *cursing system* was Paul's invention, and it is universally agreed that James pursued a just and reasonable course, neither pressing into Mosaism an unwilling Christian Gentile, nor forbidding, to one who desired it, incorporation with the Hebrew body : whereas Paul invented a prohibition, supported it by an extravagant assumption of authority, and (one can hardly doubt) by conveniently misunderstanding the doctrin of his opponents.

What James would hav replied to the words addressed by Paul to Peter, we need not doubt : "if righteousness "come by the law," says Paul, "then Christ is dead in "vain." James would say : "Righteousness, we all "agree, *consists in* obedience to God's law : therefor, of "necessity, righteousness can only come by God's law. "Nevertheless, God has not laid on Gentiles that law to "which we Jews ar bound. A Gentile Christian is free to "join our Hebrew nation, free also not to join : *whichever* "*he does, affects not his state before God.* You hav no "right to reproach him for desiring to join our com- "munity. As to saying that 'Christ is then dead in "vain,' this simply means that *according to your private* "*theory* Christ died in order to annihilate the law of Moses. "WE HAV NOT SO LEARNED CHRIST, and your contempt for "the everlasting covenant which God made with Abraham "does not commend itself to us."

After all, what is the basis of Paul's unmeasured self-assertion? He himself tells us, and throws a flood of light over his position and his character. His first claim is, that his apostleship is wholly INDEPENDENT; his Gospel is superior to that taught in Jerusalem. He is an apostle, *not of men*, neither *by man*. He has learnt nothing from any man, not even from those at Jerusalem who seem to be pillars. His assertion that he saw no apostle in Jerusalem but Peter and James, three years after his conversion, seems to him so important, that he confirms it by a solemn oath, "behold! before God! "I lie not."—On what then does his apostleship rest? He explains: "When it pleased God *to reveal his Son in* "*me*, immediately I conferred not with flesh and blood." He had *an inward revelation!* Just so, in 2 Cor. xii. he claims "to hav been caught up *into the third heaven.*" To us it might seem needless to add so solemnly: "whether in the body or out of the body, I cannot tell, "*God knoweth;*" but there he heard "unutterable words;" again to us necessarily unimportant, because unutterable. Of course he regarded this revelation and this ecstacy as preternatural: but he makes no allusion to the vision of Jesus in the clouds, striking him blind, nor to the scales that fell off his eyes when Ananias laid hands on him, and conferred on him the Holy Spirit. The last is virtually denied by him, and since he is silent concerning the external miracles, they must be a later fiction. But no inward revelation made to *one* man can ever be a fit argument for belief to *another*. Paul himself is anxious (1 Cor. ii. 5) that "the faith of his converts should not "stand in the wisdom of men, but in the power of God." This at once condemns his authoritativ teaching of things beyond human cognizance. If one of his Galatian converts were asked, "*Why* do you believe that Jesus of "Nazareth lived long before his human birth and was "the very and unique Son of God?" he has no answer, but: "Because Paul, who had a vision, or some sort of "inward revelation, *tells* me so, and *knows all about it;*"

thus the convert's faith stands not on the power of God, but on Paul's sagacity in discriminating divine visions from human dreams. Paul's presumption goes so far, as not to desire his private convictions, interpretations and impressions to be corrected by comparison with the creed of those who had had personal relations with Jesus. In fear of lowering his claims of independence, he purposely holds aloof, and remains contentedly ignorant of the teachings of the living Jesus. Meanwhile his innovations in Christian doctrin ar enormous and momentous: he well might proudly claim them as *his own* Gospel. First of all, it is not clear, that anyone before Paul adopted for Jesus the title "Son of God" in an exclusiv sense. The Jews called angels "Sons of God," and would no more hav shrunk from so entitling all good men, than we to use the phrase *children of God*. But with Paul, Son of God is a unique title, and is elsewhere interpreted by him that Christ is "the *image* of the invisible God, " and *firstborn of all creation*," also that he was the agent of God in all after-creation; so that Paul (1 Cor. viii. 5,6) sums up his contrast to the Polytheism of the Pagans, in words which to Jews would only mean "One chief God, " and a second inferior god." He says: Instead of gods many and lords many, "We hav one God, the Father, " *of* whom (*ex* quo) ar all things, and one Lord, Jesus, " *through* whom (per quem, by whom *as an agent or* " *instrument*) ar all things." Never for a moment does he pretend that THESE TWO AR ONE. Nevertheless, towards Jesus he cherishes and exercises all the sentiments in which divine worship consists. He trusts in his power and protection; he rests hope upon him; he makes petition to him; he receives commands from him; he inwardly and habitually holds communion with him as *ever present*. What is this, but to believe in a second god, inferior in rank, holding derived power, though morally perfect? To *us* it may seem, that to believe in a hundred gods, all morally perfect and among themselves harmonious, is consistent with the purest piety, and is far better than to believe in One God who indulges in petty passions: but the Jews had not reached that stage of thought, and it is unreasonable to doubt that many of the Jerusalem Christians judged Paul to offend against monotheism as taught by Moses and Samuel.

If anyone now were to advance a new revelation, on the strict lines of Paul, such as, that "the archangel "Raphael was the first being created by the Son of God," it would be easier to accept, than if for Raphael one substituted some historical man; say—Moses. Yet to believe this of Raphael, simply because *some pious man* had had an inward revelation to that effect, would not be judged compatible with ordinary good sense. In rejecting such evidence, no one would think that we were disparaging the man. Paul therefor, in expecting men to believe heavenly mysteries essentially shut out from human knowledge, (such as, the *First Creativ Action* of him who is Supreme and Invisible,) on the testimony of *Paul* that they were inwardly revealed *to him*, does not commend to us his sobriety of thought. He teaches us to beware of accepting him as competent to disclose to us the counsels and mind of God. He mistakes the laws imposed on the human mind.

We see in Paul's Epistle to the Romans that he could not escape the question, "What advantage then hath the "Jew?" Knowing, as we do, his doctrin, to us it must seem that his honest reply ought to be, "*None whatever.* "Zion and Jacob in the prophets mean the *spiritual* "Israel; *that is*, Christian converts of any nation." But he was not quite brave enough to avow this: we see his evasiv reply, Rom. iii. 2—"*Much every way;* chiefly "that unto them *were* committed the oracles (τὰ λόγια, the "sacred utterances) of God." Thus the *chief* advantage is not a *present* advantage at all, but one enjoyed in a former generation. The question was: What advantage *hath* the Jew? not, What *had* he once? In Paul's mind, the Gentile Christian had access to the oracles, and advantage from them, in entire equality with the Jew. Thus, in his controversy with Jews, Paul could not always afford to meet argument squarely. The topic recurs, less formally, in Rom. ix. 4, 5; but there too the advantages ascribed to the Jews ar all in the past.

In this Epistle to the Galatians, and elsewhere, a "glorying in the cross" appears to be claimed by Paul as something peculiar to himself, something from which the Jewish Christians shrink: certainly nothing of the sort comes out in James's epistle: James does not suggest that the deplorable death on the cross was in any way beneficial to mankind. But Paul further has a dialect of his own, and a new vocabulary needed for new doctrin. He is dead to the law by the body of Christ; he is dead with Christ; he is crucified with Christ; he has put on Christ; he is married to Christ; he is baptized into the death of Christ; he is in Christ, and Christ in him, Christ liveth in him, and he livs his life by faith in Christ.—What more can possibly be said concerning the Supreme God?

And yet by Athanasius Paul ought to hav been accounted a direful heretic. Paul's epistles thoroughly justify Arius, who believed the Son of God to hav been the earliest indeed of created beings, but still *created*, and *not eternal* in the past. St. John in the Apocalypse agrees with Paul, calling Jesus Christ "the beginning of the creation of God." So entirely did the Catholic church deviate from the early Gentile church in less than three centuries.

What was Paul's doctrin concerning the *Reconciliation* (of man to God) by the blood of the cross, is still much controverted; treatises ar written on opposit sides. He certainly teaches that by the blood of his cross Christ somehow *made peace* not only between Jew and Gentile, but also between God and man; and that "faith in his "blood" is essential to peace with God. The metaphor afterwards culminates in the Apocalypse, where the saints *wash their robes white* in this blood.

Whatever was the efficacy imagined in "the blood," it certainly was a great change for the worse from the simple Hebrew doctrin, which taught that God is a Father, who beyond all other epithets, deserves that of Ever Merciful; who knows man's frailty, pities it, makes allowance for it, and to the penitent forgivs transgression. Here is no difficulty imagined about Reconciliation, nor any apparatus of *death or blood* to effect it: no idea that it is self-righteous to find no need of a Mediator and Intercessor, a Divine Usher, Testator and Representativ. A simple and reasonable belief has been here corrupted into something artificial, arbitrary, obscure and opposed to general good sense. Truly he makes Christians pay a high price for getting rid of typical ceremonies.

It is a mysterious reproach which Paul casts on the Judaizers, that they teach circumcision *in order to escape persecution*. Thus too he says: "If I teach circumcision, "why do I yet suffer persecution? then is the offence "of the cross ceased." Romans had no wish to promote circumcision. The Jerusalem Church did not require it of Cornelius. Pharisees did not try to enforce it on proselytes; therefor its *non*-enforcement by Paul *cannot* hav been the main cause of anger against him. Some deeper collision is concealed under this talk about circumcision. Elsewhere the truth is manifest. That which may reasonably be held to be *Stephen's* offence was *Paul's* offence with the Jews. He not merely invoked a dead saint, as an occasional act, but established an entire system of worshipping an inferior God.

Thus by three separate practices he exasperated the Jews: 1. By the deadly sin of idolatry, as they necessarily viewed it. This would everywhere be *reported* against him, but before a tribunal could seldom be proved, unless his actual epistles were produced. Once he was stoned, like Stephen, and left for dead, probably on this accusation. 2. He taught "the Jews who were "among the Gentiles" that the Mosaic law was abolished by the death of Jesus. This may hav been punished (mercifully, in Jewish esteem) by thirty-nine stripes, which he five times received. 3. He alternately broke or kept the legal rules, according as convenient for winning favor. What Peter may hav done once through weakness,—if Paul's assertion (Gal. ii. 12) is true,—Paul tells us, he himself did from systematic policy, (1 Cor. ix. 20). This must hav degraded him in moral repute.—In Alexandria pre-eminently, but in many other cities also, Jewish tribunals had large power over men of their own nation. In this way Paul fell under their Jurisdiction.

But his worship of Jesus suggests another explanation of his charge against the Judaizers,—that they planned to avoid persecution. No doubt, as Paul himself could not in Jerusalem escape attack as *idolatrous*, it would be dangerous there to be accounted one of his partizans. Hero-worship could not be tolerated in the Holy City. Paul by it moved not only animosity among the unconverted Jews, but grave disapproval in Christians of the primitiv school; and if (what was to be expected) some of them complained that *his doctrin exposed all the Christians in Jerusalem to unjust attack*, it gave him an opening to say scornfully, that their opposition to him turned on their fear of persecution. Yet certain it was, that no preaching of circumcision would save a Christian from persecution in Jerusalem, if with Paul he also preached the worship of Jesus. On this account he cannot be esteemed accurate and candid in his representation of his opponents; though the first group of these in Galatia *may* hav been the rash zealots whose extravagance James and the Jerusalem Church ar said to hav disowned. Neither he, nor the writer of the Acts, was likely to make clear *all* the offence which Paul gave. They state only the idea of *compulsory* circumcision, in which the ultra-zealots were wrong, and say nothing about the charge of idolatry incident to Paul's new gospel.

With many eminent virtues, Paul had the defects often met in enthusiasts of novel opinion. While he was, not tender only and affectionate, but warm in love, to all who accepted him as a guide, it is more than doubtful whether he could brook an equal. Rather it may seem, that anyone who opposed any of his special tenets roused quickly his indignation, as opposing *divine truth*. He does not pretend to possess the gift of miraculous healing; though in the Acts (xiii. 11) not only was Elymas the sorcerer struck blind by his word, but (xiv. 8) a cripple is healed, an evil spirit (xvi. 18) is cast out; even napkins (xix. 12) taken from Paul's body heal divers maladies! But Paul made no attempt to cure his fellow-laborer Epaphroditus (Philip. ii. 23-27) when dangerously sick by his side, nor yet to relieve Trophimus (2 Tim. iv. 20) whom he left at Miletus sick. So little can we trust the book of Acts concerning miracles.

Sad to say, men who by honest enthusiasm rush into a false position seldom can complete their career without pretensions less clearly honest. Paul cannot wholly afford to avow that he is *not* a miracle-worker. In singularly vague high-sounding words he says to a strange church (Romans xv. 18): " I will not dare to "speak of any of those things which God hath *not* wrought "by me, through mighty signs and wonders by the "power of the Spirit of God;" and to the Corinthians he seems to put forth a threat that he will inflict miraculous sickness on a certain immoral church-member. "I hav decided already" (says he, 1 Cor. v. 3—5) "*to "deliver such a one to Satan, for the destruction of the flesh*, "that the spirit may be saved in the day of the Lord "Jesus." Satan here, as prince of demons, stands for any demon who can cause disease. Paul thus announces: "I will inflict disease on him for his spiritual benefit." So later (2 Cor. xiii. 10) "If I come again, I will not "spare, *since ye seek a proof of Christ speaking in me.* . . . "Therefor I write, lest I use sharpness, according to *the "power which the Lord hath given me* for edification, not "for destruction." The threat is worded with ingenious obscurity. Again, though his good sense led him to disparage the noisy babble called Spiritual Tongues (1 Cor. xiv.), yet he adds " I thank my God that *I speak "with tongues more than ye all.*"

The quotations given in the last paragraph savor more of cunning, than of honorable simplicity. "The Jews "seek for a sign," elsewhere says Paul, "and the Greeks "seek after wisdom;" frankly admitting that he has *no* pretensions to giv a *sign*, *i.e.*, a miraculous credential: yet in these passages he *insinuates* that it is not from want of power, but only from tenderness. Thus does erring Enthusiasm generate Fanaticism even in nobler souls.

Mr. Hampden (afterwards Bishop) in our day appealed from Paul disputing and philosophizing to Paul exhorting morally. Weak as he is in logic and in literary interpretation, yet as a practicable moralist he is generally admirable. The chief exception rises out of the primitiv Gospel itself. By teaching that Christ was speedily to overturn all existing rule and govern the world justly himself, it *annihilated zeal for earthly improvement.* Who could care for improving the laws or the tribunals, or for any enterprize needing time to achieve and still longer time to bear fruit, if he expected Messiah in a few years to make all things new? Even slavery is with Paul indifferent; marriage also is unimportant, because the fashion of this world passeth away. Patriotism is superseded, because *the Christian's citizenship is in heaven* (Philip. iii. 20): therefor "to mind earthly things" is a shame. On this side all apostolic morality is weak. We could not expect him to rise above his age in regard to the rights of women; yet it is truly extraordinary that in treating on the expediency of giving or not giving a maiden into marriage (1 Cor. vii. 38), he does not regard *her* wishes or judgment to need for a moment to be consulted! Truth forces one to say something more. We may not *blame* him, that his idea of marriage was so little edifying; that he treated even the desire of it as an infirmity. We see that he intended to be humble, when he attributed his own freedom from so troublesome a desire to a peculiar gift of God. But the stubborn fact recurs upon us, that on this topic a young Englishman will find Walter Scott and plenty of other non-religious modern writers more elevating and *more purifying* then Paul. Paul's doctrin was made offensivly prominent by Luther, and no doubt has been calamitous to many an unhappy monk. Undeniably, marriage, instead of being exalted, is degraded by Paul's treatment. But with these exceptions, his moral excellencies ar broad, solid and fruitful; his moral enthusiasm glorious. The form of his doctrin gave him a vast advantage over James and Jesus. They exhorted men to work *for* life, Paul exhorted to accept life freely given, and work *from* it. Faith is with him the *seed* of life, works the *after-fruit*. They could only say, "Do right, "Obey the law, Shun worldly pollutions, Renounce evil "wealth, and you shall be saved." Paul can tell of an "unspeakable gift of God," which men hav only gladly to accept; after which he calls them in *gratitude* to walk worthy of their high calling. "I beseech you," says he, "by the mercies of God —!" Beyond a doubt the human heart answers far more readily to this appeal than to any prudential warning against a predicted divine judgment. No Gospels had yet been written. Paul did not hamper himself by caring about Jesus in the flesh. He did not do what all Christians now do, tie themselves down to the portrait of Jesus as set forth in our books; but drew, either from his private "revelation" or his own free interpretation of old Scriptures, his own picture of a Saviour far too amiable to be ever repulsiv; who is assumed to be morally perfect, much on the same grounds as is God himself. No one can believe that the Supreme God has ever *suffered for us:* towards a Saviour who *has* suffered for us, gratitude more easily becomes a passion; then the Son is loved more than the Father; the Mediator gets the heart, and God himself only the bowing of the head.

James, like the Greek philosophers, was too high and pure for his age: he would not preach to it the worship of a dead saint. The pagans liked gods in human form, and Paul humored them by setting up a human god, who had suffered, and therefor could sympathize with suffering;—one nearer to us than (to our dull minds) he who is Infinit, Eternal and Unsusceptible of Passion seems able to be. The same cause, after Jesus had been absorbed into the Trinity, made the worship of the

Virgin and of many dead saints popular. Paul's doctrin avoided the worst evils of idolatry by representing Jesus as morally perfect, the very image of God, a marvellous sympathizing benefactor, preternatural, yet human. He could even draw his history with a free hand as in a heathen mythology. To the Gentiles the Hebrew command of *loving* God appeared impossible. Love, however tempered, seemed impertinent, out of place and even ludicrous.* Reverence and Gratitude were appropriate, but these did not easily become impulsiv, nor at all passionate. Addressing men accustomed to receive magic and marvellous tales without asking for proof, or scrutinizing the moral consistency of a story, Paul announced that the Son of God came down from heaven, took human flesh, endured contempt and suffering, solely to bless mankind in eternal life. Many believed; and the belief often changed them morally, by implanting new affections, new meditations, new hopes, new associations. With such cases in his mind, Paul wrote, "If any man "be in Christ, he is a new creation." The amplitude of this mythology gave to the uneducated a new fund of thought, pure and ennobling in contrast to all the Pagan mythologies, and far more acceptable to these Gentiles, than the meagre and severe doctrin of James,—we may add, of Plato or Epictetus. The unhappy fact was, that the educated asked *proof* of Paul's doctrin, and Paul had no answer but that "it was revealed to him." The Greeks (said he) "*seek after wisdom,*"—a sad reproach! But ought he not rather to hav said, *seek after truth?* If, after hearing Paul's doctrin, a heathen at once accepted it joyfully, without further inquiry, without suspicion, without caution, he would seem in that age "*to receive the kingdom of God as a little child,*" he would

---

* So Aristotle calls it. Εἴ τις φαίη φιλεῖν Δία, γέλοιον ἂν εἴη.

earn congratulation; thanks would be paid to God: but no man of ordinary culture will dare to say that such a convert had sought earnestly after truth, as we ought to seek, and as many Greek philosophers did seek. "*Most "unpainstaking*," old Thucydides would repeat, "is the "quest of truth with these enthusiasts." When Paul found very few educated men to accept *his word* as a guarantee of truth, he moralized on it, nearly as in old days *jealousy* was attributed to God. Jehovah overthrew Tyre "to stain the pride of all glory and bring into "contempt the honorable of the earth." Seest thou not how the God in heaven strikes with his lightning all things that ar lifted up,—high towers, high trees, high hills,—but the little ones fret him not at all? Even so, God hides his mysteries from the wise, *that no flesh may glory in his presence*. So far, the moralizing of Paul is nearly the same as that which is imputed to Jesus. Each of them expects belief without evidence. Each confounds Credulity with Faith. Perhaps each regarded Faith as the special gift of God to an Elect remnant. However beautiful and lovely in some cases the immediate results of some *un*truth may be, yet because it has no solid back-bone, it cannot stand in firm shape. Neither the doctrin nor its results can be permanent. Truth alone can stand the strain of Time: Truth cannot rest on Visions and Dreams, nor on mere Hearsay: Truth cannot be *tested* and *established* without much Incredulity and Criticism, which most religious teachers hav unwisely condemned, which also all Sham Sciences dread.

Yet Paul had great qualities. Though he preached a Christ of his own fancy, careless to learn what Jesus really was, he was the most effectiv preacher of the *name* of Christ that ever existed, and was the chief founder of Gentile Christianity. Possibly guided in part by the spurious book of Enoch, he defined Messiah to be Son of

God, Lord of angels and men, earliest of Created Beings, agent of God in all further Creation, future Judge of living and dead, predestined Ruler on earth, dispenser of all God's favors; and he taught that Jesus the crucified was this Messiah. To this he added much about the Law, its Curse, its Overthrow; the Cross and Reconciliation and Justification by Faith, Human Depravity and Helplessness, arbitrary Decrees of God under whose wrath we ar born, Predestination to be Saints, our Ruin through Adam's sin, our Recovery by the Lord from heaven; nor did he forget, that when the same Lord should come back to claim his kingdom, then the saints would judge the world. (1 Cor. vi. 2). Therein he retained the primitiv Gospel of Jerusalem, with its literal thrones for the saints. In this mass of new mythology was material for future controversy painfully abundant. Out of it came Augustinianism and what we now call Calvinism. Nevertheless in one cardinal matter Paul was the direct opposit to Calvin; for he taught *Final Universal Salvation.* This is manifest in several places, especially Rom. xi. and 1 Cor. xv. 22—28; a fact which totally changes the moral aspect of much which at first sight appears in his doctrin to be harsh, dreadful and darkening to the character of God. He has indeed sentences and arguments to which, as coming from so hot and hasty a writer, it is reasonable to believe, he would not hav tied himself. He did not know that his Epistles would be turned into a new Sacred Letter for distant ages.

His moral teaching must in every respect be preferred to that which is ascribed to Jesus. It may hardly be too much to say, that all the meaner side of Catholic doctrin comes from Jesus, and all the nobler morals of successiv Reformers from Paul, who had imbibed Greek as well as Hebrew thought. Paul's precepts ar never extravagant, but commend themselves always to practical good sense, however pure and lofty. He never condemns Wealth, nor suggests that in seeking Perfection we must renounce it; he confines himself to charging rich men to be "rich in "good works." He says, "If I giv all my goods to "feed the poor, and hav not Charity (caritas, *kindliness?)* "it profiteth me nothing." Compensation in the other world for poverty in this, is nowhere suggested by Paul. He neither blesses poverty, nor approves of religious mendicants; but of such he says: "If any man will not "work, neither let him eat." While preaching, he supported himself by his own labor, living so simply, that he earned the privilege of even supporting the weaker. He severely avows that with Food and Raiment we ought to be content. He warns of the danger of zeal to become rich, yet he never forbids to lay up for old age or for contingent weakness; but even acknowledges that it is seemly for parents to lay up for children (2 Cor. xii. 14). All of his utterances ar those of a disinterested, generous, very warm-hearted man, pure in his aims, and longing for inward perfection, persistent in enduring hardship, ambitious to infuse spiritual life into others, and aware that the privilege of the strong is to support the weak and patiently endure their follies. The duty of renouncing the enjoyment of things lawful, when they tend either to bring us into bondage to them, or to lead another into wrong ways, is presented as natural to one who livs in the new life. His heart seems ever full and gushing with glorious thought and affectionate desire, so as to leave in a reader the conviction: "This is a man who "was sure to inspire deep love and communicate high "enthusiasm,"—an enthusiasm, not for mere notions (of which he had plenty) but for justice, simplicity, purity, benevolence and tender mercy; indeed for all that he calls the Fruits of the Spirit. Having also intense conviction, boldness of assertion and unflinching bravery, he united all the moral elements needed in the apostle of a new religion. His extant Epistles ar a precious and beautiful treasure of Christian morality.

He knew that he was incapable of fascinating minds which demanded evidence before they could believe. Of those gathered into the church by him, very few were strong in intellect. Many were illiterate or slaves, others were highly emotional and credulous; some had a tinge of Oriental philosophy; many were allured by the promise of a heavenly Deliverer from oppression; some were attracted by the equality and fraternity of the church; perhaps most of all by admiration of the pure morals which were preached. But while writing and talking urgently concerning Faith, Paul does not discern the great ambiguity of this word, which in Greek, as in English, means (1) fidelity, (2) trust, (3) belief in a proposition. In the two first senses it may be a moral virtue, testing human character: in the third sense it cannot be a virtue: to believe when the particular proposition has no proof, may rather be called a vice. Through entire want of scientific culture, he (like Jesus) mistook Credulity for Faith, and wood, hay, stubble, for gold and silver. But his moral precepts ar gold that endures the fire.

Immoralities into which heathen converts relapsed, were a form of misery to Paul which we all should expect: but he encountered them also from *perverse opinion*, as in those who, having thrown off ceremonialism by the argument that external things cannot defile the spirit, deduced that no sexual act can be sin. He was further distressed to find some members at Corinth who denied human resurrection. We know that Paul's church at Thessalonica grieved over those who died before Christ's return, as though they hereby lost participation in his earthly rule. No resurrection of individuals entered into the scene of Paradise as presented by the Hebrew prophets. Paul teaches the Thessalonicans, and argues with the Corinthians. Perhaps the latter identified Resurrection with Regeneration, as in Eph. v. 14 and Matt. xix. 28, thence inferring (2 Tim. ii. 18) that "the "Resurrection is past already." Paul in his reply to the Corinthians lets us know his theory, that the kingdom of Christ is to hav a limit of time during which Death is to continue and (since with him Death implies Sin) more or less of Sin. But when *all enemies* (of which Sin is the typical name) hav been destroyed, Death also shall finally vanish. Then no longer will there be need of Rule. The Son of God will become subject to his Father and deliver up the kingdom.

This full and far-reaching anticipation was apparently worked out of a prophetical verse: "Messiah shall rule, "until God has put all enemies under his feet." If this comes from Psalm cx. 1 (as we may suspect) it is a new illustration how doctrin was generated in those days.

The Pauline churches were generally found in places where Greek was understood; in Syria, in Asia Minor or in Greece itself. We do not know that he understood Latin, or any language but Greek and Hebrew. He desired to visit Rome. At last, coming into danger from a tumult in Jerusalem, he used his privilege as a Roman citizen to appeal to Cæsar, and was carried to Rome as a prisoner. Hitherto he had known Roman magistrates as protectors, and fancied that while Christians acted aright, they would hav nothing to fear from Roman power. Hebrew Patriotism he had entirely cast off with zeal for Mosaism. But he lived to learn, how violent, pitiless and unjust was Roman rule. All Christian tradition holds that he was beheaded in Nero's atrocious massacre of Christians, A.D. 64.

A year or two earlier, James had been stoned to death in Jerusalem, on what pretence we do not know. Josephus givs details, as follows, The Roman prefect Festus was dead: his successor was on the road. The high-priest Ananos was one of the Sadducees, a sect rigidly maintaining the old law in its worst severity. He seized his opportunity, while no Roman officer was at hand to restrain him, convoked a Great Council, brought James and others before it as transgressors of the law, and carried against them a Verdict that commanded stoning them to death, which was actually inflicted. But the sentence caused great indignation in Jerusalem. So formidable a protest was made against Ananos to the new Roman prefect and to King Herod Agrippa the Second, that the high-priest was deposed for the deed. By what pleas he prevailed on the Council, no hint is given; but the punishment suggests that he imputed Hero Worship.—We may here note that the Christian Bishops of a later century were sure to dislike the Epistle of James, as testifying his wide difference from their mythology, and tried to discountenance it. But had it not been genuine, had it been a later fabrication, it never could hav gained any acceptance.

James and Paul were both true Jews in glorifying Abraham's readiness to sacrifice his son on a supposed divine command. The respect which to the present day this monstrous fable receives, warns us how little depth there still is in religious thought. A voice from heaven which urges us to an immorality ought rather to be ascribed to a Demon than to God. Paul and James would both hav seen this, if the story had been concerning a contemporary: but being told concerning an ancient patriarch, it passed without criticism. *Datur hæc venia antiquitati.* James also believes in the validity of prayer for external phenomena, such as Rain and Disease; and the Christian Church to this day upholds the doctrin.

CHAPTER XI.

CLOSE OF THE APOSTOLIC ERA.

WHEN Paul and James had been removed, the chief pillars of the Church may be recounted as Apollos, John son of Zebedee, and Simon called Peter.

Apollos was a Jew of Alexandria, who had received superior literary culture, suggestiv of Greek rhetoric. He may hav been baptized by John himself, whose disciple he regarded himself to be; and we find in the Acts of the Apostles that by reason of the close likeness of John's disciples to those of Jesus, Apollos and others passed as Christian. They were easily converted to Paul's gospel; and before long Apollos must hav become very eminent as a Christian teacher among the Gentiles, with some originality in his doctrin. For Paul (in 1st Epistle to Corinth) represents different Christians as saying, I am of Paul, and I of Apollos, and I of Peter. It was cleverly conjectured by Martin Luther, that Apollos is the author of the anonymous Epistle to the Hebrews, which cannot be Paul's, as the Greek style at once proves; though the Anglican translation (even the Recent Version) most improperly advertises it as Paul's. The Greek is far superior to that of Paul, the eloquence more polished and delicate, less fervid. The argumentation is less harsh and abrupt, though it has the fanciful subtlety to be expected from any Christian Rabbi. To no one can the Epistle be so plausibly ascribed as to

Apollos. After the death of Paul, Timotheus (Paul's younger friend) might reasonably attach himself to Apollos.

The chief novelty in this Epistle consists in representing Jesus as *High-Priest* of the Church, and *Intercessor* with God. Thus he becomes at once *Priest and Victim, offering himself* without spot to God. He rests his doctrin on the 110th Psalm, "Thou art a Priest for ever, after "the Order of Melchisedek." To many of us it is clear that that Psalm was composed by a priest, seer, or musician in honor of some Jewish king, possibly of David himself. Melchisedek was a king and priest. To say that David was a king after the Order of Melchisedek, was a poetical form of ascribing to him a right of sacrifice; and we know that David did sacrifice at the altar of Araunah the Jebusite. But in this Epistle the Psalm is assumed to be a glorification of Messiah (as probably Paul esteemed it) whence further a discussion concerning the priest-king Melchisedek. The writer's power of making much out of little is quite equal to Paul's, but perhaps this is only Rabbinical. Melchisedek in Genesis is brought-in abruptly, and nothing is said concerning his parentage, nor his birth and death. Out of these *omissions*, the writer grandiloquently raises a mighty fabric, calling him "Without father, without "mother, without descent, having neither beginning of "days nor end of life, but being made like unto the Son "of God, abideth a priest continually." On such a swollen bladder he would build a solid religion! What better illustration could we need of a "Castle in the Air" than this? His rhetoric culminates in his register of Faith, after giving a most unsatisfactory definition (if definition is intended), " Faith is the substance of things "hoped for, the evidence of things not seen." Then follows a long list of ancient worthies, among whom so many deserve sympathy and veneration, that to protest against special names is painful. Still, it is necessary to point at one monstrous assumption, contrary to the whole tenor of Hebrew literature,—that the patriarchs looked forward "to a better country, that is, a heavenly;" besides his fantasy that Moses in Egypt "endured the "reproach of Christ."

In the exaltation of Christ, as God's agent in creation, and therefor his first-begotten, also as the "off-shining" (or reflection?) of God's glory, he agrees with Paul; yet steps beyond him in saying that Jesus is the same Yesterday, To-day and For Ever, which adds to him one more attribute of Godhead, Immutability. Yet he calls "God the Judge of all," while with Paul God Judges men by Jesus. His moral exhortations ar worthy of Paul. The "*blood* of sprinkling" is his phrase, seemingly by allusion to the process for saving the first-born in Egypt from the destroying angel. This blood (he says) is "to *cleanse the conscience* from *dead* works to serve the "*living* God;" rhetorically elegant, morally very obscure. He informs us that "Christ *through the Eternal Spirit* "offered himself without spot to God,"—a new glorification of his ghastly death.

Apparently, with or without Paul, the cross was destined to a poetical glorification. Christians in the retrospect could not bear to think of their Lord's death as *simply* a cruel murder, as it is regarded in the opening of the "Acts." They felt bound to find out some divine purpose in it, some reason for saying that he had not "died in vain." This writer, who is still fuller than Paul of Hebrew sacerdotalism Rabbinically Christianized, signalizes the following curious analogy. "The bodies "of those beasts were burned *without the camp;* wherefor "Jesus also, that he might sanctify the people with his "own blood, suffered *without the gate.*" How deplorable a use of a fine intellect! *Sanitary* reasons obviously dictated where the bodies of the beasts should be burned; therefor (forsooth!) Jesus was crucified outside the *gate*. Want of good sense is too manifest. He also teaches us that in or "by the blood of the everlasting covenant" God raised Jesus from the dead, xiii. 20; quite a new covenant (it seems) here revealed, between God and Christ. But why in the blood? because covenants were confirmed *among men* by killing something! ix. 18. On this word *covenant* (Διαθήκη) he sadly blunders. In Greek it means also Last Will or Testament. He has (unawares to himself) in ix. 15—20 drawn up an argument in which this word vacillates between these two very diverse senses: whence hopeless nonsense is detected by an attempt at translation.

But on the whole we cannot wonder that this Epistle attained high honor and loyal acceptance with the Christian Church. Being in many respects like Paul and worthy of Paul, it was supposed to be Paul's. The date cannot be fixed. It has no historical allusion, either to the persecution by Nero or to the coming troubles of Jerusalem. If written in Paul's life, in alluding to Timothy one might expect allusion to Paul. This is not decisiv, yet may seem to turn the scale in favor of believing that it was written after Paul's death.

Nero's persecution of the Christians in Rome is dated A.D. 64. It was a very critical time for the Church, which hitherto, both in Palestine and among the Gentiles, had striven to avoid all offence to the Roman authorities. The belief that the Lord from heaven would quickly supersede all earthly rule, made it easier to them, than to the mass of the Jews, to endure Roman supremacy; nay, to many Roman rule may hav seemed more tolerable than the power of Sadducees. To converted Gentiles an idolatrous power in Italy was no worse, than if it had been in Alexandria or Babylon, Antioch or Sardis. Paul, as a Roman citizen, had lent all his influence to inculcate loyal submission to Rome: Peter, still later, followed in his track. But events were too stormy and overpowering. The temperament and judgment of the Church concerning Roman rule was changed violently, inevitably,—by cruelty which could not hav been pre-imagined.

This change is first indicated to us in the book which has for title "The Apocalypse (or Revelation) of Jesus "Christ." The author's name is given as John. He writes, as if with authority, to the Seven Churches of Asia. Internal evidence proves that the book was penned not long after the death of Nero, and before the destruction of Jerusalem. All Christian antiquity ascribes to John the son of Zebedee a long life. During his life it was hardly possible for any one to write as personating him. The Greek is the worst of all in the New Testament, and is that of a Hebrew. Absolutely nothing in the book exists to throw doubt on its being the genuine work of the son of Zebedee; and Justin Martyr, the earliest Christian writer who names it, ascribes it distinctly to the *Apostle* John. This apostle was one of the three who according to Paul, were accounted Pillars of the Church. Of any superiority in Peter, Paul was evidently quite ignorant. That must hav been a later fancy, equally that John was peculiarly beloved.

Innocent Englishmen seldom ar able to imagin what Roman "persecution" meant. We know that Romish legend is apt to exaggerate, and a vague distrust is often felt, when the horrors of old days ar alluded to. It therefor is not amiss to go into some detail as to the intense hardheartedness of Roman rule, which is often trumpeted as mild and tolerant, sagacious and civilizing.

There can be no just suspicion that the cruelties of that persecution were less than the tale. Will any one say, Perhaps hatred of the Emperor Nero, who commanded it, led the historians to exaggerate? But the very eminent historian Tacitus, who narrates hideous details, while confessing the Christians innocent of the crime imputed, *viz.*, the burning of Rome, tells all without pity, rather with ferocious exultation, slandering Christians as *per flagitia invisos*, "hateful for profligacies," "convicted of the crime of hating the human race." This philosophic and typical Roman proceeds, "Their "punishments were made a sport: some were covered "by skins of beasts, to make dogs mangle them to death: "others were crucified; others again, wrapped up in "cloths covered with pitch and brimstone, were burnt "in the night to serve as torches. For this spectacle "Nero opened his own gardens. Hence arose pity for a "set of men, *guilty though they were* and *deserving of the* "*most extreme punishments;* yet they now seemed to be "sacrificed, not for the public good, but for the in- "human pleasure of one man." By their "guilt," the historian means *guilt of opinion*, guilt of religion, not guilt of deed: of this he acquits them. Yet he thinks pity for them quite misplaced. When such a writer could hold such sentiments, incredulity seems vain. The horrors ar not narrated by a Christian priest, but by the highest genius then living in Rome, who tells events which occurred in his father's life-time.—Suetonius in few words is equally slanderous and unpitying. Trajan and Pliny, without knowing what Christianity is, assume as an Axiom that it is deadly guilt.

No wonder that Paul's roseate view of Roman power became untenable to Christian hearts. Roman rule had previously seemed as good or as bad as other Pagan rule. To those who learned the facts, it now glared forth signally as the guilty and deadly foe "of God and his Christ." Christians, before long, painted it to themselves in the same lurid colors as did the bitterest Jewish insurgent. In the Apocalypse of John the Roman Empire is set forth as a fierce Beast: the city Rome is drunk with the blood of the saints. In one and only one chapter of this singular book (ch. xvii.) is an authoritativ *interpretation* added, which the Christian historian Neander has lucidly explained, nor is the explanation open to any reasonable doubt. The chapter sets forth that the seven heads of the beast represent kings, of whom five ar fallen, one still exists, a seventh is yet to come. We must count them: 1, Augustus Cæsar; 2, Tiberius; 3, Caligula; 4, Claudius; 5, Nero: for Caius Julius was known only as one out of several successful combatants in civil war. The Monarchy was recognized in the Eastern provinces only after Antony was defeated by Octavianus B.C. 30.—Nero is the head which received a deadly wound: yet "this deadly "wound was *healed*." This is explained by the fact that for some twenty years after the death of Nero the Eastern provinces did not believe in his death, but supposed that he had escaped into Parthia. Hence two false Neros attained a great and dangerous following. Nero is denoted also by the 8th head, which *is to be* one of the seven. Who ar intended by the 6th and 7th must remain uncertain, since tidings concerning Galba, Otho and Vitellius came thick and confusing in that year of civil war. The burning down of the temple of Jupiter in Rome by the contending armies is apparently alluded to in ch. xvii. 16, which givs close limits of time for the composition of this book. Tacitus says that in that year the Roman Empire nearly came to an end. —We thus readily understand the mental excitement under which "the Apocalypse" was written, and the vehemence with which in the opening and in the close it avows that the events prophesied ar *about to be* accomplished *speedily*. Not merely the impending fall of the Empire was declared, but the final triumph in which the kingdoms of this world become the kingdoms of God and his Christ.

Our Gospels did not yet exist. The dreadful persecution under Nero (which was not wholly confined to Rome) left open the possibility of a rumour that Jesus had foreseen and predicted such sufferings for his faithful disciples: though we see, that if he did not plan or imagin a Gentile church, it is scarcely credible that he foretold these events. After forty or fifty years, in the midst of the mental strain which the imperial violence laid on the Christians, no one need wonder at the rise of numerous unhistorical traditions, which in time would be chronicled as truth. The predictions concerning the destruction of Jerusalem and the temple (as observed above), *cannot* hav proceeded from the mouth of Jesus: consequently there is none but the feeblest reason for attributing to him a foresight that his disciples would suffer extreme persecution.

In the phraseology of the Apocalypse a novelty appears in the use of the word Lamb for Christ: as "God and the Lamb;" "the Lamb that was slain;" "the Lamb that is in the midst of the throne;" and in a very startling metaphor: "they hav *washed** their robes "and made them *white* in the *blood* of the Lamb." Paul set the example of comparing Christ to the *Paschal* Lamb. This lamb in the Hebrew law was not a sacrifice on the altar, but a food in each house. Its blood was (in Exodus) sprinkled on every Israelite doorpost that

---

* In Rev. i. 5, the Sinaitic version for "washed" has "loosed, freed, "liberated," by reading simple υ for ου.

the inmates might be spared by the angel sent to destroy the Egyptians. That is why Paul said: "Christ our "Passover is *slaughtered* for us." But John's use of the Lamb may be borrowed from Isaiah liii., "He is brought "as a lamb to the slaughter."

Another novelty of greater importance is found in its entitling Jesus in one passage only (Rev. xix. 13) the *Word* of God. This is the beginning of *sublimating* him into an abstract *principle*, and dealing with Christianity as Philo had dealt with Judaism. The early Christian might now claim a Trinity in a verse of the Hebrew Psalms: "By the *Word* of Jehovah were the heavens "made, and all the host of them by the *Breath* (Spirit) "of his mouth." In Paul, the Lord Jesus is a solid person, no less separate from God, the Source of being, than is every individual man. So indeed is the Lamb of the Apocalypse: but as soon as the Son of God is entitled the *Word* of God, (especially since the same Greek term means Word and Reason) a foundation is laid for endless fantasy and endless controversy.

John in the Apocalypse closely follows Paul's exaltation of Christ. Paul calls him the *first-born of all creation* (Coloss. i. 15), so in Rev. iii. 14, he is *the beginning of the creation of God*. Each shows that *Arius* went the full length of Apostolic orthodoxy, and that Athanasius was an innovator. John goes on to call Jesus the King of kings and Lord of lords, "the first and the "last," who has the keys of Hades and of Death.—Whatever may be said by calm critics as to the want of sobriety in this book, it has a strange magnificence and purity of its own, and an admirable moral depth. In these dreadful times it must hav had an overpowering fascination to the suffering Christian.

Some phenomena in it ar hard to explain. (1) Is he literally Judaical, when he represents twelve thousand saints to be sealed from each of the twelve tribes of Israel? or if not, what can the statement mean? (2) When he makes out twelve tribes by omitting Dan, and numbering Manasseh and Joseph (*i.e.* Ephraim) as *two*, does he merely follow the reckoning already popular? The tribe of Dan was never able to conquer its allotted territory: a portion of it conquered by cruel attack a single town, in the farthest north of "the Holy Land:" but this perhaps was *never* accounted one of the twelve.— (3) Can any but a literal sense be put on his phrase: "These ar they which ar not defiled with women: for "they ar virgins," (Rev. xiv. 4). One can understand that in those terrible days such Christians as followed Paul in refraining from marriage, lest tenderness to wife and children lessen their power of endurance and faithfulness, were considered pre-eminent saints: but to brand marriage as "defilement" is simply dreadful, and one is unwilling to impute this to the apostle John. Whatever he *meant*, it would seem that this text had a very fatal effect on all the old historical churches. From a different side it buttressed Paul's pernicious doctrin that God does not grant the gift of chastity to men in general; whence a detestable tenet, current in modern false science for defence of male unchastity, gains support among Christian dignitaries.

Not only is the Roman Empire denounced in the Apocalypse as the deadly enemy of God and his saints (in marked contrast to Paul's notion and hope), but much stress is laid on the wickedness of worshipping the Beast (*i.e.* the Empire) and *his image*. There can be no reasonable doubt that this meant the image of Cæsar. A monstrous and abominable tyranny had crept in, which Augustus or Tiberius Cæsar would hav abhorred,—that of demanding, as a test of loyalty, to worship the Emperor's image. We see in the Apocalypse the terrible prominence which this had obtained.

This book became classical, as promising a First and Second Resurrection, and between them a Thousand Years' reign on Earth of Jesus and his Saints. That is why it was disparaged when Christians became ashamed of that expectation. It also, more than any other Christian book, undertakes to depict to the imagination the delights of a Christian heaven. The effort at spirituality is plausible, but a cessation of toil, pain and sorrow (as in Hebraic death) is the only solid idea in it. In continued life the total absence of pain and want is fatal to the idea of progressiv virtue. There is absolutely nothing to be *done*. No self-sacrifice is possible. No motiv for any exertion is imaginable, except to increase *knowledge* and *science;* so, after all, nothing beyond a Ciceronian heaven is propounded to us. Personal vision of "the Lamb" is *in itself* not more satisfying than was personal vision of the living Jesus.

Concerning this John we may remark that when Paul wrote to the Galatians, John apparently was still resident in Jerusalem; but afterwards he must hav had long familiarity with the seven churches of Asia to whom he inscribed the book of Apocalypse. Among them he learned to deviate widely from the primitiv creed of Jerusalem, as we see it in James's Epistle. Nevertheless it is not probable that he ever formally sanctioned Paul; for he pointedly upholds only twelve apostles, whereas if Paul's apostleship were admitted, there were thirteen. He also puts into the mouth of Jesus severe words against those who say they ar apostles, and ar not: which seems to strike at Paul.

A few words ar needed concerning Simon, called Cephas in Hebrew, Petros in Greek. No reason appears for doubt, that Jesus gave to Simon the surname Rock, because of his forwardness in avowing that Jesus was the Messiah. Paul never calls him Simon; James in the

"Acts" is made to call him Simeon. In his first and genuine Epistle, he calls himself Petros. The second Epistle, which even by Augustus Neander is judged spurious, opens by the name Simon Petros. The word Simon is Greek, meaning *snubnosed*. In Galilee this may hav been of Greek origin: but Simeon is clearly Hebrew. Was then the spelling Simon the mistake of men familiar with Greek?

Peter's character as depicted in the Gospels is that of generous ardour unsupported by moral tenacity. Paul also in writing to the Galatians represents him as aiming at the impossible task of pleasing both sides; the error of one amiable, but not strong. He had moved on quite readily in admitting Gentiles into the Church. He could not go along with Paul's vehemence at Antioch, and encountered Paul's severe rebuke; yet he certainly had no desire to impose on Gentiles the ceremonial law. German critics hav disputed the authenticity of even Peter's first Epistle, on the ground (solely, I believe,) of its being too like Paul's doctrin. It however is Paul without Pauline argumentation or Pauline subtleties. It is far more popular and less scholastic than is Paul normally, and seems to come from a tender and sweet nature which would both forgiv Paul's rudeness and be willing to learn of him.

No trace of Rabbinical argument appears in it, though it has what may be thought a Pharisaic doctrin concerning Spirits in Prison (rebel angels?) to whom Christ was supposed to preach the Gospel (iii. 19) by going down into Hades or Gehenna. These ar the angels (or sons of God) in Gen. vi. who through love of women (Jude 6 and 7) kept not their first estate. A peculiar obscurity is in iii. 6, where he speaks of the Gospel as preached to *the dead*, which whether literal or figurativ is very perplexing. His most Pauline trait is the comparison of Baptism to Noah's ark, but the Baptism of which he speaks is not the mere external rite, but the confession of a sincere heart.

It may be objected that nothing in this Epistle denotes the writer ever to have seen and listened to Jesus. But the objection assumes that in those days the business of an apostle was to play the part of an "evangelist," making much of the deeds and words of the living Jesus. It assumes that the practical morality taught by Jesus was more valuable than that of Paul and Peter. Rather, these apostles believed that they had to teach truths and hopes concerning the *risen* Jesus which he, while alive, did not teach, and that change of circumstances made change of moral exhortation suitable. The *perfect virtue* of Jesus himself could not be attested by an apostle as though eye or ear were a competent judge; so transcendent a quality could only be inferred by the *prophecies* concerning Messiah.

The last words of this remarkably beautiful and edifying Epistle send a salutation from the Church in *Babylon*. No valid reason appears for doubting that he wrote from the historical city of Babylon. The tone of iv. 17 denotes that he saw the destruction of Jerusalem under Vespasian and Titus to impend. He may hav written A.D. 69. In iv. 12 his expectation of the fiery trial (to all Jewish Christians—for it is to these that he writes) attests that the fierce enmity of the Roman Government to Christians was no secret to him. Yet he perseveres in Paul's theory concerning governors (ii. 14) and is most earnest that Christian Jews shall giv no symptom of disloyalty. His modesty in addressing Elders as himself an Elder, and exhorting them not to be lords over God's heritage, is in very pleasing contrast to that of bishops in the following centuries. Whether Peter ever set foot in Italy, is historically quite doubtful.

No well attested fact denotes that he ever held or desired any supremacy in the Church, Jewish or Gentile. The four Gospels accuse him of having three times denied Christ with vehement oaths: but the lead which in Acts i. 15 is conceded to him ungrudgingly, makes this story as improbable as ar the details concerning the motivs of Judas.

The reasons for rejecting as spurious the second Epistle called Peter's, cannot here be fully treated. It is enough to say, that the second chapter is judged to be a mere importation of Jude's Epistle, and Jude writes, looking back to the apostles as an earlier generation: also the third chapter is written after much disappointment had been felt that Christ's second coming was delayed. The excuse for this, that "with the Lord a thousand years "ar as one day" is fatal to all truth, making God a wilful deceiver of men. Such doctrin is self-confuting.

CHAPTER XII.

DESTRUCTION OF JERUSALEM AND ITS EFFECT ON CHRISTIANITY.

UNHAPPILY it was not the Romans alone who hated the Jews. No conquering empire has yet made itself beloved, except that of the Incas in Peru, who (according to Spanish accounts) conquered by that blessed Christian rule, which bids us show greatness by becoming servant of the weaker. To imperial kindness the barbarian heart pays grateful allegiance, as surely as do horses and dogs. But Assyrians, Babylonians, Medes and Persians, Macedonians and Romans, following the doctrin that

Might makes right, and, *Woe to the conquered!* were hated by those whom they trod down. It is not wonderful, that so too were the Jews during their short term of imperialism. The Hebrew annals frankly inform us how very far was their pious king David from gentleness towards Edom, Ammon and even Moab; how light-handed also his plundering of Syrian towns. All this comes as it were naturally to one who has proved superior in war.

The tale was repeated by the Jewish power after the marvellous Maccabean successes. These exalted the Jewish spirit everywhere and gave honor to the Jewish name. The successiv kings of Egypt looked on Jews with respect, and (in modern phraseology) admitted them to diplomatic equality. Maccabean princes ruled in Sheba. A million Jews dwelt in Alexandria with nativ autonomy under the Ptolemies. The Romans were glad to make the Jewish power their ally. The sacrosanct head of the Jews, already a Priest-King in fact, dealt with a very high hand towards foreigners, grudging municipal local freedom even to nativ towns, in order to centralize power in Jerusalem. Syrian towns, of which many were conquered, ar not likely to hav had much freedom left to them, though their language was that of Jerusalem. All that is reported of them implies, that at every time they felt themselves to be under a foreign yoke. Jewish dealing with Edomite towns was severer still; for after conquest, circumcision and the whole of the Mosaic ritual was violently imposed. Yet here it may seem that the violence was successful; for, as the descendants of Saxons who had been driven to baptism by the spear of Charlemagne, and Hungarians forcibly converted by St. Stephen, came to pride themselves on their Christianity, so (in two generations perhaps) were these Edomites proud of their Judaism, and practically were incorporated into Israel. The fierce demolition of Samaria by the high-priest Hyrcanus was mentioned above. Jerusalem was not virtuous enough for her own successes and temporary power. When Rome came down in might on Syria, it may well be believed that from the evil reports of the Syrians, many of whom avowed disaffection to Jewish rule, the Romans quickly imbibed strong aversion to the Jewish character. Moreover, it is every way credible, that the Jews under their new regimen were more offensiv to their neighbours than under their former royalty. David, however acceptable his piety to the strict worshippers of Jehovah, and however unbridled his personal elation, was not king over a whole nation possessed by ceremonial zeal. His people were only too prone to adopt the superstitions of their neighbours, as indeed were many of the kings who succeeded him. But in the later period, when all the nation had become devoted to the law of Moses, and had seemed to experience that Jehovah indeed *fought* for them; then, to avoid religious arrogance was hardly possible. They had rejected marriage with Gentiles as a defilement and a breach of sacred law. To eat at a common table involved ceremonial uncleanness. On a smaller scale, like causes separate Turks from their Christian subjects, and Englishmen in India from nativs. To be conquered and governed by foreigners is a grievous sore; but to be insulted by the perpetual suggestion: " We domineer, because we ar pure, and you ar defiled," drops poison into the wound. It can scarcely be doubted, that the ordinary insolence of conquerors was inflamed by ecclesiastical pride. The Hebrew scriptures fanned the flame. Every Israelite remembered such texts as: " God shall subdue the nations under us, and the peoples " under our feet! Moab is my washpot; over Edom will " I cast my shoe," &c. Texts ar too numerous here to quote; indeed that glorious (later) Isaiah abounds with ampler and varied chants of triumph. Earthly dominion, earthly wealth and splendor, earthly vassalage of Gentiles, ar announced in words unmistakable. It is childish to pretend that Jerusalem and Zion do *not* mean the cities so called, but mean miscellaneous saints who profess a different and higher religion than that of Isaiah. Most certainly no such idea could enter the Hebrew nation, even if a few eccentric Rabbis, with Paul, imagined it. But Christians, instead of confessing that these beautiful prophecies were *patriotic* error and an unhappy source of delusion, continue to insist that they ar divine, scold at the Jews for accepting their obvious and only sense, and twist the words to their own glory.*

The language of Jerusalem hardly differed from that of the Syrians: we call both at that time Syriac. The Asmonean princes conquered much or all of Hollow Syria, — the lofty plain between Libanus and Anti-Libanus. Some towns were alternately conquered and lost. Many Syrian towns had Jewish residents in time of peace: but probably all Syrian towns preferred Syrian to Jewish rule; and at least at first, preferred Roman masters to Jews. The city of Cæsarea approached the ancient Tyrian frontier. It had been built up into splendor by Herod the Great, and named in honor of Augustus Cæsar. It contained a temple adorned with statues in Greek style, which seemed to alienate it from Judæa. It had a Jewish synagogue; but the Syrian residents, under the patronage of Herod and his successors, may hav been more numerous than the Jews. In this city a fatal flame was first lighted (if we can

---

* The amiable and learned Crévier says that the Jews, when they made insurrection against Trajan, had only to complain of "the heavy yoke laid "upon them contrary *in their opinion (!)* to the express promises and predic-"tions of the prophets."

believe the details in Josephus) by the very wicked machinations of the Roman prefect Florus.

Every Roman officer expected to return home rich enough to liv in high state. Man differed from man in shamelessness and cruelty, but very few indeed made justice or humanity paramount. Florus (according to our historian) was so extreme in his odious malversations, that accusation against him in Rome was likely to be fatal, unless he could paralyze his accusers by involving them in imputation as insurgents. His policy therefor was, to get up an insurrection, and earn credit for crushing it. In order to provoke the Jews to resistance, he stirred up a quarrel in Cæsarea; he also himself committed slaughter in Jerusalem. Aware of his policy, the Jews at first tried to curb him by appealing to Cestius Gallus, governor of Syria, who was superior to Florus: but much delay followed. The Jews in all parts, when they heard of massacres in Jerusalem and in Cæsarea, with complicity of the Roman authorities partly clear, partly suspected, were exasperated beyond endurance. Bands of guerilla took arms. A Roman fortress near the Dead Sea was captured with a highly stored arsenal. Violent counsels prevailed in Jerusalem itself, the son of the high-priest regarding the state of things unendurable. Presently wild and frantic auxiliaries came in, led by a son of Judas of Galilee: thus the counsels of the more timid or more prudent (whichever epithet is more proper) were overpowered. Cestius Gallus himself came to mediate *too late*. His conscience seems to hav been on the side of the Jews: perhaps he abhorred the deeds of Florus. Either his moderation, or his inward vacillation, courted attack. The fierce bandits, after defeating him, violated military faith; hereby making it morally impossible for the authorities at Rome not to take up in earnest the war which had begun by Roman defeat. After this Jewish perfidy,—though it was the deed of wild unmanageable banditti,—no declaration of loyalty from Jerusalem could be listened to. So began the eminently dreadful war against brave fanaticism and patriotic despair.

The historian Crévier thinks the calculation of Josephus credible, that eleven hundred thousand Jews perished in the siege of Jerusalem alone. Another quarter of a million must be added for the war in other parts; besides ninety-seven thousand who were reduced to slavery. This destruction deprived *primitiv Christianity* of its nativ centre and purest traditions, and gave scope for credulous invention in the Gentile Churches. Jewish Christians lost all authority. They were scolded down as unsound in the faith, for not accepting the additions made to their creed from the visions of Paul and John. The remains of the Jerusalem churches after the destruction of Jerusalem, according to the learned Mosheim, fell into two sects, called *Ebionites* and *Nazarenes*.* The former regarded Jesus as born in the ordinary way from Joseph and Mary; and they clung to Mosaism as necessary to salvation, *for Gentiles as well as Jews ;*—but we hav this statement only from their enemies. In both points the Nazarenes less offended the Gentiles. They believed Jesus "to hav been born of a Virgin, and to be "*in a certain manner* united to the Divine nature." They did not press Mosaic ceremonies on Gentile Christians; but held them to be obligatory on them-

---

* The account given of these two sects belongs to the second century after the *further* massacre of the Jews, first in Cyrene, Alexandria, Cyprus and Mesopotamia under Trajan, next in Palestine itself under Hadrian, 65 years later than the destruction of the temple by Titus. In the three years of this last war, says Crévier, 580 thousand Jews perished by the sword. Their leader, Barcoceb, was accepted by them as Messiah.—These two wars were final: Palestine was nearly a wilderness. Babylon became the feeble centre of Jewish learning.

selves as Jews.—The Ebionites were quickly denounced as heretics; the Nazarenes somewhat later. But neither sect by traditional position, numbers, wealth or learning had any controul over the Gentile Church. Thus it became easy to suffocate the primitiv Creed, and the doctrin of Jesus himself, by the new incrustations.

When the second century opened, the doctrin of Paul, Apollos and John son of Zebedee, that "Jesus was the "beginning of the creation of God," was accepted in all the Gentile Churches. Under Trajan we find that the Christians known to Pliny were supposed by him to chant a hymn to Christ *as God* (or as a god). His miraculous birth from a virgin was perhaps already received in all these Churches. The Son of God was understood to be the Mediator through whom alone God can be known and approached. It is not wonderful that words to this effect should be attributed to Jesus himself, though nothing of the sort is in the celebrated Lord's Prayer, which does not suggest to pray *in his name*. In Matthew and in Luke (as we receive the books) there is a passage, evidently from the same source, of a tone strikingly new; namely, Matt. xi. 25—30, and Luke x. 21, 22: "*All things ar delivered to me by my Father;* "*and no man knoweth the Son, but the Father; neither* "*knoweth any man the Father, save the Son; and he to* "*whom the Son will reveal him.*" In the spurious prophecy Matt. xxiv. 36, the *prescience* of the Son is denied, precisely where, if "all things ar delivered unto him," he ought to know *when* to act as well as *what* to do. Thus a growth is discernible in the power attributed to Jesus, after that prophecy was imagined, that is, after the great siege of Jerusalem.

A new Epic was ere long imagined and executed by John the Elder, whom ecclesiastical tradition refers to Ephesus. His style is quite his own, though so like to the verses just quoted that they might pass as his. If in this day anyone claimed Divine Power either for himself or for another, it would seem rather madness than childishness to believe without any evidence at all. Yet if anyone ask, What evidence *would suffice?* it is impossible to reply, so extreme is our demand. If evidence quite stupendous in amount and unprecedented in quality would be justly required now, less cannot hav been really needed 1800 years ago: nor hav we any adequate proof that the pretension was ever advanced *by* or *for* Jesus *during his life*. It would seem that the Christian books regard as piety to accept such statements as if *self-evident*, or at least, as if the assertion "Jesus of "Nazareth is the Son of God, begotten of his Father "before all worlds," were a proposition of the same rank, and to be approved by the same faculties, as "The "visible Universe is the work of Super Human power."

John the Elder wrote three extant Epistles, to which the Fourth Gospel is so like in style that it is natural to attribute them to the same hand. This Gospel, like many a bold romance, has been accepted as history, and has cast the three first narrativs into the shade, by its specious pretence of spirituality. Undoubtedly the address and prayer of Jesus, by which the writer audaciously supplants the agony in the garden, is singularly majestic and captivating. As with certain writers of history, so here style gains attention and accredits a tale, when there is no ostensible proof and no probability.

Whether any of Justin Martyr's quotations (during the reign of one of the Antonines) came from the fourth Gospel, is hotly debated. Justin does not quote as from a separate book, nor attribute his quotations to the *apostle* John. But he definitly attributes to this apostle the authorship of the Apocalypse,—a book written in a marvellously different Greek style.

From the Apocalypse, this Gospel borrows the title "Word of God" for Jesus in its opening. Neither in it, nor in the Epistles of John do we meet the topic of looking for the return of the Lord from Heaven, which was the cardinal gospel in the first age. A subtle effort is perhaps made to replace it by the promise of "the "Comforter," which is to supply a mystical interpretation of the words: "I will come unto you." All the facts converge to the belief, that this Gospel was written after the most thoughtful members of the Church had abandoned the primitiv expectation of that great event which the Apocalypse solemnly declared to impend.

With this book the Canon of the New Testament may seem to close; yet the Epistle of Jude was perhaps as late, and the second (or spurious) Epistle of Peter must be later than this of Jude.

A survey of near two centuries exhibits a rapid change of fundamental doctrin. First of all, the Gospel, or Good News, is, that the Kingdom of God is nigh at hand. This formula belongs both to John the Baptist, and to Jesus with slight changes. After the death of Jesus, the Good News is, that Jesus, who has ascended to Heaven will speedily return in the clouds to reign on the Earth with his Saints. Such was the Gospel common to James and Paul. But Paul added details concerning Jesus, which were not accepted and incorporated in the Gospel of Jerusalem, making "One God and one Lord" a dual object of worship. "God and the Lamb" ar much the same as this. Sixty years later the belief in the return of Christ to reign on earth was dying out through the disappointment of hope. The primitiv gospel vanished; but instead remained, Washing away Sin by the Blood of the Cross, Predestination to Life, and a mysterious tenet concerning "the Son and the "Father." This doctrin of "the Blood" was subversiv of all that had been taught in Judaism concerning God's free forgivness. Protestants hav now another fundamental condition of saintship,—a belief that "the Bible" is the Word of God.

Such a change of front is truly damaging; but as though this were not enough, *Sacerdotalism* also was set up. The primitiv peculiarity of the doctrin of Jesus is hereby overthrown. With him religion was a personal relation between the individual soul and God; but his degenerate followers hav gone back to the earlier conception of Jews and Pagans that *religion is corporate* and is attained only by becoming a member of a special community, which virtually mediates between the soul and its God. When we see such phenomena we may modify Paul's phrase, and say "ever shifting, and never "advancing towards truth."

What ar the Gates of *Hades* which, according to Jesus, shall never prevail against his Church, is a very obscure matter; but certainly nothing in its history suggests any divine exemption from unlimited error.

CHAPTER XIII.

OUR MODERN PROBLEM.

CHRISTIANITY is no longer in its cradle. More than eighteen centuries hav passed since the Apostle John wrote these words: "The Revelation of Jesus the "Messiah, which God gave unto him, to show unto his "saints what things must quickly come to pass . . . . "For the crisis is near."—Rev. i. 1—3. Already (the Apostle assures us) it was promulgated in heaven that "the kingdoms of this world ar become the kingdoms of "our Lord and of his Messiah; for the Lord God "omnipotent reigneth." Again and again it is repeated: "I come quickly;" he comes to accept his crown and to seat his saints on the throne with him. The Spirit and the Bride say, "Come!" Let him that heareth say, "Come!" He that testifieth these things saith, "YEA, I COME QUICKLY." The Apostle eagerly responds, "Come, Lord Jesus."

If we had no history of these eighteen centuries, and we formed a picture of them from such prophecies, very false would be our belief concerning the earthly events. We should suppose that the Heavenly King had long since come down with angelic guards, had overthrown the ungodly oppressiv rule of violent men, and had installed his saints at his side, to establish his Rule of Righteousness. Such was the firm expectation of the Apostles. But in the actual history we see not a single trace in this direction. The persecution of "the saints" ever became fiercer for two centuries and a half; and the baptized Rulers who succeeded the Emperor Constantine were collectivly a crew of self-seeking worldly men, not one of them superior to the best of the Pagan Emperors. Neither the dominant Paganism nor the Empire was overthrown by the descent of Messiah on his heavenly white horse (Rev. xix. 11), but by the civil wars of the Imperialists and by the inroad of fierce barbarians; and there followed, not a kingdom of Heaven on Earth, but more than a thousand years of tumult and confusion, of gross ignorance and vile superstition, sanguinary violence on one side establishing Might as Right, priestly assumption on the other teaching prostration of the private conscience and making itself mediator between God and man.

The modern Reformer has sought, naturally and reasonably, to reform by reverting to the *primitiv* doctrin:

but how is the word *primitiv* to be interpreted? Luther and Calvin and the Anglican Reformers thought it an Axiom that the Nicene Creed and indeed even the Creed called (with no right) Athanasian, was to be retained. In fact they barely went back as far as Constantine. The earlier the creed, the simpler and less ample it was found; but side by side with modern Science, modern experience in Literature, modern investigations in History, the demand of Evidence before belief in miracle becomes ever more imperious. Not only is it found that such miracles as the resurrection of the deceased Jesus and the ascension of his body into heaven hav no adequate proof, but even with the more thoughtful and deep-thinking Christians three questions raise grave embarrassment, (1) In what sense can any one reasonably *interpret* the assertion that a man named in history was a Divine person in disguise? (2) What *proof* was offered to the world by the first preachers, that Jesus was superhuman? (3) What evidence can, or could, *ever* suffice to prove that a certain man was an eternal, incomprehensible, omnipresent being?

Any creed which is imbibed with the mother's milk will stand long and widely *without* evidence; because the bulk of mankind ar too busy to think fundamentally. In every nation a decisiv majority clings to the traditional creed. But such has been the reaction against sacerdotal pride and doctrin called orthodox, that wherever priests ar powerless to suppress literature, Christians who exercise unbiassed and reverent thought, largely embrace the modern doctrin called Unitarian, which, while seeking to glorify Jesus as a unique Saint and pre-eminent Teacher of true and undefiled Religion, yet insists that in nature and origin he was purely human and tied down by human conditions. In Calvinistic Switzerland this doctrin has largely triumphed over Calvin; in Huguenot

France the same result appears. In Germany as in England the dignified Protestant clergy ar no longer forward to expound Athanasian doctrin and dilate on the Eternal Generation of the Son or the "Procession" (*i. e.* Emanation) of the Third Person of the Trinity. Is there any reasonable hope that Unitarian Christianity, as set forth by its noblest teachers, can be accepted as a National Creed *anywhere?*

The Anglican clergy hav long wielded against this class of Christians an argument to which (as far as the present writer knows) no reply has been *publicly* attempted. The argument (mildly put) is virtually this: " If Jesus was not essentially more than human, his " deportment (as narrated in the Gospels) was abnormal " in arrogance, and variously indefensible; unexplanatory " to those whom it was his duty to instruct concerning " his claims, repelling to those whom it was his duty " to conciliate, and a very evil example of accepting " supremacy and worship. When Peter is honored by " prostration, Acts x. 26, (or whatever posture is meant " by falling down to worship) he deprecates it by 'stand " 'up! for I myself am also a man.' Jesus calls himself " meek and lowly; but if he was a man, subject to all " our limitations, his very different demeanor as narrated " in the Gospels shows him to hav been morally *greatly* " *inferior* to numbers of his professed disciples."

To this objection one reply is made privately;—never in its full strength to the public. It runs thus: "The " Gospels ar full of erroneous details, often very unjust " and damaging to the memory of Jesus. Our business " is to cast these out *by a higher criticism,* assured that " so pre-eminent a moral genius cannot hav been guilty " of the grave improprieties attributed to him in the " Gospels. We do not *assume* his pre-eminent goodness " without proof, and then eject as false whatever would

"confute us; nor do we *accept* his superhuman excellence
"on the testimony of Paul, who did not know or wish
"to know the fleshly Messiah; nor yet of Peter who
"argues it out as if from prophecy; but we *infer* it from
"the saintliness of unnumbered Christians who *must* hav
"imbibed it by spiritual transmission from the personal
"Jesus."

According to this view, in the present volume far too much reliance has been placed on the testimony of the three Gospels, although my effort has been to lay no stress, and hold no strong belief, except where the tale and its coloring, if false, were very unlikely to hav been invented or transmitted by Christian devotees. I hav freely avowed the difficulty of basing accurate history on these narrativs. But when they ar vaguely disowned as untrustworthy, and no clue is given us (such as I hav tried to use) in discriminating *some* parts as reasonably credible,—then to found a biography on the history of an after-church is like building on chaos:—a task which in no like case has ever yet attained general approval of historians. Christianity as a system of *spiritual morals*, may, just as other morals, be accepted and retained without any knowledge or belief concerning its historical origin; nor will many expect spiritual gain from re-making a man's lost image by subtle inductions or deductions, unintelligible to "babes and sucklings," however convincing to transcendental philosophers. The case of Jesus is then like that of Zoroaster and Sakya Muni, perhaps that of Moses and Mohammed. The loom and the plough, the winnowing shovel, the oar, the sail, and the horse's bit do good service, though we know not who originated them. Much the same is it with Moral and Spiritual doctrin. To hold the truth concerns us much; to know who first promulgated it, very little. Moreover we know for certain that nearly all the utterances of Jesus had been anticipated by numerous teachers before his birth. Nay, I must except the fundamental tenet of his own Messiahship: but as I learn, the foremost Unitarian doctrin now denies that he claimed to be the Messiah foretold by the Hebrew prophets: that is now maintained to hav been a damaging error diffused by the enthusiasm or (must we rather say?) fanaticism of James and the other apostles on the one part, and of their doubtful ally Paul on the other.

In this survey of opinion one broad fact seems to emerge; that unless we can receive the tradition current in one or other of the great national churches which deifies Jesus, we hav to reconstruct our religion, so far as the personal history of Jesus is concerned, on a totally new basis, which rejects as unhistorical, delusiv and disparaging the documents hitherto called sacred. Nor only so; but in every case one who thinks wisely has also largely to supplement and even modify Christian morals, for several decisiv reasons. First, because eighteen centuries of social and civil experience hav vastly affected men's thoughts concerning cardinal matters on which Morals ought to dogmatize,—such as the relation of master to slave, of parent to child, of man to woman, of magistrate to private person, or to speak more definitly, the relation of him who claims and holds rule by force of weapons and those who ar made or kept subjects ("subditi") against their will by superior force; also concerning the moral duties of king and people when the legitimacy of their relation is conceded. Egyptian, Persian, Greek, Roman, Hebrew, Christian moralists in common applaud *Justice;* but this grand and cardinal virtue in its application and interpretation varies notably with the width of experience and knowledge in the interpreter. Secondly, because the helpless position of the ancient Christians under dominant and raw Pagan Imperialism was enormously different from that which modern Christians hold under royalty or republicanism, which, however Pagan in fact, is Christian in profession; especially where the national institutions giv safety to free thought and defined political power to private persons. Thirdly, and chiefly, because it is a plain fact, deniable only by those who read their sacred documents "with a veil over their hearts," that the first Christian teachers, whose saintly aims we revere, whose virtuous constancy we applaud, whose moral enthusiasm is kindling and truly edifying, whose teaching is to this day highly profitable, when legitimately used; —nevertheless, held the erroneous, baseless, fully and long refuted idea, that Messiah was shortly to be displayed as King himself, with his risen saints and martyrs as his pre-eminent ministers of Political power, in place of the deposed tyranny which was hitherto trampling down the earth.

This error has had a very pernicious effect, and to this day acts mischievously. Every apostle, while holding it, necessarily thought it waste effort in a Christian to improve institutions or culture, when their future would hav no continuous relation with the present,—a world whose material and connexions could not be transmitted to future generations,—a world whose wickedness the Most High was resolved no longer to endure, but by the descent of his Son from heaven to burn up its surface and cast down its thrones. They could not exhort Christians to any political duties, but that of *submission* to violent power and *abstinence* from wrong, *i.e.*, refusal to become partners and tools of other men's sins. The precepts which in their day were dictated by good sense ar so little suited to our day, that Bible Christians ar apt to go wrong, in exact proportion as they submit their minds to the dictation of special texts. Large souls and strong minds seize on the noble and broad generalities of apostolic teaching; but the pettier minds and hearts cling to what Paul called "the letter that killeth." Among the most sincere Biblical Christians the idea is prevalent (grounded on submission to authority accounted divine) that to "improve this world" is no work for Christians; that their sole task is to save and cultivate their own souls first, and that of their neighbours or of the heathen, if they can; to abound in works of mercy and kindliness, no doubt; but only as a physician deals with disease. His business is to heal after sickness has been induced; *not* to prevent disease by removing its causes: just so, the prevailing idea with the Biblist is, that a Christian ought indeed to show pity to the wretched or vicious, but not to attempt the wild and impossible idea of tearing up the roots which mainly gender wretchedness and vice, especially unjust and unwise national institutions, with which no apostle tried to meddle.* As once the isolation of a hermit or retirement in a convent was mistaken for Religion, so now the cultivation of personal private piety too largely occupies religious thought, superseding our duty to improve the world.

Far and wide there is outcry for a religion free from superstition, and not based on historical error or empty assumption. Our modern task really is to attain such a religion. To avoid historical error, there is one and only one sure way: namely, to avoid History altogether. History is a field of erudition, precisely the matter in which the mass of mankind ("babes and sucklings") ar necessarily weak and very deceivable. If religion is not

---

* Strange to add,—even the trade of the paid soldier, engaged to kill and ravage at the word of command,—a trade into which no primitiv Christian after conversion could enter,—has received no ecclesiastical check or reproof for more than 1500 years.

to be dictated by the few learned in antiquity to the unlearned many; if we ar ever to attain the state predicted by Hebrew prophets, in which the Spirit of God, diffused in the multitude, shall make each separately to "know the Lord," we must hav a religion of which the bulk of the adult community can judge *fundamentally*, without the aid of ancient learning. What indeed *can* Religion hav to do with History? Religion treats of the relations of Man to God, which ar the same everywhere and at all times. History details special human events on special areas in past time; none of which can possibly affect the relations of the unchangeable God to an unchanged race of his creatures; none of which ar open to the cognizance of the unlearned human millions. Religion dependent on human history is as much a chimæra and a delusion, as astronomy founded on human history.

A positiv condition requisit for a True Religion, is, that it be acceptable to the good sense of all the most cultivated races of men. In old times national minds were separated by barriers insurmountable. Oceanic navigation has thrown these barriers down. Existing national religions divide mankind and propagate enmity: they *must* do so, if they rest on special history: but the times ar ripe for a religion which shall unite us, and forbid the unnatural collision. A proof that the times ar ripe is found in the reception given in China and Japan to Derzhavin's hymn to God. [I here quote a paragraph which I cut out from a newspaper, but hav lost the reference. A translation of the Hymn is in my hands.] "The Hymn to God by a Russian born in 1763 "was translated into Japanese by order of the Emperor, "and is hung up, embroidered with gold, in the temple "of Jeddo. It has been translated also into the Chinese "and Tartar languages, written on a piece of rich silk, "and suspended in the imperial palace at Pekin." If men would but lay aside bitterness and bigotry, the intellectual state of the world now eminently invites effort in the direction of religious agreement. But alas! the rival pretensions of the Cross and the Crescent ar everywhere big with war and bloodshed. Claims to exclusiv and divine authority ar the fundamental mischief. With the renunciation of (alledged) History as part of Religion all *haughty pretension to Authority* vanishes. What other conditions ar needed for Worldwide Religion?

(1.) First of all, be it remembered, what alone makes religion desirable;—it is not for the benefit and honor of God, but for the benefit and ennoblement of Man. A religion is good, only in proportion as it stimulates men to be good. It must be a practical aid to pure morality. Since God has nothing to gain by our devotion, but men hav very much to gain by other men's righteousness, Duty to men ought to take precedence of Duty to God, and what Christians call the Second Commandment is rightfully the First. A good God cannot but regard man's duty to man as far more important than any services of man to God; and what He considers primary and paramount, we ought to make primary and paramount.

John the Elder very nearly alighted on this doctrin, in asking: "If a man love not his brother whom he hath "seen, how shall he love God whom he hath not seen?" Love to God is a chimæra in one who does not yet love virtuous conduct *for its own sake*. The love of God implies the love of perfect goodness.

(2.) Next, we hav to reverse the doctrin of Christianity, or else go back to Judaism, by teaching that the interests of *this* life ar of *primary* importance, whatever after-life may be in store; because, undeniably, this world is given into our hands *as a trust and a task*, while the future world is not. This life is known to us as fact; the future life (as Paul says) is known only by hope; and no one can suggest any reasonable preparation for a future life but that of performing all known present duties. Therefor the maxim of Lycurgus may be applied: "Sparta has been assigned as thy lot; busy thyself to "adorn this trust." The American sect called Shakers express their notion well: "We ar now in the millennium "(say they) and our business is to beautify and glorify "the earth." In our dialect we need but small change of phrase: "As trustees in our generation, our task is *to* "*improve the world.*" The more we think of making the world better, the better is our religion. The more we neglect this world through expecting a better world to be provided from on high, the vainer and the more mischievous is our religion. A bishop of Beziers (if the tale in History is true) illustrates this topic by his behavior to his Catholic brethren. The Crusaders who wished to massacre the Albigensian heretics, asked how they were to distinguish them from good Catholics. He replied: "Kill all; God will distinguish his own at the "day of judgment."

(3.) Closely related hereto is the principle, that the less we think of any reward to ourselves in a future life for the performance of duty in this life, the better is our religion; for it ought to teach us, not only that when we hav done our best, we hav failed of much, but that all virtue is its own reward, inasmuch as virtue is man's best state. Greek philosophy more than two millenniums ago, taught, that we must do good *because it is good*, not from expecting extraneous advantage from it;—"in "respect to the recompense of reward."—Heb. xi. 26.

(4.) Again, because Good Action is better than Right Opinion, and Right Loves or Hatreds better than Full

Beliefs, it follows that we must esteem men for their moral worth even when they fail of religious orthodoxy; and we must disesteem the orthodox when they ar deficient in moral worth. Therefor a Creed neither can by its acceptance accredit a saint, nor by its rejection detect a reprobate.

While congregations depend for their instruction on one or at most two men, who may not be contradicted nor answered, some previous intellectual agreement, clearly defined, which may be called a *Creed*, will be required of the teachers by the dumb laity. As Edmund Burke coarsely said, "The freedom of the clergy would "be the slavery of the laity." But the present Congregational routine is not certain to be eternal. The *platform* may hereafter enter the Congregation and be merely organized by its President for free speech. Be this as it may, no Congregation can fill up the received ideal of a Church. Those whose hearts beat together for Virtuous Action and Virtuous Sentiment ar the true Church, even if they be intellectually severed too much for Congregational Union.

Remark was made above on the woful blunder rising out of the ambiguous word Faith. In theory it is insisted that Faith is a moral quality and a test of virtuous character: in practice the Churches merge it in belief of one or more propositions; to which James tartly replies: "The Devils believe and tremble." Endless facts show, that heathens, however dark as to religious opinion, may be truly estimable men. In Paul's words: "Having "not the law, yet by nature they do the deeds of the "law." If possible, we need what a German has called, "The Religion of *Deed*." Jesus himself sets virtuous heathens higher than oppressiv Jews. Every day we see energies that might uproot destitution and demoralization, *diverted into the propagation of a creed*. In Christendom this is a world-wide phenomenon.

I expect that certain writers who do not call themselves Atheists, will taunt me with inconsistency in wishing to make a Dogma of Theism; and it may be worth while here to add a few words on that topic. Morality, so far as it rests upon collectiv mankind, is, ought to be, and must be dogmatic. The same is true of Theism, with the very important distinction, that the highest punishment of immorality is Death, and the highest punishment of Atheism is contempt. The belief in MIND, loftier than man, older than man, and the Creator and Disposer of man, is held by unscientific and even barbarian races; who see it beyond all question in ANIMAL INSTINCTS. Scientific men, since the Newtonian theory has been developed, hav a new demonstration, which, previous to the modern astronomy, was unimagined. The doctrin of GRAVITATION proclaims a Divine Mind ever acting on every particle of matter, so clearly, that a modern scientist who denies it, is as absurd and as little deserving of attention as one who denies the received Geometry of Triangles. Particles of matter in the clouds or in the planets conduct themselves *as if* they knew the precise distance which separates them from other particles in the Earth or Sun, and put forth a million million *tugs* carefully adjusted upon bodies far out of their reach. Newton, no doubt, believed and taught that this mysterious Gravitation was a *Divine force.* To ascribe it to the blind and inert particles *as if* they had *knowledge* of the distance of other particles and there were no higher Mind behind to guide them, degrades a man of Science to the level of a fetish savage in the very lowest stage of the human intellect, and forfeits all right of respect from thoughtful men.

(5.) Though Religion cannot *dictate* Morals any more than it can dictate Philosophy or Science, yet it may and must *uphold* Morals. Just so must every Polity, while measuring moral right by the judgment of collectiv mankind. We cannot pretend that this judgment will ever be absolutely final; but any modification applies to details chiefly, and in every age is exceptional. Certain broad foundations remain immovable, such as, that Men ar not machines destitute of self-controul; that *because* of this, Praise and Blame, Punishment and Reward, hav their reasonable places; that Moral Interests ar higher than Material; that Virtue is better than Health or Ease; that Self-Sacrifice for others is nobler than Self-seeking: that Justice is of all qualities paramount and indispensable, and is the right of *all* God's creatures.

(6.) Some further hints ar given us in the history of wide-spread religions. These attained reverence and strength for action nearly as did that one which is best known to us,—the Mediæval Christian Church: which strove to bridle the evil tendencies of wayward Power and greedy Wealth; and instead of confining its citizenship to Heaven *(Paul* to *Philipp.* iii. 20) as the first Christians had been forced to do, emphatically became an agent of this world. Instead of treating worldly interests as too transitory to be worthy of struggle, a wise Religion of the Future must turn a blind eye to the fact that earthly interests never can be *strictly* eternal. By accepting them *as if* eternal, we shall better forget Self and better fulfil the task imposed on us by God and Nature. A future religion must not be satisfied with lopping twigs of an evil tree, but must strive to pull up the roots, under the firm belief that in working for good *here*, it is working for *an indefinit futurity.*

Unjust national institutions and depraving national habits ar the deepest and most permanent sources of Moral Evil. Therefor the Catholic Church discerned, that, to be *philanthropic*, a Church must be eminently *political* in her aims and actions. Of course philanthropic aims degenerate into ambitious schemes when the establishment of the Church *herself* as an organized power is an accepted policy. On this rock our Ideal Church of the Future cannot split, because, having no defined creed, she cannot hav corporate organization, nor fixed existence in any visible form. Good men and women will, as in the past, but more cordially and widely than in the past, recognize each other, being thrown together in action, while striving for a common good. God has so formed our hearts, that Compassion and Justice in the millions of mankind ar *stronger* than base cupidity; hence to the voice of one who calls for Justice, the heart of every nation responds. Therefor the pure, the tender, the noble and ennobling passions in the long run overpower Injustice and Sensuality: the Woman in us is stronger than the Man. Therefor also,—though not in a year, not without lengthy struggle to enlighten the multitude,—yet more and more, as new generations rise, Religion will shake herself free from enfeebling tradition and become more conscious of her true duties, more able to execute them. Thus we shall approximate to the ideal of Glory to God, Peace among men, Kindliness to all God's creatures.

Among Religious Works by the same Author may be named

HISTORY OF THE HEBREW MONARCHY. Third Edition.
Crown 8vo, cloth. 8s. 6d.

THE SOUL, HER SORROWS AND ASPIRATIONS. Tenth
Edition. Post 8vo, cloth. 3s. 6d.

PHASES OF FAITH, or SOME OUTLINE OF MY RELIGIOUS
CREED. New Edition. Crown 8vo, cloth. 3s. 6d.

THEISM, DOCTRINAL AND PRACTICAL. 4to, cloth. 4s. 6d.

HEBREW THEISM. New and Revised Edition. Royal 8vo,
stiff wrappers. 4s. 6d.

CHRISTIANITY WITHOUT CHRIST. 8vo, wrapper. 1s.

A CHRISTIAN COMMONWEALTH. Crown 8vo, cloth. 1s.

If the Writer live to superintend it, he hopes to edit, if his Publishers have encouragement, a Volume containing his Moral and Religious Tracts, Essays, and Lay-Sermons; also *perhaps*, after this, a continuation of his Miscellanies, Political and Academical.

A CATALOGUE OF IMPORTANT WORKS,

PUBLISHED BY

TRÜBNER & CO.

57 AND 59 LUDGATE HILL.

ABEL.—LINGUISTIC ESSAYS. By Carl Abel. CONTENTS: Language as the Expression of National Modes of Thought—The Conception of Love in some Ancient and Modern Languages—The English Verbs of Command—The Discrimination of Synonyms—Philological Methods—The Connection between Dictionary and Grammar—The Possibility of a Common Literary Language for the Slav Nations—Coptic Intensification—The Origin of Language—The Order and Position of Words in the Latin Sentence. Post 8vo, pp. xii. and 282, cloth. 1882. 9s.

ABEL.—SLAVIC AND LATIN. Ilchester Lectures on Comparative Lexicography. Delivered at the Taylor Institution, Oxford. By Carl Abel, Ph.D. Post 8vo, pp. vi.-124, cloth. 1883. 5s.

ABRAHAMS.—A MANUAL OF SCRIPTURE HISTORY FOR USE IN JEWISH SCHOOLS AND FAMILIES. By L. B. Abrahams, B.A., Principal Assistant Master, Jews' Free School. With Map and Appendices. Third Edition. Crown 8vo, pp. viii. and 152, cloth. 1883. 1s. 6d.

AGASSIZ.—AN ESSAY ON CLASSIFICATION. By Louis Agassiz. 8vo, pp. vii. and 381, cloth. 1859. 12s.

AHLWARDT.—THE DIVANS OF THE SIX ANCIENT ARABIC POETS, ENNĀBIGA, 'ANTARA, THARAFA, ZUHAIR, 'ALQUAMA, and IMRUULQUAIS; chiefly according to the MSS. of Paris, Gotha, and Leyden, and the Collection of their Fragments, with a List of the various Readings of the Text. Edited by W. Ahlwardt, Professor of Oriental Languages at the University of Greifswald. Demy 8vo, pp. xxx. and 340, sewed. 1870. 12s.

AHN.—PRACTICAL GRAMMAR OF THE GERMAN LANGUAGE. By Dr. F. Ahn. A New Edition. By Dr. Dawson Turner, and Prof. F. L. Weinmann. Crown 8vo, pp. cxii. and 430, cloth. 1878. 3s. 6d.

AHN.—NEW, PRACTICAL, AND EASY METHOD OF LEARNING THE GERMAN LANGUAGE. By Dr. F. Ahn. First and Second Course. Bound in 1 vol. 12mo, pp. 86 and 120, cloth. 1866. 3s.

AHN.—KEY to Ditto. 12mo, pp. 40, sewed. 8d.

AHN.—MANUAL OF GERMAN AND ENGLISH CONVERSATIONS, or Vade Mecum for English Travellers. 12mo, pp. x. and 137, cloth. 1875. 1s. 6d.

AHN.—NEW, PRACTICAL, AND EASY METHOD OF LEARNING THE FRENCH LANGUAGE. By Dr. F. Ahn. First Course and Second Course. 12mo, cloth. Each 1s. 6d. The Two Courses in 1 vol. 12mo, pp. 114 and 170, cloth. 1865. 3s.

AHN.—NEW, PRACTICAL, AND EASY METHOD OF LEARNING THE FRENCH LANGUAGE. Third Course, containing a French Reader, with Notes and Vocabulary. By H. W. Ehrlich. 12mo, pp. viii. and 125, cloth. 1866. 1s. 6d.

AHN.—MANUAL OF FRENCH AND ENGLISH CONVERSATIONS, FOR THE USE OF SCHOOLS AND TRAVELLERS. By Dr. F. Ahn. 12mo, pp. viii. and 200, cloth. 1862. 2s. 6d.

AHN.—NEW, PRACTICAL, AND EASY METHOD OF LEARNING THE ITALIAN LANGUAGE. By Dr. F. Ahn. First and Second Course. 12mo, pp. 198, cloth. 1872. 3s. 6d.

AHN.—NEW, PRACTICAL, AND EASY METHOD OF LEARNING THE DUTCH LANGUAGE, being a complete Grammar, with Selections. By Dr. F. Ahn. 12mo, pp. viii. and 166, cloth. 1862. 3s. 6d.

AHN.—AHN'S COURSE. Latin Grammar for Beginners. By W. Ihne, Ph.D. 12mo, pp. vi. and 184, cloth. 1864. 3s.

ALABASTER.—THE WHEEL OF THE LAW : Buddhism illustrated from Siamese Sources by the Modern Buddhist, a Life of Buddha, and an Account of the Phra Bat. By Henry Alabaster, Esq., Interpreter of Her Majesty's Consulate-General in Siam. Demy 8vo, pp. lviii. and 324, cloth. 1871. 14s.

ALI.—THE PROPOSED POLITICAL, LEGAL, AND SOCIAL REFORMS IN THE OTTOMAN EMPIRE AND OTHER MOHAMMEDAN STATES. By Moulaví Cherágh Ali, H.H. the Nizam's Civil Service. Demy 8vo, pp. liv. and 184, cloth. 1883. 8s.

ALLAN-FRASER.—CHRISTIANITY AND CHURCHISM. By Patrick Allan-Fraser. Second (revised and enlarged) Edition. Crown 8vo, pp. 52, cloth. 1884. 1s.

ALLEN.—THE COLOUR SENSE. See English and Foreign Philosophical Library, Vol. X.

ALLIBONE.—A CRITICAL DICTIONARY OF ENGLISH LITERATURE AND BRITISH AND AMERICAN AUTHORS (LIVING AND DECEASED). From the Earliest Accounts to the latter half of the 19th century. Containing over 46,000 Articles (Authors), with 40 Indexes of subjects. By S. A. Allibone. In 3 vols. royal 8vo, cloth. £5, 8s.

ALTHAUS.—THE SPAS OF EUROPE. By Julius Althaus, M.D. 8vo, pp. 516, cloth. 1862. 7s. 6d.

AMATEUR MECHANIC'S WORKSHOP (THE). A Treatise containing Plain and Concise Directions for the Manipulation of Wood and Metals ; including Casting, Forging, Brazing, Soldering, and Carpentry. By the Author of "The Lathe and its Uses." Sixth Edition. Demy 8vo, pp. vi. and 148, with Two Full-Page Illustrations, on toned paper and numerous Woodcuts, cloth. 1880. 6s.

AMATEUR MECHANICAL SOCIETY.—JOURNAL OF THE AMATEUR MECHANICAL SOCIETY. 8vo. Vol. i. pp. 344 cloth. 1871-72. 12s. Vol. ii. pp. vi. and 290, cloth. 1873-77. 12s. Vol. iii. pp. iv. and 246, cloth. 1878-79. 12s. 6d.

AMERICAN ALMANAC AND TREASURY OF FACTS, STATISTICAL, FINANCIAL, AND POLITICAL. Edited by Ainsworth R. Spofford, Librarian of Congress. Crown 8vo, cloth. Published yearly. 1878-1884. 7s. 6d. each.

AMERY.—NOTES ON FORESTRY. By C. F. Amery, Deputy Conservator N. W. Provinces, India. Crown 8vo, pp. viii. and 120, cloth. 1875. 5s.

AMBERLEY.—AN ANALYSIS OF RELIGIOUS BELIEF. By Viscount Amberley. 2 vols. demy 8vo, pp. xvi. and 496 and 512, cloth. 1876. 30s.

AMONGST MACHINES. A Description of Various Mechanical Appliances used in the Manufacture of Wood, Metal, and other Substances. A Book for Boys, copiously Illustrated. By the Author of "The Young Mechanic." Second Edition. Imperial 16mo, pp. viii. and 336, cloth. 1878. 7s. 6d.

ANDERSON.—PRACTICAL MERCANTILE CORRESPONDENCE. A Collection of Modern Letters of Business, with Notes, Critical and Explanatory, and an Appendix, containing a Dictionary of Commercial Technicalities, pro forma Invoices, Account Sales, Bills of Lading, and Bills of Exchange; also an Explanation of the German Chain Rule. 24th Edition, revised and enlarged. By William Anderson. 12mo, pp. 288, cloth. 5s.

ANDERSON and TUGMAN.—MERCANTILE CORRESPONDENCE, containing a Collection of Commercial Letters in Portuguese and English, with their translation on opposite pages, for the use of Business Men and of Students in either of the Languages, treating in modern style of the system of Business in the principal Commercial Cities of the World. Accompanied by pro forma Accounts, Sales, Invoices, Bills of Lading, Drafts, &c. With an Introduction and copious Notes. By William Anderson and James E. Tugman. 12mo, pp. xi. and 193, cloth. 1867. 6s.

APEL.—PROSE SPECIMENS FOR TRANSLATION INTO GERMAN, with copious Vocabularies and Explanations. By H. Apel. 12mo, pp. viii. and 246, cloth. 1862. 4s. 6d.

APPLETON (Dr.)—LIFE AND LITERARY RELICS. See English and Foreign Philosophical Library, Vol. XIII.

ARAGO.—LES ARISTOCRATIES. A Comedy in Verse. By Etienne Arago. Edited, with English Notes and Notice on Etienne Arago, by the Rev. E. P. H. Brette, B.D., Head Master of the French School, Christ's Hospital, Examiner in the University of London. Fcap. 8vo, pp. 244, cloth. 1868. 4s.

ARMITAGE.—LECTURES ON PAINTING: Delivered to the Students of the Royal Academy. By Edward Armitage, R.A. Crown 8vo, pp. 256, with 29 Illustrations, cloth. 1883. 7s. 6d.

ARNOLD.—INDIAN IDYLLS. From the Sanskrit of the Mahâbhârata. By Edwin Arnold, C.S.I., &c. Crown 8vo, pp. xii. and 282, cloth. 1883. 7s. 6d.

ARNOLD.—PEARLS OF THE FAITH; or, Islam's Rosary: being the Ninety-nine beautiful names of Allah. With Comments in Verse from various Oriental sources as made by an Indian Mussulman. By Edwin Arnold, C.S.I., &c. Third Edition. Crown 8vo, pp. xvi. and 320, cloth. 1884. 7s. 6d.

ARNOLD.—THE LIGHT OF ASIA; or, THE GREAT RENUNCIATION (Mahâbhinishkramana). Being the Life and Teaching of Gautama, Prince of India, and Founder of Buddhism (as told in verse by an Indian Buddhist). By Edwin Arnold, M.A., &c. Twenty-fifth Edition. Crown 8vo, pp. xvi. and 240, limp parchment. 1885. 3s. 6d. Library Edition. 1883. 7s. 6d. Illustrated Edition. Small 4to, pp. xx.–196, cloth. 1884. 21s.

ARNOLD.—THE SECRET OF DEATH: Being a Version, in a popular and novel form, of the Katha Upanishad, from the Sanskrit. With some Collected Poems. By Edwin Arnold, M.A., &c. Third Edition. Crown 8vo. pp. viii.–406, cloth. 1885. 7s. 6d.

ARNOLD.—THE SONG CELESTIAL; or, BHAGAVAD-GITÂ (from the Mahâbhârata). Being a Discourse between Arjuna, Prince of India, and the Supreme Being under the form of Krishna. Translated from the Sanskrit Text. By Edwin Arnold, M.A. Second Edition, crown 8vo, pp. 192, cloth. 1885. 5s.

ARNOLD.—THE ILIAD AND ODYSSEY OF INDIA. By Edwin Arnold, M.A., F.R.G.S., &c., &c. Fcap. 8vo, pp. 24, sewed. 1s.

ARNOLD.—A SIMPLE TRANSLITERAL GRAMMAR OF THE TURKISH LANGUAGE. Compiled from Various Sources. With Dialogues and Vocabulary. By Edwin Arnold, M.A., C.S.I., F.R.G.S. Post 8vo, pp. 80, cloth. 1877. 2s. 6d.

ARNOLD.—INDIAN POETRY. See Trübner's Oriental Series.

ARTHUR.—THE COPARCENERS: Being the Adventures of two Heiresses. By F. Arthur. Crown 8vo, pp. iv.–312, cloth. 1885. 10s. 6d.

ARTOM.—SERMONS. By the Rev. B. Artom, Chief Rabbi of the Spanish and Portuguese Congregations of England. First Series. Second Edition. Crown 8vo, pp. viii. and 314, cloth. 1876. 6s.

4   *A Catalogue of Important Works,*

ASIATIC SOCIETY OF BENGAL. List of Publications on application.

ASIATIC SOCIETY.—JOURNAL OF THE ROYAL ASIATIC SOCIETY OF GREAT BRITAIN AND IRELAND, from the Commencement to 1863. First Series, complete in 20 Vols. 8vo, with many Plates. £10, or in parts from 4s. to 6s. each.

ASIATIC SOCIETY.—JOURNAL OF THE ROYAL ASIATIC SOCIETY OF GREAT BRITAIN AND IRELAND. New Series. 8vo. Stitched in wrapper. 1864-84.
Vol. I., 2 Parts, pp. iv. and 490, 16s.—Vol. II., 2 Parts, pp. 522, 16s.—Vol. III., 2 Parts, pp. 516, with Photograph, 22s.—Vol. IV., 2 Parts. pp. 521, 16s.—Vol. V., 2 Parts, pp. 463, with 10 full-page and folding Plates, 18s. 6d.—Vol. VI., Part 1, pp. 212, with 2 Plates and a Map, 8s.—Vol. VI. Part 2, pp. 272, with Plate and Map, 8s.—Vol. VII., Part 1, pp. 194, with a Plate, 8s.—Vol. VII., Part 2, pp. 204, with 7 Plates and a Map, 8s.—Vol. VIII., Part 1, pp. 156, with 3 Plates and a Plan, 8s.—Vol. VIII., Part 2, pp. 152, 8s.—Vol. IX., Part 1, pp. 154, with a Plate, 8s.—Vol. IX., Part 2, pp. 292, with 3 Plates, 10s. 6d.—Vol. X., Part 1, pp. 156, with 2 Plates and a Map, 8s.—Vol. X., Part 2, pp. 146, 6s.—Vol. X., Part 3, pp. 204, 8s.—Vol. XI., Part 1, pp. 128, 5s.—Vol. XI., Part 2, pp. 158, with 2 Plates, 7s. 6d.—Vol. XI., Part 3, pp. 250, 8s.—Vol. XII., Part 1, pp. 152, 5s.—Vol. XII., Part 2, pp. 182, with 2 Plates and Map, 6s.—Vol. XII., Part 3, pp. 100, 4s.—Vol. XII., Part 4, pp. x., 152., cxx. 16, 8s.—Vol. XIII., Part 1, pp. 120, 5s.—Vol. XIII., Part 2, pp. 170, with a Map, 8s.—Vol. XIII., Part 3, pp. 178, with a Table, 7s. 6d.—Vol. XIII., Part 4, pp. 282, with a Plate and Table, 10s. 6d.—Vol. XIV., Part 1, pp. 124, with a Table and 2 Plates, 5s.—Vol. XIV., Part 2, pp. 164, with 1 Table, 7s. 6d.—Vol. XIV., Part 3, pp. 206, with 6 Plates, 8s.—Vol. XIV., Part 4, pp. 492, with 1 Plate, 14s.—Vol. XV., Part 1, pp. 136, 6s. ; Part 2, pp. 158, with 3 Tables, 5s. : Part 3, pp. 192, 6s. ; Part 4, pp. 140, 5s.—Vol. XVI., Part 1, pp. 138, with 2 Plates, 7s. Part 2, pp. 184, with 1 Plate, 9s. Part 3, July 1884, pp. 74-clx., 10s. 6d. Part 4, pp. 132, 8s.—Vol. XVII., Part 1, pp. 144, with 6 Plates, 10s. 6d. Part 2, pp. 194, with a Map, 9s.

ASPLET.—THE COMPLETE FRENCH COURSE. Part II. Containing all the Rules of French Syntax, &c., &c. By Georges C. Asplet, French Master, Frome. Fcap. 8vo, pp. xx. and 276, cloth. 1880. 2s. 6d.

ASTON.—A Short Grammar of the Japanese Spoken Language. By W. G. Aston, M.A. Third Edition. Crown 8vo, pp. 96, cloth. 1873. 12s.

ASTON.—A GRAMMAR OF THE JAPANESE WRITTEN LANGUAGE. By W. G. Aston, M.A., Assistant Japanese Secretary H.B.M.'s Legation, Yedo, Japan. Second Edition. 8vo, pp. 306, cloth. 1877. 28s.

ASTONISHED AT AMERICA. BEING CURSORY DEDUCTIONS, &c., &c. By Zigzag. Fcap. 8vo, pp. xvi.-108, boards. 1880. 1s.

AUCTORES SANSCRITI.
Vol. I. THE JAIMINÎYA-NYÂYA-MÂLÂ-VISTARA. Edited for the Sanskrit Text Society, under the supervision of Theodor Goldstücker. Large 4to, pp. 582, cloth. £3, 13s. 6d.
Vol. II. THE INSTITUTES OF GAUTAMA. Edited, with an Index of Words, by A. F. Stenzler, Ph.D., Prof. of Oriental Languages in the University of Breslau. 8vo, pp. iv. and 78, cloth. 1876. 4s. 6d. Stitched, 3s. 6d.
Vol. III. VAITÂNA SUTRA : THE RITUAL OF THE ATHARVA VEDA. Edited, with Critical Notes and Indices, by Dr. R. Garbe. 8vo, pp. viii. and 120, sewed. 1878. 5s.
Vols. IV. and V.—VARDHAMANA'S GANARATNAMAHODADHI, with the Author's Commentary. Edited, with Critical Notes and Indices, by Julius Eggeling, Ph.D. 8vo. Part I., pp. xii. and 240, wrapper. 1879. 6s. Part II., pp. 240, wrapper. 1881. 6s.

AUGIER.—DIANE. A Drama in Verse. By Émile Augier. Edited with English Notes and Notice on Augier. By T. Karcher, LL.B., of the Royal Military Academy and the University of London. 12mo, pp. xiii. and 146, cloth. 1867. 2s. 6d.

AUSTIN.—A PRACTICAL TREATISE on the Preparation, Combination, and Application of Calcareous and Hydraulic Limes and Cements. To which is added many useful Recipes for various Scientific, Mercantile, and Domestic Purposes. By James G. Austin, Architect. 12mo, pp. 192, cloth. 1862. 5s.

AUSTRALIA.—The publications of the various Australian Government Lists on application.

AUSTRALIA.—THE YEAR BOOK OF AUSTRALIA for 1885. Published under the auspices of the Governments of the Australian Colonies. Demy 8vo, pp. 774; with 6 Large Maps; boards. 5s.

AXON.—THE MECHANIC'S FRIEND. A Collection of Receipts and Practical Suggestions relating to Aquaria, Bronzing, Cements, Drawing, Dyes, Electricity, Gilding, Glass-working, &c. Numerous Woodcuts. Edited by W. E. A. Axon, M.R.S.L., F.S.S. Crown 8vo, pp. xii. and 339, cloth. 1875. 4s. 6d.

BABA.—An Elementary Grammar of the Japanese Language, with Easy Progressive Exercises. By Tatui Baba. Crown 8vo, pp. xiv. and 92, cloth. 1873. 5s.

BACON.—THE LIFE AND TIMES OF FRANCIS BACON. Extracted from the Edition of his Occasional Writings by James Spedding. 2 vols. post 8vo, pp. xx., 710, and xiv., 708, cloth. 1878. 21s.

BADEN-POWELL.—PROTECTION AND BAD TIMES, with Special Reference to the Political Economy of English Colonisation. By George Baden-Powell, M.A., F.R.A.S., F.S.S., Author of "New Homes for the Old Country," &c., &c. 8vo, pp. xii.-376, cloth. 1879. 6s. 6d.

BADER.—THE NATURAL AND MORBID CHANGES OF THE HUMAN EYE, AND THEIR TREATMENT. By C. Bader. Medium 8vo, pp. viii. and 506, cloth. 1868. 16s.

BADER.—PLATES ILLUSTRATING THE NATURAL AND MORBID CHANGES OF THE HUMAN EYE. By C. Bader. Six chromo-lithographic Plates, each containing the figures of six Eyes, and four lithographed Plates, with figures of Instruments. With an Explanatory Text of 32 pages. Medium 8vo, in a portfolio. 21s. Price for Text and Atlas taken together, £1, 12s.

BADLEY.—INDIAN MISSIONARY RECORD AND MEMORIAL VOLUME. By the Rev. B. H. Badley, of the American Methodist Mission. 8vo, pp. xii. and 280, cloth. 1876. 10s. 6d.

BALFOUR.—WAIFS AND STRAYS FROM THE FAR EAST; being a Series of Disconnected Essays on Matters relating to China. By Frederick Henry Balfour. Demy 8vo, pp. 224, cloth. 1876. 10s. 6d.

BALFOUR.—THE DIVINE CLASSIC OF NAN-HUA; being the Works of Chuang Tsze, Taoist Philosopher. With an Excursus, and Copious Annotations in English and Chinese. By F. H. Balfour. 8vo, pp. xlviii. and 426, cloth. 1881. 14s.

BALFOUR.—TAOIST TEXTS, Ethical, Political, and Speculative. By F. H. BALFOUR, Editor of the *North-China Herald*. Imp. 8vo, pp. vi.-118, cloth. 10s. 6d.

BALL.—THE DIAMONDS, COAL, AND GOLD OF INDIA; their Mode of Occurrence and Distribution. By V. Ball, M.A., F.G.S., of the Geological Survey of India. Fcap. 8vo, pp. viii. and 136, cloth. 1881. 5s.

BALL.—A MANUAL OF THE GEOLOGY OF INDIA. Part III. Economic Geology. By V. Ball, M.A., F.G.S. Royal 8vo, pp. xx. and 640, with 6 Maps and 10 Plates, cloth. 1881. 10s.

BALLAD SOCIETY—Subscriptions, small paper, one guinea; large paper, two guineas per annum. List of publications on application.

BALLANTYNE.—ELEMENTS OF HINDI AND BRAJ BHAKHA GRAMMAR. Compiled for the use of the East India College at Haileybury. By James R. Ballantyne. Second Edition. Crown 8vo, pp. 38, cloth. 1868. 5s.

BALLANTYNE.—FIRST LESSONS IN SANSKRIT GRAMMAR; together with an Introduction to the Hitopadeśa. Fourth Edition. By James R. Ballantyne, LL.D., Librarian of the India Office. 8vo, pp. viii. and 110, cloth. 1884. 3s. 6d.

BALLANTYNE.—THE SANKHYA APHORISMS OF KAPILA. See Trübner's Oriental Series.

BARANOWSKI.—VADE MECUM DE LA LANGUE FRANÇAISE, rédigé d'après les Dictionnaires classiques avec les Exemples de Bonnes Locutions que donne l'Académie Française, on qu'on trouve dans les ouvrages des plus célèbres auteurs. Par J. J. Baranowski, avec l'approbation de M. E. Littré, Sénateur, &c. Second Edition. 32mo, pp. 224. 1883. Cloth, 2s. 6d.

BARANOWSKI.—ANGLO-POLISH LEXICON. By J. J. Baranowski, formerly Under-Secretary to the Bank of Poland, in Warsaw. Fcap. 8vo, pp. viii. and 492, cloth. 1883. 6s.

BARANOWSKI.—SLOWNIK POLSKO-ANGIELSKI. (Polish-English Lexicon.) By J. J. Baranowski. Fcap. 8vo, pp. iv.-402, cloth. 1884. 6s. 6d.

BARENTS' RELICS.—Recovered in the summer of 1876 by Charles L. W. Gardiner, Esq., and presented to the Dutch Government. Described and explained by J. K. J. de Jonge, Deputy Royal Architect at the Hague. Published by command of His Excellency, W. F. Van F.R.P. Taelman Kip, Minister of Marine. Translated, with a Preface, by S. R. Van Campen. With a Map, Illustrations, and a fac-simile of the Scroll. 8vo, pp. 70, cloth. 1877. 5s.

BARRIERE and CAPENDU.—LES FAUX BONSHOMMES, a Comedy. By Théodore Barrière and Ernest Capendu. Edited, with English Notes and Notice on Barrière, by Professor Ch. Cassal, LL.D., of University College, London. 12mo, pp. xvi. and 304, cloth. 1868. 4s.

BARTH.—THE RELIGIONS OF INDIA. See Trübner's Oriental Series.

BARTLETT.—DICTIONARY OF AMERICANISMS. A Glossary of Words and Phrases colloquially used in the United States. By John Russell Bartlett. Fourth Edition, considerably enlarged and improved. 8vo, pp. xlvi. and 814, cloth. 1877. 20s.

BATTYE.—WHAT IS VITAL FORCE? or, a Short and Comprehensive Sketch, including Vital Physics, Animal Morphology, and Epidemics; to which is added an Appendix upon Geology, IS THE DENTRITAL THEORY OF GEOLOGY TENABLE? By Richard Fawcett Battye. 8vo, pp. iv. and 336, cloth. 1877. 7s. 6d.

BAZLEY.—NOTES ON THE EPICYCLODIAL CUTTING FRAME of Messrs. Holtzapffel & Co. With special reference to its Compensation Adjustment, and with numerous Illustrations of its Capabilities. By Thomas Sebastian Bazley, M.A. 8vo, pp. xvi. and 192, cloth. Illustrated. 1872. 10s. 6d.

BAZLEY.—THE STARS IN THEIR COURSES: A Twofold Series of Maps, with a Catalogue, showing how to identify, at any time of the year, all stars down to the 5.6 magnitude, inclusive of Heis, which are clearly visible in English latitudes. By T. S. Bazley, M.A., Author of "Notes on the Epicycloidal Cutting Frame." Atlas folio, pp. 46 and 24, Folding Plates, cloth. 1878. 15s.

BEAL.—A CATENA OF BUDDHIST SCRIPTURES FROM THE CHINESE. By S. Beal, B.A., Trinity College, Cambridge; a Chaplain in Her Majesty's Fleet, &c. 8vo, pp. xiv. and 436, cloth. 1871. 15s.

BEAL.—THE ROMANTIC LEGEND OF SAKYA BUDDHA. From the Chinese-Sanskrit. By the Rev. Samuel Beal. Crown 8vo, pp. 408, cloth. 1875. 12s.

BEAL.—DHAMMAPADA. See Trübner's Oriental Series.

BEAL.—BUDDHIST LITERATURE IN CHINA: Abstract of Four Lectures, Delivered by Samuel Beal, B.A., Professor of Chinese at University College, London. Demy 8vo, pp. xx. and 186, cloth. 1882. 10s. 6d.

BEAL.—SI-YU-KI. Buddhist Records of the Western World. See Trübner's Oriental Series.

BEAMES.—OUTLINES OF INDIAN PHILOLOGY. With a Map showing the Distribution of Indian Languages. By John Beames, M.R.A.S., B.C.S., &c. Second enlarged and revised Edition. Crown 8vo, pp. viii. and 96, cloth. 1868. 5s.

BEAMES.—A COMPARATIVE GRAMMAR OF THE MODERN ARYAN LANGUAGES OF INDIA, to wit, Hindi, Panjabi, Sindhi, Gujarati, Marathi, Oriya, and Bengali. By John Beames, B.C.S., M.R.A.S., &c., &c. Demy 8vo. Vol. I. On Sounds. Pp. xvi. and 360, cloth. 1872. 16s.—Vol. II. The Noun and the Pronoun. Pp. xii. and 348, cloth. 1875. 16s.—Vol. III. The Verb. Pp. xii. and 316, cloth. 1879. 16s.

BELLEW.—FROM THE INDUS TO THE TIGRIS. A Narrative of a Journey through Balochistan, Afghanistan, Khorassan, and Iran in 1872; together with a Synoptical Grammar and Vocabulary of the Brahoe Language, and a Record of the Meteorological Observations on the March from the Indus to the Tigris. By Henry Walter Bellew, C.S.I., Surgeon, B,S.C. 8vo, pp. viii. and 496, cloth. 1874. 14s.

BELLEW.—KASHMIR AND KASHGHAR; a Narrative of the Journey of the Embassy to Kashghar in 1873-74. By H. W. Bellew, C.S.I. Demy 8vo, pp. xxxii. and 420, cloth. 1875. 16s.

BELLEW.—THE RACES OF AFGHANISTAN. Being a Brief Account of the Principal Nations Inhabiting that Country. By Surgeon-Major H. W. Bellew, C.S.I., late on Special Political Duty at Kabul. 8vo, pp. 124, cloth. 1880. 7s. 6d.

BELLOWS.—ENGLISH OUTLINE VOCABULARY for the use of Students of the Chinese, Japanese, and other Languages. Arranged by John Bellows. With Notes on the Writing of Chinese with Roman Letters, by Professor Summers, King's College, London. Crown 8vo, pp. vi. and 368, cloth. 1867. 6s.

BELLOWS.—OUTLINE DICTIONARY FOR THE USE OF MISSIONARIES, EXPLORERS, AND STUDENTS OF LANGUAGE. By Max Müller, M.A., Taylorian Professor in the University of Oxford. With an Introduction on the proper use of the ordinary English Alphabet in transcribing Foreign Languages. The Vocabulary compiled by John Bellows. Crown 8vo, pp. xxxi. and 368, limp morocco. 1867. 7s. 6d.

BELLOWS.—TOUS LES VERBES. Conjugations of all the Verbs in the French and English Languages. By John Bellows. Revised by Professor Beljame, B.A., LL.B., of the University of Paris, and Official Interpreter to the Imperial Court, and George B. Strickland, late Assistant French Master, Royal Naval School, London. Also a New Table of Equivalent Values of French and English Money, Weights, and Measures. 32mo, 76 Tables, sewed. 1867. 1s.

BELLOWS.—FRENCH AND ENGLISH DICTIONARY FOR THE POCKET. By John Bellows. Containing the French-English and English-French divisions on the same page; conjugating all the verbs; distinguishing the genders by different types; giving numerous aids to pronunciation; indicating the *liaison* or *non-liaison* of terminal consonants; and translating units of weight, measure, and value, by a series of tables differing entirely from any hitherto published. The new edition, which is but six ounces in weight, has been remodelled, and contains many thousands of additional words and renderings. Miniature maps of France, the British Isles, Paris, and London, are added to the Geographical Section. Second Edition. 32mo, pp. 608, roan tuck, or persian without tuck. 1877. 10s. 6d.; morocco tuck, 12s. 6d.

BENEDIX.—DER VETTER. Comedy in Three Acts. By Roderich Benedix. With Grammatical and Explanatory Notes by F. Weinmann, German Master at the Royal Institution School, Liverpool, and G. Zimmermann, Teacher of Modern Languages. 12mo, pp. 128, cloth. 1863. 2s. 6d.

BENFEY.—A PRACTICAL GRAMMAR OF THE SANSKRIT LANGUAGE, for the use of Early Students. By Theodor Benfey, Professor of Sanskrit in the University of Göttingen. Second, revised, and enlarged Edition. Royal 8vo, pp. viii. and 296, cloth. 1868. 10s. 6d.

BENTHAM.—THEORY OF LEGISLATION. By Jeremy Bentham. Translated from the French of Etienne Dumont by R. Hildreth. Fourth Edition. Post 8vo, pp. xv. and 472, cloth. 1882. 7s. 6d.

BETTS.—*See* VALDES.

BEVERIDGE.—THE DISTRICT OF BAKARGANJ. Its History and Statistics. By H. Beveridge, B.C.S., Magistrate and Collector of Bakarganj. 8vo, pp. xx. and 460, cloth. 1876. 21s.

BHANDARKAR.—EARLY HISTORY OF THE DEKKAN DOWN TO THE MAHOMEDAN CONQUEST. By Ramkrishna Gopal Bhandarkar, M.A., Hon. M.R.A.S., Professor of Oriental Languages, Dekkan College. Written for the *Bombay Gazette*. Royal 8vo, pp. 128, wrapper. 1884. 5s.

BICKNELL.—*See* HAFIZ.

BIERBAUM.—HISTORY OF THE ENGLISH LANGUAGE AND LITERATURE.—By F. J. Bierbaum, Ph.D. Crown 8vo, pp. viii. and 270, cloth. 1883. 3s.

BIGANDET.—THE LIFE OF GAUDAMA. See Trübner's Oriental Series.

BILLINGS.—THE PRINCIPLES OF VENTILATION AND HEATING, and their Practical Application. By John S. Billings, M.D., LL.D. (Edinb.), Surgeon U.S. Army. Demy 8vo, pp. x. and 216, cloth. 1884. 15s.

BIRCH.—FASTI MONASTICI AEVI SAXONICI ; or, An Alphabetical List of the Heads of Religious Houses in England previous to the Norman Conquest, to which is prefixed a Chronological Catalogue of Contemporary Foundations. By Walter de Gray Birch. 8vo, pp. vii. and 114, cloth. 1873. 5s.

BIRD.—PHYSIOLOGICAL ESSAYS. Drink Craving, Differences in Men, Idiosyncrasy, and the Origin of Disease. By Robert Bird, M.D. Demy 8vo, pp. 246, cloth. 1870. 7s. 6d.

BIZYENOS.—ATΘIΔEΞ AYPAI. Poems. By George M. Bizyenos. With Frontispiece Etched by Prof. A. Legros. Royal 8vo, pp. viii.-312, printed on hand-made paper, and richly bound. 1883. £1, 11s. 6d.

BLACK.—YOUNG JAPAN, YOKOHAMA AND YEDO. A Narrative of the Settlement and the City, from the Signing of the Treaties in 1858 to the Close of 1879; with a Glance at the Progress of Japan during a Period of Twenty-one Years. By J. R. Black, formerly Editor of the "Japan Herald," &c. 2 vols. demy 8vo, pp. xviii. and 418 ; xiv. and 522, cloth. 1881. £2, 2s.

BLACKET.—RESEARCHES INTO THE LOST HISTORIES OF AMERICA ; or, The Zodiac shown to be an Old Terrestrial Map, in which the Atlantic Isle is delineated ; so that Light can be thrown upon the Obscure Histories of the Earthworks and Ruined Cities of America. By W. S. Blacket. Illustrated by numerous Engravings. 8vo, pp. 336, cloth. 1883. 10s. 6d.

BLADES.—SHAKSPERE AND TYPOGRAPHY. Being an Attempt to show Shakspere's Personal Connection with, and Technical Knowledge of, the Art of Printing ; also Remarks upon some common Typographical Errors, with especial reference to the Text of Shakspere. By William Blades. 8vo, pp. viii. and 78, with an Illustration, cloth. 1872. 3s.

BLADES.—THE BIOGRAPHY AND TYPOGRAPHY OF WILLIAM CAXTON, England's First Printer. By W. Blades. Founded upon the Author's "Life and Typography of William Caxton." Brought up to the Present Date. Elegantly and appropriately printed in demy 8vo, on hand-made paper, imitation old bevelled binding. 1877. £1, 1s. Cheap Edition. Crown 8vo, cloth. 1881. 5s.

BLADES.—THE ENEMIES OF BOOKS. By William Blades, Typograph. Crown 8vo, pp. xvi. and 112, parchment wrapper. 1880.

BLADES.—AN ACCOUNT OF THE GERMAN MORALITY PLAY ENTITLED DEPOSITIO CORNUTI TYPOGRAPHICI, as Performed in the Seventeenth and Eighteenth Centuries. With a Rhythmical Translation of the German Version of 1648. By William Blades (Typographer). To which is added a Literal Reprint of the unique Original Version, written in Plant Deutsch by Paul de Wise, and printed in 1621. Small 4to, pp. xii.-144, with facsimile Illustrations, in an appropriate binding. 1885. 7s. 6d.

BLAKEY.—MEMOIRS OF DR. ROBERT BLAKEY, Professor of Logic and Metaphysics, Queen's College, Belfast. Edited by the Rev. Henry Miller. Crown 8vo, pp. xii. and 252, cloth. 1879. 5s.

BLEEK.—REYNARD THE FOX IN SOUTH AFRICA ; or, Hottentot Fables and Tales, chiefly Translated from Original Manuscripts in the Library of His Excellency Sir George Grey, K.C.B. By W. H. I. Bleek, Ph.D. Post 8vo, pp. xxvi. and 94, cloth. 1864. 3s. 6d.

BLEEK.—A BRIEF ACCOUNT OF BUSHMAN FOLK LORE, and other Texts. By W. H. I. Bleek. Ph.D. Folio, pp. 21, paper. 2s. 6d.

BLUMHARDT.—See CHARITABALI.

BOEHMER.—*See* VALDES, and SPANISH REFORMERS.

BOJESEN.—A GUIDE TO THE DANISH LANGUAGE. Designed for English Students. By Mrs. Maria Bojesen. 12mo, pp. 250, cloth. 1863. 5s.

BOLIA.—THE GERMAN CALIGRAPHIST: Copies for German Handwriting. By C. Bolia. Oblong 4to, sewed. 1s.

BOOLE.—MESSAGE OF PSYCHIC SCIENCE TO MOTHERS AND NURSES. By Mary Boole. Crown 8vo, pp. xiv. and 266, cloth. 1883. 5s.

BOTTRELL.—STORIES AND FOLK-LORE OF WEST CORNWALL. By William Bottrell. With Illustrations by Joseph Blight. Third Series. 8vo, pp. viii. and 200, cloth. 1884. 6s.

BOY ENGINEERS.—See under LUKIN.

BOYD.—NÁGÁNANDA ; or, the Joy of the Snake World. A Buddhist Drama in Five Acts. Translated into English Prose, with Explanatory Notes, from the Sanskrit of Sá-Harsha-Deva. By Palmer Boyd, B.A., Cambridge. With an Introduction by Professor Cowell. Crown 8vo, pp. xvi. and 100, cloth. 1872. 4s. 6d.

BRADSHAW.—DICTIONARY OF BATHING PLACES AND CLIMATIC HEALTH RESORTS. Much Revised and Considerably Enlarged. With a Map in Eleven Colours. Third Edition. Crown 8vo, pp. lxxviii. and 364, cloth. 1884. 2s. 6d.

BRENTANO.—ON THE HISTORY AND DEVELOPMENT OF GILDS, AND THE ORIGIN OF TRADE-UNIONS. By Lujo Brentano, of Aschaffenburg, Bavaria, Doctor Juris Utriusque et Philosophiæ. 1. The Origin of Gilds. 2. Religious (or Social) Gilds. 3. Town-Gilds or Gild-Merchants. 4. Craft-Gilds. 5. Trade-Unions. 8vo, pp. xvi. and 136, cloth. 1870. 3s. 6d.

BRETSCHNEIDER.—EARLY EUROPEAN RESEARCHES INTO THE FLORA OF CHINA. By E. Bretschneider, M.D., Physician of the Russian Legation at Peking. Demy 8vo, pp. iv. and 194, sewed. 1881. 7s. 6d.

BRETSCHNEIDER.—BOTANICON SINICUM. Notes on Chinese Botany, from Native and Western Sources. By E. Bretschneider, M.D. Crown 8vo, pp. 228, wrapper. 1882. 10s. 6d.

BRETTE.—FRENCH EXAMINATION PAPERS SET AT THE UNIVERSITY OF LONDON FROM 1839 TO 1871. Arranged and edited by the Rev. P. H. Ernest Brette, B.D. Crown 8vo, pp. viii. and 278, cloth. 3s. 6d.; interleaved, 4s. 6d.

BRITISH MUSEUM.—LIST OF PUBLICATIONS OF THE TRUSTEES OF THE BRITISH MUSEUM, on application.

BROWN.—THE DERVISHES ; OR, ORIENTAL SPIRITUALISM. By John P. Brown, Secretary and Dragoman of the Legation of the United States of America at Constantinople. Crown 8vo, pp. viii. and 416, cloth, with 24 Illustrations. 1868. 14s.

BROWN.—SANSKRIT PROSODY AND NUMERICAL SYMBOLS EXPLAINED. By Charles Philip Brown, M.R.A.S., Author of a Telugu Dictionary, Grammar, &c., Professor of Telugu in the University of London. 8vo, pp. viii. and 56, cloth. 1869. 3s. 6d.

BROWNE.—HOW TO USE THE OPHTHALMOSCOPE; being Elementary Instruction in Ophthalmoscopy. Arranged for the use of Students. By Edgar A. Browne, Surgeon to the Liverpool Eye and Ear Infirmary, &c. Second Edition. Crown 8vo, pp. xi. and 108, with 35 Figures, cloth. 1883. 3s. 6d.

BROWNE.—A BÁNGÁLI PRIMER, in Roman Character. By J. F. Browne, B.C.S. Crown 8vo, pp. 32, cloth. 1881. 2s.

BROWNE.—A HINDI PRIMER IN ROMAN CHARACTER. By J. F. Browne, B.C.S. Crown 8vo, pp. 36, cloth. 1882. 2s. 6d.

BROWNE.—AN URIYÁ PRIMER IN ROMAN CHARACTER. By J. F. Browne, B.C.S. Crown 8vo, pp. 32, cloth. 1882. 2s. 6d.

BROWNING SOCIETY'S PAPERS.—Demy 8vo, wrappers. 1881-84. Part I., pp. 116. 10s. Bibliography of Robert Browning from 1833-81. Part II., pp. 142. 10s. Part III., pp. 168. 10s. Part IV., pp. 148. 10s. Part V., pp. . 10s.

BROWNING'S POEMS, ILLUSTRATIONS TO. 4to, boards. Parts I. and II. 10s. each.

10   A Catalogue of Important Works,

BRUNNOW.—*See* SCHEFFEL.

BRUNTON.—MAP OF JAPAN. See under JAPAN.

BUDGE.—ARCHAIC CLASSICS. Assyrian Texts; being Extracts from the Annals of Shalmaneser II., Sennacherib, and Assur-Bani-Pal. With Philological Notes. By Ernest A. Budge, B.A., M.R.A.S., Assyrian Exhibitioner, Christ's College, Cambridge. Small 4to, pp. viii. and 44, cloth. 1880. 7s. 6d.

BUDGE.—HISTORY OF ESARHADDON. See Trübner's Oriental Series.

BUNYAN.—SCENES FROM THE PILGRIM'S PROGRESS. By. R. B. Rutter. 4to, pp. 142, boards, leather back. 1882. 5s.

BURGESS:—
ARCHÆOLOGICAL SURVEY OF WESTERN INDIA:—
   REPORT OF THE FIRST SEASON'S OPERATIONS IN THE BELGÂM AND KALADI DISTRICTS. January to May 1874. By James Burgess, F.R.G.S. With 56 Photographs and Lithographic Plates. Royal 4to, pp. viii. and 45; half bound. 1875. £2, 2s.
   REPORT ON THE ANTIQUITIES OF KÂTHIÂWÂD AND KACHH, being the result of the Second Season's Operations of the Archæological Survey of Western India, 1874-75. By James Burgess, F.R.G.S. Royal 4to, pp. x. and 242, with 74 Plates; half bound. 1876. £3, 3s.
   REPORT ON THE ANTIQUITIES IN THE BIDAR AND AURANGABAD DISTRICTS, in the Territories of His Highness the Nizam of Haiderabad, being the result of the Third Season's Operations of the Archæological Survey of Western India, 1875-76. By James Burgess, F.R.G.S., M.R.A.S., Archæological Surveyor and Reporter to Government, Western India. Royal 4to, pp. viii. and 138, with 63 Photographic Plates; half bound. 1878. £2, 2s.
   REPORT ON THE BUDDHIST CAVE TEMPLES AND THEIR INSCRIPTIONS; containing Views, Plans, Sections, and Elevation of Façades of Cave Temples; Drawings of Architectural and Mythological Sculptures; Facsimiles of Inscriptions, &c.; with Descriptive and Explanatory Text, and Translations of Inscriptions, &c., &c. By James Burgess, LL.D., F.R.G.S., &c. Royal 4to, pp. x. and 140, with 86 Plates and Woodcuts; half-bound. } 2 Vols. 1883. £6, 6s.
   REPORT ON ELURA CAVE TEMPLES, AND THE BRAHMANICAL AND JAINA CAVES IN WESTERN INDIA. By James Burgess, LL.D., F.R.G.S., &c. Royal 4to, pp. viii. and 90, with 66 Plates and Woodcuts; half-bound.

BURMA.—THE BRITISH BURMA GAZETTEER. Compiled by Major H. R. Spearman, under the direction of the Government of India. 2 vols. 8vo, pp. 764 and 878, with 11 Photographs, cloth. 1880. £2, 10s.

BURMA.—HISTORY OF. See Trübner's Oriental Series, page 70.

BURNE.—SHROPSHIRE FOLK-LORE. A Sheaf of Gleanings. Edited by Charlotte S. Burne, from the Collections of Georgina F. Jackson. Demy 8vo. Part I., pp. xvi.-176, wrapper. 1883. 7s. 6d. Part II., pp. 192, wrapper. 1885. 7s. 6d.

BURNELL.—ELEMENTS OF SOUTH INDIAN PALÆOGRAPHY, from the Fourth to the Seventeenth Century A.D., being an Introduction to the Study of South Indian Inscriptions and MSS. By A. C. Burnell. Second enlarged and improved Edition. 4to, pp. xiv. and 148, Map and 35 Plates, cloth. 1878. £2, 12s. 6d.

BURNELL.—A CLASSIFIED INDEX TO THE SANSKRIT MSS. IN THE PALACE AT TANJORE. Prepared for the Madras Government. By A. C. Burnell, Ph.D., &c., &c. 4to, stiff wrapper. Part I., pp. iv.-80, Vedic and Technical Literature. Part II., pp. iv.-80, Philosophy and Law. Part III., Drama, Epics, Purānas, and Zantras; Indices. 1879. 10s. each.

BURTON.—HANDBOOK FOR OVERLAND EXPEDITIONS; being an English Edition of the "Prairie Traveller," a Handbook for Overland Expeditions. With Illustrations and Itineraries of the Principal Routes between the Mississippi and the Pacific, and a Map. By Captain R. B. Marcy (now General and Chief of the Staff, Army of the Potomac). Edited, with Notes, by Captain Richard F. Burton. Crown 8vo, pp. 270, numerous Woodcuts, Itineraries, and Map, cloth. 1863. 6s. 6d.

BUTLER.—EREWHON; or, Over the Range. By Samuel Butler. Seventh Edition. Crown 8vo, pp. xii. and 244, cloth. 1884. 5s.

BUTLER.—THE FAIR HAVEN. A Work in Defence of the Miraculous Element in Our Lord's Ministry upon Earth, both as against Rationalistic Impugners and certain Orthodox Defenders. By the late John Pickard Owen. With a Memoir of the Author by William Bickersteth Owen. By Samuel Butler. Second Edition. Demy 8vo, pp. x. and 248, cloth. 1873. 7s. 6d.

BUTLER.—LIFE AND HABIT. By Samuel Butler. Second Edition. Crown 8vo, pp. x. and 308, cloth. 1878. 7s. 6d.

BUTLER.—GAVOTTES, MINUETS, FUGUES, AND OTHER SHORT PIECES FOR THE PIANO. By Samuel Butler, Author of "Erewhon," "Life and Habit," &c. (Op. I. mus.), and Henry Festing Jones (Op. I.)

BUTLER.—EVOLUTION, OLD AND NEW; or, The Theories of Buffon, Dr. Erasmus Darwin, and Lamarck, as compared with that of Mr. Charles Darwin. By Samuel Butler. Second Edition, with an Appendix and Index. Crown 8vo, pp. xii. and 430, cloth. 1882. 10s. 6d.

BUTLER.—UNCONSCIOUS MEMORY: A Comparison between the Theory of Dr. Ewald Hering, Professor of Physiology at the University of Prague, and the "Philosophy of the Unconscious" of Dr. Edward von Hartmann. With Translations from these Authors, and Preliminary Chapters bearing on "Life and Habit," "Evolution, New and Old," and Mr. Charles Darwin's edition of Dr. Krause's "Erasmus Darwin." By Samuel Butler. Crown 8vo, pp. viii. and 288, cloth. 1880. 7s. 6d.

BUTLER.—ALPS AND SANCTUARIES OF PIEDMONT AND THE CANTON TICINO. Profusely Illustrated by Charles Gogin, H. F. Jones, and the Author. By Samuel Butler. Foolscap 4to, pp. viii. and 376, cloth. 1882. 21s.

BUTLER.—SELECTIONS FROM HIS PREVIOUS WORKS, with Remarks on Mr. G. J. Romanes' recent work, "Mental Evolution in Animals," and "A Psalm of Montreal." By Samuel Butler. Crown 8vo, pp. viii. and 326, cloth. 1884. 7s. 6d.

BUTLER.—THE SPANISH TEACHER AND COLLOQUIAL PHRASE-BOOK. An Easy and Agreeable Method of acquiring a Speaking Knowledge of the Spanish Language. By Francis Butler. Fcap. 8vo, pp. xviii. and 240, half-roan. 2s. 6d.

BUTLER.—HUNGARIAN POEMS AND FABLES FOR ENGLISH READERS. Selected and Translated by E. D. Butler, of the British Museum; with Illustrations by A. G. Butler. Foolscap, pp. vi. and 88, limp cloth. 1877. 2s.

BUTLER.—THE LEGEND OF THE WONDROUS HUNT. By John Arany. With a few Miscellaneous Pieces and Folk-Songs. Translated from the Magyar by E. D. Butler, F.R.G.S. Crown 8vo, pp. viii. and 70. Limp cloth. 2s. 6d.

CAITHNESS.—LECTURES ON POPULAR AND SCIENTIFIC SUBJECTS. By the Earl of Caithness, F.R.S. Delivered at various times and places. Second enlarged Edition. Crown 8vo, pp. 174, cloth. 1879. 2s. 6d.

CALCUTTA REVIEW.—SELECTIONS FROM Nos. I.-XXXVII. 5s. each.

CALDER.—THE COMING ERA. By A. Calder, Officer of the Legion of Honour, and Author of "The Man of the Future." 8vo, pp. 422, cloth. 1879. 10s. 6d.

CALDWELL.—A COMPARATIVE GRAMMAR OF THE DRAVIDIAN OR SOUTH INDIAN FAMILY OF LANGUAGES. By the Rev. R. Caldwell, LL.D. A second, corrected, and enlarged Edition. Demy 8vo, pp. 804, cloth. 1875. 28s.

CALENDARS OF STATE PAPERS. List on application.

CALL.—REVERBERATIONS. Revised. With a chapter from My Autobiography. By W. M. W. Call, M.A., Cambridge, Author of "Lyra Hellenica" and "Golden Histories." Crown 8vo, pp. viii. and 200, cloth. 1875. 4s. 6d.

CALLAWAY.—NURSERY TALES, TRADITIONS, AND HISTORIES OF THE ZULUS. In their own words, with a Translation into English, and Notes. By the Rev. Canon Callaway, M.D. Vol. I., 8vo, pp. xiv. and 378, cloth. 1868. 16s.

CALLAWAY.—THE RELIGIOUS SYSTEM OF THE AMAZULU.

Part I.—Unkulunkulu; or, The Tradition of Creation as existing among the Amazulu and other Tribes of South Africa, in their own words, with a Translation into English, and Notes. By the Rev. Canon Callaway, M.D. 8vo, pp. 128, sewed. 1868. 4s.

Part II.—Amatongo; or, Ancestor-Worship as existing among the Amazulu, in their own words, with a Translation into English, and Notes. By the Rev. Canon Callaway, M.D. 8vo, pp. 127, sewed. 1869. 4s.

Part III.—Izinyanga Zokubula; or, Divination, as existing among the Amazulu, in their own words, with a Translation into English, and Notes. By the Rev. Canon Callaway, M.D. 8vo, pp. 150, sewed. 1870. 4s.

Part IV.—On Medical Magic and Witchcraft. 8vo, pp. 40, sewed, 1s. 6d.

CAMBRIDGE PHILOLOGICAL SOCIETY (TRANSACTIONS). Vol. I., from 1872-1880. 8vo, pp. xvi.-420, wrapper. 1881. 15s. Vol. II., for 1881 and 1882. 8vo, pp. viii.-286, wrapper. 1883. 12s.

CAMERINI.—L'ECO ITALIANO; a Practical Guide to Italian Conversation. By E. Camerini. With a Vocabulary. 12mo, pp. 98, cloth. 1860. 4s. 6d.

CAMPBELL.—THE GOSPEL OF THE WORLD'S DIVINE ORDER. By Douglas Campbell. New Edition. Revised. Crown 8vo, pp. viii. and 364, cloth. 1877. 4s. 6d.

CANADA.—A GUIDE BOOK TO THE DOMINION OF CANADA. Containing Information for intending Settlers, with many Illustrations and Map. Published under the Direction of the Government of Canada. Demy 8vo, pp. xiv.-138, thick paper, sewed. 1885. 6d.

CANDID EXAMINATION OF THEISM. By Physicus. Post 8vo, pp. xviii. and 198, cloth. 1878. 7s. 6d.

CANTICUM CANTICORUM, reproduced in facsimile, from the Scriverius copy in the British Museum. With an Historical and Bibliographical Introduction by I. Ph. Berjeau. Folio, pp. 36, with 16 Tables of Illustrations, vellum. 1860. £2, 2s.

CAREY.—THE PAST, THE PRESENT, AND THE FUTURE. By H. C. Carey. Second Edition. 8vo, pp. 474, cloth. 1856. 10s. 6d.

CARLETTI.—HISTORY OF THE CONQUEST OF TUNIS. Translated by J. T. Carletti. Crown 8vo, pp. 40, cloth. 1883. 2s. 6d.

CARNEGY.—NOTES ON THE LAND TENURES AND REVENUE ASSESSMENTS OF UPPER INDIA. By P. Carnegy. Crown 8vo, pp. viii. and 136, and forms, cloth. 1874. 6s.

CATHERINE II., MEMOIRS OF THE EMPRESS. Written by herself. With a Preface by A. Herzen. Trans. from the French. 12mo, pp. xvi. and 352, bds. 1859. 7s. 6d.

CATLIN.—O-KEE-PA. A Religious Ceremony; and other Customs of the Mandans. By George Catlin. With 13 coloured Illustrations. Small 4to, pp. vi. and 52, cloth. 1867. 14s.

CATLIN.—THE LIFTED AND SUBSIDED ROCKS OF AMERICA, with their Influence on the Oceanic, Atmospheric, and Land Currents, and the Distribution of Races. By George Catlin. With 2 Maps. Cr. 8vo, pp. xii. and 238, cloth. 1870. 6s. 6d.

CATLIN.—SHUT YOUR MOUTH AND SAVE YOUR LIFE. By George Catlin, Author of "Notes of Travels amongst the North American Indians," &c., &c. With 29 Illustrations from Drawings by the Author. Eighth Edition, considerably enlarged. Crown 8vo, pp. 106, cloth. 1882. 2s. 6d.

CAXTON.—THE BIOGRAPHY AND TYPOGRAPHY OF. See BLADES.

CAXTON CELEBRATION, 1877.—CATALOGUE OF THE LOAN COLLECTION OF ANTIQUITIES, CURIOSITIES, AND APPLIANCES CONNECTED WITH THE ART OF PRINTING. Edited by G. Bullen, F.S.A. Post 8vo, pp. xx. and 472, cloth, 3s. 6d.

CAZELLES.—OUTLINE OF THE EVOLUTION-PHILOSOPHY. By Dr. W. E. Cazelles. Translated from the French by the Rev. O. B. Frothingham. Crown 8vo, pp. 156, cloth. 1875. 3s. 6d.

CESNOLA.—SALAMINIA (Cyprus). The History, Treasures, and Antiquities of Salamis in the Island of Cyprus. By A. Palma di Cesnola, F.S.A., &c. With an Introduction by S. Birch, Esq., D.C.L., LL.D., Keeper of the Egyptian and Oriental Antiquities in the British Museum. Royal 8vo, pp. xlviii. and 325, with upwards of 700 Illustrations and Map of Ancient Cyprus, cloth. 1882. 31s. 6d.

CHALMERS.—STRUCTURE OF CHINESE CHARACTERS, under 300 Primary Forms after the Shwoh-wan, 100 A.D., and the Phonetic Shwoh-wan, 1833. By J. Chalmers, M.A., LL.D., A.B. Demy 8vo, pp. x. and 200, with two plates, limp cloth. 1882. 12s. 6d.

CHAMBERLAIN.—THE CLASSICAL POETRY OF THE JAPANESE. By Basil Hall Chamberlain, Author of "Yeigo Henkaku, Ichiran." Post 8vo, pp. xii. and 228, cloth. 1880. 7s. 6d.

CHAPMAN.—CHLOROFORM AND OTHER ANÆSTHETICS : Their History and Use during Childbirth. By John Chapman, M.D. 8vo, pp. 51, sewed. 1859. 1s.

CHAPMAN.—DIARRHŒA AND CHOLERA : Their Nature, Origin, and Treatment through the Agency of the Nervous System. By John Chapman, M.D., M.R.C.P., M.R.C.S. 8vo, pp. xix. and 248, cloth. 7s. 6d.

CHAPMAN.—MEDICAL CHARITY : its Abuses, and how to Remedy them. By John Chapman, M.D. 8vo, pp. viii. and 108, cloth. 1874. 2s. 6d.

CHAPMAN.—SEA-SICKNESS, AND HOW TO PREVENT IT. An Explanation of its Nature and Successful Treatment, through the Agency of the Nervous System, by means of the Spinal Ice Bag; with an Introduction on the General Principles of Neuro-Therapeutics. By John Chapman, M.D., M.R.C.P., M.R.C.S. Second Edition. 8vo, pp. viii. and 112, cloth. 1868. 3s.

CHAPTERS ON CHRISTIAN CATHOLICITY. By a Clergyman. 8vo, pp. 282, cloth. 1878. 5s.

CHARITABALI (THE), or, Instructive Biography. By Isvarachandra Vidyasagara. With a Vocabulary of all the Words occurring in the Text. By J. F. Blumhardt, Bengal Lecturer at the University College, London; and Teacher of Bengali for the Cambridge University. 12mo, pp. 174, cloth. 1884. 5s. The Vocabulary only, 2s. 6d.

CHARNOCK.—A GLOSSARY OF THE ESSEX DIALECT. By Richard Stephen Charnock, Ph.D., F.S.A. Fcap., pp. xii. and 64, cloth. 1880. 3s. 6d.

CHARNOCK.—PRŒNOMINA ; or, The Etymology of the Principal Christian Names of Great Britain and Ireland. By R. S. Charnock, Ph.D., F.S.A. Crown 8vo, pp. xvi. and 128, cloth. 1882. 6s.

CHATTERJEE. See PHILLIPS.

CHATTOPADHYAYA.—THE YÂTRÂS; or, The Popular Dramas of Bengal. By N. Chattopadhyaya. Post 8vo, pp. 50, wrapper. 1882. 2s.

CHAUCER SOCIETY.—Subscription, two guineas per annum. List of Publications on application.

CHILDERS.—A PALI-ENGLISH DICTIONARY, with Sanskrit Equivalents, and with numerous Quotations, Extracts, and References. Compiled by Robert Cæsar Childers, late of the Ceylon Civil Service. Imperial 8vo, double columns, pp. 648, cloth. 1875. £3, 3s.

CHILDERS.—THE MAHAPARINIBBANASUTTA OF THE SUTTA PITAKA. The Pali Text. Edited by the late Professor R. C. Childers. 8vo, pp. 72, limp cloth. 1878. 5s.

CHINTAMON.—A COMMENTARY ON THE TEXT OF THE BHAGAVAD-GITÁ; or, The Discourse between Khrishna and Arjuna of Divine Matters. A Sanskrit Philosophical Poem. With a few Introductory Papers. By Hurrychund Chintamon, Political Agent to H. H. the Guicowar Mulhar Rao Maharajah of Baroda. Post 8vo, pp. 118, cloth. 1874. 6s.

CHRONICLES AND MEMORIALS OF GREAT BRITAIN AND IRELAND DURING THE MIDDLE AGES. List on application.

CLARK.—MEGHADUTA, THE CLOUD MESSENGER. Poem of Kalidasa. Translated by the late Rev. T. Clark, M.A. Fcap. 8vo, pp. 64, wrapper. 1882. 1s.

CLARK.—A FORECAST OF THE RELIGION OF THE FUTURE. Being Short Essays on some important Questions in Religious Philosophy. By W. W. Clark. Post 8vo, pp. xii. and 238, cloth. 1879. 3s. 6d.

CLARKE.—TEN GREAT RELIGIONS: An Essay in Comparative Theology. By James Freeman Clarke. Demy 8vo, pp. x. and 528, cloth. 1871. 15s.

CLARKE.—TEN GREAT RELIGIONS. Part II., A Comparison of all Religions. By J. F. Clarke. Demy 8vo, pp. xxviii.-414, cloth. 1883. 10s. 6d.'

CLARKE.—THE EARLY HISTORY OF THE MEDITERRANEAN POPULATIONS, &c., in their Migrations and Settlements. Illustrated from Autonomous Coins, Gems, Inscriptions, &c. By Hyde Clarke. 8vo, pp. 80, cloth. 1882. 5s.

CLAUSEWITZ.—ON WAR. By General Carl von Clausewitz. Translated by Colonel J. J. Graham, from the third German Edition. Three volumes complete in one. Fcap 4to, double columns, pp. xx. and 564, with Portrait of the author, cloth. 1873. 10s. 6d.

CLEMENT AND HUTTON.—ARTISTS OF THE NINETEENTH CENTURY AND THEIR WORKS. A Handbook containing Two Thousand and Fifty Biographical Sketches. By Clara Erskine Clement and Lawrence Hutton. Third, Revised Edition. 2 vols. crown 8vo. pp. 844, cloth. 1885. 21s.

COKE.—CREEDS OF THE DAY: or, Collated Opinions of Reputable Thinkers. By Henry Coke. In Three Series of Letters. 2 vols. Demy 8vo, pp. 302-324, cloth. 1883. 21s.

COLEBROOKE.—THE LIFE AND MISCELLANEOUS ESSAYS OF HENRY THOMAS COLEBROOKE. The Biography by his Son, Sir T. E. Colebrooke, Bart., M.P. 3 vols. Vol. I. The Life. Demy 8vo, pp. xii. and 492, with Portrait and Map, cloth. 1873. 14s. Vols. II. and III. The Essays. A new Edition, with Notes by E. B. Cowell, Professor of Sanskrit in the University of Cambridge. Demy 8vo, pp. xvi. and 544, and x. and 520, cloth. 1873. 28s.

COLENSO.—NATAL SERMONS. A Series of Discourses Preached in the Cathedral Church of St Peter's, Maritzburg. By the Right Rev. John William Colenso, D.D., Bishop of Natal. 8vo, pp. viii. and 373, cloth. 1866. 7s. 6d. The Second Series. Crown 8vo, cloth. 1868. 5s.

COLLINS.—A GRAMMAR AND LEXICON OF THE HEBREW LANGUAGE, Entitled Sefer Hassoham. By Rabbi Moseh Ben Yitshak, of England. Edited from a MS. in the Bodleian Library of Oxford, and collated with a MS. in the Imperial Library of St. Petersburg, with Additions and Corrections, by G. W. Collins, M.A. Demy 4to, pp. 112, wrapper. 1882. 7s. 6d.

COLYMBIA.—Crown 8vo, pp. 260, cloth. 1873. 5s.

"The book is amusing as well as clever."—*Athenæum.* "Many exceedingly humorous passages."—*Public Opinion.* "Deserves to be read."—*Scotsman.* "Neatly done."—*Graphic.* "Very amusing."—*Examiner.*

COMTE.—THE CATECHISM OF POSITIVE RELIGION: Translated from the French of Auguste Comte. By Richard Congreve. Second Edition. Revised and Corrected. and conformed to the Second French Edition of 1874. Crown 8vo, pp. 316, cloth. 1883. 2s. 6d.

COMTE.—THE EIGHT CIRCULARS OF AUGUSTE COMTE. Translated from the French, under the auspices of R. Congreve. Fcap. 8vo, pp. iv. and 90, cloth. 1882. 1s. 6d.

COMTE.—PRELIMINARY DISCOURSE ON THE POSITIVE SPIRIT. Prefixed to the "Traité Philosophique d'Astronomie Populaire." By M. Auguste Comte. Translated by W. M. W. Call, M.A., Camb. Crown 8vo, pp. 154, cloth. 1883. 2s. 6d.

COMTE.—THE POSITIVE PHILOSOPHY OF AUGUSTE COMTE. Translated and condensed by Harriet Martineau. 2 vols. Second Edition. 8vo, cloth. Vol. I., pp. xxiv. and 400 ; Vol. II., pp. xiv. and 468. 1875. 25s.

CONGREVE.—THE ROMAN EMPIRE OF THE WEST. Four Lectures delivered at the Philosophical Institution, Edinburgh, February 1855, by Richard Congreve, M.A. 8vo, pp. 176, cloth. 1855. 4s.

CONGREVE.—ELIZABETH OF ENGLAND. Two Lectures delivered at the Philosophical Institution, Edinburgh, January 1862. By Richard Congreve. 18mo, pp. 114, sewed. 1862. 2s. 6d.

CONTOPOULOS.—A LEXICON OF MODERN GREEK-ENGLISH AND ENGLISH MODERN GREEK. By N. Contopoulos. Part I. Modern Greek-English. Part II. English Modern Greek. 8vo, pp. 460 and 582, cloth. 1877. 27s.

CONWAY.—THE SACRED ANTHOLOGY : A Book of Ethnical Scriptures. Collected and Edited by Moncure D. Conway. Fifth Edition. Demy 8vo, pp. viii. and 480, cloth. 1876. 12s.

CONWAY.—IDOLS AND IDEALS. With an Essay on Christianity. By Moncure D. Conway, M.A., Author of "The Eastern Pilgrimage," &c. Crown 8vo, pp. 352, cloth. 1877. 4s.

CONWAY.—EMERSON AT HOME AND ABROAD. See English and Foreign Philosophical Library.

CONWAY.—TRAVELS IN SOUTH KENSINGTON. By M. D. Conway. Illustrated. 8vo, pp. 234, cloth. 1882. 12s.
CONTENTS.—The South Kensington Museum—Decorative Art and Architecture in England —Bedford Park.

COOMARA SWAMY.—THE DATHAVANSA ; or, The History of the Tooth Relic of Gotama Buddha, in Pali verse. Edited, with an English Translation, by Mutu Coomara Swamy, F.R.A.S. Demy 8vo, pp. 174, cloth. 1874. 10s. 6d. English Translation. With Notes. pp. 100. 6s.

COOMARA SWAMY.—SUTTA NIPATA ; or, Dialogues and Discourses of Gotama Buddha (2500 years old). Translated from the original Pali. With Notes and Introduction. By Mutu Coomara Swamy, F.R.A.S. Crown 8vo, pp. xxxvi. and 160, cloth. 1874. 6s.

COPARCENERS (THE): Being the Adventures of Two Heiresses. See "Arthur."

CORNELIA. A Novel. Post 8vo, pp. 250, boards. 1863. 1s. 6d.

COTTA.—GEOLOGY AND HISTORY. A Popular Exposition of all that is known of the Earth and its Inhabitants in Pre-historic Times. By Bernhard Von Cotta, Professor of Geology at the Academy of Mining, Freiberg, in Saxony. 12mo, pp. iv. and 84, cloth. 1865. 2s.

COUSIN.—THE PHILOSOPHY OF KANT. Lectures by Victor Cousin. Translated from the French. To which is added a Biographical and Critical Sketch of Kant's Life and Writings. By A. G. Henderson. Large post 8vo, pp. xciv. and 194, cloth. 1864. 6s.

COUSIN.—ELEMENTS OF PSYCHOLOGY : included in a Critical Examination of Locke's Essay on the Human Understanding, and in additional pieces. Translated from the French of Victor Cousin, with an Introduction and Notes. By Caleb S. Henry, D.D. Fourth improved Edition, revised according to the Author's last corrections. Crown 8vo, pp. 568, cloth. 1871. 8s.

COWELL.—A SHORT INTRODUCTION TO THE ORDINARY PRAKRIT OF THE SANSKRIT DRAMAS. With a List of Common Irregular Prâkrit Words. By E. B. Cowell, Professor of Sanskrit in the University of Cambridge, and Hon. LL.D. of the University of Edinburgh. Crown 8vo, pp. 40, limp cloth. 1875. 3s. 6d.

COWELL.—Prakrita-Prakasa; or, The Prakrit Grammar of Vararuchi, with the Commentary (Manorama) of Bhamaha; the first complete Edition of the Original Text, with various Readings from a collection of Six MSS. in the Bodleian Library at Oxford, and the Libraries of the Royal Asiatic Society and the East India House; with Copious Notes, an English Translation, and Index of Prakrit Words, to which is prefixed an Easy Introduction to Prakrit Grammar. By Edward Byles Cowell, of Magdalen Hall, Oxford, Professor of Sanskrit at Cambridge. New Edition, with New Preface, Additions, and Corrections. Second Issue. 8vo, pp. xxxi. and 204, cloth. 1868. 14s.

COWELL.—The Sarvadarsana Samgraha. See Trübner's Oriental Series.

COWLEY.—Poems. By Percy Tunnicliff Cowley. Demy 8vo, pp. 104, cloth. 1881. 5s.

CRAIG.—The Irish Land Labour Question, Illustrated in the History of Ralahine and Co-operative Farming. By E. T. Craig. Crown 8vo, pp. xii. and 202, cloth. 1882. 2s. 6d. Wrappers, 2s.

CRANBROOK.—Credibilia; or, Discourses on Questions of Christian Faith. By the Rev. James Cranbrook, Edinburgh. Reissue. Post 8vo, pp. iv. and 190, cloth. 1868. 3s. 6d.

CRANBROOK.—The Founders of Christianity; or, Discourses upon the Origin of the Christian Religion. By the Rev. James Cranbrook, Edinburgh. Post 8vo, pp. xii. and 324. 1868. 6s.

CRAVEN.—The Popular Dictionary in English and Hindustani, and Hindustani and English. With a Number of Useful Tables. Compiled by the Rev. T. Craven, M.A. 18mo, pp. 430, cloth. 1881. 3s. 6d.

CRAWFORD.—Recollections of Travel in New Zealand and Australia. By James Coutts Crawford, F.G.S., Resident Magistrate, Wellington, &c., &c. With Maps and Illustrations. 8vo, pp. xvi. and 468, cloth. 1880. 18s.

CROSLAND.—Apparitions; An Essay explanatory of Old Facts and a New Theory. To which are added Sketches and Adventures. By Newton Crosland. Crown 8vo, pp. viii. and 166, cloth. 1873. 2s. 6d.

CROSLAND.—Pith: Essays and Sketches Grave and Gay, with some Verses and Illustrations. By Newton Crosland. Crown 8vo, pp. 310, cloth. 1881. 5s.

CROSLAND.—The New Principia; or, The Astronomy of the Future. An Essay Explanatory of a Rational System of the Universe. By N. Crosland, Author of "Pith," &c. Foolscap 8vo, pp. 88, cloth limp elegant, gilt edges. 1884. 2s. 6d.

CROSS.—Hesperides. The Occupations, Relaxations, and Aspirations of a Life. By Launcelot Cross, Author of "Characteristics of Leigh Hunt," "Brandon Tower," "Business," &c. Demy 8vo, pp. iv.-486, cloth. 1883. 10s. 6d.

CSOMA DE KÖRÖS.—Life of. See Trübner's Oriental Series.

CUMMINS.—A Grammar of the Old Friesic Language. By A. H. Cummins, A.M. Crown 8vo, pp. x. and 76, cloth. 1881. 3s. 6d.

CUNNINGHAM.—The Ancient Geography of India. I. The Buddhist Period, including the Campaigns of Alexander and the Travels of Hwen-Thsang. By Alexander Cunningham, Major-General, Royal Engineers (Bengal Retired). With 13 Maps. 8vo, pp. xx. and 590, cloth. 1870. £1, 8s.

CUNNINGHAM.—The Stupa of Bharhut: A Buddhist Monument ornamented with numerous Sculptures illustrative of Buddhist Legend and History in the Third Century b.c. By Alexander Cunningham, C.S.I., C.I.E., Maj.-Gen., R.E. (B.R.), Dir.-Gen. Archæol. Survey of India. Royal 8vo, pp. viii. and 144, with 57 Plates, cloth. 1879. £3, 3s.

CUNNINGHAM.—Archæological Survey of India. Reports from 1862-80. By A. Cunningham, C.S.I., C.I.E., Major-General, R.E. (Bengal Retired), Director-General, Archæological Survey of India. With numerous Plates, cloth, Vols. I.-XI. 10s. each. (Except Vols. VII., VIII., and IX., and also Vols. XII. to XVIII., which are 12s. each.)

CUSHMAN.—CHARLOTTE CUSHMAN: Her Letters and Memories of her Life. Edited by her friend, Emma Stebbins. Square 8vo, pp. viii. and 308, cloth. With Portrait and Illustrations. 1879. 12s. 6d.

CUST.—LANGUAGES OF THE EAST INDIES. See Trübner's Oriental Series.

CUST.—LINGUISTIC AND ORIENTAL ESSAYS. See Trübner's Oriental Series.

CUST.—LANGUAGES OF AFRICA. See Trübner's Oriental Series.

CUST.—PICTURES OF INDIAN LIFE, Sketched with the Pen from 1852 to 1881. By R. N. Cust, late I.C.S., Hon. Sec. Royal Asiatic Society. Crown 8vo, pp. x. and 346, cloth. With Maps. 1881. 7s. 6d.

CUST.—THE SHRINES OF LOURDES, ZARAGOSSA, THE HOLY STAIRS AT ROME, THE HOLY HOUSE OF LORETTO AND NAZARETH, AND ST. ANN AT JERUSALEM. By R. N. Cust, Member of Committees of the Church Missionary Society, and British and Foreign Bible Society. With Four Autotypes from Photographs obtained on the spot. Fcap. 8vo, pp. iv. and 63, stiff wrappers. 1885. 2s.

DANA.—A TEXT-BOOK OF GEOLOGY, designed for Schools and Academies. By James D. Dana, LL.D., Professor of Geology, &c., at Yale College. Illustrated. Crown 8vo, pp. vi. and 354, cloth. 1876. 10s.

DANA.—MANUAL OF GEOLOGY, treating of the Principles of the Science, with special Reference to American Geological History; for the use of Colleges, Academies, and Schools of Science. By James D. Dana, LL.D. Illustrated by a Chart of the World, and over One Thousand Figures. 8vo, pp. xvi. and 800, and Chart, cl. 21s.

DANA.—THE GEOLOGICAL STORY BRIEFLY TOLD. An Introduction to Geology for the General Reader and for Beginners in the Science. By J. D. Dana, LL.D. Illustrated. 12mo, pp. xii. and 264, cloth. 7s. 6d.

DANA.—A SYSTEM OF MINERALOGY. Descriptive Mineralogy, comprising the most Recent Discoveries. By J. D. Dana, aided by G. J. Brush. Fifth Edition, rewritten and enlarged, and illustrated with upwards of 600 Woodcuts, with three Appendixes and Corrections. Royal 8vo, pp. xlviii. and 892, cloth. £2, 2s.

DANA.—A TEXT BOOK OF MINERALOGY. With an Extended Treatise on Crystallography and Physical Mineralogy. By E. S. Dana, on the Plan and with the Co-operation of Professor J. D. Dana. Third Edition, revised. Over 800 Woodcuts and 1 Coloured Plate. 8vo, pp. viii. and 486, cloth. 1879. 18s.

DANA.—MANUAL OF MINERALOGY AND LITHOLOGY; Containing the Elements of the Science of Minerals and Rocks, for the Use of the Practical Mineralogist and Geologist, and for Instruction in Schools and Colleges. By J. D. Dana. Fourth Edition, rearranged and rewritten. Illustrated by numerous Woodcuts. Crown 8vo, pp. viii. and 474, cloth. 1882. 7s. 6d.

DARWIN.—CHARLES DARWIN: A Paper contributed to the Transactions of the Shropshire Archæological Society. By Edward Woodall. With Portrait and Illustrations. Post 8vo, pp. iv.-64, cloth. 1884. 3s. 6d.

DATES AND DATA RELATING TO RELIGIOUS ANTHROPOLOGY AND BIBLICAL ARCHÆOLOGY. (Primæval Period.) 8vo, pp. viii. and 106, cloth. 1876. 5s.

DAVIDS.—BUDDHIST BIRTH STORIES. See Trübner's Oriental Series.

DAVIES.—HINDU PHILOSOPHY. 2 vols. See Trübner's Oriental Series.

DAVIS.—NARRATIVE OF THE NORTH POLAR EXPEDITION, U.S. SHIP *Polaris*, Captain Charles Francis Hall Commanding. Edited under the direction of the Hon. G. M. Robeson, Secretary of the Navy, by Rear-Admiral C. H. Davis, U.S.N. Third Edition. With numerous Steel and Wood Engravings, Photolithographs, and Maps. 4to, pp. 696, cloth. 1881. £1, 8s.

DAY.—THE PREHISTORIC USE OF IRON AND STEEL; with Observations on certain matter ancillary thereto. By St. John V. Day, C.E., F.R.S.E., &c. 8vo, pp. xxiv. and 278, cloth. 1877. 12s.

DE FLANDRE.—MONOGRAMS OF THREE OR MORE LETTERS, DESIGNED AND DRAWN ON STONE. By C. De Flandre, F.S.A. Scot., Edinburgh. With Indices, showing the place and style or period of every Monogram, and of each individual Letter. 4to, 42 Plates, cloth. 1880. Large paper, £7, 7s.; small paper, £3, 3s.

B

DELBRUCK.—INTRODUCTION TO THE STUDY OF LANGUAGE : A Critical Survey of the History and Methods of Comparative Philology of the Indo-European Languages. By B. Delbrück. Authorised Translation, with a Preface by the Author. 8vo, pp. 156, cloth. 1882. 5s. Sewed, 4s.

DELEPIERRE.—HISTOIRE LITTERAIRE DES FOUS. Par Octave Delepierre. Crown 8vo, pp. 184, cloth. 1860. 5s.

DELEPIERRE.—MACARONEANA ANDRA ; overum Nouveaux Mélanges de Litterature Macaronique. Par Octave Delepierre. Small 4to, pp. 180, printed by Whittingham, and handsomely bound in the Roxburghe style. 1862. 10s. 6d.

DELEPIERRE.—ANALYSE DES TRAVAUX DE LA SOCIETE DES PHILOBIBLON DE LONDRES. Par Octave Delepierre. Small 4to, pp. viii. and 134, bound in the Roxburghe style. 1862. 10s. 6d.

DELEPIERRE.—REVUE ANALYTIQUE DES OUVRAGES ÉCRITS EN CENTONS, depuis les Temps Anciens, jusqu'au xixième Siècle. Par un Bibliophile Belge. Small 4to, pp. 508, stiff covers. 1868. £1, 10s.

DELEPIERRE.—TABLEAU DE LA LITTÉRATURE DU CENTON, CHEZ LES ANCIENS ET CHEZ LES MODERNES. Par Octave Delepierre. 2 vols, small 4to, pp. 324 and 318. Paper cover. 1875. £1, 1s.

DELEPIERRE.—L'ENFER : Essai Philosophique et Historique sur les Légendes de la Vie Future. Par Octave Delepierre. Crown 8vo, pp. 160, paper wrapper. 1876. 6s. Only 250 copies printed.

DENNYS.—A HANDBOOK OF THE CANTON VERNACULAR OF THE CHINESE LANGUAGE. Being a Series of Introductory Lessons for Domestic and Business Purposes. By N. B. Dennys, M.R.A.S., &c. Royal 8vo, pp. iv. and 228, cloth. 1874. 30s.

DENNYS.—A HANDBOOK OF MALAY COLLOQUIAL, as spoken in Singapore, being a Series of Introductory Lessons for Domestic and Business Purposes. By N. B. Dennys, Ph.D., F.R.G.S., M.R.A.S. Impl. 8vo, pp. vi. and 204, cloth. 1878. 21s.

DENNYS.—THE FOLK-LORE OF CHINA, AND ITS AFFINITIES WITH THAT OF THE ARYAN AND SEMITIC RACES. By N. B. Dennys, Ph.D., F.R.G.S., M.R.A.S. 8vo, pp. 166, cloth. 1876. 10s. 6d.

DE VALDES.—See VALDES.

DE VINNE.—THE INVENTION OF PRINTING : A Collection of Texts and Opinions. Description of Early Prints and Playing Cards, the Block-Books of the Fifteenth Century, the Legend of Lourens Janszoon Coster of Haarlem, and the Works of John Gutenberg and his Associates. Illustrated with Fac-similes of Early Types and Woodcuts. By Theo. L. De Vinne. Second Edition. In royal 8vo, elegantly printed, and bound in cloth, with embossed portraits, and a multitude of Fac-similes and Illustrations. 1877. £1 1s.

DICKSON.—WHO WAS SCOTLAND'S FIRST PRINTER? Ane Compendious and breue Tractate, in Commendation of Androw Myllar. Compylit be Robert Dickson, F.S.A. Scot. Fcap. 8vo, pp. 24, parchment wrapper. 1881. 1s.

DOBSON.—MONOGRAPH OF THE ASIATIC CHIROPTERA, and Catalogue of the Species of Bats in the Collection of the Indian Museum, Calcutta. By G. E. Dobson, M.A., M.B., F.L.S., &c. 8vo, pp. viii. and 228, cloth. 1876. 12s.

D'ORSEY.—A PRACTICAL GRAMMAR OF PORTUGUESE AND ENGLISH, exhibiting in a Series of Exercises, in Double Translation, the Idiomatic Structure of both Languages, as now written and spoken. Adapted to Ollendorff's System by the Rev. Alexander J. D. D'Orsey, of Corpus Christi College, Cambridge, and Lecturer on Public Reading and Speaking at King's College, London. Third Edition. 12mo, pp. viii. and 298, cloth. 1868. 7s.

DOUGLAS.—CHINESE-ENGLISH DICTIONARY OF THE VERNACULAR OR SPOKEN LANGUAGE OF AMOY, with the principal variations of the Chang-Chew and Chin-Chew Dialects. By the Rev. Carstairs Douglas, M.A., LL.D., Glasg., Missionary of the Presbyterian Church in England. High quarto, double columns, pp. 632, cloth. 1873. £3, 3s.

DOUGLAS.—CHINESE LANGUAGE AND LITERATURE. Two Lectures delivered at the Royal Institution, by R. K. Douglas, of the British Museum, and Professor of Chinese at King's College. Crown 8vo, pp. 118, cloth. 1875. 5s.

DOUGLAS.—THE LIFE OF JENGHIZ KHAN. Translated from the Chinese. With an Introduction. By Robert K. Douglas, of the British Museum, and Professor of Chinese at King's College. Crown 8vo, pp. xxxvi. and 106, cloth. 1877. 5s.
DOUGLAS.—POEMS: Lyrical and Dramatic. By Evelyn Douglas. Foolscap 8vo, pp. 256, cloth. 1885. 5s.
DOUGLAS.—THE QUEEN OF THE HID ISLE: An Allegory of Life and Art. And LOVE'S PERVERSITY; or, Eros and Anteros. A Drama. By Evelyn Douglas. Fcap. 8vo, pp. viii.-258, cloth. 1885. 5s.
DOWSON.—DICTIONARY OF HINDU MYTHOLOGY, &c. See Trübner's Oriental Series.
DOWSON.—A GRAMMAR OF THE URDŪ OR HINDŪSTĀNĪ LANGUAGE. By John Dowson, M.R.A.S., Professor of Hindūstānī, Staff College, Sandhurst. Crown 8vo, pp. xvi. and 264, with 8 Plates, cloth. 1872. 10s. 6d.
DOWSON.—A HINDŪSTĀNĪ EXERCISE BOOK; containing a Series of Passages and Extracts adapted for Translation into Hindūstānī. By John Dowson, M.R.A.S., Professor of Hindūstānī, Staff College, Sandhurst. Crown 8vo, pp. 100, limp cloth. 1872. 2s. 6d.
DUKA.—THE LIFE AND TRAVELS OF ALEXANDER CSOMA DE KÖRÖS: A Biography, compiled chiefly from hitherto Unpublished Data; With a Brief Notice of each of his Published Works and Essays, as well as of his still Extant Manuscripts. By Theodore Duka, Doctor of Medicine; Fellow of the Royal College of Surgeons of England; Surgeon-Major, Her Majesty's Bengal Medical Service, Retired; Knight of the Order of the Iron Crown; Corresponding Member of the Academy of Sciences of Hungary. Post 8vo, with Portrait, pp. xii.-234, cloth. 1885. 9s.
DUSAR.—A GRAMMAR OF THE GERMAN LANGUAGE; with Exercises. By P. Friedrich Dusar, First German Master in the Military Department of Cheltenham College. Second Edition. Crown 8vo, pp. viii. and 208, cloth. 1879. 4s. 6d.
DUSAR.—A GRAMMATICAL COURSE OF THE GERMAN LANGUAGE. By P. Friedrich Dusar. Third Edition. Crown 8vo, pp. x. and 134, cloth. 1883. 3s. 6d.
DYMOCK.—THE VEGETABLE MATERIA MEDICA OF WESTERN INDIA. By W. Dymock, Surgeon-Major Bombay Army, &c. &c. To be completed in four parts. 8vo, Part I., pp. 160; Part II., pp. 168; wrappers, 4s. each.
EARLY ENGLISH TEXT SOCIETY.—Subscription, one guinea per annum. *Extra Series.* Subscriptions—Small paper, one guinea; large paper, two guineas, per annum. List of publications on application.
EASTWICK.—KHIRAD AFROZ (the Illuminator of the Understanding). By Maulaví Hafízu'd-dín. A New Edition of the Hindústaní Text, carefully revised, with Notes, Critical and Explanatory. By Edward B. Eastwick, F.R.S., M.R.A.S., &c. Imperial 8vo, pp. xiv. and 319, cloth. Reissue, 1867. 18s.
EASTWICK.—THE GULISTAN. See Trübner's Oriental Series.
EBERS.—THE EMPEROR. A Romance. By Georg Ebers. Translated from the German by Clara Bell. In two volumes, 16mo, pp. iv. 319 and 322, cloth. 1881. 7s. 6d. Paper, 5s.
EBERS.—A QUESTION: The Idyl of a Picture by his friend, Alma Tadema. Related by Georg Ebers. From the German, by Mary J. SAFFORD. 16mo, pp. 125, with Frontispiece, cloth. 1881. 4s. Paper, 2s. 6d.
EBERS.—SERAPIS. A Romance. By Georg Ebers. From the German by Clara Bell. 16mo, pp. iv.-388, cloth. 1885. 4s. Paper, 2s. 6d.
ECHO (DEUTSCHES). THE GERMAN ECHO. A Faithful Mirror of German Conversation. By Ludwig Wolfram. With a Vocabulary. By Henry P. Skelton. Post 8vo, pp. 130 and 70, cloth. 1863. 3s.
ECHO FRANÇAIS. A PRACTICAL GUIDE TO CONVERSATION. By Fr. de la Fruston. With a complete Vocabulary. By Anthony Maw Border. Post 8vo, pp. 120 and 72, cloth. 1860. 3s.
ECO ITALIANO (L'). A PRACTICAL GUIDE TO ITALIAN CONVERSATION. By Eugene Camerini. With a complete Vocabulary. By Henry P. Skelton. Post 8vo, pp. vi., 128, and 98, cloth. 1860. 4s. 6d.
ECO DE MADRID. THE ECHO OF MADRID. A Practical Guide to Spanish Conversation. By J. E. Hartzenbusch and Henry Lemming. With a complete Vocabulary, containing copious Explanatory Remarks. By H_nry Lemming. Post 8vo, pp. xii., 144, and 83, cloth. 1860. 5s.

ECKSTEIN.—PRUSIAS: A Romance of Ancient Rome under the Republic. By Ernst Eckstein. From the German by Clara Bell. Two vols. 16mo, pp. 356 and 336, cloth. 1884. 7s. 6d.; paper, 5s.

ECKSTEIN. —QUINTUS CLAUDIUS. A Romance of Imperial Rome. By Ernst Eckstein. From the German by Clara Bell, Two vols. 16mo, pp. 314 and 304, cloth. 1884. 7s. 6d.; paper, 5s.

EDDA SÆMUNDAR HINNS FRODA. The Edda of Sæmund the Learned. Translated from the Old Norse, by Benjamin Thorpe. Complete in 1 vol. fcap. 8vo, pp. viii. and 152, and pp. viii. and 170, cloth. 1866. 7s. 6d.

EDGREN.—SANSKRIT GRAMMAR. See Trübner's Collection.

EDKINS.—CHINA'S PLACE IN PHILOLOGY. An attempt to show that the Languages of Europe and Asia have a common origin. By the Rev. Joseph Edkins. Crown 8vo, pp. xxiii. and 403, cloth. 1871. 10s. 6d.

EDKINS.—INTRODUCTION TO THE STUDY OF THE CHINESE CHARACTERS. By J. Edkins, D.D., Peking, China. Royal 8vo, pp. 340, paper boards. 1876. 18s.

EDKINS.—RELIGION IN CHINA. See English and Foreign Philosophical Library, Vol. VIII., or Trübner's Oriental Series.

EDKINS.—CHINESE BUDDHISM. See Trübner's Oriental Series.

EDMONDS.—GREEK LAYS, IDYLLS, LEGENDS, &c. A Selection from Recent and Contemporary Poets. Translated by E. M. Edmonds. With Introduction and Notes. Crown 8vo, pp. xiv. and 264, cloth. 1885. 6s. 6d.

EDMUNDSON.—MILTON AND VONDEL: a Curiosity of Literature. By George Edmundson, M.A., Late Fellow and Tutor of Brasenose College, Oxford, Vicar of Northolt, Middlesex. Crown 8vo, pp.   , cloth.

EDWARDS.—MEMOIRS OF LIBRARIES, together with a Practical Handbook of Library Economy. By Edward Edwards. Numerous Illustrations. 2 vols. royal 8vo, cloth. Vol. i. pp. xxviii. and 841; Vol. ii. pp. xxxvi. and 1104. 1859. £2, 8s.
DITTO, large paper, imperial 8vo, cloth. £4, 4s.

EDWARDS.—CHAPTERS OF THE BIOGRAPHICAL HISTORY OF THE FRENCH ACADEMY. 1629-1863. With an Appendix relating to the Unpublished Chronicle "Liber de Hyda." By Edward Edwards. 8vo, pp. 180, cloth. 1864. 6s.
DITTO, large paper, royal 8vo. 10s. 6d.

EDWARDS.—LIBRARIES AND FOUNDERS OF LIBRARIES. By Edward Edwards. 8vo, pp. xix. and 506, cloth. 1865. 18s.
DITTO, large paper, imperial 8vo, cloth. £1, 10s.

EDWARDS.—FREE TOWN LIBRARIES, their Formation, Management, and History in Britain, France, Germany, and America. Together with Brief Notices of Book Collectors, and of the respective Places of Deposit of their Surviving Collections. By Edward Edwards. 8vo, pp. xvi. and 634, cloth. 1869. 21s.

EDWARDS.—LIVES OF THE FOUNDERS OF THE BRITISH MUSEUM, with Notices of its Chief Augmentors and other Benefactors. 1570-1870. By Edward Edwards. With Illustrations and Plans. 2 vols. 8vo, pp. xii. and 780, cloth. 1870. 30s.

EDWARDES.—See ENGLISH AND FOREIGN PHILOSOPHICAL LIBRARY, Vol. XVII.

EGER.—TECHNOLOGICAL DICTIONARY IN THE ENGLISH AND GERMAN LANGUAGES. Edited by Gustav Eger, Professor of the Polytechnic School of Darmstadt, and Sworn Translator of the Grand Ducal Ministerial Departments. Technically Revised and Enlarged by Otto Brandes, Chemist. Two vols., royal 8vo, pp. viii. and 712, and pp. viii. and 970, cloth. 1884. £1, 7s.

EGER AND GRIME.—An Early English Romance. Edited from Bishop Percy's Folio Manuscripts, about 1650 A.D. By J. W. Hales, M.A., Fellow of Christ's College, Cambridge, and F. J. Furnivall, M.A., of Trinity Hall, Cambridge. 4to, large paper, half bound, Roxburghe style, pp. 64. 1867. 10s. 6d.

EGERTON.—SUSSEX FOLK AND SUSSEX WAYS. Stray Studies in the Wealden Formation of Human Nature. By the Rev. J. Coker Egerton, M.A., Rector of Burwash. Crown 8vo, pp. 140, cloth. 1884. 2s.

EGGELING.—See AUCTORES SANSKRITI, Vols. IV. and V.

EGYPT EXPLORATION FUND :—
THE STORE-CITY OF PITHOM, and the Route of the Exodus. By Edouard Naville. 4to, pp. viii. and 32, with Thirteen Plates and Two Maps, boards. 1885. 25s.

EGYPTIAN GENERAL STAFF PUBLICATIONS :—
GENERAL REPORT ON THE PROVINCE OF KORDOFAN. Submitted to General C. P. Stone, Chief of the General Staff Egyptian Army. By Major H. G. Prout, Commanding Expedition of Reconnaissance. Made at El-Obeiyad (Kordofan), March 12th, 1876. Royal 8vo, pp. 232, stitched, with 6 Maps. 1877. 10s. 6d.

PROVINCES OF THE EQUATOR: Summary of Letters and Reports of the Governor-General. Part 1. 1874. Royal 8vo, pp. viii. and 90, stitched, with Map. 1877. 5s.

REPORT ON THE SEIZURE BY THE ABYSSINIANS of the Geological and Mineralogical Reconnaissance Expedition attached to the General Staff of the Egyptian Army. By L. H. Mitchell, Chief of the Expedition. Containing an Account of the subsequent Treatment of the Prisoners and Final Release of the Commander. Royal 8vo, pp. xii. and 126, stitched, with a Map. 1878. 7s. 6d.

EGYPTIAN CALENDAR for the year 1295 A.H. (1878 A.D.): Corresponding with the years 1594, 1595 of the Koptic Era. 8vo, pp. 98, sewed. 1878. 2s. 6d.

EHRLICH.—FRENCH READER : With Notes and Vocabulary. By H. W. Ehrlich. 12mo, pp. viii. and 125, limp cloth. 1877. 1s. 6d.

EITEL.—BUDDHISM: Its Historical, Theoretical, and Popular Aspects. In Three Lectures. By E. J. Eitel, M.A., Ph.D. Third Revised Edition. Demy 8vo, pp. x.-146. 1884. 5s.

EITEL.—FENG-SHUI; or, The Rudiments of Natural Science in China. By E. J. Eitel, M.A., Ph.D. Royal 8vo, pp. vi. and 84, sewed. 1873. 6s.

EITEL.—HANDBOOK FOR THE STUDENT OF CHINESE BUDDHISM. By the Rev. E. J. Eitel, of the London Missionary Society. Crown 8vo, pp. viii. and 224, cloth. 1870. 18s.

ELLIOT.—MEMOIRS ON THE HISTORY, FOLK-LORE, AND DISTRIBUTION OF THE RACES OF THE NORTH-WESTERN PROVINCES OF INDIA. By the late Sir Henry M. Elliot, K.C.B. Edited, revised, and rearranged by John Beames, M.R.A.S., &c., &c. In 2 vols. demy 8vo, pp. xx., 370, and 396, with 3 large coloured folding Maps, cloth. 1869. £1 16s.

ELLIOT.—THE HISTORY OF INDIA, as told by its own Historians. The Muhammadan Period. Edited from the Posthumous Papers of the late Sir H. M. Elliot, K.C.B., East India Company's Bengal Civil Service. Revised and continued by Professor John Dowson, M.R.A.S., Staff College, Sandhurst. 8vo. Vol. I.—Vol. II., pp. x. and 580, cloth. Vol. III., pp. xii. and 627, cloth. 24s.—Vol. IV., pp. xii. and 564, cloth. 1872. 21s.—Vol. V., pp. x. and 576, cloth. 1873. 21s.—Vol. VI., pp. viii. 574, cloth. 21s.—Vol VII., pp. viii.-574. 1877. 21s. Vol. VIII., pp. xxxii.-444. With Biographical, Geographical, and General Index. 1877. 24s. Complete sets, £8, 8s. Vols. I. and II. not sold separately.

ELLIS.—ETRUSCAN NUMERALS. By Robert Ellis, B.D., late Fellow of St. John's College, Cambridge. 8vo, pp. 52, sewed. 1876. 2s. 6d.

ELY.—FRENCH AND GERMAN SOCIALISM IN MODERN TIMES. By R. T. Ely, Ph.D., Associate Professor of Political Economy in the Johns Hopkins University, Baltimore; and Lecturer on Political Economy in Cornell University, Ithaca, N. Y. Crown 8vo, pp. viii.-274, cloth. 1884. 3s. 6d.

EMERSON AT HOME AND ABROAD. See English and Foreign Philosophical Library, Vol. XIX.

EMERSON.—INDIAN MYTHS; or, Legends, Traditions, and Symbols of the Aborigines of America, compared with those of other Countries, including Hindostan, Egypt, Persia, Assyria, and China. By Ellen Russell Emerson. Illustrated. Post 8vo, pp. viii.-678, cloth. 1884. £1, 1s.

ENGLISH DIALECT SOCIETY.—Subscription, 10s. 6d. per annum. List of publications on application.

ENGLISH AND FOREIGN PHILOSOPHICAL LIBRARY (THE).
Post 8vo, cloth, uniformly bound.

I. to III.—A HISTORY OF MATERIALISM, and Criticism of its present Importance. By Professor F. A. Lange. Authorised Translation from the German by Ernest C. Thomas. In three volumes. Vol. I. Second Edition. pp. 350. 1878. 10s. 6d.—Vol. II., pp. viii. and 298. 1880. 10s. 6d.—Vol. III., pp. viii. and 376. 1881. 10s. 6d.

IV.—NATURAL LAW: an Essay in Ethics. By Edith Simcox. Second Edition. Pp. 366. 1878. 10s. 6d.

V and VI.—THE CREED OF CHRISTENDOM; its Foundations contrasted with Superstructure. By W. R. Greg. Eighth Edition, with a New Introduction. In two volumes, pp. cxiv.-154 and vi.-282. 1883. 15s.

VII.—OUTLINES OF THE HISTORY OF RELIGION TO THE SPREAD OF THE UNIVERSAL RELIGIONS. By Prof. C. P. Tiele. Translated from the Dutch by J. Estlin Carpenter, M.A., with the author's assistance. Third Edition. Pp. xx. and 250. 1884. 7s. 6d.

VIII.—RELIGION IN CHINA; containing a brief Account of the Three Religions of the Chinese; with Observations on the Prospects of Christian Conversion amongst that People. By Joseph Edkins, D.D., Peking. Third Edition. Pp. xvi. and 260. 1884. 7s. 6d.

IX.—A CANDID EXAMINATION OF THEISM. By Physicus. Pp. 216. 1878. 7s. 6d.

X.—THE COLOUR-SENSE; its Origin and Development; an Essay in Comparative Psychology. By Grant Allen, B.A., author of "Physiological Æsthetics." Pp. xii. and 282. 1879. 10s. 6d.

XI.—THE PHILOSOPHY OF MUSIC; being the substance of a Course of Lectures delivered at the Royal Institution of Great Britain in February and March 1877. By William Pole, F.R.S., F.R.S.E., Mus. Doc., Oxon. Pp. 336. 1879. 10s. 6d.

XII.—CONTRIBUTIONS TO THE HISTORY OF THE DEVELOPMENT OF THE HUMAN RACE: Lectures and Dissertations, by Lazarus Geiger. Translated from the German by D. Asher, Ph.D. Pp. x. and 156. 1880. 6s.

XIII.—DR. APPLETON: his Life and Literary Relics. By J. H. Appleton, M.A., and A. H. Sayce, M.A. Pp. 350. 1881. 10s. 6d.

XIV.—EDGAR QUINET: His Early Life and Writings. By Richard Heath. With Portraits, Illustrations, and an Autograph Letter. Pp. xxiii. and 370. 1881. 12s. 6d.

XV.—THE ESSENCE OF CHRISTIANITY. By Ludwig Feuerbach. Translated from the German by Marian Evans, translator of Strauss's "Life of Jesus." Second Edition. Pp. xx. and 340. 1881. 7s. 6d.

XVI.—AUGUSTE COMTE AND POSITIVISM. By the late John Stuart Mill, M.P. Third Edition. Pp. 200. 1882. 3s. 6d.

XVII.—ESSAYS AND DIALOGUES OF GIACOMO LEOPARDI. Translated by Charles Edwardes. With Biographical Sketch. Pp. xliv. and 216. 1882. 7s. 6d.

XVIII.—RELIGION AND PHILOSOPHY IN GERMANY: A Fragment. By Heinrich Heine. Translated by J. Snodgrass. Pp. xii. and 178, cloth. 1882. 6s.

XIX.—EMERSON AT HOME AND ABROAD. By M. D. Conway. Pp. viii. and 310. With Portrait. 1883. 10s. 6d.

XX.—ENIGMAS OF LIFE. By W. R. Greg. Fifteenth Edition, with a Postscript. CONTENTS: Realisable Ideals—Malthus Notwithstanding—Non-Survival of the Fittest—Limits and Directions of Human Development—The Significance of Life—De Profundis—Elsewhere—Appendix. Pp. xx. and 314, cloth. 1883. 10s. 6d.

ENGLISH AND FOREIGN PHILOSOPHICAL LIBRARY—continued.

XXI.—ETHIC DEMONSTRATED IN GEOMETRICAL ORDER AND DIVIDED INTO FIVE PARTS, which treat (1) Of God, (2) Of the Nature and Origin of the Mind, (3) Of the Origin and Nature of the Affects, (4) Of Human Bondage, or of the Strength of the Affects, (5) Of the Power of the Intellect, or of Human Liberty. By Benedict de Spinoza. Translated from the Latin by William Hale White. Pp. 328. 1883. 10s. 6d.

XXII.—THE WORLD AS WILL AND IDEA. By Arthur Schopenhauer. Translated from the German by R. B. Haldane, M.A., and John Kemp, M.A. 3 vols. Vol. I., pp. xxxii.-532. 1883. 18s.

XXV. to XXVII.—THE PHILOSOPHY OF THE UNCONSCIOUS. By Eduard Von Hartmann. Speculative Results, according to the Inductive Method of Physical Science. Authorised Translation, by William C. Coupland, M.A. 3 vols. pp. xxxii.-372; vi.-368; viii.-360. 1884. 31s. 6d.

XXVIII. to XXX.—THE GUIDE OF THE PERPLEXED OF MAIMONIDES. Translated from the Original Text and Annotated by M. Friedlander, Ph.D. 3 vols., pp.

Extra Series.

I. and II.—LESSING: His Life and Writings. By James Sime, M.A. Second Edition. 2 vols., pp. xxii. and 328, and xvi. and 358, with portraits. 1879. 21s.

III. and VI.—AN ACCOUNT OF THE POLYNESIAN RACE: its Origin and Migrations, and the Ancient History of the Hawaiian People to the Times of Kamehameha I. By Abraham Fornander, Circuit Judge of the Island of Maui, H.I. Vol. I., pp. xvi. and 248. 1877. 7s. 6d. Vol. II., pp. viii. and 400, cloth. 1880. 10s. 6d.

IV. and V.—ORIENTAL RELIGIONS, and their Relation to Universal Religion—India. By Samuel Johnson. In 2 vols., pp. viii. and 408; viii. and 402. 1879. 21s.

VI.—AN ACCOUNT OF THE POLYNESIAN RACE. By A. Fornander. Vol. II., pp. viii. and 400, cloth. 1880. 10s. 6d.

ER SIE ES.—FACSIMILE OF A MANUSCRIPT supposed to have been found in an Egyptian Tomb by the English soldiers last year. Royal 8vo, in ragged canvas covers, with string binding, with dilapidated edges (? just as discovered). 1884. 6s. 6d.

EYTON.—DOMESDAY STUDIES: AN ANALYSIS AND DIGEST OF THE STAFFORDSHIRE SURVEY. Treating of the Method of Domesday in its Relation to Staffordshire. &c. By the Rev. R. W. Eyton. 4to, pp. vii. and 135, cloth. 1881. £1, 1s.

FABER.—THE MIND OF MENCIUS. See Trübner's Oriental Series.

FALKE.—ART IN THE HOUSE. Historical, Critical, and Æsthetical Studies on the Decoration and Furnishing of the Dwelling. By J. von Falke, Vice-Director of the Austrian Museum of Art and Industry at Vienna. Translated from the German. Edited, with Notes, by C. C. Perkins, M.A. Royal 8vo, pp. xxx, 356, cloth. With Coloured Frontispiece, 60 Plates, and over 150 Illustrations. 1878. £3.

FARLEY.—EGYPT, CYPRUS, AND ASIATIC TURKEY. By J. L. Farley, author of "The Resources of Turkey," &c. 8vo, pp. xvi. and 270, cloth gilt. 1878. 10s. 6d.

FAUSBOLL.—See JATAKA.

FEATHERMAN.—THE SOCIAL HISTORY OF THE RACES OF MANKIND. By A. Featherman. Demy 8vo, cloth. Vol. I. THE NIGRITIANS. Pp. xxvi. and 800. 1885. £1, 11s. 6d. Vol. V. THE ARAMÆANS. Pp. xvii. and 664. 1881. £1, 1s.

FENTON.—EARLY HEBREW LIFE: a Study in Sociology. By John Fenton. 8vo, pp. xxiv. and 102, cloth. 1880. 5s.

FERGUSSON.—ARCHÆOLOGY IN INDIA. With especial reference to the works of Babu Rajendralala Mitra. By James Fergusson, C.I.E., F.R.S., D.C.L., LL.D., V.-P.R.A.S., &c. Demy 8vo, pp. 116, with Illustrations, sewed. 1884. 5s.

FERGUSSON.—The Temple of Diana at Ephesus. With Especial Reference to Mr. Wood's Discoveries of its Remains. By James Fergusson, C.I.E., D.C.L., LL.D., F.R.S., &c. From the Transactions of the Royal Institute of British Architects. Demy 4to, pp. 24, with Plan, cloth. 1883. 5s.

FERGUSSON AND BURGESS.—The Cave Temples of India. By James Fergusson, D.C.L., F.R.S., and James Burgess, F.R.G.S. Impl. 8vo, pp. xx. and 536, with 98 Plates, half bound. 1880. £2, 2s.

FERGUSSON.—Chinese Researches. First Part. Chinese Chronology and Cycles. By Thomas Fergusson, Member of the North China Branch of the Royal Asiatic Society. Crown 8vo, pp. viii. and 274, sewed. 1881. 10s. 6d.

FEUERBACH.—The Essence of Christianity. See English and Foreign Philosophical Library, vol. XV.

FICHTE.—J. G. Fichte's Popular Works: The Nature of the Scholar—The Vocation of Man—The Doctrine of Religion. With a Memoir by William Smith, LL.D. Demy 8vo, pp. viii. and 564, cloth. 1873. 15s.

FICHTE.—Characteristics of the Present Age. By J. G. Fichte. Translated from the German by W. Smith. Post 8vo, pp. xi. and 271, cloth. 1847. 6s.

FICHTE.—Memoir of Johann Gottlieb Fichte. By William Smith. Second Edition. Post 8vo, pp. 168, cloth. 1848. 4s.

FICHTE.—On the Nature of the Scholar, and its Manifestations. By Johann Gottlieb Fichte. Translated from the German by William Smith. Second Edition. Post 8vo, pp. vii. and 131, cloth. 1848. 3s.

FICHTE.—New Exposition of the Science of Knowledge. By J. G. Fichte. Translated from the German by A. E. Krœger. 8vo, pp. vi. and 182, cloth. 1869. 6s.

FIELD.—Outlines of an International Code. By David Dudley Field. Second Edition. Royal 8vo, pp. iii. and 712, sheep. 1876. £2, 2s.

FIGANIERE.—Elva: A Story of the Dark Ages. By Viscount de Figanière, G.C. St. Anne, &c. Crown 8vo, pp. viii. and 194, cloth. 1878. 5s.

FINN.—Persian for Travellers. By Alexander Finn, F.R.G.S., &c., H.B.M. Consul at Resht. Oblong 32mo, pp. xxii.-232, cloth. 1884. 5s.

FISKE.—The Unseen World, and other Essays. By John Fiske, M.A., LL.B. Crown 8vo, pp. 350. 1876. 10s.

FISKE.—Myths and Myth-Makers; Old Tales and Superstitions, interpreted by Comparative Mythology. By John Fiske, M.A., LL.B., Assistant Librarian, and late Lecturer on Philosophy at Harvard University. Crown 8vo, pp. 260, cloth. 1873. 10s.

FITZGERALD.—Australian Orchids. By R. D. Fitzgerald, F.L.S. Folio.—Part I. 7 Plates.—Part II. 10 Plates.—Part III. 10 Plates.—Part IV. 10 Plates.—Part V. 10 Plates.—Part VI. 10 Plates. Each Part, Coloured 21s.; Plain, 10s. 6d. —Part VII. 10 Plates. Vol. II., Part I. 10 Plates. Each, Coloured, 25s.

FITZGERALD.—An Essay on the Philosophy of Self-Consciousness. Comprising an Analysis of Reason and the Rationale of Love. By P. F. Fitzgerald. Demy 8vo, pp. xvi. and 196, cloth. 1882. 5s.

FORJETT.—External Evidences of Christianity. By E. H. Forjett. 8vo, pp. 114, cloth. 1874. 2s. 6d.

FORNANDER.—The Polynesian Race. See English and Foreign Philosophical Library, Extra Series, Vols. III. and VI.

FORSTER.—Political Presentments.—By William Forster, Agent-General for New South Wales. Crown 8vo, pp. 122, cloth. 1878. 4s. 6d.

FOULKES.—The Daya Bhaga, the Law of Inheritance of the Sarasvati Vilasa. The Original Sanskrit Text, with Translation by the Rev. Thos. Foulkes, F.L.S., M.R.A.S., F.R.G.S., Fellow of the University of Madras, &c. Demy 8vo, pp. xxvi. and 194-162, cloth. 1881. 10s. 6d.

FOX.—Memorial Edition of Collected Works, by W. J. Fox. 12 vols. 8vo, cloth. £3.

FRANKLYN.—OUTLINES OF MILITARY LAW, AND THE LAWS OF EVIDENCE. By H. B. Franklyn, LL.B. Crown 16mo, pp. viii. and 152, cloth. 1874. 3s. 6d.

FREEMAN.—LECTURES TO AMERICAN AUDIENCES. By E. A. Freeman, D.C.L., LL.D., Honorary Fellow of Trinity College, Oxford. I. The English People in its Three Homes. II. The Practical Bearings of General European History. Post 8vo. pp. viii.–454, cloth. 1883. 8s. 6d.

FRIEDRICH.—PROGRESSIVE GERMAN READER, with Copious Notes to the First Part. By P. Friedrich. Crown 8vo, pp. 166, cloth. 1868. 4s. 6d.

FRIEDRICH.—A GRAMMATICAL COURSE OF THE GERMAN LANGUAGE. See under DUSAR.

FRIEDRICH.—A GRAMMAR OF THE GERMAN LANGUAGE, WITH EXERCISES. See under DUSAR.

FRIEDERICI.—BIBLIOTHECA ORIENTALIS, or a Complete List of Books, Papers, Serials, and Essays, published in England and the Colonies, Germany and France, on the History, Geography, Religions, Antiquities, Literature, and Languages of the East. Compiled by Charles Friederici. 8vo, boards. 1876, 2s. 6d. 1877, 3s. 1878, 3s. 6d. 1879, 3s. 1880, 3s. 1881, 3s. 1882, 3s. 1883, 3s. 6d.

FRŒMBLING.—GRADUATED GERMAN READER. Consisting of a Selection from the most Popular Writers, arranged progressively; with a complete Vocabulary for the first part. By Friedrich Otto Frœmbling. Eighth Edition. 12mo, pp. viii. and 306, cloth. 1883. 3s. 6d.

FRŒMBLING.—GRADUATED EXERCISES FOR TRANSLATION INTO GERMAN. Consisting of Extracts from the best English Authors, arranged progressively; with an Appendix, containing Idiomatic Notes. By Friedrich Otto Frœmbling, Ph.D., Principal German Master at the City of London School. Crown 8vo, pp. xiv. and 322, cloth. With Notes, pp. 66. 1867. 4s. 6d. Without Notes, 4s.

FROUDE.—THE BOOK OF JOB. By J. A. Froude, M.A., late Fellow of Exeter College, Oxford. Reprinted from the *Westminster Review*. 8vo, pp. 38, cloth. 1s.

FRUSTON.—ECHO FRANÇAIS. A Practical Guide to French Conversation. By F. de la Fruston. With a Vocabulary. 12mo, pp. vi. and 192, cloth. 3s.

FRYER.—THE KHYENG PEOPLE OF THE SANDOWAY DISTRICT, ARAKAN. By G. E. Fryer, Major, M.S.C., Deputy Commissioner, Sandoway. With 2 Plates. 8vo, pp. 44, cloth. 1875. 3s. 6d.

FRYER.—PÁLI STUDIES. No. I. Analysis, and Páli Text of the Subodhálankara, or Easy Rhetoric, by Sangharakkhita Thera. 8vo, pp. 35, cloth. 1875. 3s. 6d.

FURNIVALL.—EDUCATION IN EARLY ENGLAND. Some Notes used as forewords to a Collection of Treatises on "Manners and Meals in Olden Times," for the Early English Text Society. By Frederick J. Furnivall, M.A. 8vo, pp. 4 and lxxiv., sewed. 1867. 1s.

GALDOS.—TRAFALGAR: A Tale. By B. Perez Galdos. From the Spanish by Clara Bell. 16mo, pp. 256, cloth. 1884. 4s. Paper, 2s. 6d.

GALDOS.—MARIANELA. By B. Perez Galdos. From the Spanish, by Clara Bell. 16mo, pp. 264, cloth. 1883. 4s. Paper, 2s. 6d.

GALDOS.—GLORIA: A Novel. By B. Perez Galdos. From the Spanish, by Clara Bell. Two volumes, 16mo, pp. vi. and 318, iv. and 362, cloth. 1883. 7s. 6d. Paper, 5s.

GALLOWAY.—A TREATISE ON FUEL. Scientific and Practical. By Robert Galloway, M.R.I.A., F.C.S., &c. With Illustrations. Post 8vo, pp. x. and 136, cloth. 1880. 6s.

GALLOWAY.—EDUCATION: SCIENTIFIC AND TECHNICAL; or, How the Inductive Sciences are Taught, and How they Ought to be Taught. By Robert Galloway, M.R.I.A., F.C.S. 8vo, pp. xvi. and 462, cloth. 1881. 10s. 6d.

GAMBLE.—A MANUAL OF INDIAN TIMBERS: An Account of the Structure, Growth, Distribution, and Qualities of Indian Woods. By J. C. Gamble, M.A., F.L.S. 8vo, pp. xxx. and 522, with a Map, cloth. 1881. 10s.

GARBE.—See AUCTORES SANSKRITI, Vol. III.

GARFIELD.—THE LIFE AND PUBLIC SERVICE OF JAMES A. GARFIELD, Twentieth President of the United States. A Biographical Sketch. By Captain F. H. Mason, late of the 42d Regiment, U.S.A. With a Preface by Bret Harte. Crown 8vo, pp. vi. and 134, cloth. With Portrait. 1881. 2s. 6d.

GARRETT.—A CLASSICAL DICTIONARY OF INDIA : Illustrative of the Mythology, Philosophy, Literature, Antiquities, Arts, Manners, Customs, &c., of the Hindus. By John Garrett, Director of Public Instruction in Mysore. 8vo, pp. x. and 794, cloth. With Supplement, pp. 160. 1871 and 1873. £1, 16s.

GAUTAMA.—THE INSTITUTES OF. See AUCTORES SANSKRITI, Vol. II.

GAZETTEER OF THE CENTRAL PROVINCES OF INDIA. Edited by Charles Grant, Secretary to the Chief Commissioner of the Central Provinces. Second Edition. With a very large folding Map of the Central Provinces of India. Demy 8vo, pp. clvii. and 582, cloth. 1870. £1, 4s.

GEIGER.—A PEEP AT MEXICO ; Narrative of a Journey across the Republic from the Pacific to the Gulf, in December 1873 and January 1874. By J. L. Geiger, F.R.G.S. Demy 8vo, pp. 368, with Maps and 45 Original Photographs. Cloth, 24s.

GEIGER.—CONTRIBUTIONS TO THE HISTORY OF THE DEVELOPMENT OF THE HUMAN RACE : Lectures and Dissertations, by Lazarus Geiger. Translated from the Second German Edition, by David Asher, Ph.D. Post 8vo, pp. x.-156, cloth. 1880. 6s.

GELDART.—FAITH AND FREEDOM. Fourteen Sermons. By E. M. Geldart, M.A. Crown 8vo, pp. vi. and 168, cloth. 1881. 4s. 6d.

GELDART.—A GUIDE TO MODERN GREEK. By E. M. Geldart, M.A. Post 8vo, pp. xii. and 274, cloth. 1883. 7s. 6d. Key, pp. 28, cloth. 1883. 2s. 6d.

GELDART.—GREEK GRAMMAR. See Trübner's Collection.

GEOLOGICAL MAGAZINE (THE) : OR, MONTHLY JOURNAL OF GEOLOGY. With which is incorporated "The Geologist." Edited by Henry Woodward, LL.D., F.R.S., F.G.S., &c., of the British Museum. Assisted by Professor John Morris, M.A., F.G.S., &c., and Robert Etheridge, F.R.S., L. & E., F.G.S., &c., of the Museum of Practical Geology. 8vo, cloth. 1866 to 1884. 20s. each.

GHOSE.—THE MODERN HISTORY OF THE INDIAN CHIEFS, RAJAS, ZAMINDARS, &c. By Loke Nath Ghose. 2 vols. post 8vo, pp. xii. and 218, and xviii. and 612, cloth. 1883. 21s.

GILES.—CHINESE SKETCHES.—By Herbert A. Giles, of H.B.M.'s China Consular Service. 8vo, pp. 204, cloth. 1875. 10s. 6d.

GILES.—A DICTIONARY OF COLLOQUIAL IDIOMS IN THE MANDARIN DIALECT. By Herbert A. Giles. 4to, pp. 65, half bound. 1873. 28s.

GILES.—SYNOPTICAL STUDIES IN CHINESE CHARACTER. By Herbert A. Giles. 8vo, pp. 118, half bound. 1874. 15s.

GILES.—CHINESE WITHOUT A TEACHER. Being a Collection of Easy and Useful Sentences in the Mandarin Dialect. With a Vocabulary. By Herbert A. Giles. 12mo, pp. 60, half bound. 1872. 5s.

GILES.—THE SAN TZU CHING ; or, Three Character Classic ; and the Ch'Jen Tsu Wen ; or, Thousand Character Essay. Metrically Translated by Herbert A. Giles. 12mo, pp. 28, half bound. 1873. 2s. 6d.

GLASS.—ADVANCE THOUGHT. By Charles E. Glass. Crown 8vo, pp. xxxvi. and 188, cloth. 1876. 6s.

GOETHE'S FAUST.—See SCOONES and WYSARD.

GOETHE'S MINOR POEMS.—See SELSS.

GOLDSTÜCKER.—A DICTIONARY, SANSKRIT AND ENGLISH, extended and improved from the Second Edition of the Dictionary of Professor H. H. Wilson, with his sanction and concurrence. Together with a Supplement, Grammatical Appendices, and an Index, serving as a Sanskrit-English Vocabulary. By Theodore Goldstücker. Parts I. to VI. 4to, pp. 400. 1856-63. 6s. each.

GOLDSTÜCKER.—See AUCTORES SANSKRITI, Vol. I.

GOOROO SIMPLE. Strange Surprising Adventures of the Venerable G. S. and his Five Disciples, Noodle, Doodle, Wiseacre, Zany, and Foozle ; adorned with Fifty Illustrations, drawn on wood, by Alfred Crowquill. A companion Volume to "Münchhausen" and "Owlglass," based upon the famous Tamul tale of the Gooroo Paramartan, and exhibiting, in the form of a skilfully-constructed consecutive narrative, some of the finest specimens of Eastern wit and humour. Elegantly printed on tinted paper, in crown 8vo, pp. 223, richly gilt ornamental cover, gilt edges. 1861. 10s. 6d.

GORKOM.—HANDBOOK OF CINCHONA CULTURE. By K. W. Van Gorkom, formerly Director of the Government Cinchona Plantations in Java. Translated by B. D. Jackson, Secretary of the Linnæan Society of London. With a Coloured Illustration. Imperial 8vo, pp. xii. and 292, cloth. 1882. £2.

GOUGH.—The SARVA-DARSANA-SAMGRAHA. See Trübner's Oriental Series.

GOUGH.—PHILOSOPHY OF THE UPANISHADS. See Trübner's Oriental Series.

GOVER.—THE FOLK-SONGS OF SOUTHERN INDIA. By C. E. Gover, Madras. Contents: Canarese Songs ; Badaga Songs ; Coorg Songs ; Tamil Songs ; The Cural ; Malayalam Songs ; Telugu Songs. 8vo, pp. xxviii. and 300, cloth. 1872. 10s. 6d.

GRAY.—DARWINIANA : Essays and Reviews pertaining [to Darwinism. By Asa Gray. Crown 8vo, pp. xii. and 396, cloth. 1877. 10s.

GRAY.—NATURAL SCIENCE AND RELIGION : Two Lectures Delivered to the Theological School of Yale College. By Asa Gray. Crown 8vo, pp. 112, cloth. 1880. 5s.

GREEN.—SHAKESPEARE AND THE EMBLEM-WRITERS : An Exposition of their Similarities of Thought and Expression. Preceded by a View of the Emblem-Book Literature down to A.D. 1616. By Henry Green, M.A. In one volume, pp. xvi. 572, profusely illustrated with Woodcuts and Photolith. Plates, elegantly bound in cloth gilt. 1870. Large medium 8vo, £1, 11s. 6d. ; large imperial 8vo, £2, 12s. 6d.

GREEN.—ANDREA ALCIATI, and his Books of Emblems : A Biographical and Bibliographical Study. By Henry Green, M.A. With Ornamental Title, Portraits, and other Illustrations. Dedicated to Sir William Stirling-Maxwell, Bart., Rector of the University of Edinburgh. Only 250 copies printed. Demy 8vo, pp. 360, handsomely bound. 1872. £1, 1s.

GREENE.—A NEW METHOD OF LEARNING TO READ, WRITE, AND SPEAK THE FRENCH LANGUAGE ; or, First Lessons in French (Introductory to Ollendorff's Larger Grammar). By G. W. Greene, Instructor in Modern Languages in Brown University. Third Edition, enlarged and rewritten. Fcap. 8vo, pp. 248, cloth. 1869. 3s. 6d.

GREENE.—THE HEBREW MIGRATION FROM EGYPT. By J. Baker Greene, LL.B., M.B., Trin. Coll., Dub. Second Edition. Demy 8vo, pp. xii. and 440, cloth. 1882. 10s. 6d.

GREG.—TRUTH VERSUS EDIFICATION. By W. R. Greg. Fcap. 8vo, pp. 32, cloth. 1869. 1s.

GREG.—WHY ARE WOMEN REDUNDANT ? By W. R. Greg. Fcap. 8vo, pp. 40, cloth. 1869. 1s.

GREG.—LITERARY AND SOCIAL JUDGMENTS. By W. R. Greg. Fourth Edition, considerably enlarged. 2 vols. crown 8vo, pp. 310 and 288, cloth. 1877. 15s.

GREG.—MISTAKEN AIMS AND ATTAINABLE IDEALS OF THE ARTISAN CLASS. By W. R. Greg. Crown 8vo, pp. vi. and 332, cloth. 1876. 10s. 6d.

GREG.—ENIGMAS OF LIFE. By W. R. Greg. Fifteenth Edition, with a postscript. Contents: Realisable Ideals. Malthus Notwithstanding. Non-Survival of the Fittest. Limits and Directions of Human Development. The Significance of Life. De Profundis. Elsewhere. Appendix. Post 8vo, pp. xxii. and 314, cloth. 1883. 10s. 6d.

GREG.—POLITICAL PROBLEMS FOR OUR AGE AND COUNTRY. By W. R. Greg. Contents: I. Constitutional and Autocratic Statesmanship. II. England's Future Attitude and Mission. III. Disposal of the Criminal Classes. IV. Recent Change in the Character of English Crime. V. The Intrinsic Vice of Trade-Unions. VI. Industrial and Co-operative Partnerships. VII. The Economic Problem. VIII. Political Consistency. IX. The Parliamentary Career. X. The Price we pay for Self-government. XI. Vestryism. XII. Direct v. Indirect Taxation. XIII. The New Régime, and how to meet it. Demy 8vo, pp. 342, cloth. 1870. 10s. 6d.

GREG.—THE GREAT DUEL: Its True Meaning and Issues. By W. R. Greg. Crown 8vo, pp. 96, cloth. 1871. 2s. 6d.

GREG.—THE CREED OF CHRISTENDOM. See English and Foreign Philosophical Library, Vols. V. and VI.

GREG.—ROCKS AHEAD; or, The Warnings of Cassandra. By W. R. Greg. Second Edition, with a Reply to Objectors. Crown 8vo, pp. xliv. and 236, cloth. 1874. 9s.

GREG.—MISCELLANEOUS ESSAYS. By W. R. Greg. First Series. Crown 8vo, pp. iv.-268, cloth. 1881. 7s. 6d.
 CONTENTS:—Rocks Ahead and Harbours of Refuge. Foreign Policy of Great Britain. The Echo of the Antipodes. A Grave Perplexity before us. Obligations of the Soil. The Right Use of a Surplus. The Great Twin Brothers: Louis Napoleon and Benjamin Disraeli. Is the Popular Judgment in Politics more Just than that of the Higher Orders? Harriet Martineau. Verify your Compass. The Prophetic Element in the Gospels. Mr. Frederick Harrison on the Future Life. Can Truths be Apprehended which could not have been Discovered?

GREG.—MISCELLANEOUS ESSAYS. By W. R. Greg. Second Series. Pp. 294. 1884. 7s. 6d.
 CONTENTS:—France since 1848. France in January 1852. England as it is. Sir R. Peel's Character and Policy. Employment of our Asiatic Forces in European Wars.

GRIFFIN.—THE RAJAS OF THE PUNJAB. Being the History of the Principal States in the Punjab, and their Political Relations with the British Government. By Lepel H. Griffin, Bengal Civil Service, Acting Secretary to the Government of the Punjab, Author of "The Punjab Chiefs," &c. Second Edition. Royal 8vo, pp. xvi. and 630, cloth. 1873. £1, 1s.

GRIFFIN.—THE WORLD UNDER GLASS. By Frederick Griffin, Author of "The Destiny of Man," "The Storm King," and other Poems. Fcap. 8vo, pp. 204, cloth gilt. 1879. 3s. 6d.

GRIFFIN.—THE DESTINY OF MAN, THE STORM KING, and other Poems. By F. Griffin. Second Edition. Fcap. 8vo, pp. vii.-104, cloth. 1883. 2s. 6d.

GRIFFIS.—THE MIKADO'S EMPIRE. Book I. History of Japan, from 660 B.C. to 1872 A.D.—Book II. Personal Experiences, Observations, and Studies in Japan, 1870-1874. By W. E. Griffis, A.M. Second Edition. 8vo, pp. 626, cloth. Illustrated. 1883. 20s.

GRIFFIS.—JAPANESE FAIRY WORLD. Stories from the Wonder-Lore of Japan. By W. E. Griffis. Square 16mo, pp. viii. and 304, with 12 Plates. 1880. 7s. 6d.

GRIFFITH.—THE BIRTH OF THE WAR GOD. See Trübner's Oriental Series.

GRIFFITH.—YUSUF AND ZULAIKHA. See Trübner's Oriental Series.

GRIFFITH.—SCENES FROM THE RAMAYANA, MEGHADUTA, &c. Translated by Ralph T. H. Griffith, M.A., Principal of the Benares College. Second Edition. Crown 8vo, pp. xviii. and 244, cloth. 1870. 6s.

CONTENTS.—Preface—Ayodhya—Ravan Doomed—The Birth of Rama—The Heir-Apparent—Manthara's Guile—Dasaratha's Oath—The Step-mother—Mother and Son—The Triumph of Love—Farewell ?—The Hermit's Son—The Trial of Truth—The Forest—The Rape of Sita—Rama's Despair—The Messenger Cloud—Khumbakarna—The Suppliant Dove—True Glory—Feed the Poor—The Wise Scholar.

GRIFFITH.—THE RÁMÁYAN OF VÁLMÍKI. Translated into English Verse. By Ralph T. H. Griffith, M.A., Principal of the Benares College. Vol. I., containing Books I. and II., demy 8vo, pp. xxxii. and 440, cloth. 1870. —Vol. II., containing Book II., with additional Notes and Index of Names. Demy 8vo, pp. 504, cloth. 1871. —Vol. III., demy 8vo, pp. 390, cloth. 1872. —Vol. IV., demy 8vo, pp. viii. and 432, cloth. 1873. —Vol. V., demy 8vo, pp. viii. and 360, cloth. 1875. The complete work, 5 vols. £7, 7s.

GROTE.—REVIEW of the Work of Mr. John Stuart Mill entitled "Examination of Sir William Hamilton's Philosophy." By George Grote, Author of the "History of Ancient Greece," "Plato, and the other Companions of Socrates," &c. 12mo, pp. 112, cloth. 1868. 3s. 6d.

GROUT.—ZULU-LAND; or, Life among the Zulu-Kafirs of Natal and Zulu-Land, South Africa. By the Rev. Lewis Grout. Crown 8vo, pp. 352, cloth. With Map and Illustrations. 7s. 6d.

GROWSE.—MATHURA: A District Memoir. By F. S. Growse, B.C.S., M.A., Oxon, C.I.E., Fellow of the Calcutta University. Second edition, illustrated, revised, and enlarged, 4to, pp. xxiv. and 520, boards. 1880. 42s.

GUBERNATIS.—ZOOLOGICAL MYTHOLOGY; or, The Legends of Animals. By Angelo de Gubernatis, Professor of Sanskrit and Comparative Literature in the Instituto di Studii Superorii e di Perfezionamento at Florence, &c. 2 vols. 8vo, pp. xxvi. and 432, and vii. and 442, cloth. 1872. £1, 8s.

This work is an important contribution to the study of the comparative mythology of the Indo-Germanic nations. The author introduces the denizens of the air, earth, and water in the various characters assigned to them in the myths and legends of all civilised nations, and traces the migration of the mythological ideas from the times of the early Aryans to those of the Greeks, Romans, and Teutons.

GULSHAN I. RAZ: THE MYSTIC ROSE GARDEN OF SA'D UD DIN MAHMUD SHABISTARI. The Persian Text, with an English Translation and Notes, chiefly from the Commentary of Muhammed Bin Yahya Lahiji. By E. H. Whinfield, M.A., Barrister-at-Law, late of H.M.B.C.S. 4to, pp. xvi., 94, 60, cloth. 1880. 10s. 6d.

GUMPACH.—TREATY RIGHTS OF THE FOREIGN MERCHANT, and the Transit System in China. By Johannes von Gumpach. 8vo, pp. xviii. and 421, sewed. 10s. 6d.

HAAS.—CATALOGUE OF SANSKRIT AND PALI BOOKS IN THE BRITISH MUSEUM. By Dr. Ernst Haas. Printed by permission of the Trustees of the British Museum. 4to, pp. viii. and 188, paper boards. 1876. 21s.

HAFIZ OF SHIRAZ.—SELECTIONS FROM HIS POEMS. Translated from the Persian by Hermann Bicknell. With Preface by A. S. Bicknell. Demy 4to, pp. xx. and 384, printed on fine stout plate-paper, with appropriate Oriental Bordering in gold and colour, and Illustrations by J. R. Herbert, R.A. 1875. £2, 2s.

HAFIZ.—See Trübner's Oriental Series.

HAGEN.—NORICA; or, Tales from the Olden Time. Translated from the German of August Hagen. Fcap. 8vo, pp. xiv. and 374. 1850. 5s.

HAGGARD.—CETYWAYO AND HIS WHITE NEIGHBOURS; or, Remarks on Recent Events in Zululand, Natal, and the Transvaal. By H. R. Haggard. Crown 8vo, pp. xvi. and 294, cloth. 1882. 7s. 6d.

HAGGARD.—See "The Vazir of Lankuran."

HAHN.—TSUNI- ‖ GOAM, the Supreme Being of the Khoi-Khoi. By Theophilus Hahn, Ph.D., Custodian of the Grey Collection, Cape Town, &c., &c. Post 8vo, pp. xiv. and 154. 1882. 7s. 6d.

HALDANE.—See SCHOPENHAUER, or ENGLISH AND FOREIGN PHILOSOPHICAL LIBRARY, vol. xxii.

HALDEMAN.—PENNSYLVANIA DUTCH: A Dialect of South Germany with an Infusion of English. By S. S. Haldeman, A.M., Professor of Comparative Philology in the University of Pennsylvania, Philadelphia. 8vo, pp. viii. and 70, cloth. 1872. 3s. 6d.

HALL.—ON ENGLISH ADJECTIVES IN -ABLE, WITH SPECIAL REFERENCE TO RELIABLE. By FitzEdward Hall, C.E., M.A., Hon. D.C.L. Oxon; formerly Professor of Sanskrit Language and Literature, and of Indian Jurisprudence in King's College, London. Crown 8vo, pp. viii. and 238, cloth. 1877. 7s. 6d.

HALL.—MODERN ENGLISH. By FitzEdward Hall, M.A., Hon. D.C.L. Oxon. Crown 8vo, pp. xvi. and 394, cloth. 1873. 10s. 6d.

HALL.—SUN AND EARTH AS GREAT FORCES IN CHEMISTRY. By T. W. Hall, M.D., L.R.C.S.E. Crown 8vo, pp. xii. and 220, cloth. 1874. 3s.

HALL.—THE PEDIGREE OF THE DEVIL. By F. T. Hall, F.R.A.S. With Seven Autotype Illustrations from Designs by the Author. Demy 8vo, pp. xvi. and 256, cloth. 1883. 7s. 6d.

HALL.—ARCTIC EXPEDITION. See NOURSE.

HALLOCK.—THE SPORTSMAN'S GAZETTEER AND GENERAL GUIDE. The Game Animals, Birds, and Fishes of North America: their Habits and various methods of Capture, &c., &c. With a Directory to the principal Game Resorts of the Country. By Charles Hallock. New Edition. Crown 8vo, cloth. Maps and Portrait. 1883. 15s.

HAM.—THE MAID OF CORINTH. A Drama in Four Acts. By J. Panton Ham. Crown 8vo, pp. 65, sewed. 2s. 6d.

HARLEY.—THE SIMPLIFICATION OF ENGLISH SPELLING, specially adapted to the Rising Generation. An Easy Way of Saving Time in Writing, Printing, and Reading. By Dr. George Harley, F.R.S., F.C.S. 8vo. pp. 128, cloth. 1877. 2s. 6d.

HARRISON.—WOMAN'S HANDIWORK IN MODERN HOMES. By Constance Cary Harrison. With numerous Illustrations and Five Coloured Plates, from designs by Samuel Colman, Rosina Emmet, George Gibson, and others. 8vo, pp. xii. and 242, cloth. 1881. 10s.

HARTMANN.—See English and Foreign Philosophical Library, vol. XXV.

HARTZENBUSCH and LEMMING.—ECO DE MADRID. A Practical Guide to Spanish Conversation. By J. E. Hartzenbusch and H. Lemming. Second Edition. Post 8vo, pp. 250, cloth. 1870. 5s.

HASE.—MIRACLE PLAYS AND SACRED DRAMAS: An Historical Survey. By Dr. Karl Hase. Translated from the German by A. W. Jackson, and Edited by the Rev. W. W. Jackson, Fellow of Exeter College, Oxford. Crown 8vo, pp. 288. 1880. 9s.

HAUG.—GLOSSARY AND INDEX of the Pahlavi Texts of the Book of Arda Viraf, the Tale of Gosht—J. Fryano, the Hadokht Nask, and to some extracts from the Dinkard and Nirangistan; prepared from Destur Hoshangji Jamaspji Asa's Glossary to the Arda Viraf Namak, and from the Original Texts, with Notes on Pahlavi Grammar by E. W. West, Ph.D. Revised by M. Haug, Ph.D., &c. Published by order of the Bombay Government. 8vo, pp. viii. and 352, sewed. 1874. 25s.

HAUG.—THE SACRED LANGUAGE, &c., OF THE PARSIS. See Trübner's Oriental Series.

HAUPT.—THE LONDON ARBITRAGEUR; or, The English Money Market, in connection with Foreign Bourses. A Collection of Notes and Formulæ for the Arbitration of Bills, Stocks, Shares, Bullion, and Coins, with all the Important Foreign Countries. By Ottomar Haupt. Crown 8vo, pp. viii. and 196, cloth. 1870. 7s. 6d.

HAWKEN.—UPA-SASTRĀ: Comments, Linguistic, Doctrinal, on Sacred and Mythic Literature. By J. D. Hawken. Crown 8vo, pp. viii. and 288, cloth. 1877. 7s. 6d.

HAZEN.—THE SCHOOL AND THE ARMY IN GERMANY AND FRANCE, with a Diary of Siege Life at Versailles. By Brevet Major-General W. B. Hazen, U.S.A., Col. 6th Infantry. 8vo, pp. 408, cloth. 1872. 10s. 6d.

HEATH.—EDGAR QUINET. See English and Foreign Philosophical Library, Vol. XIV.

HEATON—AUSTRALIAN DICTIONARY OF DATES AND MEN OF THE TIME. Containing the History of Australasia from 1542 to May 1879. By I. H. Heaton. Royal 8vo, pp. iv. and 554, cloth. 15s.

HEBREW LITERATURE SOCIETY.

HECHLER.—THE JERUSALEM BISHOPRIC DOCUMENTS. With Translations, chiefly derived from "Das Evangelische Bisthum in Jerusalem," Geschichtliche Darlegung mit Urtunden. Berlin, 1842. Published by Command of His Majesty Frederick William IV., King of Prussia. Arranged and Supplemented by the Rev. Prof. William H. Hechler, British Chaplain at Stockholm. 8vo, pp. 212, with Maps, Portrait, and Illustrations, cloth. 1883. 10s. 6d.

HECKER.—THE EPIDEMICS OF THE MIDDLE AGES. Translated by G. B. Babington, M.D., F.R.S. Third Edition, completed by the Author's Treatise on Child-Pilgrimages. By J. F. C. Hecker. 8vo, pp. 384, cloth. 1859. 9s. 6d.
CONTENTS.—The Black Death—The Dancing Mania—The Sweating Sickness—Child Pilgrimages.

HEDLEY.—MASTERPIECES OF GERMAN POETRY. Translated in the Measure of the Originals, by F. H. Hedley. With Illustrations by Louis Wanke. Crown 8vo, pp. viii. and 120, cloth. 1876. 6s.

HEINE.—RELIGION AND PHILOSOPHY IN GERMANY. See English and Foreign Philosophical Library, Vol. XVIII.

HEINE.—WIT, WISDOM, AND PATHOS from the Prose of Heinrich Heine. With a few pieces from the "Book of Songs." Selected and Translated by J. Snodgrass. With Portrait. Crown 8vo, pp. xx. and 340, cloth. 1879. 7s. 6d.

HEINE.—PICTURES OF TRAVEL. Translated from the German of Henry Heine, by Charles G. Leland. 7th Revised Edition. Crown 8vo, pp. 472, with Portrait, cloth. 1873. 7s. 6d.

HEINE.—HEINE's BOOK OF SONGS. Translated by Charles G. Leland. Fcap. 8vo, pp. xiv. and 240, cloth, gilt edges. 1874. 7s. 6d.

HEITZMANN.—MICROSCOPICAL MORPHOLOGY OF THE ANIMAL BODY IN HEALTH AND DISEASE. By C. HEITZMANN, M.D. Royal 8vo, pp. xx.-850, cloth. 1884. 31s. 6d.

HENDRIK.—MEMOIRS OF HANS HENDRIK, THE ARCTIC TRAVELLER; serving under Kane, Hayes, Hall, and Nares, 1853-76. Written by Himself. Translated from the Eskimo Language, by Dr. Henry Rink. Edited by Prof. Dr. G. Stephens, F.S.A. Crown 8vo, pp. 100, Map, cloth. 1878. 3s. 6d.

HENNELL.—PRESENT RELIGION: As a Faith owning Fellowship with Thought. Vol. I. Part I. By Sara S. Hennell. Crown 8vo, pp. 570, cloth. 1865. 7s. 6d.

HENNELL.—COMPARATIVISM; An Introduction to the Second Part of "Present Religion," explaining the Principle by which Religion appears still to be set in Necessary Antagonism to Positivism. By Sara S. Hennell. 8vo, pp. 160, cloth. 1869. 3s.

HENNELL.—COMPARATIVE ETHICS—I. Section I. Moral Standpoint. Present Religion, Vol. III. By Sara S. Hennell. 8vo, pp. 66, wrapper. 1882. 2s.

HENNELL.—COMPARATIVE ETHICS—I. Sections II. and III. Moral Principle in Regard to Sexhood. Present Religion, Vol. III. By S. Hennell. Crown 8vo, pp. 92, wrapper. 1884. 2s.

HENNELL.—PRESENT RELIGION: As a Faith owning Fellowship with Thought. Part II. First Division. Intellectual Effect: shown as a Principle of Metaphysical Comparativism. By Sara S. Hennell. Crown 8vo, pp. 618, cloth. 1873. 7s. 6d.

HENNELL.—PRESENT RELIGION, Vol. III. Part II. Second Division. The Effect of Present Religion on its Practical Side. By S. S. Hennell. Crown 8vo, pp. 68, paper covers. 1882. 2s.

HENNELL.—COMPARATIVISM shown as Furnishing a Religious Basis to Morality. (Present Religion. Vol. III. Part II. Second Division: Practical Effect.) By Sara S. Hennell. Crown 8vo, pp. 220, stitched in wrapper. 1878. 3s. 6d.

HENNELL.—COMPARATIVE ETHICS. II. Sections I. and II. Moral Principle in regard to Brotherhood. (Present Religion, Vol. III.) By Sara S. Hennell. Crown 8vo, pp. 52, wrapper. 1884. 2s.

HENNELL.—THOUGHTS IN AID OF FAITH. Gathered chiefly from recent Works in Theology and Philosophy. By Sara S. Hennell. Post 8vo, pp. 428, cloth. 1860. 6s.

HENWOOD.—THE METALLIFEROUS DEPOSITS OF CORNWALL AND DEVON; with Appendices on Subterranean Temperature; the Electricity of Rocks and Veins; the Quantities of Water in the Cornish Mines; and Mining Statistics. (Vol. V. of the Transactions of the Royal Geographical Society of Cornwall.) By William Jory Henwood, F.R.S., F.G.S. 8vo, pp. x. and 515; with 113 Tables, and 12 Plates, half bound. £2, 2s.

HENWOOD.—OBSERVATIONS ON METALLIFEROUS DEPOSITS, AND ON SUBTERRANEAN TEMPERATURE. (Vol. VIII. of the Transactions of the Royal Geological Society of Cornwall.) By William Jory Henwood, F.R.S., F.G.S., President of the Royal Institution of Cornwall. In 2 Parts. 8vo, pp. xxx., vii. and 916; with 38 Tables, 31 Engravings on Wood, and 6 Plates. £1, 16s.

HEPBURN.—A JAPANESE AND ENGLISH DICTIONARY. With an English and Japanese Index. By J. C. Hepburn, M.D., LL.D. Second Edition. Imperial 8vo, pp. xxxii., 632, and 201, cloth. £8, 8s.

HEPBURN.—JAPANESE-ENGLISH AND ENGLISH-JAPANESE DICTIONARY. By J. C. Hepburn, M.D., LL.D. Abridged by the Author. Square fcap., pp. vi. and 536, cloth. 1873. 18s.

HERNISZ.—A GUIDE TO CONVERSATION IN THE ENGLISH AND CHINESE LANGUAGES, for the Use of Americans and Chinese in California and elsewhere. By Stanislas Hernisz. Square 8vo, pp. 274, sewed. 1855. 10s. 6d.

HERSHON.—TALMUDIC MISCELLANY. See Trübner's Oriental Series.

HERZEN.—DU DEVELOPPEMENT DES IDÉES REVOLUTIONNAIRES EN RUSSIE. Par Alexander Herzen. 12mo, pp. xxiii. and 144, sewed. 1853. 2s. 6d.

HERZEN.—A separate list of A. Herzen's works in Russian may be had on application.

HILL.—THE HISTORY OF THE REFORM MOVEMENT in the Dental Profession in Great Britain during the last twenty years. By Alfred Hill, Licentiate in Dental Surgery, &c. Crown 8vo, pp. xvi. and 400, cloth. 1877. 10s. 6d.

HILLEBRAND.—FRANCE AND THE FRENCH IN THE SECOND HALF OF THE NINETEENTH CENTURY. By Karl Hillebrand. Translated from the Third German Edition. Post 8vo, pp. xx. and 262, cloth. 1881. 10s. 6d.

HINDOO MYTHOLOGY POPULARLY TREATED. Being an Epitomised Description of the various Heathen Deities illustrated on the Silver Swami Tea Service presented, as a memento of his visit to India, to H.R.H. the Prince of Wales, K.G., G.C.S.I., by His Highness the Gaekwar of Baroda. Small 4to, pp. 42, limp cloth. 1875. 3s. 6d.

HITTELL.—THE COMMERCE AND INDUSTRIES OF THE PACIFIC COAST OF NORTH AMERICA. By J. S. Hittell, Author of "The Resources of California." 4to, pp. 820. 1882. £1, 10s.

HODGSON.—ACADEMY LECTURES. By J. E. Hodgson, R.A., Librarian and Professor of Painting to the Royal Academy. Cr. 8vo, pp. viii. and 312, cloth. 1884. 7s. 6d.

HODGSON.—ESSAYS ON THE LANGUAGES, LITERATURE, AND RELIGION OF NÉPAL AND TIBET. Together with further Papers on the Geography, Ethnology, and Commerce of those Countries. By B. H. Hodgson, late British Minister at the Court of Nepál. Royal 8vo, cloth, pp. xii. and 276. 1874. 14s.

HODGSON.— ESSAYS ON INDIAN SUBJECTS. See Trübner's Oriental Series.

HODGSON.—THE EDUCATION OF GIRLS; AND THE EMPLOYMENT OF WOMEN OF THE UPPER CLASSES EDUCATIONALLY CONSIDERED. Two Lectures. By W. B. Hodgson, LL.D. Second Edition. Cr. 8vo, pp. xvi. and 114, cloth. 1869. 3s. 6d.

HODGSON.—TURGOT: His Life, Times, and Opinions. Two Lectures. By W. B. Hodgson, LL.D. Crown 8vo, pp. vi. and 83, sewed. 1870. 2s.

HOERNLE.—A COMPARATIVE GRAMMAR OF THE GAUDIAN LANGUAGES, with Special Reference to the Eastern Hindi. Accompanied by a Language Map, and a Table of Alphabets. By A. F. Rudolf Hoernle. Demy 8vo, pp. 474, cloth. 1880. 18s.

HOLBEIN SOCIETY.—Subscription, one guinea per annum. List of publications on application.

HOLMES-FORBES.—THE SCIENCE OF BEAUTY. An Analytical Inquiry into the Laws of Æsthetics. By Avary W. Holmes-Forbes, of Lincoln's Inn, Barrister-at-Law. Post 8vo, cloth, pp. vi. and 200. 1881. 6s.

HOLST.—THE CONSTITUTIONAL AND POLITICAL HISTORY OF THE UNITED STATES. By Dr. H. von Holst. Translated by J. J. Lalor and A. B. Mason. Royal 8vo. Vol. I. 1750-1833. State Sovereignty and Slavery. Pp. xvi. and 506. 1876. 18s.—Vol. II. 1828-1846. Jackson's Administration—Annexation of Texas. Pp. 720. 1879. £1, 2s.—Vol. III. 1846-1850. Annexation of Texas—Compromise of 1850. Pp. x. and 598. 1881. 18s.

HOLYOAKE.—TRAVELS IN SEARCH OF A SETTLER'S GUIDE-BOOK OF AMERICA AND CANADA. By George Jacob Holyoake, Author of "The History of Co-operation in England." Post 8vo, pp. 148, wrapper. 1884. 2s. 6d.

HOLYOAKE.—THE HISTORY OF CO-OPERATION IN ENGLAND: its Literature and its Advocates. By G. J. Holyoake. Vol. I. The Pioneer Period, 1812-44. Crown 8vo, pp. xii. and 420, cloth. 1875. 4s.—Vol. II. The Constructive Period, 1845-78. Crown 8vo, pp. x. and 504, cloth. 1878. 8s.

HOLYOAKE.—THE TRIAL OF THEISM ACCUSED OF OBSTRUCTING SECULAR LIFE. By G. J. Holyoake. Crown 8vo, pp. xvi. and 256, cloth. 1877. 2s. 6d.

HOLYOAKE.—REASONING FROM FACTS: A Method of Everyday Logic. By G. J. Holyoake. Fcap., pp. xii. and 94, wrapper. 1877. 1s. 6d.

HOLYOAKE.—SELF-HELP BY THE PEOPLE. Thirty-three Years of Co-operation in Rochdale. In Two Parts. Part I., 1844-1857; Part II., 1857-1877. By G. J. Holyoake. Ninth Edition. Crown 8vo, pp. 174, cloth. 1883. 2s. 6d.

HOPKINS.—ELEMENTARY GRAMMAR OF THE TURKISH LANGUAGE. With a few Easy Exercises. By F. L. Hopkins, M.A., Fellow and Tutor of Trinity Hall, Cambridge. Crown 8vo, pp. 48, cloth. 1877. 3s. 6d.

HORDER.—A SELECTION FROM "THE BOOK OF PRAISE FOR CHILDREN," as Edited by W. Garrett Horder. For the Use of Jewish Children. Fcap. 8vo, pp. 80, cloth. 1883. 1s. 6d.

HOSMER.—THE PEOPLE AND POLITICS; or, The Structure of States and the Significance and Relation of Political Forms. By G. W. Hosmer, M.D. Demy 8vo, pp. viii. and 340, cloth. 1883. 15s.

HOWELLS.—A LITTLE GIRL AMONG THE OLD MASTERS. With Introduction and Comment. By W. D. Howells. Oblong crown 8vo, cloth, pp. 66, with 54 plates. 1884. 10s.

C

HOWELLS.—Dr. Breen's Practice; A Novel. By W. D. Howells. English Copyright Edition. Crown 8vo, pp. 272, cloth. 1882. 6s.

HOWSE.—A Grammar of the Cree Language. With which is combined an Analysis of the Chippeway Dialect. By Joseph Howse, F.R.G.S. 8vo, pp. xx. and 324, cloth. 1865. 7s. 6d.

HULME.—Mathematical Drawing Instruments, and How to Use Them. By F. Edward Hulme, F.L.S., F.S.A., Art-Master of.Marlborough College, Author of "Principles of Ornamental Art," &c. With Illustrations. Second Edition. Imperial 16mo, pp. xvi. and 152, cloth. 1881. 3s. 6d.

HUMBERT.—On "Tenant Right." By C. F. Humbert. 8vo, pp. 20, sewed. 1875. 1s.

HUMBOLDT.—The Sphere and Duties of Government. Translated from the German of Baron Wilhelm Von Humboldt by Joseph Coulthard, jun. Post 8vo, pp. xv. and 203, cloth. 1854. 5s.

HUMBOLDT.—Letters of William Von Humboldt to a Female Friend. A complete Edition. Translated from the Second German Edition by Catherine M. A. Couper, with a Biographical Notice of the Writer. 2 vols. crown 8vo, pp. xxviii. and 592, cloth. 1867. 10s.

HUNT.—The Religion of the Heart. A Manual of Faith and Duty. By Leigh Hunt. Fcap. 8vo, pp. xxiv. and 259, cloth. 2s. 6d.

HUNT.—Chemical and Geological Essays. By Professor T. Sterry Hunt. Second Edition. 8vo, pp. xxii. and 448, cloth. 1879. 12s.

HUNTER.—A Comparative Dictionary of the Non-Aryan Languages of India and High Asia. With a Dissertation, Political and Linguistic, on the Aboriginal Races. By W. W. Hunter, B.A., M.R.A.S., Hon. Fel. Ethnol. Soc., Author of the "Annals of Rural Bengal," of H.M.'s Civil Service. Being a Lexicon of 144 Languages, illustrating Turanian Speech. Compiled from the Hodgson Lists, Government Archives, and Original MSS., arranged with Prefaces and Indices in English, French, German, Russian, and Latin. Large 4to, toned paper, pp. 230, cloth. 1869. 42s.

HUNTER.—The Indian Musalmans. By W. W. Hunter, B.A., LL.D., Director-General of Statistics to the Government of India, &c., Author of the "Annals of Rural Bengal," &c. Third Edition. 8vo, pp. 219, cloth. 1876. 10s. 6d.

HUNTER.—Famine Aspects of Bengal Districts. A System of Famine Warnings. By W. W. Hunter, B.A., LL.D. Crown 8vo, pp. 216, cloth. 1874. 7s. 6d.

HUNTER.—A Statistical Account of Bengal. By W. W. Hunter, B.A., LL.D., Director-General of Statistics to the Government of India, &c. In 20 vols. 8vo, half morocco. 1877. £5.

HUNTER.—Catalogue of Sanskrit Manuscripts (Buddhist). Collected in Nepal by B. H. Hodgson, late Resident at the Court of Nepal. Compiled from Lists in Calcutta, France, and England, by W. W. Hunter, C.I.E., LL.D. 8vo, pp. 28, paper. 1880. 2s.

HUNTER.—The Imperial Gazetteer of India. By W. W. Hunter, C.I.E., LL.D., Director-General of Statistics to the Government of India. In Nine Volumes. 8vo, pp. xxxiii. and 544, 539, 567, xix. and 716, 509, 513, 555, 537, and xii. and 478, half morocco. With Maps. 1881.

HUNTER.—The Indian Empire: Its History, People, and Products. By W. W. Hunter, C.I.E., LL.D. Post 8vo, pp. 568, with Map, cloth. 1882. 16s.

HUNTER.—An Account of the British Settlement of Aden, in Arabia. Compiled by Capt. F. M. Hunter, Assistant Political Resident, Aden. 8vo, pp. xii. and 232, half bound. 1877. 7s. 6d.

HUNTER.—A Statistical Account of Assam. By W. W. Hunter, B.A., LL.D., C.I.E., Director-General of Statistics to the Government of India, &c. 2 vols. 8vo, pp. 420 and 490, with 2 Maps, half morocco. 1879. 10s.

HUNTER.—A Brief History of the Indian People. By W. W. Hunter, C.I.E., LL.D. Fourth Edition. Crown 8vo, pp. 222, cloth. With Map. 1884. 3s. 6d.

HURST.—History of Rationalism: embracing a Survey of the Present State of Protestant Theology. By the Rev. John F. Hurst, A.M. With Appendix of Literature. Revised and enlarged from the Third American Edition. Crown 8vo, pp. xvii. and 525, cloth. 1867. 10s. 6d.

HYETT.—Prompt Remedies for Accidents and Poisons: Adapted to the use of the Inexperienced till Medical aid arrives. By W. H. Hyett, F.R.S. A Broadsheet, to hang up in Country Schools or Vestries, Workshops, Offices of Factories, Mines and Docks, on board Yachts, in Railway Stations, remote Shooting Quarters, Highland Manses, and Private Houses, wherever the Doctor lives at a distance. Sold for the benefit of the Gloucester Eye Institution. In sheets, 21½ by 17¼ inches, 2s. 6d.; mounted, 3s. 6d.

HYMANS.—Pupil *Versus* Teacher. Letters from a Teacher to a Teacher. Fcap. 8vo, pp. 92, cloth. 1875. 2s.

IHNE.—A Latin Grammar for Beginners. By W. H. Ihne, late Principal of Carlton Terrace School, Liverpool. Crown 8vo, pp. vi. and 184, cloth. 1864. 3s.

IKHWÁNU-S Safá; or, Brothers of Purity. Translated from the Hindustani by Professor John Dowson, M.R.A.S., Staff College, Sandhurst. Crown 8vo, pp. viii. and 156, cloth. 1869. 7s.

INDIA.—Archæological Survey of Western India. See Burgess.

INDIA.—Publications of the Archæological Survey of India. A separate list on application.

INDIA.—Publications of the Geographical Department of the India Office, London. A separate list, also list of all the Government Maps, on application.

INDIA.—Publications of the Geological Survey of India. A separate list on application.

INDIA OFFICE PUBLICATIONS :—
Aden, Statistical Account of. 5s.
Assam, do.   do.   Vols. I. and II. 5s. each.
Baden Powell, Land Revenues, &c., in India. 12s.
    Do.   Jurisprudence for Forest Officers. 12s.
Beal's Buddhist Tripitaka. 4s.
Bengal, Statistical Account of. Vols. I. to XX. 100s. per set.
    Do.   do.   do.   Vols. VI. to XX. 5s. each.
Bombay Code. 21s.
Bombay Gazetteer. Vol. II., 14s. Vol. VIII., 9s. Vol. XIII. (2 parts), 16s.
        Vol. XV. (2 parts), 16s.
    Do.   do.   Vols. III. to VII., and X., XI., XII., XIV., XVI. 8s. each.
    Do.   do.   Vols. XXI., XXII., and XXIII. 9s. each.
Burgess' Archæological Survey of Western India. Vols. I. and III. 42s. each.
    Do.   do.   do.   Vol. II. 63s.
    Do.   do.   do.   Vols. IV. and V. 126s.
Burma (British) Gazetteer. 2 vols. 50s.
Catalogue of Manuscripts and Maps of Surveys. 12s.
Chambers' Meteorology (Bombay) and Atlas. 30s.
Cole's Agra and Muttra. 70s.
Cook's Gums and Resins. 5s.
Corpus Inscriptionem Indicarum. Vol. I. 32s.
Cunningham's Archæological Survey. Vols. I. to XVIII. 10s. and 12s. each.
    Do.   Stupa of Bharut. 63s.
Egerton's Catalogue of Indian Arms. 2s. 6d.
Ferguson and Burgess, Cave Temples of India. 42s.
    Do.   Tree and Serpent Worship. 105s.
Finance and Revenue Accounts of the Government of India for 1883-4. 2s. 6d.
Gamble, Manual of Indian Timbers. 10s.
Hunter's Imperial Gazetteer. 9 vols.

INDIA OFFICE PUBLICATIONS—continued.
Indian Education Commission, Report of the. 12s. Appendices. 10 vols. 10s.
Jaschke's Tibetan-English Dictionary. 30s.
King. Chinchona-Planting. 1s.
Kurz. Forest Flora of British Burma. Vols. I. and II. 15s. each.
Liotard's Materials for Paper. 2s. 6d.
Liotard's Silk in India. Part I. 2s.
Loth. Catalogue of Arabic MSS. 10s. 6d.
Markham's Tibet. 21s.
    Do.   Memoir of Indian Surveys. 10s. 6d.
    Do.   Abstract of Reports of Surveys. 1s. 6d.
Mitra (Rajendralala), Buddha Gaya. 60s.
Moir, Torrent Regions of the Alps. 1s.
Mueller. Select Plants for Extra-Tropical Countries. 8s.
Mysore and Coorg Gazetteer. Vols. I. and II. 10s. each.
    Do.   do.   Vol. III. 5s.
N. W. P. Gazetteer. Vols. I. and II. 10s. each.
    Do.   do.   Vols. III. to XI., XIII., and XIV. 12s. each.
Oudh   do.   Vols. I. to III. 10s. each.
People of India, The. Vols. I. to VIII. 45s. each.
Raverty's Notes on Afghanistan and Baluchistan. Sections I. and II. 2s. Section III. 5s. Section IV. 3s.
Rajputana Gazetteer. 3 vols. 15s.
Saunders' Mountains and River Basins of India. 3s.
Sewell's Amaravati Tope. 3s.
Smyth's (Brough) Gold Mining in Wynaad. 1s.
Taylor. Indian Marine Surveys. 2s. 6d.
Trigonometrical Survey, Synopsis of Great. Vols. I. to VI. 10s. 6d. each.
Trumpp's Adi Granth. 52s. 6d.
Waring. Pharmacopœia of India, The. 6s.
Watson's Cotton Gins. Boards, 10s. 6d. Paper, 10s.
    Do.   Rhea Fibre. 2s. 6d.
    Do.   Tobacco. 5s.
Wilson. Madras Army. Vols. I. and II. 21s.

INDIAN GAZETTEERS.—See GAZETTEER, and INDIA OFFICE PUBLICATIONS.

INGLEBY.—See SHAKESPEARE.

INMAN.—NAUTICAL TABLES. Designed for the use of British Seamen. By the Rev. James Inman, D.D., late Professor at the Royal Naval College, Portsmouth. Demy 8vo, pp. xvi. and 410, cloth. 1877. 15s.

INMAN.—HISTORY OF THE ENGLISH ALPHABET: A Paper read before the Liverpool Literary and Philosophical Society. By T. Inman, M.D. 8vo, pp. 36, sewed. 1872. 1s.

IN SEARCH OF TRUTH. Conversations on the Bible and Popular Theology, for Young People. By A. M. Y. Crown 8vo, pp. x. and 138, cloth. 1875. 2s. 6d.

INTERNATIONAL NUMISMATA ORIENTALIA (THE).—Royal 4to, in paper wrapper. Part I. Ancient Indian Weights. By E. Thomas, F.R.S. Pp. 84, with a Plate and Map of the India of Manu. 9s. 6d.—Part II. Coins of the Urtukí Turkumáns. By Stanley Lane Poole, Corpus Christi College, Oxford. Pp. 44, with 6 Plates. 9s.—Part III. The Coinage of Lydia and Persia, from the Earliest Times to the Fall of the Dynasty of the Achæmenidæ. By Barclay V. Head, Assistant-Keeper of Coins, British Museum. Pp. viii.-56, with 3 Autotype Plates. 10s. 6d.— Part IV. The Coins of the Tuluni Dynasty. By Edward Thomas Rogers. Pp. iv.-22, and 1 Plate. 5s.—Part V. The Parthian Coinage. By Percy Gardner, M.A. Pp. iv.-66, and 8 Autotype Plates. 18s.—Part VI. The Ancient Coins and Measures of Ceylon. By T. W. Rhys Davids. Pp. iv. and 60, and 1 Plate. 10s.—Vol. I., containing the first six parts. as specified above. Royal 4to, half bound. £3, 13s. 6d.

INTERNATIONAL NUMISMATA—*continued*.

Vol. II. COINS OF THE JEWS. Being a History of the Jewish Coinage and Money in the Old and New Testaments. By Frederick W. Madden, M.R.A.S., Member of the Numismatic Society of London, Secretary of the Brighton College, &c., &c. With 279 woodcuts and a plate of alphabets. Royal 4to, pp. xii. and 330, sewed. 1881. £2.

Vol. III. Part I. THE COINS OF ARAKAN, OF PEGU, AND OF BURMA. By Lieut.-General Sir Arthur Phayre, C.B., K.C.S.I., G.C.M.G., late Commissioner of British Burma. Also contains the Indian Balhara, and the Arabian Intercourse with India in the Ninth and following Centuries. By Edward Thomas, F.R.S. Royal 4to, pp. viii. and 48, with Five Autotype Illustrations, wrapper. 1882. 8s. 6d.

Part II. THE COINS OF SOUTHERN INDIA. By Sir W. Elliot. Royal 4to.

JACKSON.—ETHNOLOGY AND PHRENOLOGY AS AN AID TO THE HISTORIAN. By the late J. W. Jackson. Second Edition. With a Memoir of the Author, by his Wife. Crown 8vo, pp. xx. and 324, cloth. 1875. 4s. 6d.

JACKSON.—THE SHROPSHIRE WORD-BOOK. A Glossary of Archaic and Provincial Words, &c., used in the County. By Georgina F. Jackson. Crown 8vo, pp. civ. and 524, cloth. 1881. 31s. 6d.

JACOB.—HINDU PANTHEISM. See Trübner's Oriental Series.

JAGIELSKI.—ON MARIENBAD SPA, and the Diseases Curable by its Waters and Baths. By A. V. Jagielski, M.D., Berlin. Second Edition. Crown 8vo, pp. viii. and 186. With Map. Cloth. 1874. 5s.

JAMISON.—THE LIFE AND TIMES OF BERTRAND DU GUESCLIN. A History of the Fourteenth Century. By D. F. Jamison, of South Carolina. Portrait. 2 vols. 8vo, pp. xvi., 287, and viii., 314, cloth. 1864. £1, 1s.

JAPAN.—MAP OF NIPPON (Japan): Compiled from Native Maps, and the Notes of most recent Travellers. By R. Henry Brunton, M.I.C.E., F.R.G.S., 1880. Size, 5 feet by 4 feet, 20 miles to the inch. In 4 Sheets, £1, 1s.; Roller, varnished. £1, 11s. 6d.; Folded, in Case, £1, 5s. 6d.

JASCHKE.—A TIBETAN-ENGLISH DICTIONARY. With special reference to the Prevailing Dialects. To which is added an English-Tibetan Vocabulary. By H. A. Jäschke, late Moravian Missionary at Kyèlang, British Lahoul. Imperial 8vo, pp. xxiv.-672, cloth. 1881. £1, 10s.

JASCHKE.—TIBETAN GRAMMAR. By H. A. Jäschke. Crown 8vo, pp. viii.-104, cloth. 1883. 5s.

JATAKA (THE), together with its COMMENTARY : being tales of the Anterior Birth of Gotama Buddha. Now first published in Pali, by V. Fausböll. Text. 8vo. Vol. I., pp. viii. and 512, cloth. 1877. 28s.—Vol. II., pp. 452, cloth. 1879, 28s.—Vol. III., pp. viii. and 544, cloth. 1883. 28s. (For Translation see Trübner's Oriental Series. "Buddhist Birth Stories.")

JENKINS.—A PALADIN OF FINANCE : Contemporary Manners. By E. Jenkins, Author of "Ginx's Baby." Crown 8vo, pp. iv. and 392, cloth. 1882. 7s. 6d.

JENKINS.—VEST-POCKET LEXICON. An English Dictionary of all except familiar Words, including the principal Scientific and Technical Terms, and Foreign Moneys, Weights and Measures; omitting what everybody knows, and containing what everybody wants to know and cannot readily find. By Jabez Jenkins. 64mo, pp. 564, cloth. 1879. 1s. 6d.

JOHNSON.—ORIENTAL RELIGIONS. India. See English and Foreign Philosophical Library, Extra Series, Vols. IV. and V.

JOHNSON.—ORIENTAL RELIGIONS AND THEIR RELATION TO UNIVERSAL RELIGION. Persia. By Samuel Johnson. With an Introduction by O. B. Frothingham. Demy 8vo, pp. xliv. and 784, cloth. 1885. 18s.

JOLLY.—See NARADÍYA.

JOMINI.—THE ART OF WAR. By Baron de Jomini, General and Aide-de-Camp to the Emperor of Russia. A New Edition, with Appendices and Maps. Translated from the French. By Captain G. H. Mendell, and Captain W. O. Craighill. Crown 8vo, pp. 410, cloth. 1879. 9s.

JOSEPH.—RELIGION, NATURAL AND REVEALED. A Series of Progressive Lessons for Jewish Youth. By N. S. Joseph. Crown 8vo, pp. xii.-296, cloth. 1879. 3s.

JUVENALIS SATIRÆ. With a Literal English Prose Translation and Notes. By J. D. Lewis, M.A., Trin. Coll. Camb. Second Edition. Two vols. 8vo, pp. xii. and 230 and 400, cloth. 1882. 12s.

KARCHER.—QUESTIONNAIRE FRANÇAIS. Questions on French Grammar, Idiomatic Difficulties, and Military Expressions. By Theodore Karcher, LL.B. Fourth Edition, greatly enlarged. Crown 8vo, pp. 224, cloth. 1879. 4s. 6d. Interleaved with writing paper, 5s. 6d.

KARDEC.—THE SPIRIT'S BOOK. Containing the Principles of Spiritist Doctrine on the Immortality of the Soul, &c., &c., according to the Teachings of Spirits of High Degree, transmitted through various mediums, collected and set in order by Allen Kardec. Translated from the 120th thousand by Anna Blackwell. Crown 8vo, pp. 512, cloth. 1875. 7s. 6d.

KARDEC.—THE MEDIUM'S BOOK ; or, Guide for Mediums and for Evocations. Containing the Theoretic Teachings of Spirits concerning all kinds of Manifestations, the Means of Communication with the Invisible World, the Development of Medianimity, &c., &c. By Allen Kardec. Translated by Anna Blackwell. Crown 8vo, pp. 456, cloth. 1876. 7s. 6d.

KARDEC.—HEAVEN AND HELL ; or, the Divine Justice Vindicated in the Plurality of Existences. By Allen Kardec. Translated by Anna Blackwell. Crown 8vo, pp. viii. and 448, cloth. 1878. 7s. 6d.

KEMP. See SCHOPENHAUER.

KENDRICK.—GREEK OLLENDORFF. A Progressive Exhibition of the Principles of the Greek Grammar. By Asahel C. Kendrick. 8vo, pp. 371, cloth. 1870. 9s.

KERMODE.—NATAL : Its Early History, Rise, Progress, and Future Prospects as a Field for Emigration. By W. Kermode, of Natal. Crown 8vo, pp. xii. and 228, with Map, cloth. 1883. 3s. 6d.

KEYS OF THE CREEDS (THE). Third Revised Edition. Crown 8vo, pp. 210, cloth. 1876. 5s.

KINAHAN.—VALLEYS AND THEIR RELATION TO FISSURES, FRACTURES, AND FAULTS. By G. H. Kinahan, M.R.I.A., F.R.G.S.I., &c. Dedicated by permission to his Grace the Duke of Argyll. Crown 8vo, pp. 256, cloth, illustrated. 7s. 6d.

KING'S STRATAGEM (The) ; OR, THE PEARL OF POLAND ; A Tragedy in Five Acts. By Stella. Second Edition. Crown 8vo, pp. 94, cloth. 1874. 2s. 6d.

KINGSTON.—THE UNITY OF CREATION. A Contribution to the Solution of the Religious Question. By F. H. Kingston. Crown 8vo, pp. viii. and 152, cloth. 1874. 5s.

KISTNER.—BUDDHA AND HIS DOCTRINES. A Bibliographical Essay. By Otto Kistner. 4to, pp. iv. and 32, sewed. 1869. 2s. 6d.

KNOX.—ON A MEXICAN MUSTANG. See under SWEET.

KLEMM.—MUSCLE BEATING ; or, Active and Passive Home Gymnastics, for Healthy and Unhealthy People. By C. Klemm. With Illustrations. 8vo, pp. 60, wrapper. 1878. 1s.

KOHL.—TRAVELS IN CANADA AND THROUGH THE STATES OF NEW YORK AND PENNSYLVANIA. By J. G. Kohl. Translated by Mrs. Percy Sinnett. Revised by the Author. Two vols. post 8vo, pp. xiv. and 794, cloth. 1861. £1, 1s.

KRAPF.—DICTIONARY OF THE SUAHILI LANGUAGE. Compiled by the Rev. Dr. L. Krapf, missionary of the Church Missionary Society in East Africa. With an Appendix, containing an outline of a Suahili Grammar. Medium 8vo, pp. xl. and 434, cloth. 1882. 30s.

KRAUS.—CARLSBAD AND ITS NATURAL HEALING AGENTS, from the Physiological and Therapeutical Point of View. By J. Kraus, M.D. With Notes Introductory by the Rev. J. T. Walters, M.A. Second Edition. Revised and enlarged. Crown 8vo, pp. 104, cloth. 1880. 5s.

KROEGER.—THE MINNESINGER OF GERMANY. By A. E. Kroeger. Fcap. 8vo, pp. 290, cloth. 1873. 7s.

KURZ.—FOREST FLORA OF BRITISH BURMA. By S. Kurz, Curator of the Herbarium, Royal Botanical Gardens, Calcutta. 2 vols. crown 8vo, pp. xxx., 550, and 614, cloth. 1877. 30s.

LACERDA'S JOURNEY TO CAZEMBE in 1798. Translated and Annotated by Captain R. F. Burton, F.R.G.S. Also Journey of the Pombeiros, &c. Demy 8vo, pp. viii. and 272. With Map, cloth. 1873. 7s. 6d.

LANARI.—COLLECTION OF ITALIAN AND ENGLISH DIALOGUES. By A. Lanari. Fcap. 8vo, pp. viii. and 200, cloth. 1874. 3s. 6d.

LAND.—THE PRINCIPLES OF HEBREW GRAMMAR. By J. P. N. Land, Professor of Logic and Metaphysics in the University of Leyden. Translated from the Dutch, by Reginald Lane Poole, Balliol College, Oxford. Part I. Sounds. Part II. Words. With Large Additions by the Author, and a new Preface. Crown 8vo, pp. xx. and 220, cloth. 1876. 7s. 6d.

LANE.—THE KORAN. See Trübner's Oriental Series.

LANGE.—A HISTORY OF MATERIALISM. See English and Foreign Philosophical Library, Vols. I. to III.

LANGE.—GERMANIA. A German Reading-book Arranged Progressively. By F. K. W. Lange, Ph.D. Part I. Anthology of German Prose and Poetry, with Vocabulary and Biographical Notes. 8vo, pp. xvi. and 216, cloth, 1881, 3s. 6d. Part II. Essays on German History and Institutions, with Notes. 8vo, pp. 124, cloth. 1881. 3s. 6d. Parts I. and II. together. 5s. 6d.

LANGE.—GERMAN PROSE WRITING. Comprising English Passages for Translation into German. Selected from Examination Papers of the University of London, the College of Preceptors, London, and the Royal Military Academy, Woolwich, arranged progressively, with Notes and Theoretical as well as Practical Treatises on themes for the writing of Essays. By F. K. W. Lange, Ph.D., Assistant German Master, Royal Academy, Woolwich; Examiner, Royal College of Preceptors London. Crown 8vo, pp. viii. and 176, cloth. 1881. 4s.

LANGE.—GERMAN GRAMMAR PRACTICE. By F. K. W. Lange, Ph.D. Crown 8vo, pp. viii. and 64, cloth. 1882. 1s. 6d.

LANGE.—COLLOQUIAL GERMAN GRAMMAR. With Special Reference to the Anglo-Saxon Element in the English Language. By F. K. W. Lange, Ph.D., &c. Crown 8vo, pp. xxxii. and 380, cloth. 1882. 4s. 6d.

LANMAN.—A SANSKRIT READER. With Vocabulary and Notes. By Charles Rockwell Lanman, Professor of Sanskrit in Harvard College. Part I. Imperial 8vo, pp. xx. and 294, cloth. 1884. 10s. 6d.

LARSEN.—DANISH-ENGLISH DICTIONARY. By A. Larsen. Crown 8vo, pp. viii. and 646, cloth. 1884. 7s. 6d.

LASCARIDES.—A Comprehensive Phraseological English-Ancient and Modern Greek Lexicon. Founded upon a manuscript of G. P. Lascarides, and Compiled by L. Myriantheus, Ph.D. 2 vols. 18mo, pp. xi. and 1338, cloth. 1882. £1, 10s.

LATHE (The) and its Uses; or, Instruction in the Art of Turning Wood and Metal, including a description of the most modern appliances for the Ornamentation of Plain and Curved Surfaces, &c. Sixth Edition. With additional Chapters and Index. Illustrated. 8vo, pp. iv. and 316, cloth. 1883. 10s. 6d.

LE-BRUN.—Materials for Translating from English into French; being a short Essay on Translation, followed by a Graduated Selection in Prose and Verse. By L. Le-Brun. Seventh Edition. Revised and corrected by Henri Van Laun. Post 8vo, pp. xii. and 204, cloth. 1882. 4s. 6d.

LEE.—Illustrations of the Physiology of Religion. In Sections adapted for the use of Schools. Part I. By Henry Lee, F.R.C.S., formerly Professor of Surgery, Royal College of Surgeons, &c. Crown 8vo, pp. viii. and 108, cloth. 1880. 3s. 6d.

LEES.—A Practical Guide to Health, and to the Home Treatment of the Common Ailments of Life: With a Section on Cases of Emergency, and Hints to Mothers on Nursing, &c. By F. Arnold Lees, F.L.S. Crown 8vo, pp. 334, stiff covers. 1874. 3s.

LEGGE.—The Chinese Classics. With a Translation, Critical and Exegetical, Notes, Prolegomena, and copious Indexes. By James Legge, D.D., of the London Missionary Society. In 7 vols. Royal 8vo. Vols. I.-V. in Eight Parts, published, cloth. £2, 2s. each Part.

LEGGE.—The Chinese Classics, translated into English. With Preliminary Essays and Explanatory Notes. Popular Edition. Reproduced for General Readers from the Author's work, containing the Original Text. By James Legge, D.D. Crown 8vo. Vol. I. The Life and Teachings of Confucius. Third Edition. Pp. vi. and 338, cloth. 1872. 10s. 6d.—Vol. II. The Works of Mencius. Pp. x. and 402, cloth, 12s.—Vol. III. The She-King; or, The Book of Poetry. Pp. vi. and 432, cloth. 1876. 12s.

LEGGE.—Confucianism in Relation to Christianity. A Paper read before the Missionary Conference in Shanghai, on May 11th, 1877. By Rev. James Legge, D.D., LL.D., &c. 8vo, pp. 12, sewed. 1877. 1s. 6d.

LEGGE.—A Letter to Professor Max Müller, chiefly on the Translation into English of the Chinese Terms *Ti* and *Shang Ti*. By James Legge, Professor of the Chinese Language and Literature in the University of Oxford. Crown 8vo, pp. 30, sewed. 1880. 1s.

LEIGH.—The Religion of the World. By H. Stone Leigh. 12mo, pp. xii. and 66, cloth. 1869. 2s. 6d.

LEIGH.—The Story of Philosophy. By Aston Leigh. Post 8vo, pp. xii. and 210, cloth. 1881. 6s.

LEÏLA-HANOUM.—A Tragedy in the Imperial Harem at Constantinople. By Leïla-Hanoum. Translated from the French, with Notes by General R. E. Colston. 16mo, pp. viii. and 300, cloth. 1883. 4s. Paper, 2s. 6d.

LELAND.—The Breitmann Ballads. The only authorised Edition. Complete in 1 vol., including Nineteen Ballads, illustrating his Travels in Europe (never before printed), with Comments by Fritz Schwackenhammer. By Charles G. Leland. Crown 8vo, pp. xxviii. and 292, cloth. 1872. 6s.

LELAND.—The Music Lesson of Confucius, and other Poems. By Charles G. Leland. Fcap. 8vo, pp. viii. and 168, cloth. 1871. 3s. 6d.

LELAND.—Gaudeamus. Humorous Poems translated from the German of Joseph Victor Scheffel and others. By Charles G. Leland. 16mo, pp. 176, cloth. 1872. 3s. 6d.

LELAND.—THE EGYPTIAN SKETCH-BOOK. By C. G. Leland. Crown 8vo, pp. viii. and 316, cloth. 1873. 7s. 6d.

LELAND.—THE ENGLISH GIPSIES AND THEIR LANGUAGE. By Charles G. Leland. Second Edition. Crown 8vo, pp. xvi. and 260, cloth. 1874. 7s. 6d.

LELAND.—FU-SANG; OR, THE DISCOVERY OF AMERICA by Chinese Buddhist Priests in the Fifth Century. By Charles G. Leland. Crown 8vo, pp. 232, cloth. 1875. 7s. 6d.

LELAND.—PIDGIN-ENGLISH SING-SONG; or, Songs and Stories in the China-English Dialect. With a Vocabulary. By Charles G. Leland. Crown 8vo, pp. viii. and 140, cloth. 1876. 5s.

LELAND.—THE GYPSIES. By C. G. Leland. Crown 8vo, pp. 372, cloth. 1882. 10s. 6d.

LEOPARDI.—See English and Foreign Philosophical Library, Vol. XVII.

LEO.—FOUR CHAPTERS OF NORTH'S PLUTARCH, Containing the Lives of Caius Marcius, Coriolanus, Julius Cæsar, Marcus Antonius, and Marcus Brutus, as Sources to Shakespeare's Tragedies; Coriolanus, Julius Cæsar, and Antony and Cleopatra; and partly to Hamlet and Timon of Athens. Photolithographed in the size of the Edition of 1595. With Preface, Notes comparing the Text of the Editions of 1579, 1595, 1603, and 1612; and Reference Notes to the Text of the Tragedies of Shakespeare. Edited by Professor F. A. Leo, Ph.D., Vice-President of the New Shakespeare Society; Member of the Directory of the German Shakespeare Society; and Lecturer at the Academy of Modern Philology at Berlin. Folio, pp. 22, 130 of facsimiles, half-morocco. Library Edition (limited to 250 copies), £1, 11s. 6d.; Amateur Edition (50 copies on a superior large hand-made paper), £3, 3s.

LEO.—SHAKESPEARE-NOTES. By F. A. Leo. Demy 8vo, pp. viii. and 120, cloth. 1885. 6s.

LEONOWENS.—LIFE AND TRAVEL IN INDIA: Being Recollections of a Journey before the Days of Railroads. By Anna Harriette Leonowens, Author of "The English Governess at the Siamese Court," and "The Romance of the Harem." 8vo, pp. 326, cloth, Illustrated. 1885. 10s. 6d.

LERMONTOFF.—THE DEMON. By Michael Lermontoff. Translated from the Russian by A. Condie Stephen. Crown 8vo, pp. 88, cloth. 1881. 2s. 6d.

LESLEY.—MAN'S ORIGIN AND DESTINY. Sketched from the Platform of the Physical Sciences. By. J. P. Lesley, Member of the National Academy of the United States, Professor of Geology, University of Pennsylvania. Second (Revised and considerably Enlarged) Edition, crown 8vo, pp. viii. and 142, cloth. 1881. 7s. 6d.

LESSING.—LETTERS ON BIBLIOLATRY. By Gotthold Ephraim Lessing. Translated from the German by the late H. H. Bernard, Ph.D. 8vo, pp. 184, cloth. 1862. 5s.

LESSING.—See English and Foreign Philosophical Library, Extra Series, Vols. I. and II.

LETTERS ON THE WAR BETWEEN GERMANY AND FRANCE. By Mommsen, Strauss, Max Müller, and Carlyle. Second Edition. Crown 8vo, pp. 120, cloth. 1871. 2s. 6d.

LEWES.—PROBLEMS OF LIFE AND MIND. By George Henry Lewes. First Series: The Foundations of a Creed. Vol. I., demy 8vo. Fourth edition, pp. 488, cloth. 1884. 12s.—Vol. II., demy 8vo, pp. 552, cloth. 1875. 16s.

LEWES.—PROBLEMS OF LIFE AND MIND. By George Henry Lewes. Second Series. THE PHYSICAL BASIS OF MIND. 8vo, with Illustrations, pp. 508, cloth. 1877. 16s. Contents.—The Nature of Life; The Nervous Mechanism; Animal Automatism; The Reflex Theory.

LEWES.—PROBLEMS OF LIFE AND MIND. By George Henry Lewes. Third Series. Problem the First—The Study of Psychology: Its Object, Scope, and Method. Demy 8vo, pp. 200, cloth. 1879. 7s. 6d.

LEWES.—PROBLEMS OF LIFE AND MIND. By George Henry Lewes. Third Series. Problem the Second—Mind as a Function of the Organism. Problem the Third—The Sphere of Sense and Logic of Feeling. Problem the Fourth—The Sphere of Intellect and Logic of Signs. Demy 8vo, pp. x. and 500, cloth. 1879. 15s.

LEWIS.—See JUVENAL and PLINY.

LIBRARIANS, TRANSACTIONS AND PROCEEDINGS OF THE CONFERENCE OF, held in London, October 1877. Edited by Edward B. Nicholson and Henry R. Tedder. Imperial 8vo, pp. 276, cloth. 1878. £1, 8s.

LIBRARY ASSOCIATION OF THE UNITED KINGDOM, Transactions and Proceedings of the Annual Meetings of the. Imperial 8vo, cloth. FIRST, held at Oxford, October 1, 2, 3, 1878. Edited by the Secretaries, Henry R. Tedder, Librarian of the Athenæum Club, and Ernest C. Thomas, late Librarian of the Oxford Union Society. Pp. viii. and 192. 1879. £1, 8s.—SECOND, held at Manchester, September 23, 24, and 25, 1879. Edited by H. R. Tedder and E. C. Thomas. Pp. x. and 184. 1880. £1, 1s.—THIRD, held at Edinburgh, October 5, 6, and 7, 1880. Edited by E. C. Thomas and C. Welsh. Pp. x. and 202. 1881. £1, 1s.—FOURTH and FIFTH, held in London, September 1881, and at Cambridge, September 1882. Edited by E. C. Thomas. Pp. x.-258. 1885. 28s.

LIEBER.—THE LIFE AND LETTERS OF FRANCIS LIEBER. Edited by T. S. Perry. 8vo, pp. iv. and 440, cloth, with Portrait. 1882. 14s.

LITTLE FRENCH READER (THE). Extracted from "The Modern French Reader." Third Edition. Crown 8vo, pp. 112, cloth. 1884. 2s.

LLOYD AND NEWTON.—PRUSSIA'S REPRESENTATIVE MAN. By F. Lloyd of the Universities of Halle and Athens, and W. Newton, F.R.G.S. Crown 8vo, pp. 648, cloth. 1875. 10s. 6d.

LOBSCHEID.—CHINESE AND ENGLISH DICTIONARY, arranged according to the Radicals. By W. Lobscheid. 1 vol. imperial 8vo, pp. 600, cloth. £2, 8s.

LOBSCHEID.—ENGLISH AND CHINESE DICTIONARY, with the Punti and Mandarin Pronunciation. By W. Lobscheid. Four Parts. Folio, pp. viii. and 2016, boards. £8, 8s.

LONG.—EASTERN PROVERBS. See Trübner's Oriental Series.

LOVETT.—THE LIFE AND STRUGGLES OF WILLIAM LOVETT in his pursuit of Bread, Knowledge, and Freedom; with some short account of the different Associations he belonged to, and of the Opinions he entertained. 8vo, pp. vi. and 474, cloth. 1876. 5s.

LOVELY.—WHERE TO GO FOR HELP: Being a Companion for Quick and Easy Reference of Police Stations, Fire-Engine Stations, Fire-Escape Stations, &c., &c., of London and the Suburbs. Compiled by W. Lovely, R.N. Third Edition. 18mo, pp. 16, sewed. 1882. 3d.

LOWELL.—THE BIGLOW PAPERS. By James Russell Lowell. Edited by Thomas Hughes, Q.C. A Reprint of the Authorised Edition of 1859, together with the Second Series of 1862. First and Second Series in 1 vol. Fcap., pp. lxviii.-140 and lxiv.-190, cloth. 1880. 2s. 6d.

LUCAS.—THE CHILDREN'S PENTATEUCH: With the Haphtarahs or Portions from the Prophets. Arranged for Jewish Children. By Mrs. Henry Lucas. Crown 8vo, pp. viii. and 570, cloth. 1878. 5s.

LUDEWIG.—THE LITERATURE OF AMERICAN ABORIGINAL LANGUAGES. By Hermann E. Ludewig. With Additions and Corrections by Professor Wm. W. Turner. Edited by Nicolas Trübner. 8vo, pp. xxiv. and 258, cloth. 1858. 10s. 6d.

LUKIN.—THE BOY ENGINEERS: What they did, and how they did it. By the Rev. L. J. Lukin, Author of "The Young Mechanic," &c. A Book for Boys; 30 Engravings. Imperial 16mo, pp. viii. and 344, cloth. 1877. 7s. 6d.

LUX E TENEBRIS; OR, THE TESTIMONY OF CONSCIOUSNESS. A Theoretic Essay. Crown 8vo, pp. 376, with Diagram, cloth. 1874. 10s. 6d.

MACCORMAC.—THE CONVERSATION OF A SOUL WITH GOD : A Theodicy. By Henry MacCormac, M.D. 16mo, pp. xvi. and 144, cloth. 1877. 3s. 6d.

MACHIAVELLI.—THE HISTORICAL,. POLITICAL, AND DIPLOMATIC WRITINGS OF NICCOLO MACHIAVELLI. Translated from the Italian by C. E. Detmold. With Portraits. 4 vols. 8vo, cloth, pp. xli., 420, 464, 488, and 472. 1882. £3, 3s.

MACKENZIE.—HISTORY OF THE RELATIONS OF THE GOVERNMENT WITH THE HILL TRIBES OF THE NORTH-EAST FRONTIER OF BENGAL. By Alexander Mackenzie, of the Bengal Civil Service; Secretary to the Government of India in the Home Department, and formerly Secretary to the Government of Bengal. Royal 8vo, pp. xviii. and 586, cloth, with Map. 1884. 16s.

MADDEN.—COINS OF THE JEWS. Being a History of the Jewish Coinage and Money in the Old and New Testaments. By Frederick W. Madden, M.R.A.S. Member of the Numismatic Society of London, Secretary of the Brighton College, &c., &c. With 279 Woodcuts and a Plate of Alphabets. Royal 4to, pp. xii. and 330, cloth. 1881. £2, 2s.

MADELUNG.—THE CAUSES AND OPERATIVE TREATMENT OF DUPUYTREN'S FINGER CONTRACTION. By Dr. Otto W. Madelung, Lecturer of Surgery at the University, and Assistant Surgeon at the University Hospital, Bonn. 8vo, pp. 24, sewed. 1876. 1s.

MAHAPARINIBBANASUTTA.—See CHILDERS.

MAHA-VIRA-CHARITA; or, The Adventures of the Great Hero Rama. An Indian Drama in Seven Acts. Translated into English Prose from the Sanskrit of Bhavabhúti. By John Pickford, M.A. Crown 8vo, cloth. 5s.

MAIMONIDES.—THE GUIDE OF THE PERPLEXED OF MAIMONIDES. See English and Foreign Philosophical Library.

MALLESON.—ESSAYS AND LECTURES ON INDIAN HISTORICAL SUBJECTS. By Colonel G. B. Malleson, C.S.I. Second Issue. Crown 8vo, pp. 348, cloth. 1876. 5s.

MAN.—ON THE ABORIGINAL INHABITANTS OF THE ANDAMAN ISLANDS. By Edward Horace Man, Assistant Superintendent, Andaman and Nicobar Islands, F.R.G.S., M.R.A.S., M.A.I. With Report of Researches into the Language of the South Andaman Islands. By A. J. Ellis, F.R.S., F.S.A. Reprinted from "The Journal of the Anthropological Institute of Great Britain and Ireland." Demy 8vo, pp. xxviii.-298, with Map and 8 Plates, cloth. 1885. 10s. 6d.

MANDLEY.—WOMAN OUTSIDE CHRISTENDOM. An Exposition of the Influence exerted by Christianity on the Social Position and Happiness of Women. By J. G. Mandley. Crown 8vo, pp. viii. and 160, cloth. 1880. 5s.

MANIPULUS VOCABULORUM. A Rhyming Dictionary of the English Language. By Peter Levins (1570). Edited, with an Alphabetical Index, by Henry B. Wheatley. 8vo, pp. xvi. and 370, cloth. 1867. 14s.

MANŒUVRES.—A RETROSPECT OF THE AUTUMN MANŒUVRES, 1871. With 5 Plans. By a Recluse. 8vo, pp. xii. and 133, cloth. 1872. 5s.

MARIETTE-BEY.—THE MONUMENTS OF UPPER EGYPT: a translation of the "Itinéraire de la Haute Egypte" of Auguste Mariette-Bey. Translated by Alphonse Mariette. Crown 8vo, pp. xvi. and 262, cloth. 1877. 7s. 6d.

MARKHAM.—QUICHUA GRAMMAR AND DICTIONARY. Contributions towards a Grammar and Dictionary of Quichua, the Language of the Yncas of Peru. Collected by Clements R. Markham, F.S.A. Crown 8vo, pp. 223, cloth. £1, 11s. 6d.

MARKHAM.—OLLANTA : A Drama in the Quichua Language. Text, Translation, and Introduction. By Clements R. Markham, C.B. Crown 8vo, pp. 128, cloth. 1871. 7s. 6d.

MARKHAM.—A MEMOIR OF THE LADY ANA DE OSORIO, Countess of Chincon, and Vice-Queen of Peru, A.D. 1629-39. With a Plea for the correct spelling of the Chinchona Genus. By Clements R. Markham, C.B., Member of the Imperial Academy Naturæ Curiosorum, with the Cognomen of Chinchon. Small 4to, pp. xii. and 100. With 2 Coloured Plates, Map, and Illustrations. Handsomely bound. 1874. 28s.

MARKHAM.—A Memoir on the Indian Surveys. By Clements R. Markham, C.B., F.R.S., &c., &c. Published by Order of H. M. Secretary of State for India in Council. Illustrated with Maps. Second Edition. Imperial 8vo, pp. xxx. and 481, boards. 1878. 10s. 6d.

MARKHAM.—Narratives of the Mission of George Bogle to Tibet, and of the Journey of Thomas Manning to Lhasa. Edited with Notes, an Introduction, and Lives of Mr. Bogle and Mr. Manning. By Clements R. Markham, C.B., F.R.S. Second Edition. 8vo, pp. clxv. and 362, cloth. With Maps and Illustrations. 1879. 21s.

MARKS.—Sermons. Preached on various occasions at the West London Synagogue of British Jews. By the Rev. Professor Marks, Minister of the Congregation. Published at the request of the Council. Second Series, demy 8vo, pp. viii.-310, cloth. 1885. 7s. 6d. Third Series, demy 8vo, pp. iv.-284, cloth. 1885. 7s. 6d.

MARMONTEL.—Belisaire. Par Marmontel. Nouvelle Edition. 12mo, pp. xii. and 123, cloth. 1867. 2s. 6d.

MARSDEN.—Numismata Orientalia Illustrata. The Plates of the Oriental Coins, Ancient and Modern, of the Collection of the late William Marsden, F.R.S., &c. &c. Engraved from Drawings made under his Directions. 4to, 57 Plates, cloth. 31s. 6d.

MARTIN and Trübner.—The Current Gold and Silver Coins of all Countries, their Weight and Fineness, and their Intrinsic Value in English Money, with Facsimiles of the Coins. By Leopold C. Martin, of Her Majesty's Stationery Office, and Charles Trübner. In 1 vol. medium 8vo, 141 Plates, printed in Gold and Silver, and representing about 1000 Coins, with 160 pages of Text, handsomely bound in embossed cloth, richly gilt, with Emblematical Designs on the Cover, and gilt edges. 1863. £2, 2s.

MARTIN.—The Chinese: their Education, Philosophy, and Letters. By W. A. P. Martin, D.D., LL.D., President of the Tungwen College, Pekin. 8vo, pp. 320, cloth. 1881. 7s. 6d.

MARTINEAU.—Essays, Philosophical and Theological. By James Martineau. 2 vols. crown 8vo, pp. iv. and 414—x. and 430, cloth. 1875. £1, 4s.

MARTINEAU.—Letters from Ireland. By Harriet Martineau. Reprinted from the *Daily News*. Post 8vo, pp. viii. and 220, cloth. 1852. 6s. 6d.

MASON.—Burma: Its People and Productions; or, Notes on the Fauna, Flora, and Minerals of Tenasserim, Pegu and Burma. By the Rev. F. Mason, D.D., M.R.A.S., Corresponding Member of the American Oriental Society, of the Boston Society of Natural History, and of the Lyceum of Natural History, New York. Vol. I. Geology, Mineralogy and Zoology. Vol. II. Botany. Rewritten and Enlarged by W. Theobald, late Deputy-Superintendent Geological Survey of India. Two Vols., royal 8vo, pp. xxvi. and 560; xvi. and 788 and xxxvi., cloth. 1884. £3.

MATHEWS.—Abraham Ibn Ezra's Commentary on the Canticles after the First Recension. Edited from the MSS., with a translation, by H. J. Mathews, B.A., Exeter College, Oxford. Crown 8vo, pp. x., 34, and 24, limp cloth. 1874. 2s. 6d.

MATERIA MEDICA, Physiological and Applied. Vol. I. Contents:—Aconitum, by R. E. Dudgeon, M.D.; Crotalus, by J. W. Hayward, M.D.; Digitalis, by F. Black, M.D.; Kali Bichromicum, by J. J. Drysdale, M.D.; Nux Vomica, by F. Black, M.D.; Plumbum, by F. Black, M.D. Demy 8vo, pp. xxiv.-726, cloth. 1884. 15s.

MAXWELL.—A Manual of the Malay Language. By W. E. Maxwell, of the Inner Temple, Barrister-at-Law; Assistant Resident, Perak, Malay Peninsula. With an Introductory Sketch of the Sanskrit Element in Malay. Crown 8vo, pp. viii. and 182, cloth. 1882. 7s. 6d.

MAY.—A Bibliography of Electricity and Magnetism. 1860 to 1883. With Special Reference to Electro-Technics. Compiled by G. May. With an Index by O. Salle, Ph.D. Crown 8vo, pp. viii.-204, cloth. 1884. 5s.

MAYER.—ON THE ART OF POTTERY: with a History of its Rise and Progress in Liverpool. By Joseph Mayer, F.S.A., F.R.S.N.A., &c. 8vo, pp. 100, boards. 1873. 5s.

MAYERS.—TREATIES BETWEEN THE EMPIRE OF CHINA AND FOREIGN POWERS, together with Regulations for the conduct of Foreign Trade, &c. Edited by W. F. Mayers, Chinese Secretary to H.B.M.'s Legation at Peking. 8vo, pp. 246, cloth. 1877. 25s.

MAYERS.—THE CHINESE GOVERNMENT: a Manual of Chinese Titles, categorically arranged and explained, with an Appendix. By Wm. Fred. Mayers, Chinese Secretary to H.B.M.'s Legation at Peking, &c., &c. Royal 8vo, pp. viii. and 160, cloth. 1878. 30s.

M'CRINDLE.—ANCIENT INDIA, AS DESCRIBED BY MEGASTHENES AND ARRIAN; being a translation of the fragments of the Indika of Megasthenes collected by Dr. Schwanbeck, and of the first part of the Indika of Arrian. By J. W. M'Crindle, M.A., Principal of the Government College, Patna, &c. With Introduction, Notes, and Map of Ancient India. Post 8vo, pp. xi. and 224, cloth. 1877. 7s. 6d.

M'CRINDLE.—THE COMMERCE AND NAVIGATION OF THE ERYTHRÆAN SEA. Being a Translation of the Periplus Maris Erythræi, by an Anonymous Writer, and of Arrian's Account of the Voyage of Nearkhos, from the Mouth of the Indus to the Head of the Persian Gulf. With Introduction, Commentary, Notes, and Index. By J. W. M'Crindle, M.A., Edinburgh, &c. Post 8vo, pp. iv. and 238, cloth. 1879. 7s. 6d.

M'CRINDLE.—Ancient India as Described by Ktesias the Knidian; being a Translation of the Abridgment of his "Indika" by Photios, and of the Fragments of that Work preserved in other Writers. With Introduction, Notes, and Index. By J. W. M'Crindle, M.A., M.R.S.A. 8vo, pp. viii. and 104, cloth. 1882. 6s.

MECHANIC (THE YOUNG). A Book for Boys, containing Directions for the use of all kinds of Tools, and for the construction of Steam Engines and Mechanical Models, including the Art of Turning in Wood and Metal. Fifth Edition. Imperial 16mo, pp. iv. and 346, and 70 Engravings, cloth. 1878. 6s.

MECHANIC'S WORKSHOP (AMATEUR). A Treatise containing Plain and Concise Directions for the Manipulation of Wood and Metals, including Casting, Forging, Brazing, Soldering, and Carpentry. By the Author of "The Lathe and its Uses." Sixth Edition. Demy 8vo, pp. iv. and 148. Illustrated, cloth. 1880. 6s.

MEDITATIONS ON DEATH AND ETERNITY. Translated from the German by Frederica Rowan. Published by Her Majesty's gracious permission. 8vo, pp. 386, cloth. 1862. 10s. 6d.

DITTO. Smaller Edition, crown 8vo, printed on toned paper, pp. 352, cloth. 1884. 6s.

MEDITATIONS ON LIFE AND ITS RELIGIOUS DUTIES. Translated from the German by Frederica Rowan. Dedicated to H.R.H. Princess Louis of Hesse. Published by Her Majesty's gracious permission. Being the Companion Volume to "Meditations on Death and Eternity." 8vo, pp. vi. and 370, cloth. 1863. 10s. 6d.

DITTO. Smaller Edition, crown 8vo, printed on toned paper, pp. 338. 1863. 6s.

MEDLICOTT.—A MANUAL OF THE GEOLOGY OF INDIA, chiefly compiled from the observations of the Geological Survey. By H. B. Medlicott, M.A., Superintendent, Geological Survey of India, and W. T. Blanford, A.R.S.M., F.R.S., Deputy Superintendent. Published by order of the Government of India. 2 vols. 8vo, pp. xviii.-lxxx.-818, with 21 Plates and large coloured Map mounted in case, uniform, cloth. 1879. 16s. (For Part III. see BALL.)

MEGHA-DUTA (THE). (Cloud-Messenger.) By Kālidāsa. Translated from the Sanskrit into English Verse by the late H. H. Wilson, M.A., F.R.S. The Vocabulary by Francis Johnson. New Edition. 4to, pp. xi. and 180, cloth. 10s. 6d.

MEREDYTH.—ARCA, A REPERTOIRE OF ORIGINAL POEMS, Sacred and Secular. By F. Meredyth, M.A., Canon of Limerick Cathedral. Crown 8vo, pp. 124, cloth. 1875. 5s.

METCALFE.—THE ENGLISHMAN AND THE SCANDINAVIAN. By Frederick Metcalfe, M.A., Fellow of Lincoln College, Oxford; Translator of "Gallus" and "Charicles;" and Author of "The Oxonian in Iceland." Post 8vo, pp. 512, cloth. 1880. 18s.

MICHEL.—LES ÉCOSSAIS EN FRANCE, LES FRANÇAIS EN ÉCOSSE. Par Francisque Michel, Correspondant de l'Institut de France, &c. In 2 vols. 8vo, pp. vii., 547, and 551, rich blue cloth, with emblematical designs. With upwards of 100 Coats of Arms, and other Illustrations. Price, £1, 12s.—Also a Large-Paper Edition (limited to 100 Copies), printed on Thick Paper. 2 vols. 4to, half morocco, with 3 additional Steel Engravings. 1862. £3, 3s.

MICKIEWICZ.—KONRAD WALLENROD. An Historical Poem. By A. Mickiewicz. Translated from the Polish into English Verse by Miss M. Biggs. 18mo, pp. xvi. and 100, cloth. 1882. 2s. 6d.

MILL.—AUGUSTE COMTE AND POSITIVISM. By the late John Stuart Mill, M.P. Third Edition. 8vo, pp. 200, cloth. 1882. 3s. 6d.

MILLHOUSE.—MANUAL OF ITALIAN CONVERSATION. For the Use of Schools. By John Millhouse. 18mo, pp. 126, cloth. 1866. 2s.

MILLHOUSE.—NEW ENGLISH AND ITALIAN PRONOUNCING AND EXPLANATORY DICTIONARY. By John Millhouse. Vol. I. English-Italian. Vol. II. Italian-English. Fourth Edition. 2 vols. square 8vo, pp. 654 and 740, cloth. 1867. 12s.

MILNE.—NOTES ON CRYSTALLOGRAPHY AND CRYSTALLO-PHYSICS. Being the Substance of Lectures delivered at Yedo during the years 1876-1877. By John Milne, F.G.S. 8vo, pp. viii. and 70, cloth. 1879. 3s.

MILTON AND VONDEL.—See EDMUNDSON.

MINOCHCHERJI.—PAHLAVI, GUJÂRATI, AND ENGLISH DICTIONARY. By Jamashji Dastur Minochcherji. Vol. I., with Photograph of Author. 8vo, pp. clxxii. and 168, cloth. 1877. 14s.

MITRA.—BUDDHA GAYA: The Hermitage of Sákya Muni. By Rajendralala Mitra, LL.D., C.I.E., &c. 4to, pp. xvi. and 258, with 51 Plates, cloth. 1879. £3.

MOCATTA.—MORAL BIBLICAL GLEANINGS AND PRACTICAL TEACHINGS, Illustrated by Biographical Sketches Drawn from the Sacred Volume. By J. L. Mocatta. 8vo, pp. viii. and 446, cloth. 1872. 7s.

MODERN FRENCH READER (THE). Prose. Junior Course. Tenth Edition. Edited by Ch. Cassal, LL.D., and Théodore Karcher, LL.B. Crown 8vo, pp. xiv. and 224, cloth. 1884. 2s. 6d.

SENIOR COURSE. Third Edition. Crown 8vo, pp. xiv. and 418, cloth. 1880. 4s.

MODERN FRENCH READER.—A GLOSSARY of Idioms, Gallicisms, and other Difficulties contained in the Senior Course of the Modern French Reader; with Short Notices of the most important French Writers and Historical or Literary Characters, and hints as to the works to be read or studied. By Charles Cassal, LL.D., &c. Crown 8vo, pp. viii. and 104, cloth. 1881. 2s. 6d.

MODERN FRENCH READER.—SENIOR COURSE AND GLOSSARY combined. 6s.

MORELET.—TRAVELS IN CENTRAL AMERICA, including Accounts of some Regions unexplored since the Conquest. From the French of A. Morelet, by Mrs. M. F Squier. Edited by E. G. Squier. 8vo, pp. 430, cloth. 1871. 8s. 6d.

MORFILL.—SIMPLIFIED POLISH GRAMMAR. See Trübner's Collection.

MORFIT.—A Practical Treatise on the Manufacture of Soaps. By Campbell Morfit, M.D., F.C.S., formerly Professor of Applied Chemistry in the University of Maryland. With Illustrations. Demy 8vo, pp. xii. and 270, cloth. 1871. £2, 12s. 6d.

MORFIT.—A Practical Treatise on Pure Fertilizers, and the Chemical Conversion of Rock Guanos, Marlstones, Coprolites, and the Crude Phosphates of Lime and Alumina generally into various valuable Products. By Campbell Morfit, M.D., F.C.S., formerly Professor of Applied Chemistry in the University of Maryland. With 28 Plates. 8vo, pp. xvi. and 547, cloth. 1873. £4, 4s.

MORRIS.—A Descriptive and Historical Account of the Godavery District, in the Presidency of Madras. By Henry Morris, formerly of the Madras Civil Service, author of "A History of India, for use in Schools," and other works. With a Map. 8vo, pp. xii. and 390, cloth. 1878. 12s.

MOSENTHAL.—Ostriches and Ostrich Farming. By J. de Mosenthal, late Member of the Legistive Council of the Cape of Good Hope, &c., and James E. Harting, F.L.S., F.Z.S., Member of the British Ornithologist's Union, &c. Second Edition. With 8 full-page illustrations and 20 woodcuts. Royal 8vo, pp. xxiv. and 246, cloth. 1879. 10s. 6d.

MOTLEY.—John Lothrop Motley: a Memoir. By Oliver Wendell Holmes. English Copyright Edition. Crown 8vo, pp. xii. and 275, cloth. 1878. 6s.

MUELLER.—The Organic Constituents of Plants and Vegetable Substances, and their Chemical Analysis. By Dr. G. C. Wittstein. Authorised Translation from the German Original, enlarged with numerous Additions, by Baron Ferd. von Mueller, K.C.M.G., M. & Ph. D., F.R.S. Crown 8vo, pp. xviii. and 332, wrapper. 1880. 14s.

MUELLER.—Select Extra-Tropical Plants readily eligible for Industrial Culture or Naturalisation. With Indications of their Native Countries and some of their Uses. By F. Von Mueller, K.C.M.G., M.D., Ph.D., F.R.S. 8vo, pp. x., 394, cloth. 1880. 8s.

MUHAMMED.—The Life of Muhammed. Based on Muhammed Ibn Ishak. By Abd El Malik Ibn Hisham. Edited by Dr. Ferdinand Wüstenfeld. One volume containing the Arabic Text. 8vo, pp. 1026, sewed. £1, 1s. Another volume, containing Introduction, Notes, and Index in German. 8vo, pp. lxxii. and 266, sewed. 7s. 6d. Each part sold separately.

MUIR.—Extracts from the Coran. In the Original, with English rendering. Compiled by Sir William Muir, K.C.S.I., LL.D., Author of "The Life of Mahomet." Second Edition. Crown 8vo, pp. viii. and 64, cloth. 1885. 2s. 6d.

MUIR.—Original Sanskrit Texts, on the Origin and History of the People of India, their Religion and Institutions. Collected, Translated, and Illustrated by John Muir, D.C.L., LL.D., Ph.D., &c. &c.

Vol. I. Mythical and Legendary Accounts of the Origin of Caste, with an Inquiry into its existence in the Vedic Age. Second Edition, rewritten and greatly enlarged. 8vo, pp. xx. and 532, cloth. 1868. £1, 1s.

Vol. II. The Trans-Himalayan Origin of the Hindus, and their Affinity with the Western Branches of the Aryan Race. Second Edition, revised, with Additions. 8vo, pp. xxxii. and 512, cloth. 1871. £1, 1s.

Vol. III. The Vedas: Opinions of their Authors, and of later Indian Writers, on their Origin, Inspiration, and Authority. Second Edition, revised and enlarged. 8vo, pp. xxxii. and 312, cloth. 1868. 16s.

Vol. IV. Comparison of the Vedic with the later representation of the principal Indian Deities. Second Edition, revised. 8vo, pp. xvi. and 524, cloth. 1873. £1, 1s.

MUIR.—ORIGINAL SANSKRIT TEXTS—*continued*.
Vol. V. Contributions to a Knowledge of the Cosmogony, Mythology, Religious Ideas, Life and Manners of the Indians in the Vedic Age. Third Edition. 8vo, pp. xvi. and 492, cloth. 1884. £1, 1s.

MUIR.—TRANSLATIONS FROM THE SANSKRIT. See Trübner's Oriental Series.

MULHALL.—HANDBOOK OF THE RIVER PLATE, Comprising the Argentine Republic, Uruguay, and Paraguay. With Six Maps. By M. G. and E. T. Mulhall, Proprietors and Editors of the Buenos Ayres *Standard*. Fifth Edition (Ninth Thousand), crown 8vo, pp. x. and 732, cloth. 1885. 7s. 6d.

MÜLLER.—OUTLINE DICTIONARY, for the Use of Missionaries, Explorers, and Students of Language. With an Introduction on the proper Use of the Ordinary English Alphabet in transcribing Foreign Languages. By F. Max Müller, M.A. The Vocabulary compiled by John Bellows. 12mo, pp. 368, morocco. 1867. 7s. 6d.

MÜLLER.—LECTURE ON BUDDHIST NIHILISM. By F. Max Müller, M.A. Fcap. 8vo, sewed. 1869. 1s.

MÜLLER.—THE SACRED HYMNS OF THE BRAHMINS, as preserved to us in the oldest collection of religious poetry, the Rig-Veda-Sanhita. Translated and explained, by F. Max Müller, M.A., Fellow of All Souls' College, Professor of Comparative Philology at Oxford, Foreign Member of the Institute of France, &c., &c. Vol. I. Hymns to the Maruts or the Storm-Gods. 8vo, pp. clii. and 264, cloth. 1869. 12s. 6d.

MÜLLER.—THE HYMNS OF THE RIG-VEDA, in the Samhita and Pada Texts. Reprinted from the Editio Princeps. By F. Max Müller, M.A., &c. Second Edition, with the two Texts on Parallel Pages. In two vols. 8vo, pp. 1704, sewed. £1, 12s.

MÜLLER.—A SHORT HISTORY OF THE BOURBONS. From the Earliest Period down to the Present Time. By R. M. Müller, Ph.D., Modern Master at Forest School, Walthamstow, and Author of "Parallèle entre 'Jules César,' par Shakespeare, et 'Le Mort de César,' par Voltaire," &c. Fcap. 8vo, pp. 30, wrapper. 1882. 1s.

MÜLLER.—ANCIENT INSCRIPTIONS IN CEYLON. By Dr. Edward Müller. 2 Vols. Text, crown 8vo, pp. 220, cloth, and Plates, oblong folio, cloth. 1883. 21s.

MÜLLER.—PALI GRAMMAR. See Trübner's Collection.

MULLEY.—GERMAN GEMS IN AN ENGLISH SETTING. Translated by Jane Mulley. Fcap., pp. xii. and 180, cloth. 1877. 3s. 6d.

NÁGÁNANDA; OR, THE JOY OF THE SNAKE WORLD. A Buddhist Drama in Five Acts. Translated into English Prose, with Explanatory Notes, from the Sanskrit of Sri-Harsha-Deva, by Palmer Boyd, B.A. With an Introduction by Professor Cowell. Crown 8vo, pp. xvi. and 100, cloth. 1872. 4s. 6d.

NAPIER.—FOLK LORE; or, Superstitious Beliefs in the West of Scotland within this Century. With an Appendix, showing the probable relation of the modern Festivals of Christmas, May Day, St. John's Day, and Hallowe'en, to ancient Sun and Fire Worship. By James Napier, F.R.S.E., &c. Crown 8vo, pp. vii. and 190, cloth. 1878. 4s.

NARADÍYA DHARMA-SASTRA; OR, THE INSTITUTES OF NARADA. Translated, for the first time, from the unpublished Sanskrit original. By Dr. Julius Jolly, University, Wurzburg. With a Preface, Notes, chiefly critical, an Index of Quotations from Narada in the principal Indian Digests, and a general Index. Crown 8vo, pp. xxxv. and 144, cloth. 1876. 10s. 6d.

NAVILLE.—PITHOM. See Egypt Exploration Fund.

NEVILL.—HAND LIST OF MOLLUSCA IN THE INDIAN MUSEUM, CALCUTTA. By Geoffrey Nevill, C.M.Z.S., &c., First Assistant to the Superintendent of the Indian Museum. Part I. Gastropoda, Pulmonata, and Prosobranchia-Neurobranchia. 8vo, pp. xvi. and 338, cloth. 1878. 15s.

NEWMAN.—THE ODES OF HORACE. Translated into Unrhymed Metres, with Introduction and Notes. By F. W. Newman. Second Edition. Post 8vo, pp. xxi. and 247, cloth. 1876. 4s.

NEWMAN.—THEISM, DOCTRINAL AND PRACTICAL; or, Didactic Religious Utterances. By F. W. Newman. 4to, pp. 184, cloth. 1858. 4s. 6d.

NEWMAN.—HOMERIC TRANSLATION IN THEORY AND PRACTICE. A Reply to Matthew Arnold. By F. W. Newman. Crown 8vo, pp. 104, stiff covers. 1861. 2s. 6d.

NEWMAN.—HIAWATHA: Rendered into Latin. With Abridgment. By F. W. Newman. 12mo, pp. vii. and 110, sewed. 1862. 2s. 6d.

NEWMAN.—A HISTORY OF THE HEBREW MONARCHY from the Administration of Samuel to the Babylonish Captivity. By F. W. Newman. Third Edition. Crown 8vo, pp. x. and 354, cloth. 1865. 8s. 6d.

NEWMAN.—PHASES OF FAITH; or, Passages from the History of my Creed. By F. W. Newman. New Edition; with Reply to Professor Henry Rogers, Author of the "Eclipse of Faith." Crown 8vo, pp. viii. and 212, cloth. 1881. 3s. 6d.

NEWMAN.—A HANDBOOK OF MODERN ARABIC, consisting of a Practical Grammar, with numerous Examples, Dialogues, and Newspaper Extracts, in European Type. By F. W. Newman. Post 8vo, pp. xx. and 192, cloth. 1866. 6s.

NEWMAN.—TRANSLATIONS OF ENGLISH POETRY INTO LATIN VERSE. Designed as Part of a New Method of Instructing in Latin. By F. W. Newman. Crown 8vo, pp. xiv. and 202, cloth. 1868. 6s.

NEWMAN.—THE SOUL: Her Sorrows and her Aspirations. An Essay towards the Natural History of the Soul, as the True Basis of Theology. By F. W. Newman. Tenth Edition. Post 8vo, pp. xii. and 162, cloth. 1882. 3s. 6d.

NEWMAN.—THE TEXT OF THE IGUVINE INSCRIPTIONS. With Interlinear Latin Translation and Notes. By F. W. Newman. 8vo, pp. 56, sewed. 1868. 2s.

NEWMAN.—MISCELLANIES; chiefly Addresses, Academical and Historical. By F. W. Newman. 8vo, pp. iv. and 356, cloth. 1869. 7s. 6d.

NEWMAN.—THE ILIAD OF HOMER, faithfully translated into Unrhymed English Metre, by F. W. Newman. Royal 8vo, pp. xvi. and 384, cloth. 1871. 10s. 6d.

NEWMAN.—A DICTIONARY OF MODERN ARABIC. 1. Anglo-Arabic Dictionary. 2. Anglo-Arabic Vocabulary. 3. Arabo-English Dictionary. By F. W. Newman. In 2 vols. crown 8vo, pp. xvi. and 376-464, cloth. 1871. £1, 1s.

NEWMAN.—HEBREW THEISM. By F. W. Newman. Royal 8vo, pp. viii. and 172 Stiff wrappers. 1874. 4s. 6d.

NEWMAN.—THE MORAL INFLUENCE OF LAW. A Lecture by F. W. Newman, May 20, 1860. Crown 8vo, pp. 16, sewed. 3d.

NEWMAN.—RELIGION NOT HISTORY. By F. W. Newman. Foolscap, pp. 58, paper wrapper. 1877. 1s.

NEWMAN.—MORNING PRAYERS IN THE HOUSEHOLD OF A BELIEVER IN GOD. By F. W. Newman. Second Edition. Crown 8vo, pp. 80, limp cloth. 1882. 1s. 6d.

NEWMAN.—REORGANIZATION OF ENGLISH INSTITUTIONS. A Lecture by Emeritus Professor F. W. Newman. Delivered in the Manchester Athenæum, October 15, 1875. Crown 8vo, pp. 28, sewed. 1880. 6d.

NEWMAN.—WHAT IS CHRISTIANITY WITHOUT CHRIST? By F. W. Newman, Emeritus Professor of University College, London. 8vo, pp. 28, stitched in wrapper. 1881. 1s.

NEWMAN.—LIBYAN VOCABULARY. An Essay towards Reproducing the Ancient Numidian Language out of Four Modern Languages. By F. W. Newman. Crown 8vo, pp. vi. and 204, cloth. 1882. 10s. 6d.

NEWMAN.—A CHRISTIAN COMMONWEALTH. By F. W. Newman. Crown 8vo, pp. 60, cloth. 1883. 1s.

NEWMAN.—CHRISTIANITY IN ITS CRADLE. By F. W. Newman, once Fellow of Balliol College, Oxford, now Emeritus Professor of University College, London. Crown 8vo, pp. iv. and 132, cloth. 1884. 2s.

NEWMAN.—COMMENTS ON THE TEXT OF ÆSCHYLUS. By F. W. Newman, Honorary Fellow of Worcester College, Oxford, and formerly Fellow of Balliol College. Demy 8vo, pp. xii. and 144, cloth. 1884. 5s.

NEWMAN.—REBILIUS CRUSO: Robinson Crusoe in Latin. A Book to Lighten Tedium to a Learner. By F. W. Newman, Emeritus Professor of Latin in University College, London; Honorary Fellow of Worcester College, Oxford. Post 8vo, pp. xii. and 110, cloth. 1884. 5s.

NEW SOUTH WALES, PUBLICATIONS OF THE GOVERNMENT OF. List on application.

NEW SOUTH WALES.—JOURNAL AND PROCEEDINGS OF THE ROYAL SOCIETY OF Published annually. Price 10s. 6d. List of Contents on application.

NEWTON.—PATENT LAW AND PRACTICE: showing the mode of obtaining and opposing Grants, Disclaimers, Confirmations, and Extensions of Patents. With a Chapter on Patent Agents. By A. V. Newton. Enlarged Edition. Crown 8vo, pp. xii. and 104, cloth. 1879. 2s. 6d.

NEWTON.—AN ANALYSIS OF THE PATENT AND COPYRIGHT LAWS: Including the various Acts relating to the Protection of Inventions, Designs, Trade Marks; Literary and Musical Compositions, Dramatic Performances; Engravings, Sculpture, Paintings, Drawings, and Photographs. By A. Newton, author of "Patent Law and Practice." Demy 8vo, pp. viii. and 70, cloth. 1884. 3s. 6d.

NEW ZEALAND INSTITUTE PUBLICATIONS:—
I. TRANSACTIONS AND PROCEEDINGS of the New Zealand Institute. Demy 8vo, stitched. Vols. I. to XVI., 1868 to 1883. £1, 1s. each.
II. AN INDEX TO THE TRANSACTIONS AND PROCEEDINGS of the New Zealand Institute. Vols. I. to VIII. Edited and Published under the Authority of the Board of Governors of the Institute. By James Hector, C.M.G., M.D., F.R.S. Demy, 8vo, 44 pp., stitched. 1877. 2s. 6d.

NEW ZEALAND.—GEOLOGICAL SURVEY. List of Publications on application.

NOIRIT.—A FRENCH COURSE IN TEN LESSONS. By Jules Noirit, B.A. Lessons I.-IV. Crown 8vo, pp. xiv. and 80, sewed. 1870. 1s. 6d.

NOIRIT.—FRENCH GRAMMATICAL QUESTIONS for the use of Gentlemen preparing for the Army, Civil Service, Oxford Examinations, &c., &c. By Jules Noirit. Crown 8vo, pp. 62, cloth. 1870. 1s. Interleaved, 1s. 6d.

NOURSE.—NARRATIVE OF THE SECOND ARCTIC EXPEDITION MADE BY CHARLES F. HALL. His Voyage to Repulse Bay; Sledge Journeys to the Straits of Fury and Hecla, and to King William's Land, and Residence among the Eskimos during the years 1864-69. Edited under the orders of the Hon. Secretary of the Navy, by Prof. J. E. Nourse, U.S.N. 4to, pp. l. and 644, cloth. With maps, heliotypes, steel and wood engravings. 1880. £1, 8s.

NUGENT'S IMPROVED FRENCH AND ENGLISH AND ENGLISH AND FRENCH POCKET DICTIONARY. Par Smith. 24mo, pp. 489 and 320, cloth. 1873. 3s.

NUTT.—TWO TREATISES ON VERBS CONTAINING FEEBLE AND DOUBLE LETTERS. By R. Jehuda Hayug of Fez. Translated into Hebrew from the original Arabic by R. Moses Gikatilia of Cordova, with the Treatise on Punctuation by the same author, translated by Aben Ezra. Edited from Bodleian MSS., with an English translation, by J. W. Nutt, M.A. Demy 8vo, pp. 312, sewed. 1870. 5s.

NUMISMATA ORIENTALIA ILLUSTRATA. See MARSDEN, and INTERNATIONAL.

NUTT.—A SKETCH OF SAMARITAN HISTORY, DOGMA, AND LITERATURE. An Introduction to "Fragments of a Samaritan Targum." By J. W. Nutt, M.A., &c., &c. Demy 8vo, pp. 180, cloth. 1874. 5s.

OEHLENSCHLÄGER.—AXEL AND VALBORG: a Tragedy, in Five Acts, and other Poems. Translated from the Danish of Adam Oehlenschläger by Pierce Butler, M.A., late Rector of Ulcombe, Kent. Edited by Professor Palmer, M.A., of St. John's Coll., Camb. With a Memoir of the Translator. Fcap. 8vo, pp. xii. and 164, cloth. 1874. 5s.

OERA LINDA BOOK (THE).—From a Manuscript of the 13th Century, with the permission of the proprietor, C. Over de Linden of the Helder. The Original Frisian Text as verified by Dr. J. O. Ottema, accompanied by an English Version of Dr. Ottema's Dutch Translation. By W. R. Sandbach. 8vo, pp. xxv. and 254, cloth. 1876. 5s.

OGAREFF.—ESSAI SUR LA SITUATION RUSSE. Lettres à un Anglais. Par N. Ogareff. 12mo, pp. 150, sewed. 1862. 3s.

OLCOTT.—A BUDDHIST CATECHISM, according to the Canon of the Southern Church. By Colonel H. S. Olcott, President of the Theosophical Society. 24mo, pp. 32. 1s.

OLCOTT.—THE YOGA PHILOSOPHY: Being the Text of Patanjali, with Bhojarajah's Commentary. A Reprint of the English Translation of the above, by the late Dr. Ballantyne and Govind Shastri Deva; to which are added Extracts from Various Authors. With an Introduction by Colonel H. S. Olcott, President of the Theosophical Society. The whole Edited by Tukaram Tatia, F.T.S. Crown 8vo, pp. xvi.-294, wrapper. 1882. 7s. 6d.

OLLENDORFF.—METODO PARA APRENDER A LEER, escribir y hablar el Inglés segun el sistema de Ollendorff. Por Ramon Palenzuela y Juan de la Carreño. 8vo, pp. xlvi. and 460, cloth. 1873. 7s. 6d.

KEY to Ditto. Crown 8vo, pp. 112, cloth. 1873. 4s.

OLLENDORFF.—METODO PARA APRENDER A LEER, escribir y hablar el Frances, segun el verdadero sistema de Ollendorff; ordenado en lecciones progresivas, consistiendo de ejercicios orales y escritos; enriquecido de la pronunciacion figurada como se estila en la conversacion; y de un Apéndice abrazando las reglas de la sintáxis, la formacion de los verbos regulares, y la conjugacion de los irregulares. Por Teodoro Simonné, Professor de Lenguas. Crown 8vo, pp. 342, cloth. 1873. 6s.

KEY to Ditto. Crown 8vo, pp. 80, cloth. 1873. 3s. 6d.

OPPERT.—ON THE CLASSIFICATION OF LANGUAGES: A Contribution to Comparative Philology. By Dr. Gustav Oppert, Ph.D., Professor of Sanskrit, Presidency College, Madras. 8vo, paper, pp. viii. and 146. 1883. 7s. 6d.

OPPERT.—LISTS OF SANSKRIT MANUSCRIPTS in Private Libraries of Southern India, Compiled, Arranged, and Indexed by Gustav Oppert, Ph.D., Professor of Sanskrit, Presidency College, Madras. Vol. I. 8vo, pp. vii. and 620, cloth. 1883. £1, 1s.

OPPERT.—ON THE WEAPONS, ARMY ORGANISATION, AND POLITICAL MAXIMS OF THE ANCIENT HINDUS; with special reference to Gunpowder and Firearms. By Dr. Gustav Oppert, Ph.D., Professor of Sanskrit, Presidency College, Madras. 8vo, paper, pp. vi. and 162. 1883. 7s. 6d.

ORIENTAL SERIES.—See TRÜBNER'S ORIENTAL SERIES.

ORIENTAL TEXT SOCIETY'S PUBLICATIONS. A list may be had on application.

ORIENTAL CONGRESS.—REPORT OF THE PROCEEDINGS OF THE SECOND INTERNATIONAL CONGRESS OF ORIENTALISTS HELD IN LONDON, 1874. Royal 8vo, pp. viii. and 68, sewed. 1874. 5s.

ORIENTALISTS.—TRANSACTIONS OF THE SECOND SESSION OF THE INTERNATIONAL CONGRESS OF ORIENTALISTS. Held in London in September 1874. Edited by Robert K. Douglas, Hon. Sec. 8vo, pp. viii. and 456, cloth. 1876. 21s.

OTTÉ.—HOW TO LEARN DANISH (Dano-Norwegian): a Manual for Students of Danish based on the Ollendorffian system of teaching languages, and adapted for self-instruction. By E. C. Otté. Second Edition. Crown 8vo, pp. xx. and 338, cloth. 1884. 7s. 6d.

Key to above. Crown 8vo, pp. 84, cloth. 3s.

OTTÉ.—SIMPLIFIED DANISH AND SWEDISH GRAMMARS. See TRÜBNER'S COLLECTION.

OVERBECK.—CATHOLIC ORTHODOXY AND ANGLO-CATHOLICISM. A Word about the Intercommunion between the English and Orthodox Churches. By J. J. Overbeck, D.D. 8vo, pp. viii. and 200, cloth. 1866. 5s.

OVERBECK.—BONN CONFERENCE. By J. J. Overbeck, D.D. Crown 8vo, pp. 48, sewed. 1876. 1s.

OVERBECK.—A PLAIN VIEW OF THE CLAIMS OF THE ORTHODOX CATHOLIC CHURCH AS OPPOSED TO ALL OTHER CHRISTIAN DENOMINATIONS. By J. J. Overbeck, D.D. Crown 8vo, pp. iv. and 138, wrapper. 1881. 2s. 6d.

OWEN.—FOOTFALLS ON THE BOUNDARY OF ANOTHER WORLD. With Narrative Illustrations. By R. D. Owen. An enlarged English Copyright Edition. Post 8vo, pp. xx. and 392, cloth. 1875. 7s. 6d.

OWEN.—THE DEBATABLE LAND BETWEEN THIS WORLD AND THE NEXT. With Illustrative Narrations. By Robert Dale Owen. Second Edition. Crown 8vo, pp. 456, cloth. 1874. 7s. 6d.

OWEN.—THREADING MY WAY: Twenty-Seven Years of Autobiography. By R. D. Owen. Crown 8vo, pp. 344, cloth. 1874. 7s. 6d.

OXLEY.—EGYPT: And the Wonders of the Land of the Pharaohs. By William Oxley, author of "The Philosophy of Spirit." Illustrated by a New Version of the Bhagavat-Gita, an Episode of the Mahâbharat, one of the Epic Poems of Ancient India. Crown 8vo, pp. viii.-328, cloth. 1884. 7s. 6d.

OYSTER (THE): WHERE, HOW, AND WHEN TO FIND, BREED, COOK, AND EAT IT. Second Edition, with a New Chapter, "The Oyster-Seeker in London." 12mo, pp. viii. and 106, boards. 1863. 1s.

PALESTINE.—MEMOIRS OF THE SURVEY OF WESTERN PALESTINE. Edited by W. Besant, M.A., and E. H. Palmer, M.A., under the Direction of the Committee of the Palestine Exploration Fund. Complete in seven volumes. Demy 4to, cloth, with a Portfolio of Plans, and large scale Map. Second Issue. Price Twenty Guineas.

PALMER.—A CONCISE ENGLISH-PERSIAN DICTIONARY; together with a simplified Grammar of the Persian Language. By the late E. H. Palmer, M.A., Lord Almoner's Reader, and Professor of Arabic, Cambridge, &c. Completed and Edited, from the MS. left imperfect at his death, by G. Le Strange. Royal 16mo, pp. 606, cloth. 1883. 10s. 6d.

PALMER.—A CONCISE PERSIAN-ENGLISH DICTIONARY. By E. H. Palmer, M.A., of the Middle Temple, Barrister-at-Law, Lord Almoner's Reader, and Professor of Arabic, and Fellow of St. John's College in the University of Cambridge. Second Edition. Royal 16mo, pp. 726, cloth. 1884. 10s. 6d.

PALMER.—THE SONG OF THE REED, AND OTHER PIECES. By E. H. Palmer, M.A., Cambridge. Crown 8vo, pp. 208, cloth. 1876. 5s.

PALMER.—HINDUSTANI, ARABIC, AND PERSIAN GRAMMAR. See Trübner's Collection.

PALMER.—THE PATRIARCH AND THE TSAR. Translated from the Russ by William Palmer, M.A. Demy 8vo, cloth. Vol. I. THE REPLIES OF THE HUMBLE NICON. Pp. xl. and 674. 1871. 12s.—Vol. II. TESTIMONIES CONCERNING THE PATRIARCH NICON, THE TSAR, AND THE BOYARS. Pp. lxxviii. and 554. 1873. 12s.—Vol. III. HISTORY OF THE CONDEMNATION OF THE PATRIARCH NICON. Pp. lxvi. and 558. 1873. 12s.—Vols. IV., V., and VI. SERVICES OF THE PATRIARCH NICON TO THE CHURCH AND STATE OF HIS COUNTRY, &c. Pp. lxxviii. and 1 to 660; xiv.-661-1028, and 1 to 254; xxvi.-1029-1656, and 1-72. 1876. 36s.

PARKER.—THEODORE PARKER'S CELEBRATED DISCOURSE ON MATTERS PERTAINING TO RELIGION. People's Edition. Cr. 8vo, pp. 351. 1872. Stitched, 1s. 6d.; cl., 2s.

PARKER.—THEODORE PARKER. A Biography. By O. B. Frothingham. Crown 8vo, pp. viii. and 588, cloth, with Portrait. 1876. 12s.

PARKER.—THE COLLECTED WORKS OF THEODORE PARKER, Minister of the Twenty-eighth Congregational Society at Boston, U.S. Containing his Theological, Polemical, and Critical Writings; Sermons, Speeches, and Addresses; and Literary Miscellanies. In 14 vols. 8vo, cloth. 6s. each.
    Vol. I. Discourse on Matters Pertaining to Religion. Preface by the Editor,
        and Portrait of Parker from a medallion by Saulini. Pp. 380.
    Vol. II. Ten Sermons and Prayers. Pp. 360.
    Vol. III. Discourses of Theology. Pp. 318.
    Vol. IV. Discourses on Politics. Pp. 312.

PARKER.—COLLECTED WORKS—*continued.*
   Vol. V. Discourses of Slavery. I. Pp. 336.
   Vol. VI. Discourses of Slavery. II. Pp. 323.
   Vol. VII. Discourses of Social Science. Pp. 296.
   Vol. VIII. Miscellaneous Discourses. Pp. 230.
   Vol. IX. Critical Writings. I. Pp. 292.
   Vol. X. Critical Writings. II. Pp. 308.
   Vol. XI. Sermons of Theism, Atheism, and Popular Theology. Pp. 257.
   Vol. XII. Autobiographical and Miscellaneous Pieces. Pp. 356.
   Vol. XIII. Historic Americans. Pp. 236.
   Vol. XIV. Lessons from the World of Matter and the World of Man. Pp. 352.

PARKER.—MALAGASY GRAMMAR. See Trübner's Collection.

PARRY.—A SHORT CHAPTER ON LETTER-CHANGE, with Examples. Being chiefly an attempt to reduce in a simple manner the principal classical and cognate words to their primitive meanings. By J. Parry, B.A., formerly Scholar of Corpus Christi College, Cambridge. Fcap. 8vo, pp. 16, wrapper. 1884. 1s.

PATERSON.—NOTES ON MILITARY SURVEYING AND RECONNAISSANCE. By Lieut.-Colonel William Paterson. Sixth Edition. With 16 Plates. Demy 8vo, pp. xii. and 146, cloth. 1882. 7s. 6d.

PATERSON.—TOPOGRAPHICAL EXAMINATION PAPERS. By Lieut.-Col. W. Paterson. 8vo, pp. 32, with 4 Plates. Boards. 1882. 2s.

PATERSON.—TREATISE ON MILITARY DRAWING. With a Course of Progressive Plates. By Captain W. Paterson, Professor of Military Drawing at the Royal Military College, Sandhurst. Oblong 4to, pp. xii. and 31, cloth. 1862. £1, 1s.

PATERSON.—THE OROMETER FOR HILL MEASURING, combining Scales of Distances, Protractor, Clinometer, Scale of Horizontal Equivalents, Scale of Shade, and Table of Gradients. By Captain William Paterson. On cardboard. 1s.

PATERSON.—CENTRAL AMERICA. By W. Paterson, the Merchant Statesman. From a MS. in the British Museum, 1701. With a Map. Edited by S. Bannister, M.A. 8vo, pp. 70, sewed. 1857. 2s. 6d.

PATON.—A HISTORY OF THE EGYPTIAN REVOLUTION, from the Period of the Mamelukes to the Death of Mohammed Ali; from Arab and European Memoirs, Oral Tradition, and Local Research. By A. A. Paton. Second Edition. 2 vols. demy 8vo, pp. xii. and 395, viii. and 446, cloth. 1870. 7s. 6d.

PATON.—HENRY BEYLE (otherwise DE STENDAHL). A Critical and Biographical Study, aided by Original Documents and Unpublished Letters from the Private Papers of the Family of Beyle. By A. A. Paton. Crown 8vo, pp. 340, cloth. 1874. 7s. 6d.

PATTON.—THE DEATH OF DEATH; or, A Study of God's Holiness in Connection with the Existence of Evil, in so far as Intelligent and Responsible Beings are Concerned. By an Orthodox Layman (John M. Patton). Revised Edition, crown 8vo, pp. xvi. and 252, cloth. 1881. 6s.

PAULI.—SIMON DE MONTFORT, EARL OF LEICESTER, the Creator of the House of Commons. By Reinhold Pauli. Translated by Una M. Goodwin. With Introduction by Harriet Martineau. Crown 8vo, pp. xvi. and 340, cloth. 1876. 6s.

PETTENKOFER.—THE RELATION OF THE AIR TO THE CLOTHES WE WEAR, THE HOUSE WE LIVE IN, AND THE SOIL WE DWELL ON. Three Popular Lectures delivered before the Albert Society at Dresden. By Dr. Max Von Pettenkofer, Professor of Hygiene at the University of Munich, &c. Abridged and Translated by Augustus Hess, M.D., M.R.C.P., London, &c. Cr. 8vo, pp. viii. and 96, limp cl. 1873. 2s. 6d.

PETRUCCELLI.—PRELIMINAIRES DE LA QUESTION ROMAINE DE M. ED. ABOUT. Par F. Petruccelli de la Gattina. 8vo, pp. xv. and 364, cloth. 1860. 7s. 6d.

PEZZI.—ARYAN PHILOLOGY, according to the most recent researches (Glottologia Aria Recentissima). Remarks Historical and Critical. By Domenico Pezzi. Translated by E. S. Roberts, M.A. Crown 8vo, pp. xvi. and 200, cloth. 1879. 6s.

PHAYRE.—A HISTORY OF BURMA. See Trübner's Oriental Series.

PHAYRE.—THE COINS OF ARAKAN, OF PEGU, AND OF BURMA. By Sir Arthur Phayre, C.B., K.C.S.I., G.C.M.G., late Commissioner of British Burma. Royal 4to, pp. viii.-48, with Autotype Illustrative Plates. Wrapper. 1882. 8s. 6d.

PHILLIPS.—THE DOCTRINE OF ADDAI, THE APOSTLE, now first edited in a complete form in the Original Syriac, with English Translation and Notes. By George Phillips, D.D., President of Queen's College, Cambridge. 8vo, pp. xv. and 52 and 53, cloth. 1876. 7s. 6d.

PHILLIPS.—KOPAL-KUNDALA: A Tale of Bengali Life. Translated from the Bengali of Bunkim Chandra Chatterjee. By H. A. D. Phillips, Bengal Civil Service. Crown 8vo, pp. xxx.-208, cloth. 1885. 6s.

PHILOLOGICAL SOCIETY, TRANSACTIONS OF, published irregularly. List of publications on application.

PHILOSOPHY (THE) OF INSPIRATION AND REVELATION. By a Layman. With a preliminary notice of an Essay by the present Lord Bishop of Winchester, contained in a volume entitled "Aids to Faith." 8vo, pp. 20, sewed. 1875. 6d.

PICCIOTTO.—SKETCHES OF ANGLO-JEWISH HISTORY. By James Picciotto. Demy 8vo, pp. xi. and 420, cloth. 1875. 12s.

PIESSE.—CHEMISTRY IN THE BREWING-ROOM: being the substance of a Course of Lessons to Practical Brewers. With Tables of Alcohol, Extract, and Original Gravity. By Charles H. Piesse, F.C.S., Public Analyst. Fcap., pp. viii. and 62, cloth. 1877. 5s.

PIRY.—LE SAINT EDIT, ÉTUDE DE LITTERATURE CHINOISE. Préparée par A. Théophile Piry, du Service des Douanes Maritimes de Chine. 4to, pp. xx. and 320, cloth. 1879. 21s.

PLAYFAIR.—THE CITIES AND TOWNS OF CHINA. A Geographical Dictionary. By G. M. H. Playfair, of Her Majesty's Consular Service in China. 8vo, pp. 506, cloth. 1879. £1, 5s.

PLINY.—THE LETTERS OF PLINY THE YOUNGER. Translated by J. D. Lewis, M.A., Trinity College, Cambridge. Post 8vo, pp. vii. and 390, cloth. 1879. 5s.

PLUMPTRE.—KING'S COLLEGE LECTURES ON ELOCUTION; on the Physiology and Culture of Voice and Speech and the Expression of the Emotions by Language, Countenance, and Gesture. To which is added a Special Lecture on the Causes and Cure of the Impediments of Speech. Being the substance of the Introductory Course of Lectures annually delivered by Charles John Plumptre, Lecturer on Public Reading and Speaking at King's College, London, in the Evening Classes Department. Dedicated by permission to H.R.H. the Prince of Wales. Fourth, greatly Enlarged Illustrated, Edition. Post 8vo, pp. xviii. and 494, cloth. 1883. 15s.

PLUMPTRE.—GENERAL SKETCH OF THE HISTORY OF PANTHEISM. By C. E. Plumptre. Vol. I., from the Earliest Times to the Age of Spinoza; Vol. II., from the Age of Spinoza to the Commencement of the 19th Century. 2 vols. demy 8vo, pp. viii. and 395; iv. and 348, cloth. 1881. 18s.

POLE.—THE PHILOSOPHY OF MUSIC. See English and Foreign Philosophical Library. Vol. XI.

PONSARD.—CHARLOTTE CORDAY. A Tragedy. By F. Ponsard. Edited, with English Notes and Notice on Ponsard, by Professor C. Cassal, LL.D. 12mo, pp. xi. and 133, cloth. 1867. 2s. 6d.

PONSARD.—L'HONNEUR ET L'ARGENT. A Comedy. By François Ponsard. Edited, with English Notes and Memoir of Ponsard, by Professor C. Cassal, LL.D. Fcap. 8vo, pp. xvi. and 172, cloth. 1869. 3s. 6d.

POOLE.—AN INDEX TO PERIODICAL LITERATURE. By W. F. Poole, LL.D., Librarian of the Chicago Public Library. Third Edition, brought down to January 1882. Royal 8vo, pp. xxviii. and 1442, cloth. 1883. £3, 13s. 6d. Wrappers, £3, 10s.

PRACTICAL GUIDES :—
FRANCE, BELGIUM, HOLLAND, AND THE RHINE. 1s.—ITALIAN LAKES. 1s.—WINTERING PLACES OF THE SOUTH. 2s.—SWITZERLAND, SAVOY, AND NORTH ITALY. 2s. 6d.—GENERAL CONTINENTAL GUIDE. 5s.—GENEVA. 1s.—PARIS. 1s.—BERNESE OBERLAND. 1s.—ITALY. 4s.

PRATT.—A GRAMMAR AND DICTIONARY OF THE SAMOAN LANGUAGE. By Rev. George Pratt, Forty Years a Missionary of the London Missionary Society in Samoa. Second Edition. Edited by Rev. S. J. Whitmee, F.R.G.S. Crown 8vo, pp. viii. and 380, cloth. 1878. 18s.

PRINSEP.—RECORD OF SERVICES OF THE HONOURABLE EAST INDIA COMPANY'S CIVIL SERVANTS IN THE MADRAS PRESIDENCY, from 1741 to 1858. Compiled and Edited from Records in the possession of the Secretary of State for India. By C. C. Prinsep, late Superintendent of Records, India Office. Post 8vo, pp. xxxvi.-164, cloth. 1885. 10s. 6d.

PSYCHICAL RESEARCH, PROCEEDINGS OF THE SOCIETY FOR. Published irregularly. Post 8vo, cloth. Vol. I., pp. 338. 1884. 10s. Vol. II., pp. 356. 1884. 10s.

PURITZ.—CODE-BOOK OF GYMNASTIC EXERCISES. By Ludwig Puritz. Translated by O. Knofe and J. W. Macqueen. Illustrated. 32mo, pp. xxiv.-292, boards. 1883. 1s. 6d.

QUINET.—EDGAR QUINET. See English and Foreign Philosophical Library, Vol. XIV.

RAM RAZ.—ESSAY ON THE ARCHITECTURE OF THE HINDUS. By Ram Raz, Native Judge and Magistrate of Bangalore, Corr. Mem. R.A.S. With 48 Plates. 4to, pp. xiv. and 64, sewed. 1834. £2, 2s.

RAMSAY.—TABULAR LIST OF ALL THE AUSTRALIAN BIRDS AT PRESENT KNOWN TO THE AUTHOR, showing the distribution of the species. By E. P. Ramsay, F.L.S., &c., Curator of the Australian Museum, Sydney. 8vo, pp. 36, and Map ; boards 1878. 5s.

RASK.—GRAMMAR OF THE ANGLO-SAXON TONGUE, from the Danish of Erasmus Rask. By Benjamin Thorpe. Third Edition, corrected and improved, with Plate. Post 8vo, pp. vi. and 192, cloth. 1879. 5s. 6d.

RASK.—A SHORT TRACTATE on the Longevity ascribed to the Patriarchs in the Book of Genesis, and its relation to the Hebrew Chronology ; the Flood, the Exodus of the Israelites, the Site of Eden, &c. From the Danish of the late Professor Rask, with his manuscript corrections, and large additions from his autograph, now for the first time printed. With a Map of Paradise and the circumjacent Lands. Crown 8vo, pp. 134, cloth. 1863. 2s. 6d.

RAVENSTEIN.—THE RUSSIANS ON THE AMUR ; its Discovery, Conquest, and Colonization, with a Description of the Country, its Inhabitants, Productions, and Commercial Capabilities, and Personal Accounts of Russian Travellers. By E. G. Ravenstein, F.R.G.S. With 4 tinted Lithographs and 3 Maps. 8vo, pp. 500, cloth. 1861. 15s.

RAVENSTEIN AND HULLEY.—THE GYMNASIUM AND ITS FITTINGS. By E. G. Ravenstein and John Hulley. With 14 Plates of Illustrations. 8vo, pp. 32, sewed. 1867. 2s. 6d.

RAVERTY.—NOTES ON AFGHANISTAN AND PART OF BALUCHISTAN, Geographical, Ethnographical, and Historical, extracted from the Writings of little known Afghan, and Tajyik Historians, &c., &c., and from Personal Observation. By Major H. G. Raverty, Bombay Native Infantry (Retired). Foolscap folio. Sections I. and II., pp. 98, wrapper. 1880. 2s. Section III., pp. vi. and 218. 1881. 5s. Section IV. 1884. 3s.

READE.—THE MARTYRDOM OF MAN. By Winwood Reade. Eighth Edition. Crown 8vo, pp. viii. and 544, cloth. 1884. 7s. 6d.

RECORD OFFICE.—A SEPARATE CATALOGUE OF THE OFFICIAL PUBLICATIONS OF THE PUBLIC RECORD OFFICE, on sale by Trübner & Co., may be had on application.

RECORDS OF THE HEART. By Stella, Author of "Sappho," "The King's Stratagem," &c. Second English Edition. Crown 8vo, pp. xvi. and 188, with six steel-plate engravings, cloth. 1881. 3s. 6d.

REDHOUSE.—THE MESNEVÍ. See Trübner's Oriental Series.

REDHOUSE.—SIMPLIFIED OTTOMAN-TURKISH GRAMMAR. See Trübner's Collection.

REDHOUSE.—THE TURKISH VADE-MECUM OF OTTOMAN COLLOQUIAL LANGUAGE: Containing a Concise Ottoman Grammar; a Carefully Selected Vocabulary Alphabetically Arranged, in two Parts, English and Turkish, and Turkish and English; Also a few Familiar Dialogues and Naval and Military Terms. The whole in English Characters, the Pronunciation being fully indicated. By J. W. Redhouse, M.R.A.S. Third Edition. 32mo, pp. viii. and 372, cloth. 1882. 6s.

REDHOUSE.—ON THE HISTORY, SYSTEM, AND VARIETIES OF TURKISH POETRY. Illustrated by Selections in the Original and in English Paraphrase, with a Notice of the Islamic Doctrine of the Immortality of Woman's Soul in the Future State. By J. W. Redhouse, Esq., M.R.A.S. 8vo, pp. 62, cloth, 2s. 6d.; wrapper, 1s. 6d. 1879.

REEMELIN.—A CRITICAL REVIEW OF AMERICAN POLITICS. By C. Reemelin, of Cincinnati, Ohio. Demy 8vo, pp. xxiv. and 630, cloth. 1881. 14s.

RELIGION IN EUROPE HISTORICALLY CONSIDERED: An Essay in Verse. By the Author of "The Thames." Fcap. 8vo, pp. iv. and 152, cloth. 1883. 2s. 6d.

RENAN.—PHILOSOPHICAL DIALOGUES AND FRAGMENTS. From the French of Ernest Renan. Translated, with the sanction of the Author, by Ras Bihari Mukharji. Post 8vo, pp. xxxii. and 182, cloth. 1883. 7s. 6d.

RENAN.—AN ESSAY ON THE AGE AND ANTIQUITY OF THE BOOK OF NABATHÆAN AGRICULTURE. To which is added an Inaugural Lecture on the Position of the Shemitic Nations in the History of Civilisation. By Ernest Renan. Crown 8vo, pp. xvi. and 148, cloth. 1862. 3s. 6d.

RENAN.—THE LIFE OF JESUS. By Ernest Renan. Authorised English Translation. Crown 8vo, pp. xii. and 312, cloth. 2s. 6d.; sewed, 1s. 6d.

REPORT OF A GENERAL CONFERENCE OF LIBERAL THINKERS, for the discussion of matters pertaining to the religious needs of our time, and the methods of meeting them. Held June 13th and 14th, 1878, at South Place Chapel, Finsbury, London. 8vo, pp. 77, sewed. 1878. 1s.

RHODES.—UNIVERSAL CURVE TABLES FOR FACILITATING THE LAYING OUT OF CIRCULAR ARCS ON THE GROUND FOR RAILWAYS, CANALS, &c. Together with Table of Tangential Angles and Multiples. By Alexander Rhodes, C.E. Oblong 18mo, band, pp. ix. and 104, roan. 1881. 5s.

RHYS.—LECTURES ON WELSH PHILOLOGY. By John Rhys, M.A., Professor of Celtic at Oxford, Honorary Fellow of Jesus College, &c., &c. Second Edition, Revised and Enlarged. Crown 8vo, pp. xiv. and 467, cloth. 1879. 15s.

RICE.—MYSORE AND COORG. A Gazetteer compiled for the Government of India. By Lewis Rice, Director of Public Instruction, Mysore and Coorg. Vol. I. Mysore in General. With 2 Coloured Maps. Vol. II. Mysore, by Districts. With 10 Coloured Maps. Vol. III. Coorg. With a Map. 3 vols. royal 8vo, pp. xii. 670 and xvi.; 544 and xxii.; and 427 and xxvii., cloth. 1878. 25s.

RICE.—MYSORE INSCRIPTIONS. Translated for the Government by Lewis Rice. 8vo, pp. xcii. and 336-xxx., with a Frontispiece and Map, boards. 1879. 30s.

RIDLEY.—KÁMILARÓI, AND OTHER AUSTRALIAN LANGUAGES. By the Rev. William Ridley, B.A. Second Edition, revised and enlarged by the author; with comparative Tables of Words from twenty Australian Languages, and Songs, Traditions, Laws, and Customs of the Australian Race. Small 4to, pp. vi. and 172, cloth. 1877. 10s. 6d.

RIG-VEDA-SANHITA. A Collection of Ancient Hindu Hymns. Constituting the 1st to the 8th Ashtakas, or Books of the Rig-Veda ; the oldest authority for the Religious and Social Institutions of the Hindus. Translated from the Original Sanskrit. By the late H. H. Wilson, M.A., F.R.S., &c., &c.
Vol. I. 8vo, pp. lii. and 348, cloth. 21s.
Vol. II. 8vo, pp. xxx. and 346, cloth. 1854. 21s.
Vol. III. 8vo, pp. xxiv. and 525, cloth. 1857. 21s.
Vol. IV. Edited by E. B. Cowell, M.A. 8vo, pp. 214, cloth. 1866. 14s.
Vols. V. and VI. in the Press.

RILEY.—MEDIÆVAL CHRONICLES OF THE CITY OF LONDON. Chronicles of the Mayors and Sheriffs of London, and the Events which happened in their Days, from the Year A.D. 1188 to A.D. 1274. Translated from the original Latin of the "Liber de Antiquis Legibus" (published by the Camden Society), in the possession of the Corporation of the City of London ; attributed to Arnold Fitz-Thedmar, Alderman of London in the Reign of Henry III.—Chronicles of London, and of the Marvels therein, between the Years 44 Henry III., A.D. 1260, and 17 Edward III., A.D. 1343. Translated from the original Anglo-Norman of the "Croniques de London," preserved in the Cottonian Collection (Cleopatra A. iv.) in the British Museum. Translated, with copious Notes and Appendices, by Henry Thomas Riley, M.A., Clare Hall, Cambridge, Barrister-at-Law. 4to, pp. xii. and 319, cloth. 1863. 12s.

RIOLA.—HOW TO LEARN RUSSIAN : a Manual for Students of Russian, based upon the Ollendorffian System of Teaching Languages, and adapted for Self-Instruction. By Henry Riola, Teacher of the Russian Language. With a Preface by W.R.S. Ralston, M.A. Second Edition. Crown 8vo, pp. 576, cloth. 1883. 12s.
KEY to the above. Crown 8vo, pp. 126, cloth. 1878. 5s.

RIOLA.—A GRADUATED RUSSIAN READER, with a Vocabulary of all the Russian Words contained in it. By Henry Riola, Author of "How to Learn Russian." Crown 8vo, pp. viii. and 314, cloth. 1879. 10s. 6d.

RIPLEY.—SACRED RHETORIC ; or, Composition and Delivery of Sermons. By Henry I. Ripley. 12mo, pp. 234, cloth. 1858. 2s. 6d.

ROCHE.—A FRENCH GRAMMAR, for the use of English Students, adopted for the Public Schools by the Imperial Council of Public Instruction. By A. Roche. Crown 8vo, pp. xii. and 176, cloth. 1869. 3s.

ROCHE.—PROSE AND POETRY. Select Pieces from the best English Authors, for Reading, Composition, and Translation. By A. Roche. Second Edition. Fcap. 8vo, pp. viii. and 226, cloth. 1872. 2s. 6d.

ROCKHILL.—UDANAVARGA. See Trübner's Oriental Series.

ROCKHILL.—THE LIFE OF THE BUDDHA. See Trübner's Oriental Series.

RODD.—THE BIRDS OF CORNWALL AND THE SCILLY ISLANDS. By the late Edward Hearle Rodd. Edited, with an Introduction, Appendix, and Memoir, by J. E. Harting. 8vo, pp. lvi. and 320, with Portrait and Map, cloth. 1880. 14s.

ROGERS.—THE WAVERLEY DICTIONARY : An Alphabetical Arrangement of all the Characters in Sir Walter Scott's Waverley Novels, with a Descriptive Analysis of each Character, and Illustrative Selections from the Text. By May Rogers. 12mo, pp. 358, cloth. 1879. 10s.

ROSING.—ENGLISH-DANISH DICTIONARY. By S. Rosing. Crown 8vo, pp. x. and 722, cloth. 8s. 6d.

ROSS.—ALPHABETICAL MANUAL OF BLOWPIPE ANALYSIS ; showing all known Methods, Old and New. By Lieut.-Colonel W. A. Ross, late R.A., Member of the German Chemical Society (Author of "Pyrology, or Fire Chemistry"). Crown 8vo, pp. xii. and 148, cloth. 1880. 5s.

ROSS.—PYROLOGY, OR FIRE CHEMISTRY ; a Science interesting to the General Philosopher, and an Art of infinite importance to the Chemist, Metallurgist, Engineer, &c., &c. By W. A. Ross, lately a Major in the Royal Artillery. Small 4to, pp. xxviii. and 346, cloth. 1875. 36s.

ROSS.—CELEBRITIES OF THE YORKSHIRE WOLDS. By Frederick Ross, Fellow of the Royal Historical Society. 12mo, pp. 202, cloth. 1878. 4s.

ROSS.—THE EARLY HISTORY OF LAND HOLDING AMONG THE GERMANS. By Denman W. Ross, Ph.D. 8vo, pp. viii. and 274, cloth. 1883. 12s.

ROSS.—COREAN PRIMER : being Lessons in Corean on all Ordinary Subjects. Transliterated on the principles of the " Mandarin Primer," by the same author. By Rev. John Ross, Newchwang. 8vo, pp. 90, wrapper. 1877. 10s.

ROSS.—HONOUR OR SHAME? By R. S. Ross. 8vo, pp. 183. 1878. Cloth. 3s. 6d. ; paper, 2s. 6d.

ROSS.--REMOVAL OF THE INDIAN TROOPS TO MALTA. By R. S. Ross. 8vo, pp. 77, paper. 1878. 1s. 6d.

ROSS.—THE MONK OF ST. GALL. A Dramatic Adaptation of Scheffel's "Ekkehard." By R. S. Ross. Crown 8vo, pp. xii. and 218. 1879. 5s.

ROSS.—ARIADNE IN NAXOS. By R. S. Ross. Square 16mo, pp. 200, cloth. 1882. 5s.

ROTH.—THE ANIMAL PARASITES OF THE SUGAR CANE. By H. Ling Roth, late Hon. Sec. to the Mackay Planters' Association. Demy 8vo, pp. 16, wrapper. 1885. 1s.

ROTH.—NOTES ON CONTINENTAL IRRIGATION. By H. L. Roth. Demy 8vo, pp. 40, with 8 Plates, cloth. 1882. 5s.

ROUGH NOTES OF JOURNEYS made in the years 1868-1873 in Syria, down the Tigris, India, Kashmir, Ceylon, Japan, Mongolia, Siberia, the United States, the Sandwich Islands, and Australasia. Demy 8vo, pp. 624, cloth. 1875. 14s.

ROUSTAING.—THE FOUR GOSPELS EXPLAINED BY THEIR WRITERS. With an Appendix on the Ten Commandments. Edited by J. B. Roustaing. Translated by W. E. Kirby. 3 vols. crown 8vo, pp. 440-456-304, cloth. 1881. 15s.

ROUTLEDGE.—ENGLISH RULE AND NATIVE OPINION IN INDIA. From Notes taken in 1870-74. By James Routledge. 8vo, pp. x. and 338, cloth. 1878. 10s. 6d.

ROWE.—AN ENGLISHMAN'S VIEWS ON QUESTIONS OF THE DAY IN VICTORIA. By C. J. Rowe, M.A. Crown 8vo, pp. 122, cloth. 1882. 4s.

ROWLEY.—ORNITHOLOGICAL MISCELLANY. By George Dawson Rowley, M.A., F.Z.S. Vol. I. Part 1, 15s.—Part 2, 20s.—Part 3, 15s.—Part 4, 20s.
Vol. II. Part 5, 20s.—Part 6, 20s.—Part 7, 10s. 6d.—Part 8, 10s. 6d.—Part 9, 10s. 6d.—Part 10, 10s. 6d.
Vol. III. Part 11, 10s. 6d.—Part 12, 10s. 6d.—Part 13, 10s. 6d.—Part 14, 20s.

ROYAL SOCIETY OF LONDON (THE).—CATALOGUE OF SCIENTIFIC PAPERS (1800-1863), Compiled and Published by the Royal Society of London. Demy 4to, cloth, per vol. £1 ; in half-morocco, £1, 8s. Vol. I. (1867), A to Cluzel. pp. lxxix. and 960 ; Vol. II. (1868), Coaklay—Graydon. pp. iv. and 1012 ; Vol. III. (1869), Greatheed—Leze. pp. v. and 1002 ; Vol. IV. (1870), L'Héritier de Brutille—Pozzetti. pp. iv. and 1006 ; Vol. V. (1871), Praag—Tizzani. pp. iv. and 1000 ; Vol. VI. (1872), Tkalec—Zylius, Anonymous and Additions. pp. xi. and 763. Continuation of above (1864-1873) ; Vol. VII. (1877), A to Hyrtl. pp. xxxi. and 1047 ; Vol. VIII. (1879), Ibañez—Zwicky. pp. 1310. A List of the Publications of the Royal Society (Separate Papers from the Philosophical Transactions), on application.

RUNDALL.—A SHORT AND EASY WAY TO WRITE ENGLISH AS SPOKEN. Méthode Rapide et Facile d'Ecrire le Français comme on le Parle. Kurze und Leichte Weise Deutsch zu Schreiben wie man es Spricht. By J. B. Rundall, Certificated Member of the London Shorthand Writers' Association. 6d. each.

RUSSELL.—THE WAVE OF TRANSLATION IN THE OCEANS OF WATER, AIR, AND ETHER. By John Scott Russell, M.A., F.R.S.S. L. and E. Demy 8vo, pp. 318, with 10 Diagrams, cloth. 1885. 12s. 6d.

RUTHERFORD.—THE AUTOBIOGRAPHY OF MARK RUTHERFORD, Dissenting Minister. Edited by his friend, Reuben Shapcott. Crown 8vo, pp. xii. and 180, boards. 1881. 5s.

RUTHERFORD.—MARK RUTHERFORD'S DELIVERANCE : Being the Second Part of his Autobiography. Edited by his friend, Reuben Shapcott. Crown 8vo, pp. viii. and 210, boards. 1885. 5s.

RUTTER.—See BUNYAN.

SÂMAVIDHÂNABRÂHMANA (The) (being the Third Brâhmana) of the Sâma Veda. Edited, together with the Commentary of Sâyana, an English Translation, Introduction, and Index of Words, by A. C. Burnell. Vol. I. Text and Commentary, with Introduction. Demy 8vo, pp. xxxviii. and 104, cloth. 1873. 12s. 6d.

SAMUELSON.—HISTORY OF DRINK. A Review, Social, Scientific, and Political. By James Samuelson, of the Middle Temple, Barrister-at-Law. Second Edition. 8vo, pp. xxviii. and 288, cloth. 1880. 6s.

SAND.—MOLIÈRE. A Drama in Prose. By George Sand. Edited, with Notes, by Th. Karcher, LL.B. 12mo, pp. xx. and 170, cloth. 1868. 3s. 6d.

SARTORIUS.—MEXICO. Landscapes and Popular Sketches. By C. Sartorius. Edited by Dr. Gaspey. With Engravings, from Sketches by M. Rugendas. 4to, pp. vi. and 202, cloth gilt. 1859. 18s.

SATOW.—AN ENGLISH JAPANESE DICTIONARY OF THE SPOKEN LANGUAGE. By Ernest Mason Satow, Japanese Secretary to H.M. Legation at Yedo, and Ishibashi Masakata of the Imperial Japanese Foreign Office. Second Edition. Imperial 32mo, pp. xv. and 416, cloth. 1879. 12s. 6d.

SAVAGE.—THE MORALS OF EVOLUTION. By M. J. Savage, Author of "The Religion of Evolution," &c. Crown 8vo, pp. 192, cloth. 1880. 5s.

SAVAGE.—BELIEF IN GOD; an Examination of some Fundamental Theistic Problems. By M. J. Savage. To which is added an Address on the Intellectual Basis of Faith. By W. H. Savage. 8vo, pp. 176, cloth. 1881. 5s.

SAVAGE.—BELIEFS ABOUT MAN. By M. J. Savage. Crown 8vo, pp. 130, cloth. 1882. 5s.

SAYCE.—AN ASSYRIAN GRAMMAR for Comparative Purposes. By A. H. Sayce, M.A., Fellow and Tutor of Queen's College, Oxford. Crown 8vo, pp. xvi. and 188, cloth. 1885.

SAYCE.—THE PRINCIPLES OF COMPARATIVE PHILOLOGY. By A. H. Sayce, M.A. Third, Revised, and Enlarged Edition. Crown 8vo, pp. xlviii.-422, cloth. 1885. 10s. 6d.

SCHAIBLE.—AN ESSAY ON THE SYSTEMATIC TRAINING OF THE BODY. By C. H. Schaible, M.D., &c., &c. A Memorial Essay, Published on the occasion of the first Centenary Festival of Frederick L. Jahn, with an Etching by H. Herkomer. Crown 8vo, pp. xviii. and 124, cloth. 1878. 5s.

SCHEFFEL.—MOUNTAIN PSALMS. By J. V. von Scheffel. Translated by Mrs. F. Brunnow. Fcap., pp. 62, with 6 Plates after designs by A. Von Werner. Parchment. 1882. 3s. 6d.

SCHILLER.—THE BRIDE OF MESSINA. Translated from the German of Schiller in English Verse. By Emily Allfrey. Crown 8vo, pp. viii. and 110, cloth. 1876. 2s.

SCHLAGINTWEIT.—BUDDHISM IN TIBET: Illustrated by Literary Documents and Objects of Religious Worship. By Emil Schlagintweit, LL.D. With a folio Atlas of 20 Plates, and 20 Tables of Native Print in the Text. Roy. 8vo, pp. xxiv. and 404. 1863. £2, 2s.

SCHLAU, SCHLAUER, AM SCHLÄUESTEN.—Facsimile of a Manuscript supposed to have been found in an Egyptian Tomb by the English Soldiers. Royal 8vo, in ragged canvas covers, with string binding, and dilapidated edges (? just as discovered). 1884. 6s.

SCHLEICHER.—A COMPENDIUM OF THE COMPARATIVE GRAMMAR OF THE INDO-EUROPEAN, SANSKRIT, GREEK, AND LATIN LANGUAGES. By August Schleicher. Translated from the Third German Edition, by Herbert Bendall, B.A., Chr. Coll., Camb. 8vo. Part I., Phonology. Pp. 184, cloth. 1874. 7s. 6d. Part II., Morphology. Pp. viii. and 104, cloth. 1877. 6s.

SCHOPENHAUER.—THE WORLD AS WILL AND IDEA. By Arthur Schopenhauer. Translated from the German by R. B. HALDANE, M.A., and J. KEMP, M.A. Vol. I., containing Four Books. Post 8vo, pp. xxxii.-532, cloth. 1883. 18s.

SCHULTZ.—UNIVERSAL DOLLAR TABLES (Complete United States). Covering all Exchanges between the United States and Great Britain, France, Belgium, Switzerland, Italy, Spain, and Germany. By C. W. H. Schultz. 8vo, cloth. 1874. 15s.

SCHULTZ.—UNIVERSAL INTEREST AND GENERAL PERCENTAGE TABLES. On the Decimal System. With a Treatise on the Currency of the World, and numerous examples for Self-Instruction. By C. W. H. Schultz. 8vo, cloth. 1874. 10s. 6d.

SCHULTZ.—ENGLISH GERMAN EXCHANGE TABLES. By C. W. H. Schultz. With a Treatise on the Currency of the World. 8vo, boards. 1874. 5s.

SCHWENDLER.—INSTRUCTIONS FOR TESTING TELEGRAPH LINES, and the Technical Arrangements in Offices. Written on behalf of the Government of India, under the Orders of the Director-General of Telegraphs in India. By Louis Schwendler. Vol. I., demy 8vo, pp. 248, cloth. 1878. 12s. Vol. II., demy 8vo, pp. xi. and 268, cloth. 1880. 9s.

SCOONES.—FAUST. A Tragedy. By Goethe. Translated into English Verse, by William Dalton Scoones. Fcap., pp. vi. and 230, cloth. 1879. 5s.

SCOTT.—THE ENGLISH LIFE OF JESUS. By Thomas Scott. Crown 8vo, pp. xxviii. and 350, cloth. 1879. 2s. 6d.

SCOTUS.—A NOTE ON MR. GLADSTONE'S "The Peace to Come." By Scotus. 8vo, pp. 106. 1878. Cloth, 2s. 6d.; paper wrapper, 1s. 6d.

SELL.—THE FAITH OF ISLAM. By the Rev. E. Sell, Fellow of the University of Madras. Demy 8vo, pp. xiv. and 270, cloth. 1881. 6s. 6d.

SELL.—IHN-I-TAJWID; OR, ART OF READING THE QURAN. By the Rev. E. Sell, B.D. 8vo, pp. 48, wrappers. 1882. 2s. 6d.

SELSS.—GOETHE'S MINOR POEMS. Selected, Annotated, and Rearranged. By Albert M. Selss, Ph.D. Crown 8vo, pp. xxxi. and 152, cloth. 1875. 3s. 6d.

SERMONS NEVER PREACHED. By Philip Phosphor. Crown 8vo, pp. vi. and 124, cloth. 1878. 2s. 6d.

SEWELL.—REPORT ON THE AMARAVATI TOPE, and Excavations on its Site in 1877. By Robert Sewell, of the Madras C.S., &c. With four plates. Royal 4to, pp. 70, boards. 1880. 3s.

SEYPPEL.—SHARP, SHARPER, SHARPEST: A Humorous Tale of Old Egypt. Penned down and Depicted in the Year 1315 A.C. By C. M. Seyppel, Court Painter and Poet Laureate of His Majesty King Rhampsinit III., and done into the English tongue by Two Mummies of the Old Dynasty. Memphis, 35, Mummies Arcade. (Ring three times). Imperial 8vo, pp. 42, in ragged canvas cover, with dilapidated edges, and string binding (? just as discovered), price 6s.

SHADWELL.—POLITICAL ECONOMY FOR THE PEOPLE. By J. L. Shadwell, Author of "A System of Political Economy." Fcap., pp. vi. and 154, limp cloth. 1880. 1s. 6d.

SHAKESPEARE.—A NEW STUDY OF SHAKESPEARE: An Inquiry into the connection of the Plays and Poems, with the origins of the Classical Drama, and with the Platonic Philosophy, through the Mysteries. Demy 8vo, pp. xii. and 372, with Photograph of the Stratford Bust, cloth. 1884. 10s. 6d.

SHAKESPEARE'S CENTURIE OF PRAYSE; being Materials for a History of Opinion on Shakespeare and his Works, culled from Writers of the First Century after his Rise. By C. M. Ingleby. Medium 8vo, pp. xx. and 384. Stiff cover. 1874. £1, 1s. Large paper, fcap. 4to, boards. £2, 2s.

SHAKESPEARE.—HERMENEUTICS; OR, THE STILL LION. Being an Essay towards the Restoration of Shakespeare's Text. By C. M. Ingleby, M.A., LL.D., of Trinity College, Cambridge. Small 4to, pp. 168, boards. 1875. 6s.

SHAKESPEARE.—THE MAN AND THE BOOK. By C. M. Ingleby, M.A., LL.D. Small 4to. Part I., pp. 172, boards. 1877. 6s.

SHAKESPEARE.—OCCASIONAL PAPERS ON SHAKESPEARE; being the Second Part of "Shakespeare: the Man and the Book." By C. M. Ingleby, M.A., LL.D., V.P.R.S.L. Small 4to, pp. x. and 194, paper boards. 1881. 6s.

SHAKESPEARE'S BONES.—The Proposal to Disinter them, considered in relation to their possible bearing on his Portraiture: Illustrated by instances of Visits of the Living to the Dead. By C. M. Ingleby, LL.D., V.P.R.S.L. Fcap. 4to, pp. viii. and 48, boards. 1883. 1s. 6d.

SHAKESPEARE.—A NEW VARIORUM EDITION OF SHAKESPEARE. Edited by Horace Howard Furness. Royal 8vo. Vol. I. Romeo and Juliet. Pp. xxiii. and 480, cloth. 1871. 18s.—Vol. II. Macbeth. Pp. xix. and 492. 1873. 18s.—Vols. III. and IV. Hamlet. 2 vols. pp. xx. and 474 and 430. 1877. 36s.—Vol. V. King Lear. Pp. vi. and 504. 1880. 18s.
SHAKESPEARE.—CONCORDANCE TO SHAKESPEARE'S POEMS. By Mrs. H. H. Furness. Royal 8vo, cloth. 18s.
SHAKESPEARE-NOTES. By F. A. Leo. Demy 8vo, pp. viii. and 120, cloth. 1885. 6s.
SHAKSPERE SOCIETY (THE NEW).—Subscription, One Guinea per annum. List of Publications on application.
SHERRING.—THE SACRED CITY OF THE HINDUS. An Account of Benares in Ancient and Modern Times. By the Rev. M. A. Sherring, M.A., LL.D. ; and Prefaced with an Introduction by FitzEdward Hall, D.C.L. With Illustrations. 8vo, pp. xxxvi. and 388, cloth. 21s.
SHERRING.—HINDU TRIBES AND CASTES; together with an Account of the Mohamedan Tribes of the North-West Frontier and of the Aboriginal Tribes of the Central Provinces. By the Rev. M. A. Sherring, M.A., LL.B., Lond., &c. 4to. Vol. II. Pp. lxviii. and 376, cloth. 1879. £2, 8s.—Vol. III., with Index of 3 vols. Pp. xii. and 336, cloth. 1881. 32s.
SHERRING.—THE HINDOO PILGRIMS. By Rev. M. A. Sherring, M.A., LL.D. Crown 8vo, pp. 126, cloth. 1878. 5s.
SHIELDS.—THE FINAL PHILOSOPHY ; or, System of Perfectible Knowledge issuing from the Harmony of Science and Religion. By Charles W. Shields, D.D., Professor in Princeton College. Royal 8vo, pp. viii. and 610, cloth. 1878. 18s.
SIBREE.—THE GREAT AFRICAN ISLAND. Chapters on Madagascar. A Popular Account of Recent Researches in the Physical Geography, Geology, and Exploration of the Country, and its Natural History and Botany ; and in the Origin and Divisions, Customs and Language, Superstitions, Folk-lore, and Religious Beliefs and Practices of the Different Tribes. Together with Illustrations of Scripture and Early Church History from Native Habits and Missionary Experience. By the Rev. James Sibree, jun., F.R.G.S., Author of "Madagascar and its People," &c. 8vo, pp. xii. and 272, with Physical and Ethnological Maps and Four Illustrations, cloth. 1879. 12s.
SIBREE.—POEMS: including "Fancy," "A Resting Place," &c. By John Sibree, M.A., London. Crown 8vo, pp. iv. and 134, cloth. 1884. 4s.
SIMCOX.—EPISODES IN THE LIVES OF MEN, WOMEN, AND LOVERS. By Edith Simcox. Crown 8vo, pp. 312, cloth. 1882. 7s. 6d.
SIMCOX.—NATURAL LAW. See English and Foreign Philosophical Library, Vol. IV.
SIME.—LESSING. See English and Foreign Philosophical Library, Extra Series, Vols. I. and II.
SIMPSON-BAIKIE.—THE DRAMATIC UNITIES IN THE PRESENT DAY. By E. Simpson-Baikie. Third Edition. Fcap. 8vo, pp. iv. and 108, cloth. 1878. 2s. 6d.
SIMPSON-BAIKIE.—THE INTERNATIONAL DICTIONARY for Naturalists and Sportsmen in English, French, and German. By Edwin Simpson-Baikie. 8vo, pp. iv. and 284, cloth. 1880. 15s.
SINCLAIR.—THE MESSENGER : A Poem. By Thomas Sinclair, M.A. Foolscap 8vo, pp. 174, cloth. 1875. 5s.
SINCLAIR.—LOVES'S TRILOGY : A Poem. By Thomas Sinclair, M.A. Crown 8vo, pp. 150, cloth. 1876. 5s.
SINCLAIR.—THE MOUNT : Speech from its English Heights. By Thomas Sinclair, M.A. Crown 8vo, pp. viii. and 302, cloth. 1877. 10s.
SINCLAIR.—GODDESS FORTUNE : A Novel. By Thomas Sinclair, M.A. Three vols., post 8vo, pp. viii.-302, 302, 274, cloth. 1884. 31s. 6d.
SINCLAIR.—QUEST: A Collection of Essays. By Thomas Sinclair, M.A. Crown 8vo, pp. 184, cloth. 1885. 2s. 6d.
SINGER.—HUNGARIAN GRAMMAR. See Trübner's Collection.
SINNETT.—THE OCCULT WORLD. By A. P. Sinnett. Fourth Edition. With an Appendix of 20 pages, on the subject of Mr. Kiddle's Charge of Plagiarism. 8vo, pp. xx. and 206, cloth. 1884. 3s. 6d.

SMITH.—THE DIVINE GOVERNMENT. By S. Smith, M.D. Fifth Edition. Crown 8vo, pp. xii. and 276, cloth. 1866. 6s.

SMITH.—THE RECENT DEPRESSION OF TRADE. Its Nature, its Causes, and the Remedies which have been suggested for it. By Walter E. Smith, B.A., New College. Being the Oxford Cobden Prize Essay for 1879. Crown 8vo, pp. vi. and 108, cloth. 1880. 3s.

SMYTH.—THE ABORIGINES OF VICTORIA. With Notes relating to the Habits of the Natives of other Parts of Australia and Tasmania. Compiled from various sources for the Government of Victoria. By R. Brough Smyth, F.L.S., F.G.S., &c., &c. 2 vols. royal 8vo, pp. lxxii.-484 and vi.-456, Maps, Plates, and Woodcuts, cloth. 1878. £3, 3s.

SNOW—A THEOLOGICO-POLITICAL TREATISE. By G. D. Snow. Crown 8vo, pp. 180, cloth. 1874. 4s. 6d.

SOLLING.—DIUTISKA: An Historical and Critical Survey of the Literature of Germany, from the Earliest Period to the Death of Goethe. By Gustav Solling. 8vo, pp. xviii. and 368. 1863. 10s. 6d.

SOLLING.—SELECT PASSAGES FROM THE WORKS OF SHAKESPEARE. Translated and Collected. German and English. By G. Solling. 12mo, pp. 155, cloth. 1866. 3s. 6d.

SOLLING.—MACBETH. Rendered into Metrical German (with English Text adjoined). By Gustav Solling. Crown 8vo, pp. 160, wrapper. 1878. 3s. 6d.

SONGS OF THE SEMITIC IN ENGLISH VERSE. By G. E. W. Crown 8vo, pp. iv. and 134, cloth. 1877. 5s.

SOUTHALL.—THE EPOCH OF THE MAMMOTH AND THE APPARITION OF MAN UPON EARTH. By James C. Southall, A.M., LL.D. Crown 8vo, pp. xii. and 430, cloth. Illustrated. 1878. 10s. 6d.

SPANISH REFORMERS OF TWO CENTURIES FROM 1520; Their Lives and Writing, according to the late Benjamin B. Wiffen's Plan, and with the Use of His Materials. Described by E. Boehmer, D.D., Ph.D. Vol. I. With B. B. Wiffen's Narrative of the Incidents attendant upon the Republication of Reformistas Antiguos Españoles, and with a Memoir of B. B. Wiffen. By Isaline Wiffen. Royal 8vo, pp. xvi. and 216, cloth. 1874. 12s. 6d. Roxburghe, 15s.—Vol. II. Royal 8vo, pp. xii.-374, cloth. 1883. 18s.

SPEDDING.—THE LIFE AND TIMES OF FRANCIS BACON. Extracted from the Edition of his Occasional Writings, by James Spedding. 2 vols. post 8vo, pp. xx.-710 and xiv.-708, cloth. 1878. 21s.

SPIERS.—THE SCHOOL SYSTEM OF THE TALMUD. By the Rev. B. Spiers. 8vo, pp. 48, cloth. 1882. 2s. 6d.

SPINOZA.—BENEDICT DE SPINOZA: his Life, Correspondence, and Ethics. By R. Willis, M.D. 8vo, pp. xliv. and 648, cloth. 1870. 21s.

SPINOZA.—ETHIC DEMONSTRATED IN GEOMETRICAL ORDER AND DIVIDED INTO FIVE PARTS, which treat—I. Of God; II. Of the Nature and Origin of the Mind; III. Of the Origin and Nature of the Affects; IV. Of Human Bondage, or of the Strength of the Affects; V. Of the Power of the Intellect, or of Human Liberty. By Benedict de Spinoza. Translated from the Latin by W. Hale White. Post 8vo, pp. 328, cloth. 1883. 10s. 6d.

SPIRITUAL EVOLUTION, AN ESSAY ON, considered in its bearing upon Modern Spiritualism, Science, and Religion. By J. P. B. Crown 8vo, pp. 156, cloth. 1879. 3s.

SPRUNER.—DR. KARL VON SPRUNER'S HISTORICO-GEOGRAPHICAL HAND-ATLAS, containing 26 Coloured Maps. Obl. cloth. 1861. 15s.

SQUIER.—HONDURAS; Descriptive, Historical, and Statistical. By E. G. Squier, M.A., F.S.A. Cr. 8vo, pp. viii. and 278, cloth. 1870. 3s. 6d.

STATIONERY OFFICE.—PUBLICATIONS OF HER MAJESTY'S STATIONERY OFFICE. List on application.

STEDMAN.—OXFORD: Its Social and Intellectual Life. With Remarks and Hints on Expenses, the Examinations, &c. By Algernon M. M. Stedman, B.A., Wadham College, Oxford. Crown 8vo, pp. xvi. and 309, cloth. 1878. 7s. 6d.
STEELE.—AN EASTERN LOVE STORY. Kusa Játakaya: A Buddhistic Legendary Poem, with other Stories. By Th. Steele. Cr. 8vo, pp. xii. and 260, cl. 1871. 6s.
STENT.—THE JADE CHAPLET. In Twenty-four Beads. A Collection of Songs, Ballads, &c. (from the Chinese). By G. C. Stent, M.N.C.B.R.A.S. Post 8vo, pp. viii. and 168, cloth. 1874. 5s.
STENZLER.—See AUCTORES SANSKRITI, Vol. II.
STOCK.—ATTEMPTS AT TRUTH. By St. George Stock. Crown 8vo, pp. vi. and 248, cloth. 1882. 5s.
STOKES.—GOIDELICA—Old and Early-Middle Irish Glosses: Prose and Verse. Edited by Whitley Stokes. 2d Edition. Med. 8vo, pp. 192, cloth. 1872. 18s.
STOKES.—BEUNANS MERIASEK. The Life of Saint Meriasek, Bishop and Confessor. A Cornish Drama. Edited, with a Translation and Notes, by Whitley Stokes. Med. 8vo, pp. xvi. and 280, and Facsimile, cloth. 1872. 15s.
STOKES.—TOGAIL TROY, THE DESTRUCTION OF TROY. Transcribed from the Facsimile of the Book of Leinster, and Translated, with a Glossarial Index of the Rarer Words, by Whitley Stokes. Crown 8vo, pp. xvi. and 188, paper boards. 1882. 18s.
STOKES.—THREE MIDDLE-IRISH HOMILIES ON THE LIVES OF SAINTS—PATRICK, BRIGIT, AND COLUMBA. Edited by Whitley Stokes. Crown 8vo, pp. xii. and 140, paper boards. 1882. 10s. 6d.
STONE.—CHRISTIANITY BEFORE CHRIST; or, Prototypes of our Faith and Culture. By Charles J. Stone, F.R.S.L., F.R.Hist.S., Author of "Cradle-Land of Arts and Creeds." Crown 8vo, pp.   , cloth.
STRANGE.—THE BIBLE; is it "The Word of God"? By Thomas Lumisden Strange. Demy 8vo, pp. xii. and 384, cloth. 1871. 7s.
STRANGE.—THE SPEAKER'S COMMENTARY. Reviewed by T. L. Strange. Cr. 8vo, pp. viii. and 159, cloth. 1871. 2s. 6d.
STRANGE.—THE DEVELOPMENT OF CREATION ON THE EARTH. By T. L. Strange. Demy 8vo, pp. xii. and 110, cloth. 1874. 2s. 6d.
STRANGE.—THE LEGENDS OF THE OLD TESTAMENT. By T. L. Strange. Demy 8vo, pp. xii. and 244, cloth. 1874. 5s.
STRANGE.—THE SOURCES AND DEVELOPMENT OF CHRISTIANITY. By Thomas Lumisden Strange. Demy 8vo, pp. xx. and 256, cloth. 1875. 5s.
STRANGE.—WHAT IS CHRISTIANITY? An Historical Sketch. Illustrated with a Chart. By T. L. Strange. Foolscap 8vo, pp. 72, cloth. 1880. 2s. 6d.
STRANGE.—CONTRIBUTIONS TO A SERIES OF CONTROVERSIAL WRITINGS, issued by the late Mr. Thomas Scott, of Upper Norwood. By Thomas Lumisden Strange. Fcap. 8vo, pp. viii. and 312, cloth. 1881. 2s. 6d.
STRANGFORD.—ORIGINAL LETTERS AND PAPERS OF THE LATE VISCOUNT STRANGFORD UPON PHILOLOGICAL AND KINDRED SUBJECTS. Edited by Viscountess Strangford. Post 8vo, pp. xxii. and 284, cloth. 1878. 12s. 6d.
STRATMANN.—THE TRAGICALL HISTORIE OF HAMLET, PRINCE OF DENMARKE. By William Shakespeare. Edited according to the first printed Copies, with the various Readings and Critical Notes. By F. H. Stratmann. 8vo, pp. vi. and 120, sewed. 3s. 6d.
STRATMANN.—A DICTIONARY OF THE OLD ENGLISH LANGUAGE. Compiled from Writings of the Twelfth, Thirteenth, Fourteenth, and Fifteenth Centuries. By F. H. Stratmann. Third Edition. 4to, pp. x. and 662, sewed. 1878. 30s.
STUDIES OF MAN. By a Japanese. Crown 8vo, pp. 124, cloth. 1874. 2s. 6d.
SUMNER.—WHAT SOCIAL CLASSES OWE TO EACH OTHER. By W. G. Sumner, Professor of Political and Social Science in Yale College. 18mo, pp. 170, cloth. 1884. 3s. 6d.
SUYEMATZ.—GENJI MONOGATARI. The Most Celebrated of the Classical Japanese Romances. Translated by K. Suyematz. Crown 8vo, pp. xvi. and 254, cloth. 1882. 7s. 6d.

SWEET.—SPELLING REFORM AND ENGLISH LITERATURE. By Henry Sweet, M.A. 8vo, pp. 8, wrapper. 1884. 2d.

SWEET.—HISTORY OF ENGLISH SOUNDS, from the Earliest Period, including an Investigation of the General Laws of Sound Change, and full Word Lists. By Henry Sweet. Demy 8vo, pp. iv.-164, cloth. 1874. 4s. 6d.

SWEET.—ON A MEXICAN MUSTANG THROUGH TEXAS FROM THE GULF TO THE RIO GRANDE. By Alex. E. Sweet and J. Armoy Knox, Editors of "Texas Siftings." English Copyright Edition. Demy 8vo, pp. 672. Illustrated, cloth. 1883. 10s.

SYED AHMAD.—A SERIES OF ESSAYS ON THE LIFE OF MOHAMMED, and Subjects subsidiary thereto. By Syed Ahmad Khan Bahadur, C.S.I. 8vo, pp. 532, with 4 Tables, 2 Maps, and Plate, cloth. 1870. 30s.

TALBOT.—ANALYSIS OF THE ORGANISATION OF THE PRUSSIAN ARMY. By Lieutenant Gerald F. Talbot, 2d Prussian Dragoon Guards. Royal 8vo, pp. 78, cloth. 1871. 3s.

TAYLER.—A RETROSPECT OF THE RELIGIOUS LIFE OF ENGLAND; or, Church, Puritanism, and Free Inquiry. By J. J. Tayler, B.A. Second Edition. Reissued, with an Introductory Chapter on Recent Development, by James Martineau, LL.D., D.D. Post 8vo, pp. 380, cloth. 1876. 7s. 6d.

TAYLOR.—PRINCE DEUKALION: A Lyrical Drama. By Bayard Taylor. Small 4to, pp. 172. Handsomely bound in white vellum. 1878. 12s.

TECHNOLOGICAL DICTIONARY of the Terms employed in the Arts and Sciences: Architecture; Civil Engineering; Mechanics; Machine-Making; Shipbuilding and Navigation; Metallurgy; Artillery; Mathematics; Physics; Chemistry; Mineralogy, &c. With a Preface by Dr. K. Karmarsch. Second Edition. 3 vols.
    Vol. I. German-English-French. 8vo, pp. 646. 12s.
    Vol. II. English-German-French. 8vo, pp. 666. 12s.
    Vol. III. French-German-English. 8vo, pp. 618. 12s.

TECHNOLOGICAL DICTIONARY.—A POCKET DICTIONARY OF TECHNICAL TERMS USED IN ARTS AND MANUFACTURES. English-German-French, Deutsch-Englisch-Französisch, Français-Allemand-Anglais. Abridged from the above Technological Dictionary by Rumpf, Mothes, and Unverzagt. With the addition of Commercial Terms. 3 vols. sq. 12mo, cloth, 12s.

TEMPLE.—THE LEGENDS OF THE PUNJAB. By Captain R. C. Temple, Bengal Staff Corps, F.G.S., &c. Vol. I., 8vo, pp. xviii.-546, cloth. 1884. £1, 6s.

THEÁTRE FRANÇAIS MODERNE.—A Selection of Modern French Plays. Edited by the Rev. P. H. E. Brette, B.D., C. Cassal, LL.D., and Th. Karcher, LL.B.
    First Series, in 1 vol. crown 8vo, cloth, 6s., containing—
CHARLOTTE CORDAY. A Tragedy. By F. Ponsard. Edited, with English Notes and Notice on Ponsard, by Professor C. Cassal, LL.D. Pp. xii. and 134. Separately, 2s. 6d.
DIANE. A Drama in Verse. By Emile Augier. Edited, with English Notes and Notice on Augier, by Th. Karcher, LL.B. Pp. xiv. and 145. Separately, 2s. 6d.
LE VOYAGE Á DIEPPE, A Comedy in Prose. By Wafflard and Fulgence. Edited, with English Notes, by the Rev. P. H. E. Brette, B.D. Pp. 104. Separately, 2s. 6d.
    Second Series, crown 8vo, cloth, 6s., containing—
MOLIÈRE. A Drama in Prose. By George Sand. Edited. with English Notes and Notice of George Sand, by Th. Karcher, LL.B. Fcap. 8vo, pp. xx. and 170, cloth. Separately, 3s. 6d.
LES ARISTOCRATIES. A Comedy in Verse. By Etienne Arago. Edited, with English Notes and Notice of Etienne Arago, by the Rev. P. H. E. Brette, B.D. 2d Edition. Fcap. 8vo, pp. xiv. and 236, cloth. Separately, 4s.

THEÂTRE Français Moderne—*continued.*
Third Series, crown 8vo, cloth, 6s., containing—
LES FAUX BONSHOMMES. A Comedy. By Théodore Barrière and Ernest Capendu. Edited, with English Notes and Notice on Barrière, by Professor C. Cassal, LL.D. Fcap. 8vo, pp. xvi. and 304. 1868. Separately, 4s.
L'HONNEUR ET L'ARGENT. A Comedy. By François Ponsard. Edited, with English Notes and Memoir of Ponsard, by Professor C. Cassal, LL.D. 2d Edition. Fcap. 8vo, pp. xvi. and 171, cloth. 1869. Separately, 3s. 6d.

THEISM.—A CANDID EXAMINATION OF THEISM. By Physicus. Post 8vo, pp. xviii. and 198, cloth. 1878. 7s. 6d.

THEOBALD.—SELECTIONS FROM THE POETS ; or, Passages Illustrating Peculiarities of their Style, Pathos, or Wit. By W. Theobald, M.R.A.S., late Deputy-Superintendent Geological Survey of India. With Notes, Historical, Explanatory, and Glossarial, for the Use of Young Readers. Demy 8vo, pp. xii. and 208, cloth. 1885. 5s.

THEOSOPHY AND THE HIGHER LIFE; or, Spiritual Dynamics and the Divine and Miraculous Man. By G. W., M.D., Edinburgh, President of the British Theosophical Society. 12mo, pp. iv. and 138, cloth. 1880. 3s.

THOM.—ST. PAUL'S EPISTLES TO THE CORINTHIANS. An Attempt to convey their Spirit and Significance. By the Rev. J. H. Thom. 8vo, pp. xii. and 408, cloth. 1851. 5s.

THOMAS.—EARLY SASSANIAN INSCRIPTIONS, SEALS, AND COINS, illustrating the Early History of the Sassanian Dynasty, containing Proclamations of Ardeshir Babek, Sapor I., and his Successors. With a Critical Examination and Explanation of the celebrated Inscription in the Hájíábad Cave, demonstrating that Sapor, the Conqueror of Valerian, was a professing Christian. By Edward Thomas. Illustrated. 8vo, pp. 148, cloth. 7s. 6d.

THOMAS.—THE CHRONICLES OF THE PATHAN KINGS OF DEHLI. Illustrated by Coins, Inscriptions, and other Antiquarian Remains. By E. Thomas, F.R.A.S. With Plates and Cuts. Demy 8vo, pp. xxiv. and 467, cloth. 1871. 28s.

THOMAS.—THE REVENUE RESOURCES OF THE MUGHAL EMPIRE IN INDIA, from A.D. 1593 to A.D. 1707. A Supplement to "The Chronicles of the Pathán Kings of Delhi." By E. Thomas, F.R.S. 8vo, pp. 60, cloth. 3s. 6d.

THOMAS.—SASSANIAN COINS. Communicated to the Numismatic Society of London. By E. Thomas, F.R.S. Two Parts, 12mo, pp. 43, 3 Plates and a Cut, sewed. 5s.

THOMAS.—JAINISM ; OR, THE EARLY FAITH OF ASOKA. With Illustrations of the Ancient Religions of the East, from the Pantheon of the Indo-Scythians. To which is added a Notice on Bactrian Coins and Indian Dates. By Edward Thomas, F.R.S. 8vo, pp. viii.-24 and 82. With two Autotype Plates and Woodcuts. 1877. 7s. 6d.

THOMAS.—THE THEORY AND PRACTICE OF CREOLE GRAMMAR. By J. J. Thomas. 8vo, pp. viii. and 135, boards. 12s.

THOMAS.—RECORDS OF THE GUPTA DYNASTY. Illustrated by Inscriptions, Written History, Local Tradition, and Coins. To which is added a Chapter on the Arabs in Sind. By Edward Thomas, F.R.S. Folio, with a Plate, pp. iv. and 64, cloth. 14s.

THOMAS.—THE INDIAN BALHARA, and the Arabian Intercourse with India in the Ninth and following Centuries. By Edward Thomas, F.R.S. (Contained in International Numismata Orientalia. Vol. II I., Part I. Coins of Arakan Royal 4to, pp. viii.-48, wrappers. 1882. 8s. 6d.

THOMAS.—BOYHOOD LAYS. By William Henry Thomas. 18mo, pp. iv. and 74, cloth. 1877. 2s. 6d.

THOMPSON.—DIALOGUES, RUSSIAN AND ENGLISH. Compiled by A. R. Thompson, sometime Lecturer of the English Language in the University of St. Vladimir, Kieff. Crown 8vo, pp. iv. and 132, cloth. 1882. 5s.

E

THOMSON.—EVOLUTION AND INVOLUTION. By George Thomson, Author of "The World of Being," &c. Crown 8vo, pp. viii. and 206, cloth. 1880. 5s.

THORBURN.—BANNÚ; OR, OUR AFGHAN FRONTIER. By S. S. Thorburn, F.C.S., Settlement Officer of the Bannú District. 8vo, pp. x. and 480, cloth. 1876. 18s.

THORPE.—DIPLOMATARIUM ANGLICUM ÆVI SAXONICI. A Collection of English Charters, from the reign of King Æthelberht of Kent, A.D. DCV., to that of William the Conqueror. Containing: I. Miscellaneous Charters. II. Wills. III. Guilds. IV. Manumissions and Acquittances. With a Translation of the Anglo-Saxon. By the late Benjamin Thorpe, Member of the Royal Academy of Sciences at Munich, and of the Society of Netherlandish Literature at Leyden. 8vo, pp. xlii. and 682, cloth. 1865. £1, 1s.

THOUGHTS ON LOGIC; or, the S.N.I.X. Propositional Theory. Crown 8vo, pp. iv. and 76, cloth. 1877. 2s. 6d.

THOUGHTS ON THEISM, with Suggestions towards a Public Religious Service in Harmony with Modern Science and Philosophy. Ninth Thousand. Revised and Enlarged. 8vo, pp. 74, sewed. 1882. 1s.

THURSTON.—FRICTION AND LUBRICATION. Determinations of the Laws and Coefficients of Friction by new Methods and with new Apparatus. By Robert H. Thurston, A.M., C.E., &c. Crown 8vo, pp. xvi. and 212, cloth. 1879. 6s. 6d.

TIELE.—See English and Foreign Philosophical Library, Vol. VII. and Trübner's Oriental Series.

TOLHAUSEN.—A SYNOPSIS OF THE PATENT LAWS OF VARIOUS COUNTRIES. By A. Tolhausen, Ph.D. Third Edition. 12mo, pp. 62, sewed. 1870. 1s. 6d.

TONSBERG.—NORWAY. Illustrated Handbook for Travellers. Edited by Charles Tönsberg. With 134 Engravings on Wood, 17 Maps, and Supplement. Crown 8vo, pp. lxx., 482, and 32, cloth. 1875. 18s.

TOPOGRAPHICAL WORKS.—A LIST OF THE VARIOUS WORKS PREPARED AT THE TOPOGRAPHICAL AND STATISTICAL DEPARTMENT OF THE WAR OFFICE may be had on application.

TORCEANU.—ROUMANIAN GRAMMAR. See Trübner's Collection.

TORRENS.—EMPIRE IN ASIA: How we came by it. A Book of Confessions. By W. M. Torrens, M.P. Med. 8vo, pp. 426, cloth. 1872. 14s.

TOSCANI.—ITALIAN CONVERSATIONAL COURSE. A New Method of Teaching the Italian Language, both Theoretically and Practically. By Giovanni Toscani, Professor of the Italian Language and Literature in Queen's Coll., London, &c. Fourth Edition. 12mo, pp. xiv. and 300, cloth. 1872. 5s.

TOSCANI.—ITALIAN READING COURSE. By G. Toscani. Fcap. 8vo, pp. xii. and 160. With table. Cloth. 1875. 4s. 6d.

TOULON.—ITS ADVANTAGES AS A WINTER RESIDENCE FOR INVALIDS AND OTHERS. By an English Resident. The proceeds of this pamphlet to be devoted to the English Church at Toulon. Crown 8vo, pp. 8, sewed. 1873. 6d.

TRADLEG.—A SON OF BELIAL. Autobiographical Sketches. By Nitram Tradleg, University of Bosphorus. Crown 8vo, pp. viii.-260, cloth. 1882. 5s.

TRIMEN.—SOUTH-AFRICAN BUTTERFLIES; a Monograph of the Extra-Tropical Species. By Roland Trimen, F.L.S., F.Z.S., M.E.S., Curator of the South African Museum, Cape Town. Royal 8vo. [*In preparation.*

TRÜBNER'S AMERICAN, EUROPEAN, AND ORIENTAL LITERARY RECORD. A Register of the most Important Works published in America, India, China, and the British Colonies. With Occasional Notes on German, Dutch, Danish, French, Italian, Spanish, Portuguese, and Russian Literature. The object of the Publishers in issuing this publication is to give a full and particular account of every publication of importance issued in America and the East. Small 4to, 6d. per number. Subscription, 5s. per volume.

TRÜBNER.—TRÜBNER'S BIBLIOGRAPHICAL GUIDE TO AMERICAN LITERATURE:
A Classed List of Books published in the United States of America, from 1817
to 1857. With Bibliographical Introduction, Notes, and Alphabetical Index.
Compiled and Edited by Nicolas Trübner. In 1 vol. 8vo, half bound, pp. 750.
1859. 18s.

TRÜBNER'S CATALOGUE OF DICTIONARIES AND GRAMMARS OF THE PRINCIPAL
LANGUAGES AND DIALECTS OF THE WORLD. Considerably Enlarged and Revised,
with an Alphabetical Index. A Guide for Students and Booksellers. Second
Edition, 8vo, pp. viii. and 170, cloth. 1882. 5s.

TRÜBNER'S COLLECTION OF SIMPLIFIED GRAMMARS OF THE PRINCIPAL ASIATIC
AND EUROPEAN LANGUAGES. Edited by Reinhold Rost, LL.D., Ph.D. Crown
8vo, cloth, uniformly bound.

    I.—HINDUSTANI, PERSIAN, AND ARABIC. By E. H. Palmer, M.A.
       Second Edition. Pp. 112. 1885. 5s.
    II.—HUNGARIAN. By I. Singer. Pp. vi. and 88. 1882. 4s. 6d.
    III.—BASQUE. By W. Van Eys. Pp. xii. and 52. 1883. 3s. 6d.
    IV.—MALAGASY. By G. W. Parker. Pp. 66, with Plate. 1883. 5s.
    V.—MODERN GREEK. By E. M. Geldart, M.A. Pp. 68. 1883. 2s. 6d.
    VI.—ROUMANIAN. By R. Torceanu. Pp. viii. and 72. 1883. 5s.
    VII.—TIBETAN GRAMMAR. By H. A. JASCHKE. Pp. viii.-104. 1883. 5s.
    VIII.—DANISH. By E. C. Otté. Pp. viii. and 66. 1884. 2s. 6d.
    IX.—TURKISH. By J. W. Redhouse, M.R.A.S. Pp. xii. and 204. 1884. 10s.6d.
    X.—SWEDISH. By E. C. Otté. Pp. xii.-70. 1884. 2s. 6d.
    XI.—POLISH. By W. R. Morfill, M.A. Pp. viii.-64. 1884. 3s. 6d.
    XII.—PALI. By E. Müller. Pp. xvi.-144. 1884. 7s. 6d.
    XIII.—SANSKRIT. By H. Edgren. Pp. xii.-178. 1885. 10s. 6d.

TRÜBNER'S ORIENTAL SERIES :—
    Post 8vo, cloth, uniformly bound.

ESSAYS ON THE SACRED LANGUAGE, WRITINGS, AND RELIGION OF
THE PARSIS. By Martin Haug, Ph.D., late Professor of Sanskrit and
Comparative Philology at the University of Munich. Third Edition.
Edited and Enlarged by E. W. West, Ph.D. To which is also added, A
Biographical Memoir of the late Dr. Haug. By Professor E. P. Evans.
Pp. xlviii. and 428. 1884. 16s.

TEXTS FROM THE BUDDHIST CANON, commonly known as Dhammapada. With Accompanying Narratives. Translated from the Chinese
by S. Beal, B.A., Trinity College, Cambridge, Professor of Chinese, University College, London. Pp. viii. and 176. 1878. 7s. 6d.

THE HISTORY OF INDIAN LITERATURE. By Albrecht Weber. Translated from the German by J. Mann, M.A., and Dr. T. Zachariae, with
the Author's sanction and assistance. 2d Edition. Pp. 368. 1882. 10s. 6d.

A SKETCH OF THE MODERN LANGUAGES OF THE EAST INDIES. Accompanied by Two Language Maps, Classified List of Languages and
Dialects, and a List of Authorities for each Language. By Robert Cust,
late of H.M.I.C.S., and Hon. Librarian of R.A.S. Pp. xii. and 198.
1878. 12s.

THE BIRTH OF THE WAR-GOD: A Poem. By Kálidasá. Translated
from the Sanskrit into English Verse, by Ralph T. H. Griffiths, M.A.,
Principal of Benares College. Second Edition. Pp. xii. and 116. 1879. 5s.

A CLASSICAL DICTIONARY OF HINDU MYTHOLOGY AND HISTORY, GEOGRAPHY AND LITERATURE. By John Dowson, M.R.A.S., late Professor
in the Staff College. Pp. 432. 1879. 16s.

METRICAL TRANSLATIONS FROM SANSKRIT WRITERS; with an Introduction, many Prose Versions, and Parallel Passages from Classical
Authors. By J. Muir, C.I.E., D.C.L., &c. Pp. xliv.-376. 1879. 14s.

MODERN INDIA AND THE INDIANS : being a Series of Impressions, Notes,
and Essays. By Monier Williams, D.C.L., Hon. LL.D. of the University
of Calcutta, Boden Professor of Sanskrit in the University of Oxford.
Third Edition, revised and augmented by considerable additions. With
Illustrations and Map, pp. vii. and 368. 1879. 14s.

TRÜBNER'S ORIENTAL SERIES—*continued.*

THE LIFE OR LEGEND OF GAUDAMA, the Buddha of the Burmese. With Annotations, the Ways to Neibban, and Notice on the Phongyies, or Burmese Monks. By the Right Rev. P. Bigandet, Bishop of Ramatha, Vicar Apostolic of Ava and Pegu. Third Edition. 2 vols. Pp. xx.-368 and viii.-326. 1880. 21s.

MISCELLANEOUS ESSAYS, relating to Indian Subjects. By B. H. Hodgson, late British Minister at Nepal. 2 vols., pp. viii.-408, and viii.-348. 1880. 28s.

SELECTIONS FROM THE KORAN. By Edward William Lane, Author of an "Arabic-English Lexicon," &c. A New Edition, Revised, with an Introduction. By Stanley Lane Poole. Pp. cxii. and 174. 1879. 9s.

CHINESE BUDDHISM. A Volume of Sketches, Historical and Critical. By J. Edkins, D.D., Author of "China's Place in Philology," "Religion in China," &c., &c. Pp. lvi. and 454. 1880. 18s.

THE GULISTAN; OR, ROSE GARDEN OF SHEKH MUSHLIU'D-DIN SADI OF SHIRAZ. Translated for the first time into Prose and Verse, with Preface and a Life of the Author, from the Atish Kadah, by E. B. Eastwick, F.R.S., M.R.A.S. 2d Edition. Pp. xxvi. and 244. 1880. 10s. 6d.

A TALMUDIC MISCELLANY; or, One Thousand and One Extracts from the Talmud, the Midrashim, and the Kabbalah. Compiled and Translated by P. J. Hershon. With a Preface by Rev. F. W. Farrar, D.D., F.R.S., Chaplain in Ordinary to Her Majesty, and Canon of Westminster. With Notes and Copious Indexes. Pp. xxviii. and 362. 1880. 14s.

THE HISTORY OF ESARHADDON (Son of Sennacherib), King of Assyria, B.C. 681-668. Translated from the Cuneiform Inscriptions upon Cylinders and Tablets in the British Museum Collection. Together with Original Texts, a Grammatical Analysis of each word, Explanations of the Ideographs by Extracts from the Bi-Lingual Syllabaries, and List of Eponyms, &c. By E. A. Budge, B.A., M.R.A.S., Assyrian Exhibitioner, Christ's College, Cambridge. Post 8vo, pp. xii. and 164, cloth. 1880. 10s. 6d.

BUDDHIST BIRTH STORIES; or, Jātaka Tales. The oldest Collection of Folk-Lore extant: being the Jātakatthavannanā, for the first time edited in the original Pali, by V. Fausböll, and translated by T. W. Rhys Davids. Translation. Vol. I. Pp. cxvi. and 348. 1880. 18s.

THE CLASSICAL POETRY OF THE JAPANESE. By Basil Chamberlain, Author of "Yeigio Henkaku, Ichiran." Pp. xii. and 228. 1880. 7s. 6d.

LINGUISTIC AND ORIENTAL ESSAYS. Written from the year 1846-1878. By R. Cust, Author of "The Modern Languages of the East Indies." Pp. xii. and 484. 1880. 18s.

INDIAN POETRY. Containing a New Edition of "The Indian Song of Songs," from the Sanskrit of the Gita Govinda of Jayadeva; Two Books from "The Iliad of India" (Mahábhárata); "Proverbial Wisdom" from the Shlokas of the Hitopadésa, and other Oriental Poems. By Edwin Arnold, C.S.I., &c. Third Edition. Pp. viii. and 270. 1884. 7s. 6d.

THE RELIGIONS OF INDIA. By A. Barth. Authorised Translation by Rev. J. Wood. Pp. xx. and 310. 1881. 16s.

HINDŪ PHILOSOPHY. The Sānkhya Kārikā of Iswara Krishna. An Exposition of the System of Kapila. With an Appendix on the Nyaya and Vaiseshika Systems. By John Davies, M.A., M.R.A.S. Pp. vi. and 151. 1881. 6s.

A MANUAL OF HINDU PANTHEISM. The Vedantasara. Translated with Copious Annotations. By Major G. A. Jacob, Bombay Staff Corps, Inspector of Army Schools. With a Preface by E. B. Cowell, M.A., Professor of Sanskrit in the University of Cambridge. Pp. x. and 130. 1881. 6s.

THE MESNEVĪ (usually known as the Mesnevīyi Sherīf, or Holy Mesnevī) of Mevlānā (Our Lord) Jelālu-'d-Din Muhammed, Er-Rūmī. Book the First. Together with some Account of the Life and Acts of the Author, of his Ancestors, and of his Descendants. Illustrated by a selection of Characteristic Anecdotes as collected by their Historian Mevlānā Shemsu-'d-Dīn Ahmed, El Efiākī El Arifī. Translated, and the Poetry Versified by James W. Redhouse, M.R.A.S., &c. Pp. xvi. and 136, vi. and 290. 1881. £1, 1s.

EASTERN PROVERBS AND EMBLEMS ILLUSTRATING OLD TRUTHS. By the Rev. J. Long, Member of the Bengal Asiatic Society, F.R.G.S. Pp. xv. and 280. 1881. 6s.

THE QUATRAINS OF OMAR KHAYYÁM. A New Translation. By E. H. Whinfield, late of H.M. Bengal Civil Service. Pp. 96. 1881. 5s.

THE QUATRAINS OF OMAR KHAYYÁM. The Persian Text, with an English Verse Translation. By E. H. Whinfield. Pp. xxxii.-335. 1883. 10s. 6d.

THE MIND OF MENCIUS; or, Political Economy Founded upon Moral Philosophy. A Systematic Digest of the Doctrines of the Chinese Philosopher Mencius. The Original Text Classified and Translated, with Comments, by the Rev. E. Faber, Rhenish Mission Society. Translated from the German, with Additional Notes, by the Rev. A. B. Hutchinson, Church Mission, Hong Kong. Author in Chinese of "Primer Old Testament History," &c., &c. Pp. xvi. and 294. 1882. 10s. 6d.

YÚSUF AND ZULAIKHA. A Poem by Jami. Translated from the Persian into English Verse. By R. T. H. Griffith. Pp. xiv. and 304. 1882. 8s. 6d.

TSUNI- ‖ GOAM: The Supreme Being of the Khoi-Khoi. By Theophilus Hahn, Ph.D., Custodian of the Grey Collection, Cape Town, Corresponding Member of the Geographical Society, Dresden; Corresponding Member of the Anthropological Society, Vienna, &c., &c. Pp. xii. and 154. 1882. 7s. 6d.

A COMPREHENSIVE COMMENTARY TO THE QURAN. To which is prefixed Sale's Preliminary Discourse, with Additional Notes and Emendations. Together with a Complete Index to the Text, Preliminary Discourse, and Notes. By Rev. E. M. Wherry, M.A., Lodiana. Vol. I. Pp. xii. and 392. 1882. 12s. 6d. Vol. II. Pp. xi. and 408. 1884. 12s. 6d.

HINDU PHILOSOPHY. THE BHAGAVAD GÎTÂ; or, The Sacred Lay. A Sanskrit Philosophical Lay. Translated, with Notes, by John Davies, M.A. Pp. vi. and 208. 1882. 8s. 6d.

THE SARVA-DARSANA-SAMGRAHA; or, Review of the Different Systems of Hindu Philosophy. By Madhava Acharya. Translated by E. B. Cowell, M.A., Cambridge, and A. E. Gough, M.A., Calcutta. Pp. xii. and 282. 1882. 10s. 6d.

TIBETAN TALES. Derived from Indian Sources. Translated from the Tibetan of the Kay-Gyur. By F. Anton von Schiefner. Done into English from the German, with an Introduction. By W. R. S. Ralston, M.A. Pp. lxvi. and 368. 1882. 14s.

LINGUISTIC ESSAYS. By Carl Abel, Ph.D. Pp. viii. and 265. 1882. 9s.

THE INDIAN EMPIRE: Its History, People, and Products. By W. W. Hunter, C.I.E., LL.D. Pp. 568. 1882. 16s.

HISTORY OF THE EGYPTIAN RELIGION. By Dr. C. P. Tiele, Leiden. Translated by J. Ballingal. Pp. xxiv. and 230. 1882. 7s. 6d.

TRÜBNER'S ORIENTAL SERIES—*continued.*

THE PHILOSOPHY OF THE UPANISHADS. By A. E. Gough, M.A., Calcutta. Pp. xxiv.-268. 1882. 9s.

UDANAVARGA. A Collection of Verses from the Buddhist Canon. Compiled by Dharmatrâta. Being the Northern Buddhist Version of Dhammapada. Translated from the Tibetan of Bkah-hgyur, with Notes, and Extracts from the Commentary of Pradjnavarman, by W. Woodville Rockhill. Pp. 240. 1883. 9s.

A HISTORY OF BURMA, including Burma Proper, Pegu, Taungu, Tenasserim, and Arakan. From the Earliest Time to the End of the First War with British India. By Lieut.-General Sir Arthur P. Phayre, G.C.M.G., K.C.S.I., and C.B. Pp. xii.-312. 1883. 14s.

A SKETCH OF THE MODERN LANGUAGES OF AFRICA. Accompanied by a Language-Map. By R. N. Cust, Author of "Modern Languages of the East Indies," &c. 2 vols., pp. xvi. and 566, with Thirty-one Autotype Portraits. 1883. 25s.

RELIGION IN CHINA; containing a brief Account of the Three Religions of the Chinese; with Observations on the Prospects of Christian Conversion amongst that People. By Joseph Edkins, D.D., Peking. Third Edition. Pp. xvi. and 260. 1884. 7s. 6d.

OUTLINES OF THE HISTORY OF RELIGION TO THE SPREAD OF THE UNIVERSAL RELIGIONS. By Prof. C. P. TIELE. Translated from the Dutch by J. Estlin Carpenter, M.A., with the Author's assistance. Third Edition. Pp. xx. and 250. 1884. 7s. 6d.

SI-YU-KI. BUDDHIST RECORDS OF THE WESTERN WORLD. Translated from the Chinese of Hiuen Tsiang (A.D. 629). By Samuel Beal, Professor of Chinese, University College, London. 2 vols., with a specially prepared Map. Pp. cviii.-242 and viii.-370. 1884. 24s. Dedicated by permission to H.R.H. the Prince of Wales.

THE LIFE OF THE BUDDHA, AND THE EARLY HISTORY OF HIS ORDER. Derived from Tibetan Works in the Bkah-Hgyur and the Bstan-Hgyur, followed by Notices on the Early History of Tibet and Khoten. By W. W. Rockhill. Pp. xii. and 274. 1884. 10s. 6d.

THE SANKHYA APHORISMS OF KAPILA. With Illustrative Extracts from the Commentaries. Translated and Edited by J. R. Ballantyne, LL.D., late Principal of Benares College. Third Edition, now entirely Re-Edited by Fitzedward Hall. Pp. viii. and 464. 1885. 16s.

THE ORDINANCES OF MANU. Translated from the Sanskrit. With an Introduction by the late A. C. Burnell, Ph.D., C.I.E. Completed and Edited by Edward W. Hopkins, Ph.D., of Columbia College, New York. Pp. xliv. and 400. 1884. 12s.

THE LIFE AND WORKS OF ALEXANDER CSOMA DE KÖRÖS between 1819 and 1842. With a Short Notice of all his Published and Unpublished Works and Essays. From Original and for the most part Unpublished Documents. By T. Duka, M.D., F.R.C.S. (Eng.), Surgeon-Major H.M.'s Bengal Medical Service, Retired, &c. Pp. xii.-234, cloth. 1885. 9s.

TURNER.—THE ENGLISH LANGUAGE. A Concise History of the English Language, with a Glossary showing the Derivation and Pronunciation of the English Words. By Roger Turner. In German and English on opposite pages. 18mo, pp. viii.-80, sewed. 1884. 1s. 6d.

UNGER.—A SHORT CUT TO READING: The Child's First Book of Lessons. Part I. By W. H. Unger. Fourth Edition. Cr. 8vo, pp. 32, cloth. 1873. 5d.

SEQUEL to Part I. and Part II. Fourth Edition. Cr. 8vo, pp. 64, cloth. 1873. 6d. Parts I. and II. Third Edition. Demy 8vo, pp. 76, cloth. 1873. 1s. 6d. In folio sheets. Pp. 44. Sets A to D, 10d. each; set E, 8d. 1873. Complete, 4s.

UNGER.—W. H. UNGER'S CONTINUOUS SUPPLEMENTARY WRITING MODELS, designed to impart not only a good business hand, but correctness in transcribing. Oblong 8vo, pp. 40, stiff covers. 1874. 6d.

UNGER.—THE STUDENT'S BLUE BOOK: Being Selections from Official Correspondence, Reports, &c. ; for Exercises in Reading and Copying Manuscripts, Writing, Orthography, Punctuation, Dictation, Précis, Indexing, and Digesting, and Tabulating Accounts and Returns. Compiled by W. H. Unger. Folio, pp. 100, paper. 1875. 2s.

UNGER.—TWO HUNDRED TESTS IN ENGLISH ORTHOGRAPHY, or Word Dictations. Compiled by W. H. Unger. Foolscap, pp. viii. and 200, cloth. 1877. 1s. 6d. plain, 2s. 6d. interleaved.

UNGER.—THE SCRIPT PRIMER: By which one of the remaining difficulties of Children is entirely removed in the first stages, and, as a consequence, a considerable saving of time will be effected. In Two Parts. By W. H. Unger. Part I. 12mo, pp. xvi. and 44, cloth. 5d. Part II., pp. 59, cloth. 5d.

UNGER.—PRELIMINARY WORD DICTATIONS ON THE RULES FOR SPELLING. By W. H. Unger. 18mo, pp. 44, cloth. 4d.

URICOECHEA.—MAPOTECA COLOMBIANA: Catalogo de Todos los Mapas, Planos, Vistas, &c., relativos a la América-Española, Brasil, e Islas adyacentes. Arreglada cronologicamente i precedida de una introduccion sobre la historia cartografica de América. Por el Doctor Ezequiel Uricoechea, de Bogóta, Nueva Granada. 8vo, pp. 232, cloth. 1860. 6s.

URQUHART.—ELECTRO-MOTORS. A Treatise on the Means and Apparatus employed in the Transmission of Electrical Energy and its Conversion into Motive-power. For the Use of Engineers and Others. By J. W. Urquhart, Electrician. Crown 8vo, cloth, pp. xii. and 178, illustrated. 1882. 7s. 6d.

VAITANA SUTRA.—See AUCTORES SANSKRITI, Vol. III.

VALDES.—LIVES OF THE TWIN BROTHERS, JUÁN AND ALFONSO DE VALDÉS. By E. Boehmer, D.D. Translated by J. T. Betts. Crown 8vo, pp. 32, wrappers. 1882. 1s.

VALDES.—SEVENTEEN OPUSCULES. By Juán de Valdés. Translated from the Spanish and Italian, and edited by John T. Betts. Crown 8vo, pp. xii. and 188, cloth. 1882. 6s.

VALDES.—JUÁN DE VALDÉS' COMMENTARY UPON THE GOSPEL OF ST. MATTHEW. With Professor Boehmer's "Lives of Juán and Alfonso de Valdés." Now for the first time translated from the Spanish, and never before published in English. By John T. Betts. Post 8vo, pp. xii. and 512-30, cloth. 1882. 7s. 6d.

VALDES.—SPIRITUAL MILK; or, Christian Instruction for Children. By Juán de Valdés. Translated from the Italian, edited and published by John T. Betts. With Lives of the twin brothers, Juán and Alfonso de Valdés. By E. Boehmer, D.D. Fcap. 8vo, pp. 60, wrappers. 1882. 2s.

VALDES.—SPIRITUAL MILK. Octaglot. The Italian original, with translations into Spanish, Latin, Polish, German, English, French, and Engadin. With a Critical and Historical Introduction by Edward Boehmer, the Editor of "Spanish Reformers." 4to, pp. 88, wrappers. 1884. 6s.

VALDES.—THREE OPUSCULES: an Extract from Valdés' Seventeen Opuscules. By Juán de Valdés. Translated, edited, and published by John T. Betts. Fcap. 8vo, pp. 58, wrappers. 1881. 1s. 6d.

VALDES.—JUÁN DE VALDÉS' COMMENTARY UPON OUR LORD'S SERMON ON THE MOUNT. Translated and edited by J. T. Betts. With Lives of Juán and Alfonso de Valdés. By E. Boehmer, D.D. Crown 8vo, pp. 112, boards. 1882. 2s. 6d.

VALDES.—JUÁN DE VALDÉS' COMMENTARY UPON THE EPISTLE TO THE ROMANS. Edited by J. T. Betts. Crown 8vo, pp. xxxii. and 296, cloth. 1883. 6s.

VALDES.—JUÁN DE VALDÉS' COMMENTARY UPON ST. PAUL'S FIRST EPISTLE TO THE CHURCH AT CORINTH. Translated and edited by J. T. Betts. With Lives of Juán and Alphonso de Valdés. By E. Boehmer. Crown 8vo, pp. 390, cloth. 1883. 6s.

VAN CAMPEN.—THE DUTCH IN THE ARCTIC SEAS. By Samuel Richard Van Campen, author of "Holland's Silver Feast." 8vo. Vol. I. A Dutch Arctic Expedition and Route. Third Edition. Pp. xxxvii. and 263, cloth. 1877. 10s. 6d. Vol. II. *in preparation.*

VAN DE WEYER.—CHOIX D'OPUSCULES PHILOSOPHIQUES, HISTORIQUES, POLITIQUES ET LITTÉRAIRES de Sylvain Van de Weyer, Précédés d'Avant propos de l'Editeur. Roxburghe style. Crown 8vo. PREMIÈRE SÉRIE. Pp. 374. 1863. 10s. 6d.—DEUXIÈME SÉRIE. Pp. 502. 1869. 12s.—TROISIÈME SÉRIE. Pp. 391. 1875. 10s. 6d.—QUATRIÈME SÉRIE. Pp. 366. 1876. 10s. 6d.

VAN EYS.—BASQUE GRAMMAR. See Trübner's Collection.

VAN LAUN.—GRAMMAR OF THE FRENCH LANGUAGE. By H. Van Laun. Parts I. and II. Accidence and Syntax. 13th Edition. Cr. 8vo, pp. 151 and 120, cloth. 1874. 4s. Part III. Exercises. 11th Edition. Cr. 8vo, pp. xii. and 285, cloth. 1873. 3s. 6d.

VAN LAUN.—LEÇONS GRADUÉES DE TRADUCTION ET DE LECTURE; or, Graduated Lessons in Translation and Reading, with Biographical Sketches, Annotations on History, Geography, Synonyms and Style, and a Dictionary of Words and Idioms. By Henri Van Laun. 4th Edition. 12mo, pp. viii. and 400, cloth. 1868. 5s.

VAN PRAAGH.—LESSONS FOR THE INSTRUCTION OF DEAF AND DUMB CHILDREN, in Speaking, Lip-reading, Reading, and Writing. By W. Van Praagh, Director of the School and Training College for Teachers of the Association for the Oral Instruction of the Deaf and Dumb, Officier d'Academie, France. Fcap. 8vo, Part I., pp. 52, cloth. 1884. 2s. 6d. Part II., pp. 62, cloth. 1s. 6d.

VARDHAMANA'S GANARATNAMAHODADHI. See AUCTORES SANSKRITI, Vol. IV.

VAZIR OF LANKURAN: A Persian Play. A Text-Book of Modern Colloquial Persian. Edited, with Grammatical Introduction, Translation, Notes, and Vocabulary, by W. H. Haggard, late of H.M. Legation in Teheran, and G. le Strange. Crown 8vo, pp. 230, cloth. 1882. 10s. 6d.

VELASQUEZ AND SIMONNÉ'S NEW METHOD TO READ, WRITE, AND SPEAK THE SPANISH LANGUAGE. Adapted to Ollendorff's System. Post 8vo, pp. 558, cloth. 1882. 6s.

KEY. Post 8vo, pp. 174, cloth. 4s.

VELASQUEZ.—A DICTIONARY OF THE SPANISH AND ENGLISH LANGUAGES. For the Use of Young Learners and Travellers. By M. Velasquez de la Cadena. In Two Parts. I. Spanish-English. II. English-Spanish. Crown 8vo, pp. viii. and 846, cloth. 1883. 7s. 6d.

VELASQUEZ.—A PRONOUNCING DICTIONARY OF THE SPANISH AND ENGLISH LANGUAGES. Composed from the Dictionaries of the Spanish Academy, Terreos, and Salvá, and Webster, Worcester, and Walker. Two Parts in one thick volume. By M. Velasquez de la Cadena. Roy. 8vo, pp. 1280, cloth. 1873. £1, 4s.

VELASQUEZ.—NEW SPANISH READER: Passages from the most approved authors, in Prose and Verse. Arranged in progressive order. With Vocabulary. By M. Velasquez de la Cadena. Post 8vo, pp. 352, cloth. 1866. 6s.

VELASQUEZ.—AN EASY INTRODUCTION TO SPANISH CONVERSATION, containing all that is necessary to make a rapid progress in it. Particularly designed for persons who have little time to study, or are their own instructors. By M. Velasquez de la Cadena. 12mo, pp. 150, cloth. 1863. 2s. 6d.

VERSES AND VERSELETS. By a Lover of Nature. Foolscap 8vo, pp. viii. and 88, cloth. 1876. 2s. 6d.

VICTORIA GOVERNMENT.—PUBLICATIONS OF THE GOVERNMENT OF VICTORIA. *List in preparation.*

VOGEL.—ON BEER. A Statistical Sketch. By M. Vogel. Fcap. 8vo, pp. xii. and 76, cloth limp. 1874. 2s.

WAFFLARD and FULGENCE.—LE VOYAGE À DIEPPE. A Comedy in Prose. By Wafflard and Fulgence. Edited, with Notes, by the Rev. P. H. E. Brette, B.D. Cr. 8vo, pp. 104, cloth. 1867. 2s. 6d.

WAKE.—THE EVOLUTION OF MORALITY. Being a History of the Development of Moral Culture. By C. Staniland Wake. 2 vols. crown 8vo, pp. xvi.-506 and xii.-474, cloth. 1878. 21s.

WALLACE.—ON MIRACLES AND MODERN SPIRITUALISM; Three Essays. By Alfred Russel Wallace, Author of "The Malay Archipelago," "The Geographical Distribution of Animals," &c., &c. Second Edition, crown 8vo, pp. viii. and 236, cloth. 1881. 5s

WANKLYN and CHAPMAN.—WATER ANALYSIS. A Practical Treatise on the Examination of Potable Water. By J. A. Wanklyn, and E. T. Chapman. Sixth Edition. Entirely rewritten. By J. A. Wanklyn, M.R.C.S. Crown 8vo, pp. 192, cloth. 1884. 5s.

WANKLYN.—MILK ANALYSIS; a Practical Treatise on the Examination of Milk and its Derivatives, Cream, Butter, and Cheese. By J. A. Wanklyn, M.R.C.S., &c. Crown 8vo, pp. viii. and 72, cloth. 1874. 5s.

WANKLYN.—TEA, COFFEE, AND COCOA. A Practical Treatise on the Analysis of Tea, Coffee, Cocoa, Chocolate, Maté (Paraguay Tea), &c. By J. A. Wanklyn, M.R.C.S., &c. Crown 8vo, pp. viii. and 60, cloth. 1874. 5s.

WAR OFFICE.—A LIST OF THE VARIOUS MILITARY MANUALS AND OTHER WORKS PUBLISHED UNDER THE SUPERINTENDENCE OF THE WAR OFFICE may be had on application.

WARD.—ICE: A Lecture delivered before the Keswick Literary Society, and published by request. To which is appended a Geological Dream on Skiddaw. By J. Clifton Ward, F.G.S. 8vo, pp. 28, sewed. 1870. 1s.

WARD.—ELEMENTARY NATURAL PHILOSOPHY; being a Course of Nine Lectures, specially adapted for the use of Schools and Junior Students. By J. Clifton Ward, F.G.S. Fcap. 8vo, pp. viii. and 216, with 154 Illustrations, cloth. 1871. 3s. 6d.

WARD.—ELEMENTARY GEOLOGY: A Course of Nine Lectures, for the use of Schools and Junior Students. By J. Clifton Ward, F.G.S. Fcap. 8vo, pp. 292, with 120 Illustrations, cloth. 1872. 4s. 6d.

WATSON.—INDEX TO THE NATIVE AND SCIENTIFIC NAMES OF INDIAN AND OTHER EASTERN ECONOMIC PLANTS AND PRODUCTS, originally prepared under the authority of the Secretary of State for India in Council. By John Forbes Watson, M.D. Imp. 8vo, pp. 650, cloth. 1868. £1, 11s. 6d.

WATSON.—SPANISH AND PORTUGUESE SOUTH AMERICA DURING THE COLONIAL PERIOD. By R. G. WATSON. 2 vols. post 8vo, pp. xvi.-308, viii.-320, cloth. 1884. 21s.

WEBER.—THE HISTORY OF INDIAN LITERATURE. By Albrecht Weber. Translated from the Second German Edition, by J. Mann, M.A., and T. Zacharaiae, Ph.D., with the sanction of the Author. Second Edition, post 8vo, pp. xxiv. and 360, cloth. 1882. 10s. 6d.

WEDGWOOD.—THE PRINCIPLES OF GEOMETRICAL DEMONSTRATION, reduced from the Original Conception of Space and Form. By H. Wedgwood, M.A. 12mo, pp. 48, cloth. 1844. 2s.

WEDGWOOD.—ON THE DEVELOPMENT OF THE UNDERSTANDING. By H. Wedgwood, A.M. 12mo, pp. 133, cloth. 1848. 3s.

WEDGWOOD.—THE GEOMETRY OF THE THREE FIRST BOOKS OF EUCLID. By Direct Proof from Definitions Alone. By H. Wedgwood, M.A. 12mo, pp. 104, cloth. 1856. 3s.

WEDGWOOD.—ON THE ORIGIN OF LANGUAGE. By H. Wedgwood, M.A. 12mo, pp. 165, cloth. 1866. 3s. 6d.

WEDGWOOD.—A DICTIONARY OF ENGLISH ETYMOLOGY. By H. Wedgwood. Third Edition, revised and enlarged. With Introduction on the Origin of Language. 8vo, pp. lxxii. and 746, cloth. 1878. £1, 1s.

WEDGWOOD.—CONTESTED ETYMOLOGIES IN THE DICTIONARY OF THE REV. W. W. SKEAT. By H. Wedgwood. Crown 8vo, pp. viii. and 194, cloth. 1882. 5s.

WEISBACH.—THEORETICAL MECHANICS: A Manual of the Mechanics of Engineering and of the Construction of Machines; with an Introduction to the Calculus. Designed as a Text-book for Technical Schools and Colleges, and for the use of Engineers, Architects, &c. By Julius Weisbach, Ph.D., Oberbergrath, and Professor at the Royal Mining Academy at Freiberg, &c. Translated from the German by Eckley B. Coxe, A.M., Mining Engineer. Demy 8vo, with 902 woodcuts, pp. 1112, cloth. 1877. 31s. 6d.

WELLER.—AN IMPROVED DICTIONARY; English and French, and French and English. By E. Weller. Royal 8vo, pp. 384 and 340, cloth. 1864. 7s. 6d.

WEST and BUHLER.—A DIGEST OF THE HINDU LAW OF INHERITANCE, PARTITION, AND ADOPTION; embodying the Replies of the Sástris in the Courts of the Bombay Presidency, with Introductions and Notes. By Raymond West and J. G. Bühler. Third Edition. Demy 8vo, pp. 1450, sewed. 1884. £1, 16s.

WETHERELL.—THE MANUFACTURE OF VINEGAR, its Theory and Practice; with especial reference to the Quick Process. By C. M. Wetherell, Ph.D., M.D. 8vo, pp. 30, cloth. 7s. 6d.

WHEELDON.—ANGLING RESORTS NEAR LONDON: The Thames and the Lea. By J. P. Wheeldon, Piscatorial Correspondent to "Bell's Life." Crown 8vo, pp. viii. and 218. 1878. Paper, 1s. 6d.

WHEELER.—THE HISTORY OF INDIA FROM THE EARLIEST AGES. By J. Talboys Wheeler. Demy 8vo, cloth. Vol. I. containing the Vedic Period and the Mahá Bhárata. With Map. Pp. lxxv. and 576, cl. 1867, o. p. Vol. II. The Ramayana, and the Brahmanic Period. Pp. lxxxviii. and 680, with 2 Maps, cl. 21s. Vol. III. Hindu, Buddhist, Brahmanical Revival. Pp. xxiv.-500. With 2 Maps, 8vo, cl. 1874. 18s. This volume may be had as a complete work with the following title, "History of India; Hindu, Buddhist, and Brahmanical." Vol IV. Part I. Mussulman Rule. Pp. xxxii.-320. 1876. 14s. Vol. IV. Part II. completing the History of India down to the time of the Moghul Empire. Pp. xxviii. and 280. 1881. 12s.

WHEELER.—EARLY RECORDS OF BRITISH INDIA: A History of the English Settlements in India, as told in the Government Records, the works of old Travellers, and other Contemporary Documents, from the earliest period down to the rise of British Power in India. By J. Talboys Wheeler, late Assistant Secretary to the Government of India in the Foreign Department. Royal 8vo, pp. xxxii. and 392, cloth. 1878. 15s.

WHEELER.—THE FOREIGNER IN CHINA. By L. N. Wheeler, D.D. With Introduction by Professor W. C. Sawyer, Ph.D. 8vo, pp. 268, cloth. 1881. 6s. 6d.

WHERRY.—A COMPREHENSIVE COMMENTARY TO THE QURAN. To which is prefixed Sale's Preliminary Discourse, with additional Notes and Emendations. Together with a complete Index to the Text, Preliminary Discourse, and Notes. By Rev. E. M. Wherry M.A., Lodiana. 3 vols. post 8vo, cloth. Vol. I. Pp. xii. and 392. 1882. 12s. 6d. Vol. II. Pp. vi. and 408. 1884. 12s. 6d.

WHINFIELD.—QUATRAINS OF OMAR KHAYYAM. See Trübner's Oriental Series.

WHINFIELD.—See GULSHAN I. RAZ.

WHIST.—SHORT RULES FOR MODERN WHIST, Extracted from the "Quarterly Review" of January 1871. Printed on a Card, folded to fit the Pocket. 1878. 6d.

WHITE.—SPINOZA. See English and Foreign Philosophical Library.

WHITNEY.—LANGUAGE AND THE STUDY OF LANGUAGE: Twelve Lectures on the Principles of Linguistic Science. By W. D. Whitney. Fourth Edition, augmented by an Analysis. Crown 8vo, pp. xii. and 504, cloth. 1884. 10s. 6d.

WHITNEY.—LANGUAGE AND ITS STUDY, with especial reference to the Indo-European Family of Languages. Seven Lectures by W. D. Whitney, Instructor in Modern Languages in Yale College. Edited with Introduction, Notes, Tables, &c., and an Index, by the Rev. R. Morris, M.A., LL.D. Second Edition. Crown 8vo, pp. xxii. and 318, cloth. 1880. 5s.

WHITNEY.—Oriental and Linguistic Studies. By W. D. Whitney. First Series. Crown 8vo, pp. x. and 420, cloth. 1874. 12s. Second Series. Crown 8vo, pp. xii. and 434. With chart, cloth. 1874. 12s.

WHITNEY.—A SANSKRIT GRAMMAR, including both the Classical Language and the older Dialects of Veda and Brahmana. By William Dwight Whitney, Professor of Sanskrit and Comparative Philology in Yale College, Newhaven, &c., &c. 8vo, pp. xxiv. and 486. 1879. Stitched in wrapper, 10s. 6d; cloth, 12s.

WHITWELL.—IRON SMELTER'S POCKET ANALYSIS BOOK. By Thomas Whitwell, Member of the Institution of Mechanical Engineers, &c. Oblong 12mo, pp. 152, roan. 1877. 5s.

WILKINSON.—THE SAINT'S TRAVEL TO THE LAND OF CANAAN. Wherein are discovered Seventeen False Rests short of the Spiritual Coming of Christ in the Saints, with a Brief Discovery of what the Coming of Christ in the Spirit is. By R. Wilkinson. Printed 1648; reprinted 1874. Fcap. 8vo, pp. 208, cloth. 1s. 6d.

WILLIAMS.—A SYLLABIC DICTIONARY OF THE CHINESE LANGUAGE; arranged according to the Wu-Fang Yuen Yin, with the pronunciation of the Characters as heard in Pekin, Canton, Amoy, and Shanghai. By S. Wells Williams, LL.D. 4to, pp. 1336. 1874. £5, 5s.

WILLIAMS.—MODERN INDIA AND THE INDIANS. See Trübner's Oriental Series.

WILSON.—WORKS OF THE LATE HORACE HAYMAN WILSON, M.A., F.R.S., &c.

Vols. I. and II. Essays and Lectures chiefly on the Religion of the Hindus, by the late H. H. Wilson, M.A., F.R.S., &c. Collected and Edited by Dr. Reinhold Rost. 2 vols. demy 8vo, pp. xiii. and 399, vi. and 416, cloth. 21s.

Vols. III., IV., and V. Essays Analytical, Critical, and Philological, on Subjects connected with Sanskrit Literature. Collected and Edited by Dr. Reinhold Rost. 3 vols. demy 8vo, pp. 408, 406, and 390, cloth. 36s.

Vols. VI., VII., VIII., IX., and X. (2 parts). Vishnu Puráná, a System of Hindu Mythology and Tradition. Translated from the original Sanskrit, and Illustrated by Notes derived chiefly from other Puránás. By the late H. H. Wilson. Edited by FitzEdward Hall, M.A., D.C.L., Oxon. Vols. I. to V. (2 parts). Demy 8vo, pp. cxl. and 200, 344, 346, 362, and 268, cloth. £3, 4s. 6d.

Vols. XI. and XII. Select Specimens of the Theatre of the Hindus. Translated from the original Sanskrit. By the late H. H. Wilson, M.A., F.R.S. Third corrected Edition. 2 vols. demy 8vo, pp. lxxi. and 384, iv. and 418, cloth. 21s.

WILSON.—THOUGHTS ON SCIENCE, THEOLOGY, AND ETHICS. By John Wilson, M.A., Trinity College, Dublin. Crown 8vo, pp. 280, cloth. 1885. 3s. 6d.

WISE.—COMMENTARY ON THE HINDU SYSTEM OF MEDICINE. By T. A. Wise, M.D. 8vo, pp. xx. and 432, cloth. 1845. 7s. 6d.

WISE.—REVIEW OF THE HISTORY OF MEDICINE. By Thomas A. Wise. 2 vols. demy 8vo, cloth. Vol. I., pp. xcviii. and 397. Vol. II., pp. 574. 10s.

WISE.—HISTORY OF PAGANISM IN CALEDONIA. By T. A. Wise, M.D., &c. Demy 4to, pp. xxviii.-272, cloth, with numerous Illustrations. 1884. 15s.

WITHERS.—THE ENGLISH LANGUAGE AS PRONOUNCED. By G. Withers. Royal 8vo, pp. 84, sewed. 1874. 1s.

WOOD.—CHRONOS. Mother Earth's Biography. A Romance of the New School. By Wallace Wood, M.D. Crown 8vo, pp. xvi. and 334, with Illustration, cloth. 1873. 6s.

WOMEN.—THE RIGHTS OF WOMEN. A Comparison of the Relative Legal Status of the Sexes in the Chief Countries of Western Civilisation. Crown 8vo, pp. 104, cloth. 1875. 2s. 6d.

WRIGHT.—FEUDAL MANUALS OF ENGLISH HISTORY, a series of Popular Sketches of our National History compiled at different periods, from the Thirteenth Century to the Fifteenth, for the use of the Feudal Gentry and Nobility. Now first edited from the Original Manuscripts. By Thomas Wright, M.A., F.S.A., &c. Small 4to, pp. xxix. and 184, cloth. 1872. 15s.

WRIGHT.—THE HOMES OF OTHER DAYS. A History of Domestic Manners and Sentiments during the Middle Ages. By Thomas Wright, M.A., F.S.A. With Illustrations from the Illuminations in Contemporary Manuscripts and other Sources. Drawn and Engraved by F. W. Fairholt, F.S.A. Medium 8vo, 350 Woodcuts, pp. xv. and 512, cloth. 1871. 21s.

WRIGHT.—ANGLO-SAXON AND OLD ENGLISH VOCABULARIES. By Thomas Wright, M.A., F.S.A., Hon. M.R.S.L. Second Edition, Edited and Collated by Richard Paul Wulcker. 2 vols. demy 8vo, pp. xx.-408, and iv.-486, cloth. 1884. 28s. Illustrating the Condition and Manners of our Forefathers, as well as the History of the forms of Elementary Education, and of the Languages Spoken in this Island from the Tenth Century to the Fifteenth.

WRIGHT.—THE CELT, THE ROMAN, AND THE SAXON; a History of the Early Inhabitants of Britain down to the Conversion of the Anglo-Saxons to Christianity. Illustrated by the Ancient Remains brought to light by Recent Research. By Thomas Wright, M.A., F.S.A., &c., &c. Third Corrected and Enlarged Edition. Cr. 8vo, pp. xiv. and 562. With nearly 300 Engravings. Cloth. 1875. 14s.

WRIGHT.—THE BOOK OF KALILAH AND DIMNAH. Translated from Arabic into Syriac. Edited by W. Wright, LL.D., Professor of Arabic in the University of Cambridge. Demy 8vo, pp. lxxxii.-408, cloth. 1884. 21s.

WRIGHT.—MENTAL TRAVELS IN IMAGINED LANDS. By H. Wright. Crown 8vo, pp. 184, cloth. 1878. 5s.

WYLD.—CLAIRVOYANCE; or, the Auto-Noetic Action of the Mind. By George Wyld, M.D. Edin. 8vo, pp. 32, wrapper. 1883. 1s.

WYSARD.—THE INTELLECTUAL AND MORAL PROBLEM OF GOETHE'S FAUST. By A. Wysard. Parts I. and II. Fcap. 8vo, pp. 80, limp parchment wrapper. 1883. 2s. 6d.

YOUNG MECHANIC (THE).—See MECHANIC.

ZELLER.—STRAUSS AND RENAN. An Essay by E. Zeller. Translated from the German. Post 8vo, pp. 110, cloth. 1866. 2s. 6d.

PERIODICALS
PUBLISHED AND SOLD BY TRÜBNER & CO.

AMATEUR MECHANICAL SOCIETY'S JOURNAL.—Irregular.

ANTANANARIVO ANNUAL AND MADAGASCAR MAGAZINE.—Irregular.

ANTHROPOLOGICAL INSTITUTE OF GREAT BRITAIN AND IRELAND (JOURNAL OF).—Quarterly, 5s.

ARCHITECT (AMERICAN) AND BUILDING NEWS.—Contains General Architectural News, Articles on Interior Decoration, Sanitary Engineering, Construction, Building Materials, &c., &c. Four full-page Illustrations accompany each Number. Weekly. Annual Subscription, £1, 11s. 6d. Post free.

ASIATIC SOCIETY (ROYAL) OF GREAT BRITAIN AND IRELAND (JOURNAL OF).—Irregular.

BIBLICAL ARCHÆOLOGICAL SOCIETY (TRANSACTIONS OF).—Irregular.
BIBLIOTHECA SACRA.—Quarterly, 3s. 6d. Annual Subscription, 14s. Post free.
BRITISH ARCHÆOLOGICAL ASSOCIATION (JOURNAL OF).—Quarterly, 8s.
BRITISH CHESS MAGAZINE.—Monthly, 8d.
BRITISH HOMŒOPATHIC SOCIETY (ANNALS OF).—Half-yearly, 2s. 6d.
BROWNING SOCIETY'S PAPERS.—Irregular.
CALCUTTA REVIEW.—Quarterly, 8s. 6d. Annual Subscription, 34s. Post free.
CAMBRIDGE PHILOLOGICAL SOCIETY (PROCEEDINGS OF).—Irregular.
ENGLISHWOMAN'S REVIEW.—Social and Industrial Questions. Monthly, 6d.
GEOLOGICAL MAGAZINE, or Monthly Journal of Geology, 1s. 6d. Annual Subscription, 18s. Post free.
GLASGOW, GEOLOGICAL SOCIETY OF (TRANSACTIONS OF).—Irregular.
INDEX MEDICUS.—A Monthly Classified Record of the Current Medical Literature of the World. Annual Subscription, 50s. Post free.
INDIAN ANTIQUARY.—A Journal of Oriental Research in Archæology, History, Literature, Languages, Philosophy, Religion, Folklore, &c. Annual Subscription, £2. Post free.
INDIAN EVANGELICAL REVIEW.—Annual Subscription, 10s.
LIBRARY JOURNAL.—Official Organ of the Library Associations of America and of the United Kingdom. Monthly, 2s. Annual Subscription, 20s. Post free.
MANCHESTER QUARTERLY.—1s. 6d.
MATHEMATICS (AMERICAN JOURNAL OF).—Quarterly, 7s. 6d. Annual Subscription, 24s. Post free.
ORIENTALIST (THE).—Monthly. Annual Subscription, 12s.
ORTHODOX CATHOLIC REVIEW.—Irregular.
PHILOLOGICAL SOCIETY (TRANSACTIONS AND PROCEEDINGS OF).—Irregular.
PSYCHICAL RESEARCH (SOCIETY OF).—PROCEEDINGS.
PUBLISHERS' WEEKLY.—THE AMERICAN BOOK-TRADE JOURNAL. Annual Subscription, 18s. Post free.
PUNJAB NOTES AND QUERIES.—Monthly. Annual Subscription, 10s.
REVUE COLONIALE INTERNATIONALE.—Monthly. Annual Subscription, 25s. Post free.
SCIENTIFIC AMERICAN.—WEEKLY. Annual subscription, 18s. Post free.
SUPPLEMENT to ditto.—WEEKLY. Annual subscription, 24s. Post free.
SCIENCE AND ARTS (AMERICAN JOURNAL OF).—Monthly, 2s. 6d. Annual Subscription, 30s.
SPECULATIVE PHILOSOPHY (JOURNAL OF).—Quarterly, 4s. Annual Subscription, 16s. Post free, 17s.
SUNDAY REVIEW.—Organ of the Sunday Society for Opening Museums and Art Galleries on Sunday.—Quarterly, 1s. Annual Subscription, 4s. 6d. Post free.
TRÜBNER'S AMERICAN, EUROPEAN, AND ORIENTAL LITERARY RECORD.—A Register of the most Important Works Published in America, India, China, and the British Colonies. With occasional Notes on German, Dutch, Danish, French, Italian, Spanish, Portuguese, and Russian Literature. Subscription for 12 Numbers, 5s. Post free.
TRÜBNER & CO.'S MONTHLY LIST of New and Forthcoming Works, Official and other Authorised Publications, and New American Books. Post free.
WESTMINSTER REVIEW.—Quarterly, 6s. Annual Subscription, 22s. Post free.
WOMAN'S SUFFRAGE JOURNAL.—Monthly, 1d.

TRÜBNER & CO.'S CATALOGUES.

Any of the following Catalogues sent per Post on receipt of Stamps.

Africa, Works Relating to the Modern Languages of. 1d.

Agricultural Works. 2d.

Arabic, Persian, and Turkish Books, printed in the East. 1s.

Assyria and Assyriology. 1s.

Bibliotheca Hispano-Americana. 1s. 6d.

Brazil, Ancient and Modern Books relating to. 2s. 6d.

British Museum, Publications of Trustees of the. 1d.

Dictionaries and Grammars of Principal Languages and Dialects of the World. 5s.

Educational Works. 1d.

Egypt and Egyptology. 1s.

Guide Books. 1d.

Important Works, published by Trübner & Co. 2d.

Linguistic and Oriental Publications. 2d.

Medical, Surgical, Chemical, and Dental Publications. 2d.

Modern German Books. 2d.

Monthly List of New Publications. 1d.

Pali, Prakrit, and Buddhist Literature. 1s.

Portuguese Language, Ancient and Modern Books in the. 6d.

Sanskrit Books. 2s. 6d.

Scientific Works. 2d.

Semitic, Iranian, and Tatar Races. 1s.

TRÜBNER'S
COLLECTION OF SIMPLIFIED GRAMMARS
OF THE
PRINCIPAL ASIATIC AND EUROPEAN LANGUAGES.

EDITED BY REINHOLD ROST, LL.D., PH.D.

The object of this Series is to provide the learner with a concise but practical Introduction to the various Languages, and at the same time to furnish Students of Comparative Philology with a clear and comprehensive view of their structure. The attempt to adapt the somewhat cumbrous grammatical system of the Greek and Latin to every other tongue has introduced a great deal of unnecessary difficulty into the study of Languages. Instead of analysing existing locutions and endeavouring to discover the principles which regulate them, writers of grammars have for the most part constructed a framework of rules on the old lines, and tried to make the language of which they were treating fit into it. Where this proves impossible, the difficulty is met by lists of exceptions and irregular forms, thus burdening the pupil's mind with a mass of details of which he can make no practical use.

In these Grammars the subject is viewed from a different standpoint; the structure of each language is carefully examined, and the principles which underlie it are carefully explained; while apparent discrepancies and so-called irregularities are shown to be only natural euphonic and other changes. All technical terms are excluded unless their meaning and application is self-evident; no arbitrary rules are admitted; the old classification into declensions, conjugations, &c., and even the usual *paradigms* and tables, are omitted. Thus reduced to the simplest principles, the Accidence and Syntax can be thoroughly comprehended by the student on one perusal, and a few hours' diligent study will enable him to analyse any sentence in the language.

Now READY.
Crown 8vo, cloth, uniformly bound.

I.—**Hindustani, Persian, and Arabic.** By the late E. H. Palmer, M.A. Second Edition. Pp. 112. 5s.
II.—**Hungarian.** By I. SINGER, of Buda-Pesth. Pp. vi. and 88. 4s. 6d.

For continuation see next page.

Trübner's Simplified Grammars—continued.

III.—**Basque.** By W. VAN EYS. Pp. xii. and 52. 3s. 6d.
IV.—**Malagasy.** By G. W. PARKER. Pp. 66. 5s.
V.—**Modern Greek.** By E. M. GELDART, M.A. Pp. 68. 2s. 6d.
VI.—**Roumanian.** By M. TORCEANU. Pp. viii. and 72. 5s.
VII.—**Tibetan.** By H. A. JÄSCHKE. Pp. viii. and 104. 5s.
VIII.—**Danish.** By E. C. OTTÉ. Pp. viii. and 66. 2s. 6d.
IX.—**Turkish.** By J. W. REDHOUSE, M.R.A.S. Pp. xii. and 10s. 6d.
X.—**Swedish.** By Miss E. C. OTTÉ. Pp. xii. and 70. 2s. 6d.
XI.—**Polish.** By W. R. MORFILL, M.A. Pp. viii. and 64. 3s. 6d.
XII.—**Pali.** By E. MÜLLER, Ph.D. Pp. xvi.-144. 7s. 6d.
XIII.—**Sanskrit.** By H. EDGREN. Pp. xii.-178. 10s. 6d.

The following are in preparation :—

SIMPLIFIED GRAMMARS OF

Albanian, by WASSA PASHA, Prince of the Lebanon.
Assyrian, by Prof. SAYCE.
Bengali, by J. F. BLUMHARDT, of the British Museum.
Burmese, by Dr. E. FORCHAMMER.
Cymric and Gaelic. by H. JENNER, of the British Museum.
Egyptian, by Dr. BIRCH.
Finnic, by Prof. OTTO DONNER, of Helsingfors.
Hebrew, by Dr. GINSBURG.
Icelandic, by Dr. WIMMER, Copenhagen.
Lettish, by Dr. M. I. A. VÖLKEL.
Lithuanian, by Dr. M. I. A. VÖLKEL.
Malay, by W. E. MAXWELL, of the Inner Temple, Barrister-at-Law.
Portuguese, by WALTER DE GRAY BIRCH.
Prakrit, by HJALMAR EDGREN, Lund, Sweden.
Russian, Bohemian, Bulgarian and Serbian, by W. R. MORFILL, Oxford.
Sinhalese, by Dr. EDWARD MÜLLER.

Arrangements are being made with competent Scholars for the preparation of Grammars of **German, Dutch, Italian, Chinese, Japanese,** *and* **Siamese.**

LONDON : TRÜBNER & CO., LUDGATE HILL.

www.ingramcontent.com/pod-product-compliance
Lightning Source LLC
Chambersburg PA
CBHW021346230426
43666CB00006B/432